The Civic Culture of Local Economic Development

In honor of the importance of mentors,
this is dedicated to Jack A. Marks, Ronald R. Stockton,
Bryan D. Jones, and Joseph F. Ohren.

LAR

To my parents, Tillye Rosenfeld and
the late Bernard Rosenfeld, whose spirit and love of
books and education are reflected in what I do.

RAR

The Civic Culture of Local Economic Development

Laura A. Reese • Raymond A. Rosenfeld

Wayne State University   Eastern Michigan University

Sage Publications
International Educational and Professional Publisher
Thousand Oaks ▪ London ▪ New Delhi

For information:

Sage Publications, Inc.
2455 Teller Road
Thousand Oaks, California 91320
E-mail: order@sagepub.com

Sage Publications Ltd.
6 Bonhill Street
London EC2A 4PU
United Kingdom

Sage Publications India Pvt. Ltd.
M-32 Market
Greater Kailash I
New Delhi 110 048 India

Printed in the United States of America

Library of Congress Cataloging-in-Publication Data

Reese, Laura A. (Laura Ann), 1958-
  The civic culture of local economic development / by Laura A. Reese and Raymond A. Rosenfeld.
    p. cm.
  Includes bibliographical references and index.
  ISBN 0-7619-1690-3 (alk. paper)
  ISBN 0-7619-1691-1 (pbk.: alk. paper)
  1. Economic development projects—United States—Case studies. 2. Political culture—United States—Case studies. 3. Community development—United States—Case studies. 4. Economic development projects—Canada—Case studies. 5. Political culture—Canada—Case studies. 6. Community development—Canada—Case studies. I. Rosenfeld, Raymond A. I. Title.
HC110.E44 R438 2001
338.973—dc21   2001001294

01 02 03 04 05 06 07 08 7 6 5 4 3 2 1

Acquiring Editor:	Marquita Flemming
Editorial Assistant:	MaryAnn Vail
Production Editor:	Denise Santoyo
Editorial Assistant:	Kathryn Journey
Copy Editor:	Marilyn Power Scott
Typesetter/Designer:	Tina Hill
Indexer:	Molly Hall
Cover Designer:	Jane Quaney
Cover Design Concept:	Cindy Bell
Cover Photography:	Laura A. Reese

CONTENTS

PREFACE

The central purpose of this book is to provide a more nuanced yet broadly applicable understanding of local policy processes via a focus on economic development policy. There are distinct local factors that shape the environment of economic-development decision making. These factors, taken together, constitute a community's local civic culture. Different cultures will produce different types of economic development policies, and the local civic culture will affect the whole array of local policies. The focus on economic development policy provides a window on local decision making and allows for the development of a theory about the role of local civic culture in framing local decisions of all types.

Using a methodology that combines large survey analysis with intensive case studies in cities in the United States and Canada, it is argued that, although regime theory and other models used to understand local economic development policy making have greatly enhanced our knowledge of local process and policy, they do not provide a sufficiently complete framework. Broadening the focus to consider local civic culture offers an approach that captures both the historic and idiosyncratic features that make each city a unique functional entity, yet it also provides a theoretical vehicle for categorizing cities and, ultimately, predicting policy outcomes.

ACKNOWLEDGMENTS

We would like to extend our sincere appreciation to several individuals who assisted in this project. First, a huge debt is owed to Joe Ohren for reading and editing numerous drafts and for both moral and intellectual support for Laura. Thanks are also due to David Fasenfest for assistance in getting the survey data together in the first place and for analysis assistance along the way. Gene Perle also helped greatly with the cluster analysis. The research has been supported by the Canadian Embassy Research Grant Program and through a Senior Research Fellowship. Wayne State University and Eastern Michigan University have also supported the research through travel funding.

We would also like to express our gratitude to all of the respondents interviewed in the nine case cities. Without their gracious cooperation, the project could not have been completed. Indeed, the level of dedication and professionalism we saw among local officials and community leaders in each city remains with us and brings to mind the words from the Oath of the Athenian City-State, which follows. Truly, the respondents in all of the cities, regardless of location, structure, economic condition, political ideology, or civic culture, embody these ideals.

We will ever strive for the ideals
And sacred things of the city,
Both alone and with many;
We will unceasingly seek to quicken
The sense of public duty;
We will revere and obey the city's laws;
We will transmit this city
Not only not less, but greater,
Better and more beautiful
Than it was transmitted to us.

1

LOCAL CIVIL CULTURE
The Missing Determinant?

The cities of Coshocton, Ohio, and Romulus, Michigan, are similar in several respects. Both have a strong-mayor form of government; poverty rates and average income levels are nearly identical. However, whereas the mayor in Romulus is the locus of power for economic development decision making and for leadership in the city more generally, the mayor in Coshocton is not. Instead, the Safety Services Director serves as a city administrator, department heads have a great deal of discretion, and economic development is conducted by an external private body. Here, a "paper" strong-mayor system really operates more like a weak-mayor/manager system. The form of government masks the real structure, which changes over time.

The cities of Kettering, Ohio, and Allen Park, Michigan, have similar governing regimes and similar economic conditions; they are reasonably healthy, with low unemployment and poverty and high average incomes. In both cities, economic development is conducted in-house, so to speak. The city manager/administrator and the bureaucrat responsible for economic development are the locus of power for development decisions. The planning commission and engineering department also play significant roles in both. Although the city councils select the city managers, in neither case do they "get in the sand box and play" when it comes to economic development policy making. There is little community or business input in either case. Hence, both cities have a development agenda led by public administrators, and broader input tends to occur only through formal planning commission or city council hearings.

Beyond this, however, other local conditions and hence approaches to economic development are very different. Local politics in Kettering are quite calm. Although the mayor's position was constrained by term limits, within that framework, there has been little turnover among elected officials. Despite having ward-based council elections, there is little division on council on a geographic basis; most votes are unanimous. Kettering takes an active, entrepreneurial stance toward development, and the resultant policies are quite innovative. The situation in Allen Park is very different. Historical politics have been quite confrontational; a one-term mayor was defeated after an administration that included a recall effort and a slander suit. City council is not necessarily supportive of recommendations from city administrators and the contracted planning firm. Various bond efforts have met with failure at the polls, and the local government is now wary of community opinion, even to the extent of trying to circumvent it. The overall approach to economic development is very passive here. Thus, cities with governing regimes composed of the same actors can have very different approaches to economic development and ultimately pursue different development policies.

The cities of Cornwall, Ontario, and Cadillac and Romulus, Michigan, suffered from relatively high levels of economic stress in the early 1990s. However, they have very different approaches to economic development. Furthermore, the locus of power for economic development decisions varies significantly among these cities. The mayor dominates economic development decision making in Romulus, and the policies represent a mix of traditional location incentives as well as so-called claw backs, local hiring goals, and an abatement formula that includes consideration of the number and type of jobs likely to be generated. Clearly, this stressed city is not giving away the store. Policies in Cadillac, which has a development regime dominated by local officials and businesses, reflect a creative and innovative approach to economic development, not one driven by desperation. Last, Cornwall, with a system basically devoid of either citizen or business actors, has an essentially passive approach to economic development, with efforts focused on marketing and the development of an industrial park. This too is not a city driven to offer incentives despite a weak economy. In short, it does not appear that economic conditions determine the composition of the governing regime, locus of decision power, nor approaches to economic development. Local history and patterns of interaction also influence how economic development decisions are made as well as the content of those decisions.

THE INFLUENCE OF LOCAL CIVIC CULTURE

As these vignettes suggest, there are distinct local factors that shape the environment of economic development decision making. These factors, taken together, constitute a community's local civic culture. Different cultures will produce different types of economic development policies, and the local civic culture will affect the whole array of local policies. The focus on economic development policy provides a window on local decision making and allows for the development of a theory about the role of local civic culture in framing local decisions of all types. The stories presented earlier highlight the importance of civic culture in local economic development decision making and provide several lessons about the assumptions and interpretations contained in much previous research. The purpose of this book is to explore the nature and role of local civic culture through the examination of one policy area—economic development. It is argued that, whereas regime theory and other models used to understand local economic development policy making have greatly enhanced our knowledge of local process and policy, they do not provide a sufficiently complete framework. Broadening the focus to consider local civic culture offers an approach that captures both the historic and idiosyncratic features that make each city a unique functional entity yet also provides a theoretical vehicle for categorizing cities and, ultimately, predicting policy outcomes.

The first story suggests that, whereas local government structure and politics matter in economic development decisions, the reality is that, in many cities, formal and informal structures differ. Local history and accepted patterns of governing can cause unique variations in forms of government that may change over time. The strong-mayor system in Romulus operates as expected. The mayor is a strong individual and provides executive leadership across policy areas. The mayor in Coshocton was not a strong leader, and patterns of administration have been adapted to that fact. The power base in the community lies with administrative staff and external actors. Structure, then, must be interpreted and understood with caution, and discussions of structure must make clear whether formal or informal arrangements are being addressed. It is civic culture that mediates between the two.

The second story highlights a significant caveat about regime theory: specifically, that governing regimes in different cities may have the same actors but may operate very differently. Indeed, it will be argued that on close inspection, many cities do not have regimes at all. Business leaders are not involved in economic development decision making in either Kettering or Allen Park; hence, any governing arrangements will be devoid of the private sector. It will be argued that this suggests that such cities really do not have regimes. Furthermore, although economic development staff are the locus of power in both these cities, they have very different approaches to economic development. Policy processes and the resultant policies are more than a function of the governing regime. Again, differences in the local political arena, local histories, accepted processes for making decisions, and shared visions of the past and future provide a framework within which regimes operate. Although these broader forces shape the governing regime, they also define how regimes govern. In the absence of regime, in many cities, the local civic culture defines the parameters of policy making.

The third description points to the limited effects of the economy on both the composition of the governing regime and economic development policy. Although it is commonly agreed that politics matters and that local policy is not simply economically determined, many extant explanations of local economic development policy rely heavily on economic determinants. It is useful to be reminded that similar economic conditions can be translated into different development policies. In other words, there is no inherent reason why economic stress creates cities desperate for any kind of development, giving away the store to private interests. Stressed cities can and do act to protect their own interests and have more discretion vis-á-vis businesses than perhaps is often assumed. The mayor in Romulus takes a very savvy and assertive stand toward the private sector to ensure that the city is getting the best deal possible. The story also highlights the fact that economic stress does not necessarily lead to governing regimes composed of development interests; developmental regimes are not the inherent result of a weak economy. Indeed, it will be demonstrated that there is little apparent relationship between the local economic environment, power arrangements, or governing regimes.

The analyses and arguments presented in this book, then, focus on the role of civic culture in local economic development policy making. It looks back in the political science literature to create a theoretical framework for local policy making that incorporates, yet moves beyond, the focus on governing regime. The following central questions are examined:

What are the essential components of local civic culture?

Can unique local civic cultures be identified?

How does local civic culture relate to governing regimes?

How does local civic culture relate to the economic environment?

Do different local civic cultures lead to different types of economic development policies?

What questions does the civic culture focus raise about what we "know" about local policy making and what new questions come to the fore?

Using both survey and case study data, local economic development policies and policy processes are examined in U.S. and Canadian cities to address these broad questions. In a sense, this research revisits many of the issues raised by urbanists and political scientists for decades, from Dahl (1961) in New Haven to Stone (1989) in Atlanta. What is the nature of local power systems? How do such systems interact with governance structure and the larger economic and global environment to produce policies and policy processes? How are decisions really made in the local arena and who appears to benefit most often? Although economic development policy is the frame, the focus remains on these perennial and root issues of local governance. In summary, it is argued that to fully understand the forces behind the choice and use of particular economic development policies in communities, the analysis must include an examination of local civic culture.

WHAT DO WE KNOW ABOUT THE CORRELATES
OF LOCAL DEVELOPMENTAL POLICY?

At the outset, it is essential to enumerate what is currently assumed to be known about local economic development process and policy. What have scholars concluded affects the decision-making process, and what local forces lead to what policies? The challenge of this effort is that the findings of the determinants literature have been mixed regarding both the variables that appear to affect local economic development policy and the nature of particular effects. Although this variation is likely due to a number of factors, including different combinations of independent variables, variation in measuring the same indicators, different time periods for study, different units of analysis, and even different policies used as dependent variables, on the whole it raises concerns about the solidity of our knowledge about local economic development. A brief summary of major trends in this literature follows to outline the forces that appear related to local economic development policy.

Overall Trends

Fiscal health has been a central focus of efforts to explain development policy. Differing trends are apparent. Some research suggests that more prosperous cities use economic development incentives to a greater degree than less prosperous cities. Such a finding is counterintuitive on its face because healthy and growing communities do not need to offer incentives. But it appears they use their greater financial ability to promote even further growth. Exacerbating this, research has also indicated that firms tend to locate in areas that are already economically successful, permitting cities to prosper without the use of incentives. It is also likely that firms will seek incentives from attractive cities (Rubin, 1988; Schneider, 1986). Indeed, state-level research has indicated that healthier areas are more likely to grant tax abatements (Brierly, 1986), research on Michigan communities suggested that more fiscally sound cities offered higher levels of tax abatements (Reese, 1991), and findings from Wisconsin cities indicate that those "successfully recruiting new businesses are more likely to adopt a wide variety of economic development policies" (Green, 1995:177). Still, other authors have found the reverse to be true; cities experiencing high levels of economic stress may be driven to offer incentives to improve their economic position (Reese, 1992; Rubin, 1986; Rubin and Rubin, 1987; Sharp, 1991). High levels of economic need among residents (unemployment and poverty for example) have been found to increase the number of economic development tools employed (Feiock, 1992; Fleischmann et al., 1992; Sharp, 1991). Last, stressed cities may be more willing to experiment with newer, more entrepreneurial, economic development strategies (Clarke and Gaile, 1998).

Researchers have also focused on the nature and level of *professionalism* among economic development decision makers in trying to explain local development policies. For example, it appears that cities that are fiscally healthy have greater resources to devote to economic development and are thus more likely to engage in systematic analyses in planning and evaluation (Ohren and Reese, 1996; Reese, 1997b). Other research suggests that cities with more professionalized economic development programs and/or greater administrative capacity (sometimes measured as size of the local bureaucracy) engage in more economic development efforts (Fleischmann et al., 1992; Pelissero and Fasenfest, 1989; Reese, 1991, 1997a; Rubin and Rubin, 1987) and do a better job of distributing benefits to lower-income areas (Rosenfeld et al., 1995). Along with professionalization, decision making and perceptions of the environment also appear important. For example, uncertainty and turbulence in the local or extralocal environment, both political and economic, appears to lead to increased reliance on decision rules or standardized routines that simplify the policy-making and implementation process (Bachelor, 1994; Reese, 1993b; Rubin, 1988; Spindler and Forrester, 1993).

Competition from other municipalities appears to increase the use of a variety of economic development techniques (Bingham, 1976; Bowman, 1988; Green and Fleischmann, 1991; Pelissero, 1986; Peterson, 1981; Reese, 1997a). For example, location and proximity to other competing cities has been found to affect both creation of enterprise zones (Green and Brintnall, 1986) and use of tax incentives (Bingham, 1976; Bowman, 1988; Pelissero, 1986). Given the information imbalance facing cities, unsure of what is necessary to attract firms, municipalities are driven to offer all possible inducements (Jones and Bachelor, 1984). This is exacerbated when cities know that others are waiting in the wings to compete for the same firms. It should be noted, however, that some research on tax abatement behavior among local governments failed to find competition a significant explanatory factor (Feiock and Clingermayer, 1992), and recent research has argued that there is "no significant evidence that cities adopt policies in response to choices made by neighboring cities" (Clarke and Gaile, 1998:13).

Governmental structure appears to play a role in local economic development policy and policy making, although these findings are also somewhat contradictory. Both "reformed" and "unreformed" structures seem predisposed to offer incentives (Feiock, 1989; Reese, 1997a). Research suggests that city manager cities may be more likely to devote resources to economic development, thus providing more opportunity for planning and evaluation (Reese, 1997a). Mayoral cities, on the other hand, have been found to be more innovative in the use of federal economic development dollars (Clarke and Gaile, 1998). Centralization of executive power appears important and seems to increase the use of tax abatements (Feiock and Clingermayer, 1986; Sharp, 1991). It has thus been argued that the combination of electoral incentives and centralized power allows for a greater focus on economic development policy, and the presence of a strong chief executive may provide the type of policy entrepreneur necessary to build coalitions and broker deals (Feiock and Clingermayer, 1986; Pagano and Bowman, 1995; Schneider and Teske, 1993). Indeed, the mayoral margin of victory has been found to be related to the total value of tax abatements granted (Reese, 1991). However, as with most of the independent variables employed, other studies have found no relationship between mayor systems and the number of incentives employed (Fleischmann et al., 1992) or indeed, no relationship between governmental structure and development policy at all (Donovan, 1993; Green and Fleischmann, 1991).

Other variables also seem to affect local economic development policy. Growing populations appear to attract business, perhaps due to greater perceived opportunities for sales and skilled employees, among other reasons (Kieschnick, 1981; Schneider, 1986). Larger cities also have been found to be more active in economic development (Feiock, 1992; Green, 1995; Green and Fleischmann, 1991). Age of a community seems important, with both newer (Levy, 1981) and older cities more aggressive in their economic development strategies (Pelissero, 1986).

Regarding more "political" variables, citizen pressure or expectations may increase the level of local economic development policy activity. Rubin and Zorn (1985) suggest that citizens expect local officials to enact policies to further economic development, and political attitudes toward business appear to be important as well (Goldstein, 1985; Schmenner, 1982). Local pressure to increase jobs is particularly likely to increase local economic development activity (Green, 1995). If economic development policies are more controversial among citizens in a community, less policy activity appears to result (Donovan, 1993).

In summary, the determinants literature has

- employed a similar array of independent variables to explain development policies, including economic or fiscal forces, governmental structure, decision-making processes, political input systems, and inter-local competition;
- suggested that even though the independent variables are similar, findings on their effects have been mixed, particularly regarding the role of local economic forces;
- used different measures of these similar variables, perhaps accounting for the conflicting findings; and
- tended to focus on overall number of economic development policies employed as the dependent variable rather then the type or level of policies pursued.

Type II Policies

Type II or progressive economic development policies have been the subject of special focus in the economic development literature and are of particular interest here. This is the case because they appear to offer local governments a way of balancing the power of the private sector and ensuring that the benefits of economic development incentives are distributed or redistributed throughout the community. Type II policies are those that serve either to redistribute or equalize the benefits of public expenditure for economic development or require performance guarantees by private sector recipients. Traditional economic development techniques, such as tax incentives, bond deals, infrastructure development, and the like, differ in that they tend to be directed at reducing the costs of doing business in a community. They primarily benefit the private sector recipient. In contrast, according to Goetz, Type II policies are a "category of economic development policy that mandates public benefits by requiring private sector developers to provide a wide range of direct economic and social goals" (Goetz, 1990:70).

More specifically, Elkins (1995) included the following as representative of Type II policies: provision of low-/middle-income housing, contribution to educational programs, minority hiring requirements, city hiring requirements, infrastructure improvements, and local regulation of building facades. Goetz (1990) included a similar set of policies: shared equity (public/private) in development projects, local and/or minority training/hiring requirements, mandated involvement of female-/minority-owned businesses, and technical assistance to community groups. Reese (1998) created an empirical typology of Type II policies based on factor analysis, including local employment requirements, minority employment requirements, worker training requirements, performance guarantees, targeted employee wage subsidies, and low-income housing linkages.

Each of these lists of activities is based on definitions by Sanyika (1986), which included a similar mix of policies, and Babcock (1987), who added linkage fees or extractions (zoning variances in exchange for contributions to infrastructure, for example). In a later article, Goetz identified Type II policies as reflecting a "new development paradigm" or "non-traditional policies" that included first-source hiring agreements, transportation mitigation fees, and social service provision requirements, in addition to the policies just noted (Goetz, 1994:93).

Scholars have focused on Type II policies because much research has suggested that traditional public subsidies to private development do not necessarily lead to benefits that trickle down to the majority of local residents (Fainstein et al., 1983; Hill, 1984). This is particularly the case for citizens at the lower end of the economic scale. Second, many traditional supply-side strategies have been found to be ineffective because they tend to move business around rather than create new capital investment, increase unhealthy and costly competition between cities, direct the benefits of public dollars to private firms, and tend not to produce job and tax base benefits commensurate with the expenditure of local revenues (see, for example, Ahlbrandt and DeAngelis, 1987; Bowman, 1988; Eisenschitz, 1993; Eisinger, 1988; Reese and Fasenfest, 1997; Schwarz and Volgy, 1992). Third, by training and employing local workers through Type II policies, communities build internal resources. This should lead to increased economic stability and stimulate local demand for goods, both internally and externally produced (Eisinger, 1988). Last, it can reasonably be argued that the expenditure of public dollars on policies, strategies, programs, or incentives to attract or create private capital investment should be predicated on goals that improve the quality of life for the community at large (Loftman, 1995; Reese and Fasenfest, 1997). In other words, Type II policies "implicitly acknowledge that the benefits of economic development are not universal, and/or are not sufficient in and of themselves to justify public subsidy" (Goetz, 1990:175).

A number of independent variables have been posited as correlates of Type II policies: land value, resident status, fiscal slack, economic vitality, demand for land, mayoral power, structure of local government, the balance of business and resident policy input, and even the experience of individual local economic development officials (Clarke, 1984; Elkins, 1995; Goetz, 1990, 1994; Reese, 1998). However, the most frequently explored correlates are local fiscal health and community involvement in or pressure on economic development decision making.

Overall, the conventional wisdom has been that local fiscal health and the desirability of a community will have the largest effect on Type II policies. That is, the only communities that are able to get away with Type II policies, which inherently place burdens on private capital, will be those that are healthy and attractive locations for development. This appears to be completely logical and reasonable. A stressed community with little demand for land or other investment should not be in any position to place additional burdens on business.

Research on these and other issues has been mixed. The findings appear to vary with the particular type of Type II policy being considered. For example, Elkins (1995) found that low-income housing requirements and guarantees of infrastructure are more prevalent in economically stressed cities. On the other hand, policies such as facade regulations, contributions to education programs, and resident and minority hiring requirements are more likely to be present in healthier communities. Clarke (1984) suggested a null hypothesis regarding the effects of local fiscal health on Type II policies. Goetz (1990), too, found mixed results. Out of 6 measures of fiscal health, 5 were unrelated to Type II policies as suggested by Clarke. The remaining measure (population growth) was significantly but negatively related to Type II policies. Goetz's (1994) later research on the broader category of "nontraditional" or alternative economic development policies was again mixed, with need and local economic performance positively related to the alternative policies but fiscal performance indicators either negatively related or not correlated at all. Similarly, Reese (1998) found that when considered as a group, Type II policies were related to financial need among local residents; need (indicated by unemployment and poverty) was significantly correlated with only three out of six individual Type II policies (low-income housing, low-income employment requirements, and minority employment requirements).

The effects of community activism appear more consistent; greater community input or activity appears to increase the use of Type II policies (Elkins, 1995; Goetz, 1990, 1994; Reese, 1998). However, Reese (1998) also found that greater business input increased the use of Type II policies, particularly low-income housing linkages and low-income employment requirements. Of the other correlates explored, the status of local residents, the demand for land, and mayoral power appear to have no significant relationship to Type II policies. Minority representation in local government appears to increase the use of hiring requirements (Elkins, 1995; Reese, 1998) and performance guarantees (Reese, 1998) but is unrelated to other Type II policies. Last, larger economic development budgets and staffing and greater planning and evaluation appear to increase the use of Type II policies (Reese, 1998).

In summary, research on Type II policies has

provided a definition of such policies;

suggested that fiscal health increases, decreases, or has no affect on Type II policies;

suggested that community activism increases policy use; and

provided mixed results regarding the effects of other variables, depending on the type of Type II policy explored.

IN SEARCH OF THEORY: MOVING BEYOND DETERMINANTS

Although the research just cited has provided a great deal of information about local economic development policy making, in a collective sense, it does not go far enough in providing a coherent theoretical framework for understanding economic development as part of a larger system of local policy making. A number of broad theories have been presented over the years to explain both the power structure of local communities and the policies that result. Early community power studies pitted the elitist and pluralist arguments of Hunter (1953) and

Domhoff (1978) and Dahl (1961) and Polsby (1980), respectively. Historically, pluralists posited that political conflict reflected a variety of relatively equal interest groups competing before an independent government answerable to voter demands. Elitists argued that a resource-laden upper class dominated decisions of elected bodies to their own advantage. Both positions, however, reflect a variety of conceptual and empirical deficiencies. Elitism has always suffered from its paranoid flavor and the lack of attention to electoral processes and the divergence in interest among elites. Pluralism, on the other hand, has never satisfactorily dealt with issues of limited representation within and resource variation among groups and strains the concept of government neutrality. Different world views were also influenced by methodological issues, such as locale and policy arena examined and technique employed to identify "powerful" participants.

The systemic power contribution of Stone (1980) did much to further the understanding of community power structures. Stone reconciled elitist and pluralist approaches by acknowledging that business leader-s have divergent interests, and governmental leaders have independent powers. However, he argued, the demands of interest groups and citizen coalitions and the need for monetary and political resources from the business community create a situation where attention to corporate needs is more a function of environmental conditions than overt control.

Currently, regime theory, arguing that coalitions of government officials and other interests form to carry out governmental policy or "social production," reigns supreme (Elkin, 1987; Imbroscio, 1998; Ramsay, 1996; Stoker and Mossberger, 1994; Stone, 1989; Turner, 2000, among many others). Although development regimes composed of local officials and the business community are thought to be most prevalent, the regime argument allows for a number of different permutations. Indeed, Stone (1993) has described four regime types—developmental, maintenance, middle-class progressive, and lower-class opportunity expansion—and other authors continue to expand on these. Indeed, it seems possible that the number of regime types could increase exponentially.

Even regime theory, with more variations in local governance arrangements and a wider array of possible actors, still does not consider the interplay between governing coalitions and the larger civic culture from which they form. In other words, it does not consider the forces and causes behind the development of a particular governing regime. Although different governing coalitions favor different combinations of interests and logically lead to different local policies, a more basic question begs to be answered: What leads to those particular governing regimes in the first place? Obviously, history plays a large role. Each community has a unique political and economic history that shapes current governing structures. But there is much more to how a particular community operates than just the governing regime. In short, the regime system is just one part of a larger way of doing things in a community, a larger civic culture. It is argued here that this is part of the reason for the conflicting or weak findings in efforts to explain economic development policies in general and Type II or more progressive policies in particular. Because the current inventory of independent variables has not been placed within the system of the larger local civic culture, analyses become limited and are presented out of context. The basic argument posited in this book is that broader civic cultures are significant and can be identified. These civic cultures are critical apart from the specific governing regime and help explain how local economic development decisions are made, who is involved, and what policies result. In short, local policy making across the board can not be fully understood without broadening the focus to embrace variations in local civic culture. How this can be done and the insights to be gained are demonstrated here through the lens of local economic development policy.

THE PLAN OF THE BOOK

The next chapter provides a historical portrait of how community power systems have been examined, moving from elitism to the current dominant regime theory. It then explores how what is known as political culture has been used in different literatures to understand both process and policy outcomes. The essential argument underlying the subsequent analysis is then presented. In short, it will be argued that the civic culture of local communities can be identified and categorized. Such civic cultures encompass local government structures and governing (regime) systems, community visions and goals, responses to the external environment as well as local economic exigencies, community power systems, decision-making processes, and ultimately, local policies. In short, it is argued that contemporary explanations of local economic development policy choice are wanting because they tend to focus on governing regime to the exclusion of larger cultural forces that both shape and define local regimes. "Regime" is only part of a larger system of civic culture.

Chapter 3 describes the methodology for the research, incorporating both large survey data analysis and intensive case studies. It begins with an examination of how local economic development policies have been defined and measured. In a broader sense, the limitations of current research using either surveys or case studies are discussed, and the ways that the combined methodology used here addresses those limitations is presented. Last, the method—both purposive and statistical—for selecting the case study cities is described and the cities introduced.

Chapter 4 extends the discussion of methods by describing how the various environmental and civic-culture variables are conceptualized and measured. It also includes a complete description of the nature of the cities in the large data set. It thus provides the necessary framework for the development of the models of civic culture and local development policy to follow.

In Chapter 5, the civic-culture argument is fleshed out and tested in an empirical fashion, using the large survey data base. The relationships between the environment of local governments, the local civic culture, and economic development policies are modeled, using path analysis, ultimately leading to a profile of the inner workings of local civic cultures. The analysis then moves to an examination of what difference civic culture makes in economic development policies and addresses the issue of the balance of power between economic, regime, and cultural explanations of local policy outcomes.

Chapter 6 serves as the bridge between the large survey and case study analyses. Specific types of civic cultures are identified and described using cluster analysis of the survey data. The case study cities representing the different types of local cultures are then identified, and profiles are presented for each of the nine cities.

The next four chapters present the case studies organized by cultural types. Chapter 7 presents the case studies for cities with strong-mayor governmental structures. Following the lines of the previous arguments, these cities, although sharing the same formal structure, vary according to the locus of power for economic development decision making. In one city, the mayor retains control, whereas in the other, economic development has been off-loaded to an external, mostly private, body.

Chapter 8 presents case studies of cities where no one group is dominant. These are politically inclusive cities where the decision-making culture reflects a pluralist model similar to that described by Dahl (1961) in New Haven. Both business and neighborhood input into decision making is high.

The elite-dominated cities—those dominated by either bureaucrats or businesses—are presented in Chapters 9 and 10. Cities where bureaucrats within city government have the greatest influence in economic development decision making predominate; five case cities represent such cultures. These cities vary in other regards, however, most important being the extent to which local elites take an active or passive approach toward economic development. Chapter 9 presents the case studies for the three cities where local elites take a proactive and entrepreneurial stance toward the economic development enterprise. The two remaining cities, which take a reactive or passive approach, are explored in Chapter 10.

Chapter 11 brings the survey and case study analyses together and discusses the contribution that consideration of the broader civic cultures of cities makes to the understanding of local economic development policy and policy making. It shows how case analyses can be used to flesh out generalized trends visible in large data sets. However, it is also clear that the statistical and case analyses are pointing to a similar set of cultural variables as being important in economic development policy making.

Last, Chapter 12 revisits what is "known" about local economic development process and policy and highlights the questions raised about that knowledge by the analyses used here and the focus on civic culture. New research questions are posed and new directions raised for continued application of a local civic culture approach toward understanding urban policy processes.

2

CIVIC CULTURE AND THEORIES OF LOCAL GOVERNANCE

[Political culture] refers to the specifically political orientations—attitudes toward the political system and its various parts, and attitudes toward the role of self in the system . . . the political system as internalized in the cognitions, feelings, and evaluations of its populations.

—Almond and Verba (1963:12-13)

[Political culture is] the particular pattern of orientation to political action in which each political system is embedded.

—Elazar (1994:9)

In sum, the political culture account identified distinctive clusters of attitudes that are widely held across individuals. These durable clusters form subjective world orientations that are highly resistant to change, and are seen as the fundamental generator of economic and political performance. They are, in this sense, more crucial than objective conditions embodied in institutions, and they endure in the face of institutional change.

—Jackman and Miller (1996:636)

17

The concept of *political* culture has been explored in the political science literature for decades, as the opening quotes illustrate. It has been used to explain international, national, and even state-level institutions, policies, and processes. To a lesser extent, local political cultures have also been explored, though usually tied to regime approaches and arguments. Yet the earlier debates about culture offer much about local policy making in general and economic development policy in particular.

Local political, or as will be argued later, civic, culture serves as a penumbra, its attributes and components defining what issues are problems, what solutions are possible, how decisions are made, and who is involved in decision making. Local civic cultures embody shared visions—past, present, and future—and are the essence of the local community. Civic culture shapes everything from governmental institutions to governing regimes and to the policies employed. It will be argued in this chapter that understanding local civic culture is critical to understanding various approaches to economic development. To frame this argument, previous uses of the term political culture will be explored, offering insight at various levels of analysis: international, national, state, and, to some extent, local. Definitions, indicators, and measures of political culture will be examined and applied to the local context. Last, *local civic culture* will be defined and positioned in relation to contemporary theories, most prominently, regime theory, to show how this broader frame adds to the understanding of and the ability to explain local development policy making.

WHAT IS POLITICAL CULTURE? BORROWING FROM THE PAST

Theoretical Approaches

The concept of political culture holds a prominent place in the history of political science research. Although it is beyond the scope of this project to provide a comprehensive description of this entire body of research, some pivotal studies will be described to highlight how the concept has been used, the heuristic importance of the concept, and how it might be applied to the study of local economic development policy making.

Elazar

The work of Daniel Elazar on political culture has spanned several decades. *American Mosaic,* a 1994 reformulation of his original ideas, suggests that political culture has a dual "manifestation" based on individual and community beliefs expressed through political symbols (patterns of understanding) and community and individual political style (patterns of action). Thus, political culture shapes governmental systems in three ways:

1. Through "perceptions of the political community"—which are the expectations for governmental actions and the appropriate role of government and the political process;
2. By "influencing recruitment" into the political process—perceptions of who should have access to the political system and the characteristics of politically active groups and individuals; and
3. By how the "art" of government is practiced—the implementation processes and policies that result. (Elazar, 1994:219)

In short, political culture shapes perceptions of how the government should function, who has access to it, and how and what policy outputs result. This definition of political culture is drawn from the earlier work of Kluckhohn (1954), which identified six pivotal themes underlying "cultures" more generally. These themes and their application to political culture more specifically are as follows:

1. *Language:* The political terms through which residents or members of a community communicate, the buzzwords used in political contexts or to describe or "vision" the community
2. *Aesthetic expression:* The political styles, symbols, and myths used in a community
3. *Standardized orientation to life problems:* Shared approaches to questions of who should have power, the balance between market and more progressive orientations, how potential leaders are recruited for political office, whose support is necessary to achieve political leadership roles, and visions about the proper role of the government in society
4. *Means to perpetuate the group:* How structures are maintained and function to maintain the society
5. *Individual demands for order:* How institutions process individual demands and how competing demands are mediated or reconciled

6. *Individual demands for survival:* Definitions of citizenship and rights to governmental services

Based on this definition, Elazar (1994) described three identifiable political subcultures among states in the United States: individualistic, moralistic, and traditionalistic. *Individualistic* cultures favored limited government engaging in only those activities that were necessary to maintain free market operations. Private concerns were emphasized through a system of mutual obligations and favoritism that regulated interactions between individuals and groups. In such cultures, there was little role for citizen initiative and participation in the political process, and most policy perspectives and decisions were nonideological. Bureaucratic structures and operations were acceptable as long as the outputs were efficient.

Moralistic political cultures placed a greater emphasis on the commonweal and the advancement of the public interest more broadly defined. It was viewed as appropriate for government to intervene as necessary in private sector activities to secure the public interest. Government was to be proactive in seeking agenda items that would enhance the public welfare. The role of the citizen vis-à-vis government was much larger; all citizens were obligated to be aware of and participate in politics. Bureaucratic structures were acceptable as long as they were operated in a neutral and rational process to determine "best" solutions.

Traditionalistic cultures did not trust the private marketplace nor the possible results of widespread citizen participation. Instead, the system would favor elites and elite interests. The role of government was to preserve both the interests of elites and their place in the community hierarchy. Social and family ties were critically important and served as the basis for interaction in society. Bureaucracy was eschewed in favor of more personal, face-to-face interactions.

Using these types, Elazar (1994) mapped the "American cultural matrix," the distribution of political cultures among states and among geographic regions within states. For example, although Michigan is shown as being a moralistic state, constituent cities are either moralistic or moralistic/individualistic combinations. Ohio has some moralistic cities in the north but is individualistic in the south; it is portrayed as individualistic overall. This analysis, however, is based on descriptive interpretations rather than on an empirical analysis of data collected to represent aspects of political culture. In other words, Elazar did not explicitly operationalize political culture, identifying indicators that could then be measured quantitatively. In this respect, his overall argument serves as a conceptual base providing direction but offers no explicit examples of how political culture can be measured.

Almond and Verba

The international political culture literature offers greater direction in the empirical measurement of the concept as well as hypothesizing and testing relationships between national political culture and various aspects of democratic performance. Almond and Verba's (1963) *The Civic Culture* serves as a seminal early work. In a study of five societies, they attempted to link political culture to democratic attributes, seeking to identify in particular a civic culture that promotes stable democratic systems, such as the United States and Great Britain.

According to Almond and Verba (1963), three components composing the political culture interact with the political system, composed of roles/structures, incumbents, and policies:

1. *Orientation:* Cognitive knowledge about how the political system operates, the individuals in office, and system outputs in terms of policy
2. *Affective:* Feelings about the political system, leaders, and output
3. *Evaluational:* Judgments and opinions about the operation of the processes, officials, and policy outputs

Based on these components, they identify three primary theoretical political cultures—*parochial, subject,* and *participant.* In addition, three subcultures are based on combinations of the primary cultures—parochial/subject, subject/participant, and parochial/participant. In the *parochial* culture, there is no separation between political and public and private roles; there is no role specialization within the system. Religious and social roles and authority are mixed with political roles. There are low expectations for the political system and very little awareness of either process or output among the citizenry. Obviously, such a culture would not emphasize nor include citizen participation in authority systems, whether religious, social, or political. The *subject*

political culture embodies specialized governmental or political authority, but there is still little awareness of system outputs nor any support for citizen participation on the input side of the process. There is
limited general civic competence; power flows from the top down. Yet
political, social, and religious powers are delineated. In *participant* political cultures, citizens are aware of and interested in both the input
and output sides of the political process. The culture supports and ad-
vocates active participation in the political system.

It is useful to note that Almond and Verba (1963) clearly differentiate
between political *culture* and political *structure*. These are separate
though obviously related entities whose nature conflicts at times, particularly during periods of large-scale cultural change. For example, citizen apathy and alienation can occur when a participatory culture is developing, whereas political structures emphasize a subject culture. This
sort of incongruency can lead to the development of subculture combinations—in this case, representing a subject/parochial combination. A
parochial/participant subculture would reflect a situation where the
political culture is still generally passive but participatory input structures have been introduced. A civic political culture, identified as most
functional for a stable democracy through both theoretical arguments
and country case studies, is one that combines elements of all three major types. A civic culture is one where there are input mechanisms,
strong system allegiance, and reasonably high levels of political participation among the general citizenry. However, stability is maintained,
and the system is protected from demand overload because there are
also cultural elements of disinterest and passivity. In short, participant
and subject cultures are combined.

Jackman and Miller

Revisiting this literature, Jackman and Miller (1996) examine and re-
test the political culture arguments of Almond and Verba's (1963) as
well as McClelland's (1961/1963) work connecting the need for
achievement in cultures and economic growth, Inglehart's (1990) study
of economic performance and democracy in industrial societies, and
Putnam's research on Italy arguing that effective government depends
on the extent of civic engagement in a culture. They ultimately conclude that "cultural accounts of political life" are overrated and that the

"political culture approach needs to be recast in institutional terms that more directly acknowledge the role of political considerations in explaining performance" (Putnam, 1993:633).

In testing prior theories, Jackman and Miller present a useful summary of the assumptions underpinning earlier arguments about political culture:

> Cultures were considered to represent relatively "coherent clusters of attitudes."
>
> Arguments focused on the extent and frequency of such attitudes in society.
>
> Cultural "syndromes" were assumed to be "durable" in that they persisted with only slight modifications over time.
>
> Cultural systems would drive other outcomes, such as economic growth and political performance at a system level. (Jackman and Miller, 1996:635)

Their analysis fails to reveal any significant effects of political culture using earlier data sets with different measures and indexes. They conclude that either the indicators don't identify different kinds of political cultures, that the performance of indicators used is unstable, or that culture is not strongly associated with political system performance. These possibilities as well as the approach to measuring the concept of political culture are important and will be addressed specifically.

State and Local Applications

The notion of political culture has also been applied to analysis of subunits within nations, notably in a body of research by Sharkansky in the late 1960s and early 1970s, although the term "political culture" is not specifically used. In an analysis of 17 regions of the United States (determined a priori), he found higher levels of consistency within than between regions for a large list of variables, such as voting rates, characteristics of the state legislatures, state expenditure and tax patterns, and spending on selected services, with the upper middle west and the mountain regions being most distinctive. Thus, he concludes that the findings "suggest the existence of regional processes—processes that may include shared experiences and norms—at work on the character of state affairs" (Sharkansky, 1970:75). Sharkansky points to the

"political attitudes and values" of early regional settlers as contributing
to levels of economic development within regions. Still, there was less
internal regional consistency in patterns of expenditure than in process
issues, suggesting that regional cultures may be more visible in *how*
things are done than in *what* things are done.

Elazar's (1994) original cultural types have been tested several times
by researchers examining state political cultures (Erikson, Wright, and
McIver, 1993; Koven, 1999, for example). Thus, Koven finds that state
civic culture, which "embodied a vision of community, premised on citizenship," appears to affect budgetary practices (1999:2). Using Elazar's
(1994) original classification of state cultures, patterns can be identified
between culture and per capita taxes and spending, interest on debt,
and educational spending. He concludes that "the cognitive environment (identified in both political culture and political ideology) shapes
administrative actions" (Koven, 1999:145).

Erikson et al. (1993) also found support for Elazar's (1994) cultural
distinctions and concluded that state political culture had an impact on
partisanship and political ideology. Again, in this case, no empirical
measures of state culture were developed. Elazar's categories were employed in one part of the analysis, whereas in others, political culture
was represented by a state dummy variable. Thus, culture was more
assumed than measured.

Conceptual Definitions

Because political culture has often been explored at the national or
international scale, operational definitions are not necessarily readily
applicable to the local context. And although Elazar's (1994) work focused on states and localities, it did not emphasize actual empirical
measurements. The studies testing Elazar's classification also did not
contain independent empirical measures of culture. However, an examination of the indicators used in the comparative study of political
culture serves as a starting point for the development of an operational
definition to be employed at the local level.

Almond and Verba (1963) used an extensive list of political culture
indicators in their five-nation study. In general terms, the indicators
of political culture included eight attributes: (a) political cognition,
(b) feelings toward government/politics, (c) patterns of partisanship,

(d) obligations to participate, (e) civic competence, (f) social relations, (g) organizational membership, and (h) political socialization. Most of these indicators are themselves concepts so are not readily applicable to field research. Thus, an even longer list of indicators was used to collect survey data, including questions relating to the impact of national and local governments on daily life (asked separately), nature of that impact (good/bad), awareness of national politics, attention to the media, ability to name national officials, willingness and ability to express political opinions, identification of aspects of the nation/culture that elicit feelings of pride, expectation for equal treatment from the government, participation in discussions about politics, perceived restrictions to talking about politics, qualities attributed to political parties and party members, social distance measures related to political party members, attitudes about voting (satisfaction, anger, apathy), perceptions about the appropriate levels of individual political activity, efficacy, knowledge about avenues for system input, trust, leisure activities, membership in voluntary associations, and influence in internal family decisions.

Inglehart (1990) employed a similar, albeit smaller, list of indicators of political culture in his cross-national study of the connections between Protestant ethics and the performance of industrial democracies. These included levels of overall life satisfaction, levels of interpersonal trust, support for revolutionary change, support for the current social order, levels of political discussion, levels of postmaterialist values, and proportion of the population that was Protestant. Putnam (1993), in examining the twenty Italian regions, used two conceptual components of political culture: civic community and historical civic traditions. The former was operationalized using an index that included preference voting, referendum turnout, newspaper readership, and the number of sports and cultural associations. The latter was represented by an index of strength of mass parties, cooperatives, membership in mutual aid societies, electoral turnout, and longevity of local associations (see Jackman and Miller, 1996:641).

Although Jackman and Miller (1996) used the same data and hence the same indicators of political culture, in their reanalysis of the Inglehart (1990) and Putnam (1993) data, they concluded that the exact composition of indicators could be improved. For example, they found some instability in the Putnam indexes because different results occurred when correlating the individual component variables and the indexes themselves with the dependent measures of institutional performance. How well political culture variables "explained" institutional performance and economic growth were dependent, in part, on how the concepts were operationalized. This led the authors to conclude that the weak explanatory power of political culture could be due to three factors: The indicators are incomplete in some way or do not properly identify or distinguish different kinds of political cultures, the performance of the indicators is not stable, or political culture is simply not strongly associated with institutional or economic performance. This is an important point to consider because the first two explanations are basically related to measurement, whereas the third represents a theory failure. Because Jackman and Miller identified problems with the indicators themselves, they concluded in part that, although culture is likely an important variable, it may be endogenous rather than exogenous, as it has been typically employed. In other words, they suggest that political culture results from the structure of economic, social, and political institutions: "It may prove fruitful to recast the puzzle in more institutional terms, and in the process to endogenize political culture" (Jackman and Miller, (1996:654). This possibility obviously needs to be carefully considered along with the measurement issues inherent in using the concept. The next section will address these issues as they relate to research on local communities.

THE POLITICAL CULTURE OF LOCAL COMMUNITIES: WHO HAS POWER?

More germane to this study is the way in which "culture" has been used to examine processes and outputs among *local* governments. Although some research has explicitly mentioned local political culture, much of the political culture context has been implicit within the community power debates and has now been subsumed within the regime theory context. Regardless of the form or nomenclature, however, questions of who has power in local communities and whose interests predominate have been central to the study of urban politics for decades. When the focus has been on local economic development policy, such questions have been integral to the analysis. Although some scholars have assumed that all local cultures were similar in that business interests would be favored in development decision making, more recent applications of regime theory open the door for different systems of local power arrangements, acknowledging a wide variety of local cultures.

The Community Power Debate:
The Inherent Implications of Culture

Although not necessarily framed explicitly in political or civic culture terms, the early work on community power systems implicitly examined political, community, and power cultures in localities. Dahl's work on New Haven (1961) presented the culture of pluralism as an alternative to elitist theories. The debate was basically framed around opposing cultural types. New Haven served as the example of the prototypical pluralist political culture, whereby citizens had input into community decision making through group membership, groups were all relatively equal in power resources or at least had countervailing power attributes, and the political system was viewed as being the neutral balancer of competing group demands. This last element or assumption was particularly critical because it implies that the state, even the local state, will be independent and powerful enough to allocate benefits and costs among groups. Furthermore, it was an accepted part of the culture that no one group would win all of its demands all the time; rather, policy outputs would represent compromise among the various groups. Pluralism then became both an empirical and normative theory. Not only was it argued that pluralism provided the more accurate explanation of local political cultures but that pluralist systems would provide the *best* model for the balancing of competing demands within a democratic system.

Those who looked at local governments, such as Hunter (1953) in Atlanta, and saw elitist power systems operating argued that interest groups, political parties, and indeed, even local government structures were immaterial. They were the window dressing behind which power brokers—elite interests—pulled the strings on both process and policy. Thus, those who held capital in communities—wealthy families and perhaps some primary information brokers, such as media owners—

organized local political systems in ways that ensured both direct benefits and continued power positions. Elitism, then, reflects a picture of a
very different local culture, one where a small group of powerful individuals operate the political system to their own benefit, and any democratic input processes are mere smokescreens or mechanisms to co-opt
"the masses."

It is useful, from a methodological standpoint, to consider why researchers looked at power structure in localities and saw such very different things. First, much of the initial community power literature was
based on case studies of individual cities. It is quite possible that elitists
and pluralists were both correct: different power systems or cultures
operated in different cities. Second, the studies were conducted at different periods of time and focused on different policies. Again, authors
on both sides of the debate could be correct. Power systems can change
over time; they are not immutable, no matter how historically ingrained. And there may well be different power configurations surrounding different local policy issues. Land owners and developers
may be very interested in local taxing and zoning policy but are perhaps
less so about recreation or waste collection services. Last, the community power studies employed significantly different research methodologies. For example, many of the scholars finding elitist power systems
were sociologists using position overlap or perceptual methods of identifying powerful individuals. Pluralists, who tended to be political scientists, were much more likely to look at decision-making processes,
such as following press and legislative debates about particular issues.
These issues are important because they highlight the fact that so much
of what is found is dependent on the methods used for looking. As argued in the following chapter, analyses that combine different research
approaches will be more likely to transcend the limitations inherent in
any one method.

Stone's (1980) theory of systemic power did much to reconcile earlier
debates, emphasizing the reality that capital and other power resources
are not equally divided within free-market economies. Based on work
by Bachrach and Baratz (1962) regarding the "second face of power," he
argued that some groups and individuals are going to have more resources than others. Thus, as Bachrach and Baratz posited, power can be
expressed without being overtly exercised, best exemplified by the
power of some groups to keep particular debates off the local political

agenda entirely, creating what are called nondecisions. On the other hand, local government officials are not simply the pawns of these interests; they have independent power and can act against purely economic motivations. Furthermore, citizen input through democratic processes matters in the nature and output of local governments. Still, some groups hold resources that are particularly critical to local political leaders—campaign resources, capital investment, and ultimately, jobs for local citizens. Because of this, economic interests are likely to operate in a favored position; they become the preeminent but not the exclusive arbiters of local policy. In short, "policy responses to the economic position of the city are thus mediated through the politics of the city" (Stone and Sanders, 1987:169).

City Limits and Growth Machines

The extent to which economic interests predominate in local decision making and whether such influence is immutable was the focus of Peterson's (1981) *City Limits.* He clearly comes down on the side of the inherent dominance of business groups, particularly those related to export industries, due to the unitary interest of cities in attracting and retaining capital investment to secure the local economy. As in Stone's (1980) systemic power theory, Peterson (1981) argues that local officials must focus on business interests because economic capital is mobile. Securing investment is necessary to maintain public services, ensure jobs for residents, and meet their own electoral needs. Developmental policies are also more popular than distributive or redistributive policies that create winners and losers because they appear to bring additional revenue to the community and thus pay for themselves.

Because cities are limited in their ability to control labor and capital in production, they focus on land-based activities in their development policies. This provides an easy transition from the "limited city" to the growth machine arguments of Logan and Molotch (1987). Here, property entrepreneurs push for the intensification of development and increase the value of their investments. Such entrepreneurs include actors who stand to benefit from local, particularly land-based, growth—financial institutions, realtors, lawyers, the media, and even institutions such as universities and foundations. Multinational corporations may not be as important as local business interests, however, because they are not necessarily tied to the prosperity of a single place (Jones and Bachelor, 1993; Molotch, 1988). Local officials share this interest in development because

> [They] are themselves a component of the growth machine—partly because most accept the dominant ideology of growth, partly because some may personally benefit from increases in land rents, and, more broadly, because of the need or desire for campaign contributions from elements of the growth machine, particularly property developers and speculators. (Wolman, 1996:118-119; see also, Logan and Molotch, 1987)

Both the city limits and growth machine arguments posit a single, pervasive, local political culture where growth, land-based, or development interests sit in systemic superiority to other groups, requiring that local officials ensure that their interests are maintained and furthered for the greater good.

Regime Theory: An Explosion of Riches

Extending his systemic-power theory, Stone (1989) introduced the concept of local political regimes through case study research on Atlanta. Regime theory rests on the critical distinction between the *government as structure* and the *act of governing*. The former represents the forms of local government and the elected and appointed local officials therein. However, to make things happen in a community, to marshal resources, bring interests together, and enact and implement policies— in other words, to meet what are called social production goals—government officials need to form coalitions with other groups within the community. Such coalitions allow local officials to govern. Central to regime theory is the distinction between power as social production rather than social control. In this sense, the end result of power is to be able to marshal resources to achieve social ends. In sum, public policies are shaped by the following three elements:

1. The composition of a community's governing coalition,
2. The nature of relationships among members of the governing coalition, and
3. The resources that members bring to the governing coalition. (Stone, 1993:2)

Inherent in the argument is the implication that each local system will vary in its responses to systemic power interests, and such responses may vary over time and by issue. Thus, contrary to earlier elitist or growth machine arguments, the door opens for consideration of *different* local cultures that define the extent to which economic interests are favored and under what circumstances. As Swanstrom notes,

> City governments do not simply respond, in knee jerk fashion, to the pressure of growth; growth pressures must be filtered through local political systems with particular rules, power arrangements, and perceptions of the governmental marketplace. The needs of the political system may clash with the needs for economic growth. (Swanstrom (1985:33)

And such rules, power arrangements, and perceptions form the basis of a local civic culture.

Urban regime theory has prospered in recent years, and the number of regime types keeps growing and may continue to do so in the future. Stone (1989) initially described three regimes: corporate, caretaker, and progressive. *Corporate regimes* included governmental officials in governing coalitions with interests represented by the growth machine: realtors, bankers, developers, and other land interests. The main governmental goal is to attract business by offering incentives and employing land-based strategies. *Caretaker regimes* typically involved citizen groups or neighborhood interests and small local—often retail—businesses. In contrast to corporate regimes, the overriding goal of local government was to limit activities and initiatives and hence taxes. *Progressive regimes* required higher educational levels among the citizenry along with significant citizen involvement. Local educational institutions were often also part of the governing coalition that supported policies that increased amenities and redistributed the benefits of development.

Later, Stone revised this typology to include four regimes, basically dividing progressive regimes into two types: middle-class progressive and lower-class opportunity expansion regimes. Similar to his initial typology, *developmental regimes* focus on changing the nature of land to promote growth; they "link private investment and public action" (Stone, 1993:18). There is an inherent desire within the regime to keep the public out of economic development decision making and allow selective benefits to be distributed to the economic interests within the governing coalition. The central role of government is to ensure that the desired investment and hence development occurs. *Maintenance regimes* are similar to the original caretaker type. Here, the regime culture supports a limited role for government, providing routine services, to keep tax levels low and maintain the development status quo within the community. Small, locally owned businesses and neighborhood groups form the core of the governing regime. *Middle-class progressive* regimes occur in cities where educated middle-class interests press for service amenities; local governments monitor and regulate economic elites to ensure that larger community goals are met. Business interests are not deterred by these regimes, however, because the city becomes more attractive as a result of enhanced educational, recreational, and cultural elements and other amenities. There are high levels of citizen involvement in the governing regime. Last, *lower-class opportunity expansion regimes* focus on a different agenda of progressive policies: education, job training, home ownership, and transportation access. Community-based organizations have a central role in such regimes, although the government is active in business regulation. Stone posits this type as hypothetical because of the difficulty in keeping citizens, particularly low-income citizens, motivated to participate over the long term and the political perils of maintaining a redistributive agenda. Such regimes would find themselves in a catch-22 situation, where the cities with the weakest economies are pursuing an agenda requiring the greatest amount of resources to maintain mass mobilization.

Scholars have continued to accept the regime framework in analyzing local power and governing systems. And the number of regime types has continued to expand. In a sense, this speaks to the power of Stone's (1989) initial concept; regime theory has been applied to a growing number of cities, even across national borders (see DiGaetano and Klemanski, 1993; Haughton and While, 1999; Levine, 1994, for example). Regime analysis has been expanded to explain cross-border governing coalitions (Clarke, 1999). Orr and Stoker (1994) added "human capital regimes" based on a study of Detroit, where community and business leaders, the school board, and the chamber of commerce coalesced to circumvent the mayor and emphasize public education. In a recent discussion of Latino politics in San Antonio, Texas, Flores (1999) identifies four regime types by time period—machine city, reform city,

entrepreneurial city, international city—based on changes in dominance within the business sector and government and electoral structures. Regardless of the exact composition of the business sector within
the governing regime, structural changes, and increasing Latino participation and representation in public office, resultant policies have not
necessarily been favorable to their interests and have not brought consistent economic improvement. This juxtaposition—apparent regime
shift without policy change—highlights a possible shortcoming of regime analysis, discussed more fully in the discussion to follow.

Imbroscio (1998) introduced three more types of local regimes: community based, petty bourgeois, and local statist. These additional regimes are based on a reformulation of regime theory that Imbroscio argues addresses several major shortcomings of Stone's (1989) original
framework: that it assumes a clear division between the state and the
market and then organizes regime types accordingly, that it minimizes
the ability of the state to be active in the market, and that it ignores the
fact that the state can act in an entrepreneurial manner in a true market
sense. His new regimes types are based on the relaxation of assumptions of a separation between the market and the state. *Community-based
regimes* present a governing coalition composed of community or neighborhood groups and their allies who have gotten power through the
electoral process. *Petty-bourgeois regimes* are composed of small local
businesses that are spatially rooted, corporate elites, and governmental
officials. Last, *local-statist regimes* have a central role for local government officials who are quite independent from other possible coalition
members. Here, local officials have found means to finance the state
through participation of the city in profit-making market-based activities. In this last case, local officials are relatively free from the need to
form governing coalitions with other actors.

Another approach to urban regimes is to emphasize their historical
time periods. For example, Fainstein and Fainstein described three
types of regimes: (a) directive (1950-1964), which pushed for development through governmental and business dominance; (b) concessionary (1965-1974), which were similar but included some policy conces-
sions to lower-class interests; and (c) conserving (1975-present), which
are dominated by elites who press for a more fiscally conservative
agenda (Fainstein and Fainstein, 1983:245-282). In a similar vein, Elkin
(1987) identities three regimes or urban axes, which are public-private

growth alliances and electoral coalitions, also organized by time period and geography. *Pluralist regimes* in the northeast and Midwest from the 1950s through the 1960s are similar to directive regimes. *Federalist regimes* were prevalent during the 1960s and 1970s and are similar to the concessionary regime's emphasis on redistribution of benefits to the lower class. *Entrepreneurial regimes,* most prevalent in the South after World War II, are very similar in composition and emphasis to growth machines.

Many other applications and extensions of regime theory have been presented:

> Stoker and Mossberger's (1994) organic, instrumental, and symbolic regimes: Organic regimes are similar to caretaker regimes where the emphasis is on limited government and the status quo. Instrumental regimes are similar to developmental regimes. Symbolic regimes—probably one of the most useful conceptual additions to the regime literature—focus on changing local images. Such regimes are most likely to be transitional, forming during periods of local revitalization. The symbolic regime concept has been applied to sports promotion strategies (Henry and Paramio-Salcines, 1994) and cross-border governing arrangements. (Clarke, 1999)

> Ramsay (1996), in case studies of two rural communities, found one to have a development regime, whereas the other, a "subsistence" regime. The latter was composed of small business owners, minorities, the poor, and those making their livelihood from fishing. It favored policies similar to a caretaker regime: low taxing and spending, very limited growth and development, and reliance on state and federal funds for infrastructure.

> Kantor et al.'s description of planner, distributor, vendor, radical, grantsman, clientelist, commercial, and free enterprise regimes is premised on the notion that regimes can be identified by bargaining environments. Such environments are structured by the positional advantage balance between the public and private sectors and include aspects of democratic conditions, market position, and intergovernmental environments of cities. (Kantor et al., 1997:350)

> Dowding et al. (1999) identify development, service, and failed regimes in their study of six London boroughs, with the last representing periodic attempts at regime formations that do not meet the test of time.

> Turner (2000) provides a discussion of shifting regime boundaries, as opposed to changes in overall regime type. Thus, boundary shifts—changes at the margins in access and benefits—are more likely to occur than wholesale regime change.

Although the growth of regime types illustrates the applicability and power of regime theory, it also begs another question. Are ever more regime types necessary because regime theory does not account for all of the important dynamics in localities? Are there policies and processes that regime theory does not seem to explain? Can regime theory be used to explain processes and policies in *all* cities? Mossberger and Stoker (2000) raise some important concerns. One is that regime theory has been stretched beyond its original definitions in an effort to apply it to ever more situations. Returning to Stone's initial work from 1989-1993, they argue effectively that regimes *must* have the following characteristics:

Be informal yet stable coalitions with access to resources

Contain governmental and business actors; they thus cross the public and private sectors

Cannot be assumed to exist in all cities—no cooperation across sectors means no regime

Have distinct policy agendas

Be based on a history of consensus and selective incentives (Mossberger and Stoker, 2000; p. 5)

If Stone's (1989) initial criteria for a regime are accepted, then several conclusions must be drawn. As noted, many cities will not have regimes because they lack stable governing coalitions. And many cities will not have regimes because the private sector is not significantly involved in governance. Thus, regime theory cannot be used to explain process and policy in all cities. Furthermore, Dowding et al. note that the "regime concept . . . at best denotes a model or concept rather than a theory" because the latter would require predictive power regarding type of regime or the policy agenda pursued (Dowding et al., 1999:517). If regime theory then also fails at being a theory, how can it be used to fully understand local process and policy?

One of the symptoms of a developing paradigm shift is an increasing number of questions and problems not explained by the predominant paradigm (Kuhn, 1962). If scholars continue to find different power or governing coalitions within cities that don't quite match a reasonably parsimonious number of regime types, then perhaps something *is* missing. To go full circle, then, the earlier political culture work has a lot to

say about what seems to be absent from the current foci on regimes—
that is, that regimes are only *one part* of the local civic culture. There are
cultural forces that shape regimes, determine likely coalition members,
affect how the regime operates (the rules of the game), and define what
policy outcomes are possible and desirable. The next section posits a
new theory that incorporates regime theory into the larger local civic
culture.

Integrating Regimes and Culture

What is the relationship between regime theory and political or civic
culture as theoretical approaches? Stone posits a distinction resting on
the role of economics in differentiating between pluralism and regime
theory: "The urban strain of classic pluralism drew heavily on a political
culture approach, whereas the analysis of urban regimes stems from
a political economy perspective" (Stone, 1993:1). However, such a distinction does not address the question of why economic perspectives
cannot be incorporated within the local culture itself. Although Stone
(1993:6) is correct in noting that economic forces are "largely absent"
from pluralist descriptions of reality, there is no inherent reason why
this must be. Indeed, it has been suggested that regime theory rests on
many of the same assumptions as later neopluralist arguments: that
business elites are in a privileged position; that as a result, democratic
processes may not function in a neutral fashion; and that fragmentation
in society is a central challenge of governance (Stoker, 1995).

Sites (1997) points to several limitations of regime theory explicitly
revolving around its failure to fully incorporate larger environmental
forces. In its focus on the composition of the governing coalition itself,
regime theory does not pay sufficient attention to the patterns of policy
benefits that result. The ruling regime may change, but unless groups
that benefit from public policies also change, a true regime shift has not
occurred—the lesson stressed in Flores's (1999) analysis of San Antonio.
Regime analysis has also underestimated federal and state impacts on
local policy as well as the effects of broader capital flows. Intergovernmental relations are an important part of the environment of local politics and policy making. Last, regime theory has focused too much on
"public-sector actors, local-state initiatives, and coalition building" and

too little on "market and community pressures, economic restructuring, and national-state retrenchment" (Sites, 1997:552).

It is argued here that the concept of governing coalitions and the critical role of the economy underlying regime analysis can be incorporated into a civic culture approach that also includes forces such as regional, state, and federal relationships. Indeed, Stone presents the seeds of this argument in particular relationship to economic development:

> By embracing a political economy perspective, regime theory rejects the notion that modern life consists of discrete spheres of activity, largely insulated from one another. The physical redevelopment of the city can be seen as part of a fundamental process of restructuring. Through the modification of land use, redevelopment spills over into all areas of community activity. (Stone, 1993:16)

It is a logical extension of this line of thinking that the civic culture, composed of the broader aspects of community life, politics, and economics, will encompass and shape the nature of the local governing regime. In his essay on regime theory and urban politics, Stoker addresses the "need to put regimes in context":

> Regimes exist within the broader external regional or national environment, as well as a local environment. The capacity of local regimes can be substantially enhanced by their access to nonlocal powers and resources. Equally nonlocal forces can constrain or influence the direction of regimes. Regimes need to be placed in the architecture of governmental complexity. (Stoker, 1995:66-67)

Some authors have already begun to explore local culture as a variable influencing urban regimes. Indeed, a recognition of the role of political culture in urban politics was used in Banfield and Wilson's *City Politics*. In general terms, they describe the local political culture as follows:

> The attachment people have to a city is in great part based on a set of common expectations about how others will behave in civic and political affairs. These common expectations might be called the city's "political culture" that, like culture generally, is "learned" by the members. A participant acquires a more or less stable set of beliefs about who runs things,

how to get things done, whom to see, who wants what, and where "the
bodies are buried." (Banfield and Wilson, 1963:58)

In a more recent example, Ferman uses political culture as a central
concept in her examination of progressive politics and regime formation in Chicago and Pittsburgh, tying it to the larger culture of liberal individualism. She argues that the "larger political culture, within which
all cities operate, is mediated by local political cultures that may create
further obstacles for progressive policy or may enhance the possibilities for such policy" (Ferman, 1996:9).

However, in Ferman's analysis, political culture does not end up receiving a sufficiently broad focus to really push the boundaries of its
power as an alternative theory of local policy making. Political culture
becomes just one aspect or force important in shaping progressive development policies, along with urban arenas (civic and electoral), external constraints, internal constraints (business and neighborhood interests), regime, and policy outcome. If one returns to the earlier work of
Kluckhohn (1954) and Elazar (1994), political culture would subsume or
encompass all of these forces.

This broader approach to local culture is pursued by Ramsay (1996)
in her analysis of economic development policies and processes in two
rural communities in Maryland. She notes, "A particular regime may itself be viewed as the product of economic, social, and political processes
occurring through time. A regime must be understood, then, as both
cause and consequence of ongoing historical processes" (Ramsay,
1996:5). Thus, aspects of the unique histories of the two communities
lead to different mores about the types of leadership and conflict styles
that are acceptable, the emergence of different regimes (development
and subsistence), and different stances toward economic development.
The focus on two small communities limits the analysis, and based on
Stone's original definition, it is questionable whether there really were
governing regimes, because in one, business influence was more systemic than governing, whereas the other appeared to operate more as a
caste system than a regime. However, the notion that regimes are
shaped by broader forces—specifically, culture—is an important one.

Savitch and Kantor also reintroduce the concept of local political culture in their study of ten cities in Western democracies. "Local culture"
is considered to be the extent to which a community evidences post

materialist attributes including white collar employment base, large managerial and professional employment, small households, and values favoring indivisible benefits (Savitch and Kantor, 1999:5). In their larger model, market conditions and the extent of intergovernmental integration shape the local culture, as defined earlier, as well as the extent of popular control of elections and input mechanisms. These then affect political processes and, ultimately, policy outcomes in the following way: The market and intergovernmental forces are considered to be "driving" variables that provide the basic resources for development to occur. These define the steering variables (culture and popular control) that determine options within that predetermined frame.

Although this model incorporates political culture, intergovernmental relations, and the larger economy, it still makes distinctions between culture and other system attributes that are likely artificial and spurious. Furthermore, it is questionable the extent to which market forces and intergovernmental relations "cause" particular cultures to develop. Last, defining culture as a postmaterialist employment mix is far too limiting.

DiGaetano and Lawless (1999) take almost the opposite approach by expanding the definition of regimes to include "governing structures" and "policy agendas." Governing structures broaden the notion of regime composition to include consideration of the relationship between the state and society (particularistic, bureaucratic, elite negotiation, or pluralistic) and the "governing logic" of decision makers (pragmatic, consensual, technocratic, or conflict management). Policy agendas include pro-growth, social reform, and caretaker. Thus, with policy agendas closely matching Stone's types, DiGaetano and Lawless provide a broader yet more contextual notion of regime that includes how the local culture defines public/private relations and hence the role of government. This conceptual framework is clearly moving in the right direction, yet its focus on regime causes the overall approach to be too narrow still, in that many important aspects of the local milieu are missing: intergovernmental relations, history, local vision and goals, input mechanisms, and so on. And at the end of the day, their analysis seems to argue as much for a deterministic tendency for economic stress to lead to corporatist structures and agendas based on the three cities explored—Detroit, Birmingham, and Sheffield. What is needed is yet another move up the ladder of abstraction to think in broader terms than regime via a "more general or umbrella concept" that would encompass regimes yet move beyond them (Santori, 1991; Mossberger and Stoker, 2000:9). This, too, takes some pressure off the regime concept because it currently is being used to explain many situations and policies that are simply beyond its capacities (Bailey, 1999). As Ramsay notes, consideration of "life patterning social structures and cultural values" allows for a more complete understanding of local development policy than regime theory that tends to emphasize a "too narrow focus on interests" (Ramsay, 1996:22).

A MODEL OF LOCAL CIVIC CULTURE

Defining Local Civic Culture

To broaden the discussion to include local political or civic culture, it is useful to explore the concept of *habitus* developed by Bourdieu (see Painter, 1997). Habitus is tied to the French definition of the word *disposition*. In French, disposition has two meanings: (a) the predisposition that causes individuals and groups to act in certain ways and (b) the results of this process of interaction (i.e., the distribution of goods or benefits). In each community, there are different dispositions that mediate back and forth between structure and practice, creating the particular habitus both within groups and between groups in the community. Every group of local actors has a habitus that focuses "on the ways in which particular groups of actors make practical sense of their political world" (Painter, 1997:137). This implies that different groups of actors, even within the same regime, will "know in different ways" (137). However, it can also be extended to argue that different communities will have their own habitus or culture that defines how individuals and groups act within the public sphere and the nature of development policies that result.

Habitus broadens the concept of local political culture used in earlier studies and provides an operational definition for this analysis. A discussion of nomenclature is necessary at this point. The literature previously cited has used the term *political culture* to express the cultural context of politics, process, and policy. It is argued here that the concept of a local "civic culture" is more appropriate. A careful examination of definitions shows that a political culture refers to state affairs or national measures pertaining to nations or states as opposed to civil or municipal affairs. Thus, politics is "having a fixed or regular system of administration of government, the science of government of a nation or a state for the preservation of its safety, peace, and prosperity" (*The New Webster's Encyclopedic Dictionary*, 1971). The use of "political" culture in this way makes perfect sense in light of past political culture literature that has focused primarily on comparisons of national cultures. However, a local culture is somewhat different. "Civic," according to Webster's, means "pertaining to a city or citizen, relating to the community or to the policy and government of the citizens and subjects of a state." Funk and Wagnalls's *Standard Dictionary* defines *civic* as "of or pertaining to a city, citizen or citizenship, civic—of or pertaining to community life." Combined with the definition of culture then, the civic culture becomes the local or community sum of "attainments and learned behavior patterns" of a people. In short, the civic culture

> relates specifically to local rather than national political arenas;
> refers more specifically to the life of a community, and thus,
> denotes the patterns or way of life in a *local* community.

Civic culture then is both a broader and more focused concept than political culture. It is more focused because it specifically applies to the local or municipal community. It is broader because it encompasses not only how people govern themselves but also larger patterns of understanding and community behavior. And although the term has been used in the comparative literature to denote a particular type of political culture—one that supports democratic institutions (see Almond and Verba, 1963; Swank, 1996, for example)—there is no inherent reason why that should be the case. The local civic culture can take on many forms.

Civic culture, then, includes the structure of the local economic development decision-making enterprise, the process through which decisions are made, the interests that are involved in decision making, and the decision-making styles evident in the local public arena. The *structure* of economic development decision making includes the nature and extent of community recourses devoted to economic development, the external competitive environment of the locality vis-à-vis other cities,

and the structure of the economic development enterprise itself. Decision-making *processes* include the locus of primary power in economic
development decisions encompassing the balance between government and other actors, the role of local bureaucrats in the decision process, and most important, the balancing between business and citizen
groups in the making of development decisions. *Decision-making styles*
are represented by the world views of the process participants, the extent of rationality in the decision process, how goals are set and the nature of those goals, how the community envisions itself now and in the
future, and the extent to which development participants feel they can
affect and/or control the destiny of their community. In this sense, local
economic development decisions and policies are more than
economism and indeed are more contextually defined than a particular
regime; they are socially embedded within the cultural fabric of a local
community. In short,

> Actors do not behave or decide as atoms outside a social context, nor do
> they adhere slavishly to a script written for them by the particular inter-
> section of social categories that they happen to occupy. Their attempts at
> purposive actions are instead embedded in concrete, ongoing systems of
> social relations. (Granovetter, 1985:487)

These components of local civic culture reflect the central attributes
of culture identified by Kluckhohn (1954). The decision-making styles
include the language used to describe the community, the "visions"
that local stakeholders identify when they talk about the community
and its future. The ways in which decisions are made are also shaped by
and reflect the local symbols and myths. The so-called standardized
orientation to life is encompassed within the decision-making process
and includes how individuals are recruited for office, whose support is
needed to run for office, and more broadly, the perceived proper role of
government in the community. The structures of development decision
making affect how group interests are maintained. A consideration of
the interests involved in development decision making includes how
institutions deal with individual demands and how competing demands are mediated. Last, the balance between citizen and business
needs in the decision-making process has much to say about who is a
citizen and hence has the greatest "right" to governmental services.

Each community, then, embodies a civic culture or habitus representing historically informed local systems for political and/or public action and processes for distribution of goods. It is thus possible that two communities could have the same interests within the ruling coalition yet, because of different customs or processes, use very different economic development policies. In the same way, similar structures of local government—strong mayor or city manager, for example—may operate very differently in practice across communities because of differences in local culture. The potential differences in local civic culture are more important than many surface similarities in structure and even economics. Indeed, to paraphrase Wallace Sayre, local governments may be similar in all *unimportant* respects: form of government, tax base, and even governing coalition, for example. It is the fine distinctions in local culture, the habitus of how interests are balanced, problems defined, symbols interpreted, goals envisioned, and decisions made that will have the greatest and perhaps most subtle effects on public policy.

A Model of Local Civic Culture

Figure 2.1 presents a heuristic model of the role and components of civic culture in local economic development policy making. This model will be further developed and tested in later chapters. Three central forces compose the model: the environment, the local civic culture, and development policy outcomes. Environmental forces, over time, shape the local civic culture, and both of these forces affect the development policies that result. Environmental forces found to be important in development policy from previous studies include the structure of local government, the nature of the chief executive, and the basis for selecting city council members. Because this study is comparative, nation—Canada or United States—is a critical environmental feature that must be considered. Regional location is still another aspect of the local environment. Economic forces, such as unemployment, poverty, income rates, local economic growth, and other demographic factors, such as population size and change, are also included as part of the environment.

It should be clear however, that the relationship between the environment and the local civic culture is not unidirectional. Rather, although the environment has a significant role in defining the civic

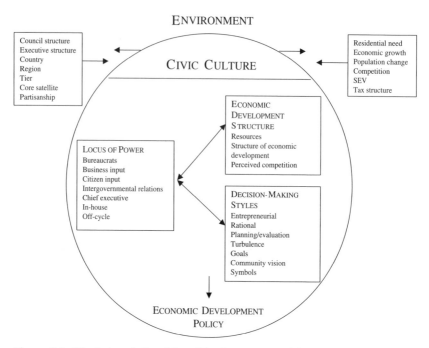

Figure 2.1. The Interrelationship of Environment and Civic Culture on Economic Development Policy

culture, that culture also affects the external environments. Such dynamics can be seen in changes in local governmental structures to better reflect community values or political power arrangements, for example. The environmental forces create the frame for the definition of the local culture. Although the concept of such variables as "drivers" is useful—they clearly contribute to the creation of the parameters of what is possible for individual communities—such a notion is too deterministic. There is the possibility that communities with very similar economic forces, say, high levels of poverty, unemployment, and slow economic growth, may pursue very different economic development policy agendas. Cities with the same economic challenges may still come up with very different policy solutions due to variation in the local civic culture. In short, the relationship between structure and agency portrayed here follows a dualist rather than a structuralist approach, arguing that history and action can modify both economic and political structures (Stone, 1989; Imbroscio, 1999).

Local civic culture is composed of three central components: the structure of the economic development enterprise, locus of power and input arrangements, and decision-making styles. The economic development arena will have a particular structure or set of conditions in each community. These include the nature and level of resources devoted to development and the governing structure of the development enterprise. These factors frame the institutional and environmental rules of the game. And although competition from other cities is almost a given in the external environment, how local officials perceive and react to competition is an important internal force. High levels of perceived competition with other cities can create a culture of crisis and lead to frenetic policy activity. Resources in the form of development staff and budget help determine what is possible in economic development as well as having significant effects on how decisions are made. Lack of resources and staff coupled with high levels of perceived competition can create a potentially pathological habitus for local development officials, leading to the sort of behavior described by Rubin (1988), where officials try anything and everything in the hopes that something will work. How the development function is placed in a community— within or external to the local government, in the executive office or in a free-standing department—also affects the basic frame of how development decisions are made and, indeed, what stakeholders are likely to hold sway. Structure and process are intricately intertwined as aspects of the local culture.

Locus issues relate to questions of who has power and access in development decisions. Critical questions regarding process include the following:

Where is the locus of power in economic development decision making?

What groups are involved in decisions?

Are governmental or extragovernmental actors more important?

What is the balance of power between appointed and elected development officials?

Does that balance change depending on the nature of the policy/project at hand?

To what extent do community or neighborhood groups have input into or
    influence in economic development decisions?

To what extent do business interests dominate in local decision making?

How are the relationships between local, regional, state, and federal govern-
    ments structured?

Are the intergovernmental relationships cooperative or antagonistic?

The decision-making styles in a community involve the symbols and
myths from earlier culture studies. Each city will have particular descriptive phrases that permeate conversation about the current and future image of the city. These will then be translated into goal sets that
can be loosely defined and more implicit than explicit in some communities or very concrete, enumerated goals within an economic development plan in others. Beyond these linguistic and vision issues, each
community will have a distinct decision-making style. This may take
the form of rational planning, decision analysis, and policy evaluation
in some communities. In others, it may be a more reactive effort to address stress and uncertainty in the economic and policy environment.
And there will be permutations of these policy processes. This variation in decision-making culture would largely account for why some
scholars have looked at cities and seen officials "shooting everything
that flies" (Rubin, 1988), whereas others find more rational efforts to
improve the community's status in the hierarchy of cities (Pagano and
Bowman, 1995).

The environment and local civic culture, then, affect local economic
development policy choices. They account for why some cities pursue
redistributive Type II policies, whereas others pursue more traditional
development agendas of financial and other location incentives to businesses. The interrelationships between the individual variables and between the environment, culture, and policy will be developed and
tested in more detail, using both the survey and case study analyses.

Defining Local Civic Culture

It is useful at this point to provide more specificity regarding what is
meant by civic culture in the foregoing model in terms of indicators that
can be and are directly measured as part of this research. Although indicators used in previous studies of civic culture are informative in a

heuristic sense, they provide little direction for urban research. To reiterate some of the discussion of the early civic culture research, although varying somewhat between studies, the indicators used were relatively similar. Thus, Almond and Verba (1963) stressed awareness of and knowledge about the national political system, feelings about structure and process, partisanship and other group membership, sense of civic duty, and political socialization. Inglehart's (1990) measures were somewhat broader, including life satisfaction and postmaterialist values, but also included trust of officials, support for the current political order, and levels of political discussion. Putnam (1993), too, considered voting behavior, political awareness, and organizational membership. Clearly, past measurement of civic culture has focused on awareness and knowledge of and affectation for politics and the political system as well as personal behaviors, such as voting, group membership, and general values. Again, these studies have focused on national political systems, and measures must be translated into the urban context.

More applicable here is Banfield and Wilson's (1963) description of the four components of an urban civic culture:

1. The appropriate forms of civic action: the strategies or avenues through which aspirations and activities can be accomplished. These define which groups are important to join or at least consider, who has power within the system, which interests must be courted, and what types of political activities are most likely to be successful.

2. Expectations about the likelihood of change, the set of problems and solutions deemed to be acceptable for the political agenda.

3. Appropriate tactics for emerging interest groups: how new groups learn from established interests to gain access to the system. Such learning includes the acceptable parameters for conflict within the system.

4. The balance between the internal forces of conflict and community: the balance between "complimentary" interests and shared identity and the conflict that occurs as the natural result of different demands among groups and interests. (59-60)

From the forgoing discussion of civic/political culture and the definitions and indicators previously employed, it seems clear that indicators of the local civic culture must cover some essential attributes: who has power in the system; how the political system is accessed; how politics are discussed, communicated, and symbolized; how political decisions are made; and how problems and solutions are defined and portrayed. To reflect this, the three central components of local civic culture—economic development structure, locus of power, and decision-making styles—are further operationalized in the discussion to follow.

Economic Development Structure: How the economic development enterprise is organized or structured says much about local political expectations and power arrangements. Specifically, the *resources* devoted toward economic development in the form of revenue and staff will be considered along with the *formal structure* for development decision making and policy implementation. A choice to place economic development within the chief executive's office as opposed to a quasi-governmental organization, such as an economic development corporation, speaks volumes about who has power in development decisions within the local community as well as how decisions are likely to be made.

Locus of Power: Who controls political decisions has been a central component of all of the research on civic culture and is pivotal to the study of urban regimes. Thus, included in the civic culture is an examination of the locus of economic development decisions: bureaucrats, elected officials, business owners or groups, citizen or neighborhood groups, or some mix of these. The *balance of power within the local government,* specifically between appointed and elected officials, will be explicitly considered. External input into economic development decision making will be examined by looking at both the extent of input mechanisms on paper for different groups as well as the reality of whose input is considered most frequently. *The balance between business and neighborhood interests* will serve as a particular focus.

Decision-Making Styles: Other central aspects of the local civic culture are how *community visions and goals* are communicated and ultimately, *how decisions are actually made.* What words, symbols, or phrases are frequently employed when participants from different sectors talk about the community? Is there some similarity across different local roles? What are the most common and consistent goals expressed by community participants? What types of mental maps are expressed by local decision makers? Is the external environment seen as uncertain and hostile? Do local officials feel like they have control of their economic futures and fortunes? How are decisions actually made: with a great deal of planning, focus, and evaluation? Or are local decisions made in a reactive mode more directed at current emergencies than future exigencies? These questions will serve as the basis for the measurement of local economic decision-making styles.

The next chapter explains the larger methodology used for this study as well as operationalizations for such concepts as *economic development* and *local development policy.* Ultimately, a comprehensive model incorporating the attributes of civic culture as defined in this chapter and local development policies is developed and tested in Chapter 5.

3

A BLENDED
METHODOLOGICAL
APPROACH

The study of local economic development has been similar to a classic "good news, bad news" story. Much research has been based on case study analyses of, often, large central cities or comparative studies of a small number of cities. Such methodology has provided detailed but possibly idiosyncratic pictures of local development politics, processes, and policies. Other research has relied on large cross-sectional surveys providing uniform data on many cities that tends to be static and shallow in explanatory power. One of the central purposes of this book is to provide an alternative blended methodology as an improvement over cross-sectional or case study approaches. By using both a large-survey data base and comparative case studies, the analysis provides both the depth and breadth necessary to gain a more complete understanding of local economic development, as well as providing the basis for the development of a comprehensive theory of local development policy making incorporating a civic culture approach. In short, the cross-sectional survey allows for robust statistical analysis in the development and testing of models explaining the use of particular economic development strategies and for the identification of cities with unique approaches to development to serve as case study subjects. The case studies, then, allow for the historical and contextual analysis required to refine existing theories, identify where academic knowledge falls short of reality, and develop new ways of viewing the local development enterprise that are sensitive to the local context while allowing for the development of generalizable new theories.

This chapter begins by explicitly delineating definitions of economic development and then moves on to explore more general methodological debates about the value of large-survey analyses versus case study approaches and the advantages that accrue from combining those approaches. Last, the particular methodologies used in this study are explained in more detail, and the case study cities are introduced.

IN SEARCH OF THE DEPENDENT VARIABLE

Defining Local Economic Development

The dependent variable in local economic development research is problematic in both definitional and measurement respects. Although local government economic development efforts have been well studied, definitions of economic development have varied or simply been assumed. Thus, there has been little agreement on exactly what the dependent variable in economic development research *is*. This challenge is compounded by the fact that consensus is also lacking with respect to actual measurement of economic development. In short, scholars are left with the possibility that we're not quite measuring whatever it is we can't quite define.

The concept of "economic development" has always been somewhat complex because scholars and practitioners have used it to mean different things: economic processes, development activities, and economic outcomes. Thus, economic development has been variously used to refer to theories about how economic growth occurs, what forces drive economic growth, and how growth might best be pursued. Economic base theory, location theory, and neoclassical economic theory are all ex-amples of economic development as *process*. Most commonly, economic development refers to the strategies, practices, activities, policies, or even tactics used by governmental units to encourage the process just noted. Last, economic development has also been used to denote the end point of the process. In other words, economic development is the desired outcome resulting from strategies and policies. Obviously, these concepts are (or should logically be) related; indeed they should be connected in some rational sense. Theories of growth should frame the selection of local policies that will hopefully lead to a desired out-come, whether that be growth or some broader notion of community development.

The term economic development has been used "to refer to efforts to increase the employment and income of area residents or in its broader sense to include land and physical development efforts" (Wolman, 1996:116). Often, economic development is defined more by its goals than its content. Several views are illustrative:

> The principal goal of local economic development is to stimulate local employment opportunities in sectors that improve the community, using existing human, natural, and institutional resources. (Blakeley, 1994:xvi)

> It is agreed the successful economic development strategies will lead to the following: job creation and retention; tax revenue growth; improved quality of life; enhanced innovation/competitiveness. (McGowan and Ottensmeyer, 1993:4)

> Economic development is the process of transforming assets into higher valued uses. Its purposes are variously viewed as producing higher liv-ing standards and quality of life; goods and services of higher quality, greater variety, and lower cost; more and/or better jobs; higher incomes; more productive enterprises; a more diverse economic base; advanced skills that will prepare workers for economic change; the opportunity to alleviate poverty and increase equity; a stronger tax base; and the capac-ity for sustained economic development in the future. (Fosler, 1991:xx)

Several goals are central to defining economic development: in-creased jobs/employment, particularly for local or disadvantaged populations; building on community resources; increased tax revenue;

increased and more diversified business; and decreased poverty and reduced income inequities. Thus, economic development has been used to indicate everything from the relatively narrow goal of business attraction to improvements in quality of life (Reese and Fasenfest, 1997).

As Wolman (1996) notes in his essay on the state of the research on the politics of local economic development, there is an important theoretical distinction to be made between local economic growth and local economic development. Herrick and Kindleberger (1983) employ an analogy to the human organism to describe the difference: "Growth involves changes in overall aggregates such as height or weight, whereas development includes changes in functional capacities—physical coordination, learning capacity, or ability to adapt to changing circumstances" (21). In the local-development context, the goal of economic *growth* typically has been to get the local community back to work and build the local tax base at the lowest price. If economic *development*, in the sense described by Herrick and Kindleberger, defines the result of local development policies, the goals are much different: (a) increase the stability as well as the gross levels of income for the population; (b) increase local control over both market and government operations, particularly in those aspects that affect citizens in poverty; and (c) increase economic and political empowerment of all sectors of a community, including individual citizens (Brown and Warner, 1991:37-38).

Although the distinction between economic development as true development or simply growth is important, particularly in an evaluative sense, the objective task of measuring economic development is extremely complex. This no doubt explains why so much research stresses growth indicators (Wolman, 1996; Reese and Fasenfest, 1997). For purposes of this research, focusing on economic development policies as opposed to outcomes, the definition of local economic development policy or approach includes activities designed to address both growth and development. Local economic development policies are defined as those designed or intended to attract capital investment, retain investment, develop new business investment, improve and or/regulate community appearance and/or growth, increase local human resource capital, and ensure or redistribute benefits of economic growth across the community.

Measuring Local Economic Development Policy

   Wolman (1996) also noted that efforts to measure local development
policies are wanting in how they gauge the extent and nature of local
policies. The two most common means of measuring local policies involve a dichotomous variable measuring whether a community employs a particular development policy or not and additive counts of the
number of economic development techniques employed. The former
do not indicate the extent of, or effort dedicated to, local development
policies. Wolman suggests that the latter measure represents an indicator of diversity of effort rather than the extent to which a policy has been
employed. Obviously, more direct indicators of policy effort, most particularly resources devoted to economic development, would be the optimal measures of local policy effort and intensity. However, as Wolman
notes, "the reason that resource deployment measures are not used is
straight forward and obvious" (125). Such data simply do not exist in a
uniform manner across municipalities. Even large-scale efforts to obtain budgetary data from individual governments would be difficult
because local economic development resources often come from multiple sources: local general fund revenue; state grants and revenue sharing; federal grants from programs ranging from Community Development Block Grants to transportation funds; and special purpose units,
such as downtown development authorities (DDA) and tax increment
finance authorities (TIFA), among others.
   Economic development policy is measured here in several ways in an
attempt to address these concerns. First, the cross-sectional survey data
set includes two variables measuring resource effort: (a) number of staff
devoting a majority of their time to economic development and (b) general fund dollars allocated to economic development. Although these
clearly do not account for the various off-budget sources of revenue,
they serve as a comparative measure of local effort. In measuring policy
effort, intensity of use was explicitly considered, following Miranda
et al. (1992). Thus, respondents were asked about the extent to which
they used 67 different economic development policies over a five-year
period, ranging from "not at all" to "high" on a five-point scale. Economic development policy is also measured more qualitatively and
subjectively in the case study analyses. Here, local officials were asked,

in unstructured fashion, to describe their economic development policies and strategies and the intensity of effort involved.

Categorizing Economic Development Policy

A number of schemes have been employed to categorize local development policies; obviously, 67 different dependent variables would be
unwieldy. Such schemes have been devised both a priori—based on
purpose, goals, extent of innovation, risk, cost and benefit distribution,
and intended outcome—and empirically, typically using factor analysis. More specifically, organization schemes have been based on the economic development goals pursued (Dubnick and Bardes, 1983; Matulef,
1987; Pelissero and Fasenfest, 1989), the direct or indirect nature of incentives and business functions targeted (Sternberg, 1987), by their sup-
ply- or demand-side or conventional or entrepreneurial natures
(Eisinger, 1988; Clarke and Gaile, 1992; Reese, 1992), and by the distribution of costs and benefits and the extent of government role (Rubin
and Rubin, 1987; Clingermayer and Feiock, 1990; Sharp and Elkins,
1991; Feiock and Clingermayer, 1992; Cable et al., 1993). However, most
typologies have been based on the similarity of techniques employed by
economic development function, such as marketing, tax incentives,
training programs, and so on (Ady, 1984; International City Management Association [ICMA], 1989; Hanson and Berkman, 1991; Green and
Fleischmann, 1991; Reese, 1993a). A brief summary of some of these is
illustrative.

Sternberg (1987) provides one of the most detailed examples of a priori categorization of economic development policy by function, identifying nine types of policy instruments: (a) direct and (b) indirect subsidies, (c) information and exhortation, (d) regulation, (e) affecting crucial
industries and institutions, (f) expanding market opportunities, (g)
shaping market structure, (h) limiting forms of enterprise, and (i) operating public enterprises or expanding public employment opportunities. These are then further categorized by the business function they are
meant to address: financing, personnel, operations, and so on (154-160).

Clingermayer and Feiock (1990) employed a less detailed but more
politically sensitive categorization of economic development incentives. They explained the adoption of five policies: (a) industrial development bonds (IDBs), Urban Development Action Grants (UDAGs),

business assistance centers, national advertising, and tax abatements. UDAGs and IDBs were classified together as policies that represented "diffused costs and concentrated benefits," whereas assistance centers and advertising denoted more diffuse benefits and concentrated costs. Tax abatements represented a category for which benefits and costs were not as clear. In a similar vein, Sharp and Elkins (1991) separated activities among those that had visible tax costs (tax exempt bonds and loans for example) and those that had very visible benefits (infrastructure improvements).

Matulef (1987) employed an objective-based typology where local incentives were categorized as being either directed toward coordination of projects or support for development initiatives. Coordination included such things as grantsmanship, consensus building, and creating media support, whereas support services were divided into nine subcategories: marketing, community organizing, land-based initiatives, and so on. In a similar vein, Pelissero and Fasenfest (1989) created a typology based on economic development goals. Their policies were classified as being either aggressive, regulatory, cooperative, retentive, or reactive.

Although supply and demand-side distinctions have come under fire because of different interpretations of what constitutes each side (see Wolman, 1996), the distinction between older, more traditional approaches to local economic development and more innovative, entrepreneurial, or even risky activities is important. Thus, Clarke and Gaile (1989, 1992) distinguish between conventional approaches, such as business attraction strategies, and more entrepreneurial efforts that involve more risky and active governmental intervention in the market.

What these studies have in common is the creation of typologies based on informed reasoning without empirical verification. Other studies have used various empirical means to identify patterns among economic development techniques. Hanson and Berkman (1991), in a study of state-level economic development policy, identified four theoretically based categories of techniques: (a) capital subsidies, (b) enhancements to return on capital investments, (c) operating subsidies, and (d) enhancements to return on capital outlays. These were then tested using factor analysis and were found to be weakly confirmed. Although useful, this approach uses activities not usually employed by local governments, such as sales tax exemptions, right-to-work laws, and tax credits for purchase of state products.

Regarding local-level policies, Reese (1993a) and Fleischmann et al. (1992) used factor analysis to identify empirical categories of activities. The latter study identified nine categories of policy or incentives: (a) loans, (b) financial schemes, (c) activities to attract or retain business, (d) revitalization efforts, (e) regulatory change, (f) land development, (g) historic preservation, (h) aesthetic improvement, and (i) management of city facilities. Using data from the 1989 ICMA survey, Reese (1993a) used factor analysis to identify thirteen conceptually distinct categories of local economic development activities: (a) traditional marketing, (b) foreign marketing, (c) tax incentives, (d) loan programs, (e) entrepreneurial financial schemes, (f) traditional land incentives, (g) land support services, (h & i) two types of entrepreneurial land incentives, (j) historic preservation, (k) transportation, (l) service enhancements, and (m) red tape reduction.

This study employs an empirical categorization scheme developed over the course of several research projects (see Reese, 1997a, 1997b, 1998). Factor analysis performed on 67 techniques included in a mailed survey indicates that there are nine identifiable factors or categories of techniques (Table 3.1 presents the techniques and factor results).[1] It should be noted that the following categorization follows the policy-type approach employed in many previous studies. Various experimental factor analyses were also run to explore for other categorization schemes, particularly those that distinguish between traditional and more innovative or entrepreneurial approaches. The 67 activities were divided theoretically, based on this distinction, for example, and continued to break into the policy-type factors identified in the discussion to follow. Thus, it appears, at least based on empirical survey data, that policies are more likely to be substantively different in their policy nature than in the extent of innovation.[2]

The policy activities loading on the factors identified were combined into single variable indexes. Indexes were created based on f-score values to standardize units of measurement. The indexes represent additive measures of both number of policies used within an index and intensity of use of each policy, based on the five-point-scaled response. It then represents a second-best method of measuring policy effort to actual resource indicators (Wolman, 1996). Although not explicitly repre-

TABLE 3.1   Factor Analysis: Economic Development Techniques

Factor	Loadings
Marketing activities	
Liaison committees	.60
Brochures	.71
Solicit foreign business	.77
Visits to firms	.82
Trade shows	.77
Development of export markets	.75
Promotion of specific sites	.67
Special events	.74
Loans	
Direct loans	.85
Small business loans	.89
Loan guarantees	.76
Start-up loans	.83
Community development loans	.81
Site development	
Lot consolidation	.68
Land expropriation	.67
Land purchase	.74
Business relocation	.69
Sale of land	.73
Donation of land	.69
Lease land	.63
Site development	.72
Infrastructure investment	
Improvement/expansion of parking	.70
Improvement/expansion of streets	.70
Improvement of pedestrian amenities	.81
Beautification improvements	.84
Improvement/expansion of recreation services	.73
Community improvement areas	.65
Financial incentives	
Tax abatements	.71
Tax deferments	.71
Employment/investment tax credits	.79
Enterprise zones	.78
In-kind service provision	.68

(Continued)

TABLE 3.1 (Continued)

Zoning policies	
Protected manufacturing districts	.74
Growth management zoning	.84
Zoning variance provisions	.71
Appearance regulations	
Sign control regulations	.80
Facade control regulations	.84
Antilitter regulations/programs	.74
Type II policies	
Local employment requirements	.76
Minority employment requirements	.80
Worker training requirements	.81
Performance guarantees	.51
Targeted employee wage subsidies	.58
Low-income housing requirements	.62
Demand-side policies	
Underwriting of employee training/retraining	.69
Public/private research and development	.73
Business incubators	.71
Sale lease-back arrangements	.68

senting resources devoted to economic development, each index can be interpreted as the intensity and diversity of use of the constituent measures.

Wolman (1996) expressed an additional concern in his critique of existing measures. Specifically, he notes that previous research has assumed that the number of tools used is highly correlated with resource deployment measures, thus acting as a reasonable proxy. However, extant studies do not attempt to make that case either theoretically or empirically. The resource questions in this survey (staff and general-fund budget devoted to economic development) were correlated with the technique indexes to explore for just this relationship. If overall effort and use of *all* techniques is used, it can be concluded that resources are positively and significantly correlated. The quantity of resources devoted to economic development is related to the number and intensity of use of all economic development incentives. Resources are not, how-

ever, significantly related to each of the separate categories of policies to
be described in the following discussion.

The Policy Categories

As previously mentioned, factor analysis indicates the presence of
ten conceptually distinct types of economic development policies or
activities. The *marketing factor* represents efforts to promote the city
through brochures, trade shows, and special events and to develop foreign markets for local goods. The *loan factor* includes five types of loan
activities, from direct loans to start-up and small business loans. A *site
preparation* factor includes most of the traditional land development activities: land acquisition; lot consolidation; relocation and clearing of
structures; and sales, donation, and leasing of sites. The *infrastructure
factor* represents efforts to use such improvements as streets, parking
and pedestrian amenities, and recreation services as economic development strategies. Traditional *financial incentives,* such as tax abatements,
deferrals and credits, and enterprise zones, form another factor. A *zoning factor* (use of manufacturing districts, growth-management zoning,
zoning variances) and a *regulatory factor* (sign, facade, and litter controls) are also present. *Type II economic development* policies, including requirements to hire local workers, minority employment requirements,
worker training requirements, performance guarantees, targeted employee wage subsidies, and requirements for the development of low-
income housing, load on a separate factor. The final factor includes economic development activities defined by Eisinger (1988) as *demand-side*
and include worker training programs, public-private research and
development initiatives, business incubators, and sale/lease-back
arrangements.

A final dependent policy variable is worth special notice. Previous
research has focused on cities using Type II policies in particular because of their presumed greater effectiveness in ensuring and distributing benefits to the local community (Goetz, 1994; Elkins, 1995; Reese,
1998). Although this research has identified interesting factors that appear to be related to Type II policies, it has failed to distinguish between
cities using Type II policies because they are trying everything possible
to induce economic development (shooting at anything that flies) from
those cities that have made a conscious decision to focus specifically on

Type II polices for their presumed benefits. If Type II policy use is simply a function of doing everything, then such high-use cities may not be good models of economic development. To differentiate between these two scenarios, a final "Focused Type II" index was created by dividing those high on the Type II index by the sum of those high on each of the other eight policy indexes. Thus, a score of 1.00 represents a complete focus on Type II (high on Type II, low on all other indexes) and .00 represents a lack of focus on Type II policies (high on all other indexes, low on Type II).

THE CROSS-SECTIONAL DATABASE: SURVEY AND SAMPLING ISSUES

The analysis here is based partially on a survey sent in the spring of 1994 to the Chief Executive Officer (CEO) of all cities in Canada with a population over 10,000 and all U.S. border (with Canada) state cities meeting the same population criteria. The CEO was asked to forward the survey to the individual responsible for economic development or answer it themselves if appropriate. The population criteria was selected to provide greater diversity of cities, including smaller and/or suburban units, and a much-needed balance to the many studies that have focused solely on large and/or central cities.

For this survey, fifteen states were broadly defined as border states, including those that border Canada through a body of water. States included in the sample were Idaho, Illinois, Indiana, Maine, Michigan, Minnesota, Montana, New Hampshire, New York, North Dakota, Ohio, Pennsylvania, Vermont, Washington, and Wisconsin. The decision to use cities in only those U.S. states along the Canadian border was based on several factors besides cost. First, because one of the goals of this project is to address policy transmission and competition issues, the choice of border cities reflected an assumption that policy emulation was related to locational proximity or a result of natural markets on both sides of the border. Second, the number of U.S. border cities provided a more comparable sample frame in relation to the much smaller number of cities throughout Canada meeting the size criteria.

The survey itself is an expansion of a similar survey distributed in the State of Michigan and the Province of Ontario in 1990. It was also designed so that portions would match surveys of U.S. cities and counties conducted by the ICMA. The previous use and analysis of survey questions and responses, particularly those relating to economic development practices, and pretest interviews with local officials provide confidence that the terms and language employed have the same meaning in both countries (see Reese, 1992, 1997a). Responses from Quebec may be problematic. Cover letters were in French though the survey itself was in English. Only 18 of the 102 cities over 10,000 population responded, a rate of 18%. Thus, the Canadian sample is questionable in its representation of the population of cities in this province.

Surveys were sent to 305 Canadian and 682 U.S. cities, and the response rate was 35% for Canadian and 52% for U.S. cities, well within normal response rates for mailed surveys. The lower response rate for Canadian cities raises the possibility that the findings will be less representative of all Canadian cities, however. There was some difference in population size between responding cities in Canada and in the United States. Canadian cities tended to be somewhat larger: Median population for the Canadian sample was 28,275, whereas the median population of U.S. cities was 19,478. Median population of cities responding to the survey seems fairly representative of those not responding. Median population size for nonresponding cities in Canada was 19,883 and for U.S. cities was 22,884.

The samples appear to be significantly different on several characteristics, including population, unemployment levels, per capita income, and percentage in poverty. Specifically, cities in the Canadian sample are significantly larger, have higher levels of unemployment, but also higher per capita income. U.S. cities have a significantly larger percentage of the population in poverty. Which officials answered the survey also differed somewhat between the two nations. In U.S. cities, surveys were completed by economic development officials (32%), city managers (27%), mayors (17%), planning officials (14%), or other city officials (10%). In Canadian cities, respondents were most likely to be the economic development director (54%), the city manager (23%), planning officials (11%), other officials (9%), or mayors (2%).

SURVEY VERSUS CASE STUDY METHODOLOGIES

The pros and cons of cross-sectional survey methodologies as opposed to case studies are well known. The great advantage of surveys is
that they provide uniform and/or comparable data on a wide array of
variables for a large number of cases. Because much of the research on
local economic development to date has been based on single or limited
case studies, findings regarding the development techniques employed
and the forces behind policy choices have often been conflicting. This
stems from variation in individual places and the inability to compare
across a large number of cases. Furthermore, survey approaches allow
for more advanced statistical analysis, including regression and path
analysis. As a whole, such studies have provided a more inclusive picture of what cities across the United States and, in some cases, other nations, are doing as far as economic development. However, there are
some significant limitations to the survey approach. These include variation in the measurement of both independent and dependent variables, lack of explanatory depth, misinterpretation of survey questions,
incorrect data, and the typically low explanatory power of analyses
based on survey research. These issues will be discussed in turn.

Obviously, the major trade-off between survey and case study research relates to the depth of information attained. Although large-scale
surveys produce a great deal of uniform information, they inherently
are limited to measuring surface effects. Questions have to be simple
and clear enough that they are uniformly understood. Clarification and
probing is impossible. Unless surveys are sent to a number of different
types of respondents in a city (mayors, managers, council members),
they reflect only the views of the particular respondent. Even then, it is
often impossible to be sure exactly who is answering the questionnaire.
Surveys intended for city managers may often be answered by assis-
tants, for example. In this case, because surveys were sent to chief executives, to be answered by the official most informed about economic development, a pass-through was potentially necessary (if the chief
executive did not have a significant role in economic development, for
example). Again, relying on a recipient to give the survey to another official just leads to another layer of possible problems. The bottom line is

that self-administered surveys do not elicit the kinds of rich, detailed information that can be attained in case studies.

Another challenge to survey research is the construction of the questionnaire itself. It is deceptively easy to construct a bad survey and extremely difficult to create a good one. Thus, even researchers trained in and experienced with survey methodology can create questionnaires with flaws. Although the survey questions employed here were based on those used in two waves of ICMA surveys, were constructed based on intensive interviews in both the United States and Canada, and have been used in previous research (see Reese, 1992, 1993a, 1993b, 1997a) some "problem" questions were still evident. For example, in answering a series of questions asking about the percentage of the local economic base composed of particular sectors (agriculture, industrial, commercial, for example), some respondents provided answers that totaled greater than 100% of their base. Similarly, a question about the percentage of land in the city vacant and available for development resulted in at least one city where apparently 100% of the land area is vacant. On the whole, these were minor issues.

The more important concern and one not easily resolved is whether respondents are interpreting the questions in the same way. Do "enterprise zones" or "community development loans" have the same meaning across cities? Preliminary interviews and survey pretesting allay concerns about different interpretations among U.S. and Canadian officials. But it is still possible that an individual official in a specific city has a different interpretation from the norm for a particular policy. Last, it is clear that some of the survey responses were just plain incorrect. This became evident in the case study interviews, where it was noted that very basic responses, such as form of government, were wrong on the original survey form. These issues are inherent to the survey methodology and tend to fall within the all-purpose "random error" category. Still, it should be noted that there are concerns about survey accuracy that simply can not be addressed.

The body of research purporting to explain or identify the determinants of local economic development policy choice using analysis of survey data sets is also problematic. It tends to offer contradictory findings based on variation in the questionnaires used and hence data collected, operationalization of indicators, mix of variables examined, statistical technique employed, and the sample drawn. Furthermore, extant models have purportedly explained widely varying amounts of policy behavior. For example, Green and Fleischmann (1991) accounted for .159 to .285 of the variance in economic development activities, whereas Reese (1991, 1992, 1997a) accounted for .05 to .89 of the variance in policy choices, depending on the particular type of policy at hand. This extent of variation supports the notion that different research methodologies and samples have gotten in the way of explanation. As Wolman (1996) notes, "with so many different model specifications, it is extremely difficult to assess the impact of any of the variables across studies" (126). The preponderantly low explanatory power of existing models suggests another problem: There are clearly important variables or dynamics missing from the analysis. Although these issues will be discussed in greater detail in Chapter 5, it seems clear that important variables or, more likely, interplay among variables are missing and likely unobtainable, given the survey methodology.

Thus, it is argued here that many interesting and indeed critical dynamics may be missed in such cross-sectional analysis. Perhaps the mixed results and limited explanatory power of past research lies within the cities themselves. Historical trends or even more idiosyncratic "causes" of policies may be hiding under our noses, so to speak, buried in macro and static analytic methodologies. A potentially more fruitful avenue for understanding such local decisions may lie in analysis of the history, characteristics, personnel, and operating forces in cities that use particular policies. The need is to describe the character of each community that produces such a decision, stepping back from the macro analysis and seeking patterns among the idiosyncrasies. If, as it appears, current theories provide only partial explanations, then perhaps deconstructing the analysis to the case level will permit reconstructing more robust theories.

STRENGTH OF A COMBINED APPROACH

It seems clear that a combined methodology that takes advantage of the strengths of mailed surveys and case studies would be the optimal approach to many research questions. However, this has not been widely done in the economic development literature to date (for an exception, see Clarke and Gaile, 1998). Although obviously more expensive and labor intensive, the combination of methodologies offers a unique and powerful research approach. The mailed survey for this project produced a data base containing 350 city responses to uniform questions, allowing for the robust statistical analysis in Chapters 5 and 6. Because the case study cities were selected from the large data base, selection was guided by a good deal of information about potential sites. Thus, as is discussed in the next section, case study selection was supported both by purposive selection based on an extensive knowledge base about the cities but also on statistical cluster analysis. The use of case study analysis produced in-depth information on each city, allowed verification of survey responses, added the perspectives of a number of different local officials and stakeholders, facilitated probing of information on the survey forms, and most important, collected information that goes beyond the survey. This latter point is quite important. Statistical analysis of survey responses prior to the case studies identified many interesting relationships and unanswered questions. The case studies then allowed for the extension of theoretical development through exploration of those questions. Furthermore, because the survey was conducted in 1994 and the case studies in 1999 and early 2000, they also add an element, albeit limited, of longitudinal understanding not present in cross-sectional efforts. Change in strategy and policy is able to be examined over that four-year period. In short, the combination of survey and case study methodologies allows for the best of both worlds and provides a powerful two-tier analysis that balances both generalizability and depth.

THE CASE STUDIES

Selection of the Cases

Selection of cases for analysis is also fraught with difficulties. By definition, a single or small number of cases is used to posit theories or relationships about a larger population. How can such a small sample possibly be representative? How can cases be selected in a manner that in any way approaches randomness? The answer is that case study research, by definition, will lead to limited or uncertain generalizability.

A purposive approach to case selection is the best that can be achieved. Because this research combines approaches, however, more options were available in selecting cities for analysis.

The method employed here began with the survey itself. Candidate cities for detailed analysis were drawn from the larger set. Thus, a good deal of background information was available, particularly about economic development practices and processes, on which to base a decision. As noted in Chapter 1, although the focus of this project was to examine the civic culture of economic development in cities, there was also a driving interest in the factors that appear to produce policy choices providing the greatest benefits to the larger local community. Hence, why some cities adopt Type II policies and how such policy choices might be encouraged are important questions motivating the research. In short, two primary forces drove the selection of cities to serve as case studies: (a) to represent the broadest possible array of local civic cultures and (b) to allow for the identification of forces that appear to lead to or encourage the use of Type II policies, in particular. If the forces leading to such policies as linkage programs or performance guarantees that better ensure benefits in return for the public costs of economic development incentives could be identified, then perhaps the use of such policies could be increased across localities. Case cities, then, needed to present profiles of cities actually using Type II policies (and such cities are not prevalent), while also including the major types of civic cultures developed in later analysis. Because the identification of cultural types could not take place a priori, because the required information was obtained from the case studies, the focus on cities using Type II policies served as the initial frame for case study selection. Before this procedure is described, it should be noted that the cities selected based on the Type II criteria were examined for their representativeness of cultural types developed in subsequent cluster and case analysis. It is clear that the nine cases originally selected do represent the spectrum of clusters identified in Chapter 6, even though the original selection process was based on Type II policy use. Why this is the case is discussed more fully in Chapter 6.

As just noted, the first step of case study selection focused on those cities that had unusually high levels of Type II policy use. This involved pulling out those cities highest on the focused Type II index. Again, that meant identifying those cities that were doing a number of Type II policies or doing some intensively to the exclusion of other types of more traditional economic development policies. The twenty cities with the highest levels of focus on Type II policies in Canada and the United States were identified. It was among this group of cities that the case studies were chosen. The ultimate choice was done in two stages. First, basic demographic and structural characteristics were examined to select a purposive sample of cities that represented variation along the following variables; population, per capita income, poverty rates, unemployment, percentage of white population, type of elections (partisan versus nonpartisan and at-large versus ward) and form of chief executive (mayor versus manager). A cluster analysis was also performed to verify that the cities identified as candidates through the purposive process really did represent different groups or types of cities. This latter analysis requires a bit more discussion, provided later in this section.

The case cities were drawn from two states (Michigan and Ohio) and one province (Ontario). The most obvious reason for this choice was ease of analysis because the locations were all relatively proximate to the researchers. More important, it was determined that it would be better to have more cities within the same state/provincial environment than to spread them out across jurisdictions. Previous research has pointed to the importance of state and provincial enabling legislation on local economic development policy choice (Reese and Malmer, 1994; Reese, 1997a). In short, the enabling environment at the state or provincial level sets the frame for what is possible as far as local development policies. Thus, selecting cities within the same state or province controls for enabling legislation as well as other economic, structural, and cultural forces that may vary along state or provincial lines. Having multiple cities within the same state/province allows for some certainty that any internal variation results from differences in the cities themselves rather than the larger environment.

Michigan Cases: The Michigan cities selected for case analysis are Allen Park, Cadillac, and Romulus. All three cities have at least moderate scores on the focused Type II policy index. *Romulus* has one of the highest Type II scores of all cities in the data set. It was also of particular interest because of its significant African American population as well as relatively high poverty and unemployment rates. The governmental structure represents a mix of reformed and unreformed elements, with a strong mayor, and at-large, nonpartisan elections. Because Michigan has a strong history of city managers as opposed to mayors, Romulus is important in that it continues with the strong-mayor form of government. *Cadillac* serves as a good counterpoint to Romulus in that it also has relatively high poverty and unemployment levels but has a population that is predominantly white. Like most cities in the state, it has a city manger. However, the city council is comprised of both at-large and ward seats. *Allen Park* has low poverty and moderate unemployment. It has a weak-mayor form of government along with a chief administrator. It has at-large and nonpartisan council elections and is predominantly white. The three cities, then, provide variation in structure, race, and general economic health. Two of the cities—Romulus and Allen Park—are in the highest category of Type II focus, whereas Cadillac is in the middle range. This pattern was followed in selecting cities in Ohio and Ontario.

Ohio Cases: *Coshocton* and Kettering both rank in the highest category of focused Type II policy use. The former is a predominantly white city with high poverty and unemployment, much like Cadillac in the Michigan sample. It has an unreformed governmental system, with a strong mayor, partisan elections, and a council with both at-large and ward seats. *Kettering* has a city manager with nonpartisan elections and both at-large and ward-based council seats. It is a much healthier city, with lower poverty and unemployment rates. *Fairborn* evidences moderate use of Type II policies and has a slightly higher nonwhite population as well as relatively high poverty and unemployment. It has a reformed governmental structure with at-large council seats, nonpartisan elections, and a city manager. The Ohio cases also provide variation in form of government as well as economic health and racial composition, to the extent possible.

Ontario Cases: There was only one city in Ontario—Cornwall—that was in the highest category on focused Type II policy use. The Canadian census does not include racial data, so race was not used in the selection. *Cornwall* exhibits very high unemployment and poverty. It is an independent unit of government, which means that it is not part of a two-tier, federated, or otherwise consolidated system, increasingly more common in Ontario (discussed in greater detail later). It has a city administrator (equivalent to a city manager), at-large seats, and nonpartisan council elections. The other two Ontario cases were selected from the midrange on the focused Type II index. At the time of the research and writing, *Gloucester* was part of a regional system of government, the Ottawa/Carleton region. It has moderate levels of poverty and unemployment and combines a city manager system with nonpartisan and ward-based council elections. *Oakville,* like Gloucester, is part of a regional governmental system. It has ward-based and partisan elections with both a mayor and a manager. Its economy is quite healthy, with low levels of poverty and unemployment and little change in unemployment over a ten-year period.

As noted earlier, cluster analysis was used as a check on the purposive sampling technique to ensure that the cities chosen really did represent conceptually different types of cities. Cluster analysis is used to identify whether cities can be grouped or clustered based on particular variables of interest. Hierarchical cluster analysis is a mathematical procedure that begins with the same number of clusters or groupings of cases (cities in this case) as there are observations. It then groups similar cases until the final cluster contains all the cases. Groups are constructed by minimizing the variance of squared Euclidean distances for each variable between cities. The two most similar cases are joined first, and the algorithm continues one step at a time until all the cities are joined.[3]

There are two significant issues to consider, one before and the other after analysis. First, meaningful variables must be selected to serve as the basis for clusters. In other words, "similar on what" must be defined before the cases can be combined. In choosing the case study cities, several basic characteristics were used to ensure that the cities represented essential variation in structure and on a few variables that have been identified in previous research as being related to economic development policy, particularly Type II activities. These included governmental structure, race (for U.S. cities only), unemployment change, and business input into the local decision-making process. These particular variables were chosen based on previously identified relationships with Type II policies and because they provided the greatest distinction among the clusters of cities, an issue to be discussed more fully.[4] It was

TABLE 3.2 U.S. Cluster Analysis

Stage	Clusters in Solution	Agglomeration Coefficient	Change in Coefficient
16	20	1.950	.09
17	19	2.042	.07
18	18	2.115	.17
19	17	2.287	.02
20	16	2.302	.30
21	15	2.597	.13
22	14	2.731	.70
23	13	3.428	.27
24	12	3.696	.47
25	11	4.166	.61
26	10	4.780	.15
27	9	4.925	.08
28	8	5.008	.98
29	7	5.988	.42
30	6	6.405	.65
31	5	7.059	1.40
32	4	8.454	.83
33	3	9.768	.48
34	2	16.633	6.87
35	1	20.510	3.88

also necessary to keep the number of clustering variables relatively small because so few cities have moderate to high levels of Type II policies to begin with.

Another issue arises after analysis. Because there are many different cluster solutions from which to choose, selecting the most appropriate solution is somewhat arbitrary. There are no neat guidelines or formal rules for picking the best cluster solution. Typically, the agglomeration schedule showing change in the agglomeration coefficient is used as a guide for identifying the optimal solution (Everitt, 1993). For example, a relatively large jump in the coefficients suggests that two heterogeneous clusters are being combined and that the appropriate solution is the one just prior. Tables 3.2 and 3.3 contain the partial agglomeration schedules for the cluster analyses performed on the cities in the data set.

TABLE 3.3 Canadian Cluster Analysis

Stage	Clusters in Solution	Agglomeration Coefficient	Change in Coefficient
3	11	1.144	.47
4	10	2.166	1.02
5	9	2.393	.23
6	8	3.140	.75
7	7	3.644	.54
8	6	3.959	.32
9	5	4.223	.26
10	4	6.096	1.87
11	3	6.461	.37
12	2	7.911	1.45
13	1	10.915	3.00

Separate analyses were performed for the sets of cities because of the absence of racial data for Canadian cities. For Tables 3.2 and 3.3, the first column lists the stage of the cluster solution, and the second provides the number of clusters in that solution. The third column indicates the agglomeration coefficient, and the final column lists the difference in the value of the agglomeration coefficient from the prior stage.

For the cluster analysis on U.S. cities ($n = 36$), it appears that a five-cluster solution is indicated, although this is, as noted, somewhat impressionistic. There are fairly large jumps in the agglomeration coefficients at the second and fifth stages. The five-cluster solution was selected because the two-stage solution placed almost all the cities within one group. Thus, the five-stage solution seemed to do the best job of actually making meaningful distinctions among groups of cities. Coshocton and Kettering, Ohio, represent a group of cities that are relatively healthy economically, with low poverty and unemployment and large reductions in unemployment from 1980 to 1990. Although Coshocton has high gross levels of poverty and unemployment, the large drop in unemployment places it among the healthier cities. This group of cities is predominantly white and has moderate levels of business input into decision-making processes. Their governmental structures are relatively reformed. Table 3.4 lists all seventeen of the cities in

TABLE 3.4 U.S. and Canadian Cluster Membership

United States				
Cluster 1	*Cluster 2*	*Cluster 3*	*Cluster 4*	*Cluster 5*
Mansfield, OH	Meadville, PA	Lancaster, PA	Bedford Heights, OH	Romulus, MI
Appleton, WI	Springfield, OH			
Anacortes, WA	Dixon, IL			
Fostoria, OH	Cadillac, MI			
Boise City, ID	DeKalb, IL			
Berea, OH	Chaska, MN			
Michigan City, IN	Beaver Falls, PA			
Morris, IL	Peekskill, NY			
River Falls, WI	Allen Park, MI			
Coshocton, OH	Prior Lake, MN			
Beech Grove, IN	West Allis, WI			
Wooster, OH	Fort Atkinson, WI			
East Moline, IL	Fairborn, OH			
Amherst, OH	Troy, NY			
Oak Harbor, WA	Berkley, MI			
Kettering, OH	York, PA			
Mount Vernon, WA				

Canada		
Cluster 1	*Cluster 2*	*Cluster 3*
Fort Erie, ON	Oshawa, ON	Osgoode Township, ON
Oakville, ON	Pointe-Claire, QU	Williams Lake, BC
St. Georges, QU	Salaberry-De-Valleyfield, QU	Thetford Mines, QU
Gloucester, ON	Cornwall, ON	Fort McMurray, AL
Mission, BC		

the data set that fall into this cluster, represented by Coshocton and Kettering.

The second cluster contains sixteen cities, including Cadillac and Allen Park, Michigan, and Fairborn, Ohio. These cities have very high business input in local decision making, tend to have reformed governmental structures, and are predominantly white, albeit with higher levels of minorities than cities in the first cluster. They have relatively high poverty and unemployment rates and did not experience much reduction in unemployment between 1980 and 1990.

The remaining three clusters contain only one city each. Romulus represents a profile of low business input within a strong-mayor system. It has, as previously noted, a relatively diverse population. Although it has moderate poverty and high unemployment, it experienced a large reduction in unemployment from 1980 to 1990. It represents a city whose general economic health is improving.

No cities were selected for analysis from the remaining two clusters of cities that contain only one city each. Lancaster, Pennsylvania, is not within the states selected for analysis, and Bedford Heights, Ohio, is not among that state's highest cities on the focused Type II index; scores for Kettering, Coshocton, and Fairborn exceed it significantly. The profile for Lancaster is very similar to that of Romulus except for a high level of business input. Bedford Heights is a very small city (population around 12,000) with a diverse population, strong mayor, and is economically healthy.

The cluster analysis for Canadian cities suggested a four-cluster solution. The first cluster of cities represents a group with relatively healthy economies: substantial unemployment reduction over a ten-year period, low poverty, and low unemployment. These cities also have city manager forms of government and high levels of business input into decision making. Among this group of five cities are the case cities of Oakville and Gloucester.

The second cluster of cities also has experienced significant reductions in unemployment but still has relatively high levels of poverty and unemployment. Business input in these cities is very low, and they are less likely to have reformed government structures as a group. Cornwall is within this group of four, although it has a city administrator/mayor form of government.

The third cluster of Canadian cities also contains four cities that have low unemployment and poverty. However, over a ten-year census period, they experienced large increases in unemployment. They have a strong-mayor form of government and reflect little business input into local decision making. No cities among this group were selected for analysis because three of the four are not in the province of Ontario and the fourth is a township in Ontario with a very small population.

The final cluster contains only one city—York, Ontario. This city has the highest unemployment and poverty rates among the Canadian cities doing Type II policies and experienced poverty increases over a ten-year period. It has a reformed governmental structure and relatively high business input into the local decision-making process. York was initially targeted for analysis, but during the period between the survey (1994) and the case studies (1999), York was consolidated into the structure of the city of Toronto. Hence, it no longer existed as a municipal entity at the time of the case studies. Such local governance trends in the Province of Ontario will be discussed in more detail later.

The next chapter continues the discussion of methodology by justifying and explaining the variables and indicators used in the analysis. It also provides a detailed picture of the characteristics of cities in the data set on the variables—and most important, those measuring civic culture—examined in further analysis.

NOTES

1. Although an initial exploratory analysis was run on all of the techniques at once, findings reported here are the results of factor analyses run on those techniques that would theoretically be expected to factor together, based on past research (Boeckelman, 1991; Green and Fleischmann, 1991; Hanson and Berkman, 1991; Fleischmann et al., 1992; Reese, 1993a, 1998). Factor analysis using principle-components analysis and varimax rotation was run on the indicated survey questions. A factor loading of .5 was the cutoff point in all cases. No questions loaded on more than one factor. Individual factor analyses were run for cities in the United States and Canada separately to verify that the same concepts were present. The same factors emerged in most cases. It should be noted that not all of the 67 techniques are included in the factors.

2. All factor analyses are available from the authors on request.

3. The method employed in the cluster analysis was between groups linkage, which is appropriate for spherical clusters with similar variances and sample sizes. Squared Euclidean distance is the appropriate cluster method to use for interval or binary data. All values were converted to standardized (z-scores) scores prior to analysis because variables measured in higher units contribute more to the calculations of distance used in the hierarchical clustering (SPSS, 1998).

4. Census data were drawn from the 1990 and 1980 census for the United States and from the 1991 and 1981 census for Canada. Racial characteristics were available from the U.S. census only.

4

QUANTITATIVE MEASURES
OF LOCAL CIVIC CULTURE

In Chapter 1, a summary of the development policy determinants literature was presented, with a particular focus on Type II
approaches. Extant research has relied on a reasonably consistent array
of independent variables to try to explain local development policies.
Such variables have most typically included some sense of community
economic stress; local government structure; political input and power
arrangements; decision-making processes; characteristics of the environment, such as interlocal competition and turbulence; and various
demographic traits of the locality, such as population size and growth
rate, age of community, tax base health and composition, sectoral employment, and the like. Indeed, in a somewhat blunt summary, Wolman
(1996) notes,

> In an analysis of sixteen articles that attempt to explain the variation in
> the extent of local economic development activity, I find that the most fre-
> quently included conceptual variables in explanatory models were local

government institutional structure (nine times), fiscal stress (nine times),
need or deprivation (five times), economic distress (five times, although this
might overlap with the need variable depending on operationalization),
openness or citizen access (four times), and city size (three times). (125)

However, the findings regarding the effects of some of these variables have been contradictory, and widely differing amounts of variation have been accounted for in the policy variables they purport to
explain. The research on Type II policies has had similar results. Local
fiscal health has been most often examined as a correlate of Type II policies and has been found to have positive, negative, and no effects.
Other variables, such as community input and governmental structure,
have had similarly mixed results. As noted by Wolman (1996), both situations are the likely result of variation in how variables such as "economy" or "fiscal health" and even "economic development" are operationalized. Thus, whereas most determinants studies have used a
common and reasonably uniform set of independent variables to explain either overall economic development policy effort or particular
policies or mixes of policies employed, they have varied in operationalization and measurement methods to the detriment of overall
theory development.

If measuring the determinants of local economic development policy
is complex, the task of operationalizing and measuring local civic culture is daunting. The theoretical basis for the concept and operational
definition was discussed in Chapter 2. The precise questions used and
indexes employed to portray civic culture are described here. The chapter identifies and describes all of the independent variables used in the
study and how they address common measurement concerns. In that
process, the characteristics of the cities in the data set are described.
From that point, the analysis moves on, in the next chapter, to the examination of the relationships among the independent variables and, ultimately, their combined effects on economic development policies.

INDEPENDENT VARIABLES

The discussion of independent variables and their operationalization is organized by the major forces portrayed in Figure 2.1 on page 44:

The local environment: local government structure, spatial characteristics, demographics, fiscal characteristics, interlocal competition for development

Attributes of civic culture: economic development structure, locus of power, input, decision-making style, goals

The Environment of Local Economic Development

As portrayed in the figure, the environment of local economic development policy making has five major components that have been explored in extant literature to varying extents. These components reflect (a) the local government structure, (b) the location of the community in space, (c) internal demographic characteristics, (d) local fiscal conditions, and (d) the amount of competition with other communities. Each of these components is discussed in turn.

Local Government Structure

Measurement of governmental structure has probably been the least problematic from a methodological standpoint. In short, there are only a limited number of ways to characterize governmental arrangements. Although it would be logical and parsimonious to simply characterize structures as being either "reformed," with city managers, nonpartisan, and at-large council elections, or "unreformed," with strong mayors, partisan, and ward-based council elections, the various attributes of reformism do not necessarily correlate with each other in practice. Indeed, factor analysis failed to show that the separate attributes of local government structure formed a single concept. Thus, the various components of structure are examined here as unique variables. Survey respondents were asked to indicate the type of executive (city manager, strong mayor, weak mayor, city commission) and legislative (at-large, ward, or some combination of the two) structures and whether they had partisan or nonpartisan elections.

As indicated in Table 4.1, strong-mayor and city manager systems are almost evenly represented; slightly more cities have strong mayors (45%) than city managers (41%). Weak-mayor and commission systems are less frequently employed at 12% and 2%, respectively. Of the cities responding to the survey, 47% have at-large council elections, making it the predominant council structure. Combinations of at-large and ward council seats are used in 30% of the cities, whereas ward-based systems are used in 24%. Cities in the data base are overwhelmingly nonpartisan; only 23% of the cities have partisan elections. Although there is no significant difference between Canadian and U.S. cities in the type of council elections used, Canadian cities are significantly more likely to have strong mayors as opposed to city managers and are more likely to have nonpartisan elections.

The final element of local government structure measured here is whether the locality is an independent political entity or whether it is part of some kind of intergovernmental structure. This question was included to fully assess the structure of the Canadian cities in particular that are much more likely to be part of some type of federated, unified, consolidated, or other type of intergovernmental arrangement. Overall, in the sample, most cities are independent (86%). However, Canadian cities are significantly more likely to be part of a multitier governing arrangement; 31% of cities in the Canadian sample are part of such an arrangement.

Spatial Characteristics

The most important locational variable measured in the survey was country of location. Of the 350 cities in the data set, 245 are in the U.S. (70%) and 105 are in Canada (30%). The large body of literature indicating that Canadian and U.S. economic development policies and policy-making processes are more similar than different notwithstanding, it is important to recognize differences due to national origin when they occur. A number of studies have focused on both the similarities and differences among cities in Canada and the United States, many examining economic development policies in particular (see Reese and Fasenfest, 1996 for a review of this literature). It was argued in early research that urban systems in the two nations were so inherently different as to be incomparable, primarily as a result of cultural factors (Goldberg and Mercer, 1986) but also due to variation in the role of the state, notions of collective rights, and systems of federalism (Feldman and Graham, 1981; Andrew, 1994; Smart, 1994). However, other researchers have pointed to many similarities in the environment of cities in the two countries that are particularly germane to economic development: manufacturing employment and population loss in central cities

(text continues on p. 84)

TABLE 4.1   Sample Profile

Structure	Percentage
Chief executive (*n* = 338)	
Strong mayor	45
Weak mayor	12
Manager	41
Commission	02
City council (*n* = 347)	
At-large	47
Ward	24
Combination	30
Partisanship (*n* = 343)	
Partisan	23
Nonpartisan	77
Tier (*n* = 347)	
Independent	86
Intergovernmental	14

Spatial Location	Percentage
Country (*n* = 350)	
Canada	30
United States	70
Region (*n* = 350)	
West	13
West Central	10
Central	23
Great Lakes	31
East	15
Core/satellite (*n* = 341)	
Core city	39
Satellite city	25
Isolated node	36

Demographic Characteristics	Mean
Residential need (*n* = 331)	
Percentage in poverty	12
Percentage unemployed	7
Population change (*n* = 330)	2004

Fiscal Characteristics	Percentage
Economic base growth (*n* = 326)	
Expanding base, past five years	77
Expanding base, past year	65
Expanding base, coming year	86
Expanding base, next five years	97

(Continued)

TABLE 4.1   (Continued)

Nonresidential tax base ($n = 300$)	
High agricultural base	10
High industrial base	32
High commercial base	30
High institutional base	21
High residential base	42
Tax structure ($n = 293$)	
Levy sales tax	19
Levy utility tax	25
Levy hospitality tax	25
Levy property tax	97
Assessed property value ($n = 252$)	

Range	Number of Cities	Cumulative
Under 9 million	7	7
10 to 99 million	40	47
100 to 999 million	156	203
Over 1 billion	47	250
Over 10 billion	2	252

Competition	Percentage That Agree/Strongly Agree
Regional competition ($n = 333$)	
Seek to attract firms from neighbors	19
Seek to attract firms from region	33
In competition with others in the region	92
Extraregional competition ($n = 331$)	
Seek to attract firms from outside region	48
Seek to attract firms from North America	21
Seek to attract firms from other nations	11
In competition with others in the nation	79

Locus of Power	Percentage That Agree/Strongly Agree
In-house locus ($n = 338$)	
City government most active	54
Local government most influential	50
Off-cycle locus ($n = 323$)	
Chair of corporation takes lead	15
Formal public/private partnership is most active	20
Activities are conducted by an outside corporation	23
Intergovernmental locus ($n = 338$)	
County is most active	04
Regional or national governments most influential	04
Activities conducted by a regional government	02
Business influence ($n = 319$)	
Private sector organization is most active	15
Local business leader takes lead in initiating	03
Finance, insurance, real estate most influential	01

TABLE 4.1   (Continued)

Locus of Power	Percentage That Agree/Strongly Agree
Professional/bureaucratic influence (n = 342)	
Decisions left to professional administrators	50
Staff more important than elected officials	59
Projects should be guided by professional staff	69
Community input (n = 350)	
Have elected neighborhood commissions	10
Pro-growth and no-growth groups evenly represented	17
Community groups determine policies	11
Business input (n = 350)	
Most pro-growth groups are represented	17
Local business leaders determine policies	34
Nonlocal business leaders determine policies	02
Business needs surveys are used	53
Economic development functional independence (n = 328)	
Activities are centralized in a separate department	17
Economic development director initiates activities	50
Chief executive locus (n = 328)	
Executive office handles economic development	21
Mayor initiates economic development activities	16
Resource index (n = 248)	
Percentage of general fund budget	09
Average staff	02

Decision-Making Styles	Percentage That Agree/Strongly Agree
Turbulence (n = 343)	
Too much time spent firefighting	47
Too often judged on immediate results	56
Undertake activities to please others	25
Emphasize showcase projects	24
Other officials do not understand job	43

Decision-Making Styles	Percentage of Moderate to High Use
Planning and evaluation (n = 350)	
Post hoc evaluation	32
Cost/benefit analysis	48
Cost-effectiveness analysis	39
Internal rate of return	33
Strategic planning	60
Economic forecasting	47
Input/output analysis	22
Decision analysis (n = 273)	
Decision trees	15
PERT	11
GANTT	10

(Continued)

TABLE 4.1   (Continued)

Decision-Making Styles	Percentage of Moderate to High Use
Rationality (*n* = 359)	
Great deal of direction and focus	66
Development plan guiding policy	49
Forecasting done for all projects	50
Entreprenuerialism (*n* = 340)	
City offers all legal incentives	49
Any program increasing jobs is good	32
Incentives offered by other cities are copied	35
Successful policies are copied	60

Economic Development Goals	Percentage Where Important/Very Important
Traditional Goals (*n* = 339)	
Diversify the economic base	77
Attract new business	84
Expand/retain existing business	92
Promote industrial growth	78
Alternative Goals (*n* = 325)	
Promote small business growth	64
Promote service sector growth	40
Promote tourism/conventions	44
Type II Goals (*n* = 316)	
Promote social equity	21
Develop minority business	15
Develop neighborhoods/communities	35
Growth Management Goals (*n* = 291)	
Limit economic growth	03
Ensure growth management	46

(Nathan and Adams, 1989; Randall 1994; Garber and Imbroscio, 1996, among others), economic stresses related to similar shifts to post-industrial economies (Davies and Murdie, 1994; Rothblatt, 1994), and increasing intercity conflicts over development and intergovernmental resources (Woodside, 1990; Rothblatt, 1994). In short,

> The character of metropolitan development and the institutional re-
> sponse to it in both countries appear to be converging. The trends we
> have observed do not represent the "Americanization" of Canadian ur-
> ban public policy or the "Canadianization" of United States metropolitan

planning, but rather the globalization of urban development and corresponding governmental adaptation. (Rothblatt, 1994:516)

Indeed, recent research suggests that cities in the two nations not
only share regional and economic characteristics but also share development ideologies, policies, and limited rational planning (Turner and
Garber, 1994). Although important systemic and cultural differences
continue to exist, the globalization of economic production and competition and the struggle to maintain local tax bases and jobs have made
economic development a preeminent activity for municipalities in both
nations. Overall, the specific mechanisms employed to foster economic
development are generally similar for U.S. and Canadian cities; public
infrastructure investment and marketing activities are emphasized,
whereas financial and land mechanisms are less widely employed. In
almost all cases, the same economic development techniques predominate in both nations—the differences tend to be of scale, not substance
(Reese and Fasenfest, 1996).

In addition to country location, cities were also coded for regional location. This was done because previous research has indicated that regional location may have independent effects on local development
policy and that such effects may transcend national boundaries
(Krmenec, 1989; Reese and Rosenfeld, 2000). Thus, cities on the west
coast of both nations may be more similar in their approach to economic
development than they are like other cities more geographically removed in their own country. Each city responding to the survey was
geocoded, along with response data and basic census information, creating a geographic information system (GIS) data set. A regional variable was then created from the GIS data set. This procedure involved dividing cities into five different regions—West, West Central, Central,
Great Lakes, and East—by drawing boundaries around them within the
GIS set. The bulk of the cities are either in the Great Lakes or Central regions (31% and 23%, respectively) followed by east (15%), west (13%),
and west central (10%). Country of origin and region are significantly
related; Canadian cities are more likely to be located in the West and
East, whereas U.S. cities compose the greater part of the West Central
and Central regions. The composition of the Great Lakes region is
evenly divided among Canadian and U.S. cities.

Last, it has been noted that research attempting to explain local development policy or policy success may be misled by ignoring the position that a city occupies in the urban hierarchy and the proportion of the metropolitan population it contains (Hill et al., 1995). Clearly, there might be differences in economic development approach between cities with similar populations but different spatial or metropolitan locations. For example, a large city in a highly urbanized area among other large cities may react strongly to interlocal competition. Another city with similar size and other demographic and fiscal traits may react to competition very differently if they are the core or only city in their immediate urban area. To examine these differences, the cities were again mapped and their place in the urban system coded. Thus, cities were identified as being either the core city in their area (no other similarly sized city in close proximity), a satellite city (reasonably large sized but smaller than a close core city), or isolated node (a city not part of an urbanized system). Based on this scheme, 39% of the cities are core cities in their regions, 25% are satellites of core cities, and 36% are cities outside a core area. Canadian cities are significantly more likely to be core cities. This is the likely result of two factors. First, the cities responding in Canada are significantly larger in population than the U.S. cities, and there are fewer highly urbanized areas in Canada.

Demographic Characteristics

Most past studies have included some measure of economic distress or demographic need within communities; however, the exact operationalization of these concepts has been problematic. As noted by Wolman (1996), "need has less obvious meaning conceptually and is a grab bag in terms of operational measures" (126). Different studies have operationalized economic distress as unemployment (Reese, 1991; Feiock, 1992), population change (Goetz, 1990), and percentage of minority population (Miranda, et al., 1992), whereas "need" has been measured by poverty rate (Green and Fleischmann, 1991), population change (Clingermayer and Feiock, 1990), employment sector mix, and minority population (Green and Fleischmann, 1991). Looking across such measures, it appears that apples and oranges are being mixed. For example, whereas poverty and unemployment represent "stress" or "need" among local residents—a contention supported by Wolman

(1996)—population gain or loss may have little inherent correlation with the economic status of local residents. Using percentage of black or minority population as an indicator of distress ignores the substantial variation in cities, and particularly suburbs, with diverse populations. To address these concerns, an index of residential need is used here, composed of the percentage in poverty and percentage of unemployment. These, among a number of different demographic indicators, including education, population change, per capita income, median income, and the like, were identified in factor analysis as being part of the same distinct concept (see Table 4.2 for complete factor analysis results). It seems reasonable to conclude that communities with residents experiencing high poverty and unemployment rates would represent localities where residential need for services is also high. Across the cities responding to the survey, the mean percentage in poverty is 12%, whereas the mean unemployment rate is 7%. Cities in Canada have significantly higher unemployment rates—a likely artifact of the timing of the survey that occurred in the middle of a national economic downturn. Poverty rates are not significantly different among cities in the two countries.

Population change is used as an independent measure of general demographic trends in a community as opposed to indicating stress or need. It is reasonable to assume that cities with rapidly growing populations will have different economic development needs (perhaps growth management) and perspectives (lower concerns about intercity competition) than cities losing population. The average city in the data set experienced population growth of about 2,003 residents between the respective ten-year census periods. Canadian cities had significantly greater population growth. Again, this makes clear the point that population change is a variable independent of measures of residential need, illustrated by the fact that although Canadian cities experienced population growth, they also experienced higher levels of residential need overall.

It is worth noting that racial composition has been used in the determinants literature as an indicator of both need and fiscal stress. Regardless of which concept it is measuring, race is clearly an important attribute of the local milieu. Race, however, has not been used in most of the analysis of the survey data. Canada has not included municipal racial characteristics in their census, and hence the data are not readily avail-

(text continues on p. 91)

TABLE 4.2　Factor Analysis: Independent Variables

Factor	Loadings
Community input	
Elected neighborhood commissions	.64
Pro-growth and no-growth groups evenly represented	.75
Community groups primarily determine policies	.62
Business input	
Mostly pro-growth groups are represented	.56
Local business leaders primarily determine policies	.76
Business needs surveys are used to develop policies	.55
Representatives of nonlocal businesses primarily determine policies	.60
Extraregional competition	
Community seeks to attract firms from outside the region.79	
Community seeks to attract firms from North America	.89
Community seeks to attract firms from foreign countries	.82
City is in competition with others in the nation	.54
Regional competition	
Community seeks to attract firms from neighboring cities.85	
Community seeks to attract firms from cities within the region	.87
Community is in competition with others in the region	.59
Residential need for service	
Percentage in poverty	.89
Percentage unemployed	.89
Resources	
Staff	.82
Budget	.82
Evaluation and forecasting	
Post hoc evaluation	.61
Cost/benefit analysis	.74
Cost-effectiveness analysis	.83
Internal rate of return	.77
Strategic planning	.77
Economic forecasting	.78
Input/output analysis	.78
Market analysis	.74
Decision analysis	
Decision trees	.86
PERT charts	.95
GANTT charts	.92
Turbulence	
I have to spend too much of my time 'firefighting' rather than on longer-term problems.	.73
People in this community too often judge my work on immediate results rather than on long-run progress.	.67
I undertake activities just to please constituents or other officials even if I think these activities accomplish little.	.72

TABLE 4.2   (Continued)

Factor	Loadings
Cities emphasize showcase projects to distract from a lack of progress in solving more pressing problems.	.69
Other city officials do not have a very good idea of what an economic development practitioner should do.	.57
Rationality	
Forecasting of future jobs and other economic development benefits is conducted for each prospective economic development project.	.68
Our economic development plan guides decisions regarding which specific development policies and projects the city will pursue.	.79
There is a great deal of direction and focus in the economic development efforts.	.84
Entrepreneurialism	
City offers all economic development incentives legally allowed.	.70
Any program increasing the number of jobs is good.	.63
Incentives offered by other cities strongly influence the activities we pursue.	.62
City tries to implement policies used successfully in other cities in the region.	.59
Bureaucratic decision making	
Economic development decisions are mostly left to professional administrators.	.76
Professional staff is more important in initiating economic development policies than elected officials.	.78
Economic development projects should be guided by professionally trained decision makers.	.74
Traditional goals	
Diversify the economic base	.62
Attract new business	.70
Expand/retain existing business	.56
Promote industrial growth	.79
Alternative goals	
Promote small business growth	.58
Promote service sector growth	.71
Promote tourism/conventions	.61
Type II goals	
Promote social equity	.76
Develop minority business	.70
Develop neighborhoods/communities	.57
Growth limitation goals	
Limit economic growth	.61
Ensure growth management	.61
Economic base growth	
Base grown over the past five years	.62
Base grown the past year	.88

(Continued)

TABLE 4.2 (Continued)

Factor	Loadings
Expected base growth the coming year	.88
Expected base growth over the next five years	.71
Nonresidential tax base	
Percentage agricultural	.50
Percentage industrial	.71
Percentage commercial	.85
Percentage institutional	.77
Off-cycle locus	
Chair of the Economic Development Commission/Corporation takes lead in initiating economic development activities.	.68
A formal, incorporated public/private partnership organization is most active in promoting economic development.	.77
Economic development activities are conducted by a commission/ corporation outside of the city government.	.66
Intergovernmental activity	
The county government is most active in promoting economic development.	.79
Regional or national governments are most influential in local economic development policy formation.	.72
Economic development activities are conducted by a regional government entity.	.52
In-house locus	
City government is most active in promoting economic development.	.79
Local governments are most influential in local economic development policy formation.	.79
Business influence	
Private sector organization (chamber of commerce, board of trade) is most active in promoting economic development.	.66
A local business leader takes the lead in initiating economic development activities.	.77
The finance, insurance, or real estate sectors are most influential in local economic development policy formation.	.46
Economic development functional independence	
Economic development activities are centralized in a separate governmental department.	.80
The economic development director takes the lead in initiating economic development activities.	.80
Chief executive locus	
The executive office handles economic development activities.	.77
The mayor takes the lead in initiating economic development activities.	.77

able for a large number of cities. For some analysis of U.S. cities that follows, race will be considered as suggestive of the larger effects of diversity within local communities.

Fiscal Characteristics

Methods of measuring the fiscal health of cities have also been mixed
and often problematic. For example,

> Fiscal stress or fiscal condition conceptual variables, for example, are var-
> iously operationalized as property tax per capita (Donovan, 1993; Sharp
> and Elkins, 1991), per capita tax revenues (Cable, Feiock, and Kim, 1993,
> for tax burden), property tax rate (Rubin and Rubin, 1987; Rubin, 1986),
> the ratio of local revenues to local expenditures (Goetz, 1990), city bond
> rating (Goetz, 1990; Feiock, 1992), and percentage of total revenue de-
> rived from property tax (Sharp and Elkins, 1991). (Wolman, 1996:126)

Because many of these measures focus on ability to raise revenue
through local taxes, they tend to have more to do with preexisting residential or other property wealth or willingness to pay for services than
actual municipal fiscal health. Furthermore, many of the indicators
measure tax burden rather than health (Wolman, 1996). What is really
needed is a more direct measure of local economic health as opposed to
the wealth of residents or tax burden.

Because the primary question of interest is what effect local economic
stress has on the policy processes and decisions of local officials, it
seems that it can be measured in a much more direct fashion. Thus, the
survey asked officials about their perceptions of economic base growth
over different periods of time. The exact wording of the question was,
"Which of these describes more closely your community's economic experiences during the following time periods—the past five years, the
past year, the coming year, the next five years." They were then provided with seven response categories ranging from a 25% decline in
economic base to a 25% expansion. Admittedly, this measures perceptual growth, not actual base expansion. However, two points are worth
making. First, it is reasonable to expect that local officials make their
economic development policy decisions based as much or more on their
own perceptions of the health of the community than on any particular

data analysis. Second, as will be discussed more fully later, most cities evidence only very modest use (if any) of the types of analytic forecasting methods that would tell officials about actual economic indicators. This, too, suggests that decisions are based more on perception than "fact." Last, the perceptual growth measures are significantly correlated with all of the pertinent census measures. Thus, in communities where officials indicated expansion, poverty was lower, incomes higher, and unemployment lower. This, then, suggests that although local officials may operate more on perception than rational analysis, their perceptions of the growth levels of the local economy are reasonably accurate in a relative sense although are somewhat inflated overall.

As indicated in Table 4.1, the majority of respondents felt that their economies had been fairly healthy, and most expected growth in the future. Indeed, 97% expected at least some economic growth over the next five-year period (which represented 1995-2000). The most pessimistic assessment was for the year prior to the survey (1994), where 65% indicated at least some growth. Not surprisingly, the questions about economic growth over the four time periods are highly correlated, and factor analysis indicated that they were part of a single concept. Thus, they were combined into a single index that represents perceived economic base growth. Respondents from U.S. cities perceived significantly higher levels of economic growth across all time periods. This, too, appears to match "reality," because the survey took place during a national recession in Canada.

In examining the fiscal environment of local economic development, policy-making "health," however measured, should not be the only concern, because it is certainly not the only force that might logically affect policy choice. The nature of the economic base—again, not as a measure of health but as a unique trait in and of itself—may well have an impact on the nature of development sought and the policies employed. Similarly, the general approach to taxation as represented by the types of taxes levied may affect the kinds of development policies, particularly financial incentives, both pursued by the city and that businesses might find necessary to consider the city as a possible location. Last, the value of local land should be considered because it represents, in part, the possible resource base a community has to work with.

Respondents were asked about the *composition* of the local economic base—specifically, the extent to which agriculture, industry, commerce,

institutions, and residences composed the local base. Again, the rationale here is that communities with large residential bases and little
industry or commerce may have greater impetus to provide locational
incentives to firms that shift some of the tax burden off individual
homeowners. Similarly, communities with high industrial bases may be
more interested in growth management policies and hence less active in
offering location incentives. Because residential uses were the most
common type across cities (42% have economic bases comprised of over
60% residential use) and because factor analysis indicated that residential use was not part of the same concept as other base compositions, an
index was created that represents the extent to which a locality is composed of nonresidential tax uses. Next to residential use, cities were
most likely to have over 60% of their economic base composed of industrial (32%) and commercial (30%) uses.

The survey also asked about the *nature of the tax methods* used to generate local revenues. Overwhelmingly, the local governments in the
sample used property tax to raise revenues, the obvious result of tax
specialization with both the U.S. and Canadian systems. Thus, the more
interesting variable (and one with greater variation) is the extent to
which cities use other types of taxes in addition to property tax. Although such a variable may be interpreted as measuring tax "effort" in
that it indicates cities willing to levy additional taxes, this assumption
should not be taken too far. The use of additional taxes may indicate
innovativeness in a community or may simply be an opportunistic reflection of having nonresidential land uses ripe for taxation. Indeed, although population and residential need are not correlated with the use
of additional taxes, cities with larger portions of nonresidential tax
bases are significantly more likely to employ a broader taxation scheme.

The survey asked whether or not communities used property, sales,
income, commuter, utility, or hospitality taxes. Factor analysis indicated that the use of sales, utility, and hospitality taxes in addition to
property tax were part of the same concept. Thus, an "extra-tax" index
was created, which indicates the extent to which a city employs taxes
beyond the property tax. The frequency data in Table 4.1 show that almost all cities use the property tax (97%). Of the cities, 25% use utility
and hospitality taxes, and 19% levy a sales tax. Cities in the U.S. are significantly more likely to levy extra taxes, likely because of the generally
greater fiscal independence granted them by states.

Last, respondents were asked to identify the "assessed value of the city's tax base" for the year prior to the survey (1994). This variable must be interpreted with caution because states and provinces use different methods to assess and/or equalize local tax bases. For example, the state of Michigan only allows cities to "value" land at one half its assessed value. Other states allow valuation at 100% of assessed value. However, as a relative measure of tax base resources available to a city, the indicate should be reasonably sound. The local assessed values range from $2,500,000 to $47,916,044,426, and responses are almost completely discrete, thus "mean assessed value" provides little valid information about the sample. Table 4.1 presents the data in categorical form. The median assessed value for cities in the sample is $658,500,000. More specifically, seven cities have assessed base values of under nine million dollars, forty cities have values from ten to ninety-nine million, 156 cities (the clear majority) have assessed values from 100 to 999 million dollars, forty-seven cities are over one billion, and two cities have assessed tax base values over ten billion. As one might expect, cities with larger populations also have significantly higher assessed values. Finally, Canadian cities have significantly higher assessed base values than do U.S. cities.

Interlocal Competition

Competition between cities for economic development has regularly been included in attempts to explain the extent and mix of local development policies. Often, competition has been measured quantitatively by averaging the number of techniques used in surrounding communities (Green and Fleischmann, 1991; Feiock and Clingermayer, 1992). However, it can be argued that this is another case where a perceptual measure makes more sense. Regardless of the extent to which other communities are pursuing economic development, if local officials are not aware of that activity or they do not perceive that they are in competition with a particular city, the actual extent of development policies does not matter. It's how officials perceive competition in the environment that shapes their reactions and decision making. Thus, respondents were asked in a number of questions to indicate the extent to which they felt in competition with other cities and/or the extent to which the activities of other cities affected their development activities.

This provides an assessment of the competitive environment as it is interpreted and experienced by local decision makers.

Factor analysis of the various questions about competition revealed that competition is actually composed of two distinct concepts: regional and extraregional competition. Officials perceiving a great deal of regional competition indicated that their cities seek to attract firms from neighboring cities as well as from cities in the larger region. Furthermore, they feel that they are in competition with other communities in the region. Respondents indicating high extraregional competition said that their cities sought to attract firms from outside the region, from across North America, and even from foreign countries. Officials felt that they were in direct competition with other cities across their respective nations. Overall, feelings of competition are quite high, although translating these perceptions into attempts to "steal" firms from other cities is somewhat lower. Almost all cities feel in competition with others in their regions (92%), but smaller numbers actively try to attract firms away from proximate cities (19%) or others within the region (33%). Thus, it seems that cities are more willing to "poach" firms the further away they are located. Many discussions with local officials bear this out. It was frequently mentioned that if they could not attract development to their city, at least they hoped to get it within the boundaries of their immediate neighbors.

Many cities feel in competition with others across the country (79%), although this appears slightly less pressing than regional competition. And perhaps based on a realistic assessment of their chances of success, more cities try to attract firms from outside their regions (48%) than from the larger continent or from other global locations. If the average amounts of competition are considered, it can be concluded that regional competition is more universal and probably more pressing on local officials. Given academic research (see Ledebur and Woodward, 1990) suggesting that business location decisions are made in two stages—first, selecting a region and then a particular site within it—it appears that local officials have a realistic sense of the most viable arena for competition. Officials in Canadian and U.S. cities are not significantly different in their perceptions of regional competition, again suggesting that this is a shared experience, an integral part of the economic development business. Respondents from Canada, on the other hand, feel significantly more in competition with cities outside the region, probably resulting from perceived competition across the border with U.S. cities.

The Civic Culture of
Local Economic Development

The civic culture of local economic development is composed of several central components: locus of power or regime issues, the structure of economic development, decision-making styles, and economic development goals. How each of these are measured is discussed in turn.

Locus of Power

The question of who has power in local development decisions has been the primary focus of much research and serves as the basis for theorizing from elitism to regime theory, as previously noted. A number of elements of the local power structure are considered here.

Although other studies have examined the internal organizational structure of economic development decision making, such as whether there is a free-standing department or whether economic development is within the planning department or in the mayors office (Fleischmann and Green, 1991), the first or most basic consideration regarding locus of power for local economic development is whether or not the city keeps primary power within its purview or whether they off-load economic development activities to a quasi-public, public-private, or even wholly private organization or body (Levy, 1990; Clarke and Gaile, 1992). Several questions in the survey address the issue of in-house versus off-cycle locus of control for economic development. Factor analysis on these questions indicates two distinct concepts, as expected: one indicating that economic development decision structures are primarily within the city, the other indicating that external structures are used. Off-cycle or external decision structures are indicated by affirmative responses to the following statements: The chair of the Economic Development Commission/Corporation takes the lead in initiating economic development activities; a formal, incorporated public/private partnership organization is most active in promoting economic development; economic development activities are conducted by a commission/corporation outside of the city government organization. Thus, two issues are being measured here: (a) the existence of external bodies for economic development (a structural question) and (b) the extent to which these external bodies have influence in the actual decision-making process (a locus question). Cities with higher scores on this index are more likely to have external structures for economic development and grant such bodies the main locus of power for development policies and decisions. Keeping economic development decisions in-house is indicated by an index that includes the following: The city government is most active in promoting economic development; local government is most influential in local economic development policy formation.

Another organizational option is possible and has been largely overlooked in extant literature. Local governments may, in some cases, offload economic development to another governmental entity. A third index indicates the extent to which the county government is most active in promoting economic development, the regional or national governments are most influential, and economic development activities are conducted by a regional government entity. Although it might be reasoned that such arrangements would be employed in smaller cities lacking the capacity for development functions, there is no significant correlation between city population and the use of intergovernmental structures, nor is there a correlation between residential need and this option. Obviously, this is a variation in structure that is chosen by local governments for reasons other than abject need.

It is clear from the frequencies in Table 4.1 that cities are most likely to keep the locus for economic development in-house; over half of the cities indicate that the city is most active and most influential in development matters. Placing the locus of economic development in some type of external body is the next most common arrangement: An average of 19% of the cities give primary locus to an external agency or commission. Placing economic development in the hands of higher level governments, most commonly a regional or county body, is quite infrequent; on average, only 3% have such an arrangement. The only significant difference between Canadian and U.S. cites on locus issues is related to this last point. Canadian cities are more likely to use intergovernmental arrangements for economic development.

Regardless of whether the locus for economic development is internal or external to the city, a secondary question is what types of actors have the primary responsibility for development decisions. Regardless of whether external commissions or city departments are most active in economic development, there remains the issue of whether business leaders or development professionals are taking the lead. Although it is likely that external corporations will open the door for greater business influence and that city departments are more likely to be staffed by professional development bureaucrats, this is not necessarily so in either case. Thus, additional questions addressed the extent to which business leaders and professional bureaucrats had influence in development decision making. The business influence index includes the extent to which private sector organizations (chambers of commerce or boards of trade) are active in promoting economic development; a local business leader takes the lead in initiating development activities; and the finance, insurance, or real estate sectors are influential in development policy formation. The professional/bureaucratic index measures the extent to which development decisions are left to professional administrators, professional staff is more important in initiating policies than elected officials, and there is a feeling among officials that development projects should be primarily guided by professionally trained decision makers.

The data indicate that cities are much more likely to lean toward professional bureaucrats as opposed to local business leaders in economic development decision making; over half of the cities let professional administrators handle development decisions and emphasize staff over elected officials. Only 1% of the cities indicate that traditional growth machine interests (finance and real estate) dominate decision making, and few have a local business person taking the lead in development projects. Thus, regardless of particular structure, professionals tend to drive decision making, at least relative to private sector leaders.

The extent of business and community input into the economic development process and the nature of their relative influence has been a topic of focus in economic development research. Studies based on large numbers of cities, typically using survey methodologies, have tended to measure citizen and business input using additive indexes or scales of avenues or *opportunities* for such input (Sharp and Elkins, 1991; Cable et al., 1993; Reese, 1998). Other scholars have taken the approach of asking local officials about which interests usually benefited from economic development policies as a measure of influence; the central business district and local businesses appear to benefit most often

(Bowman, 1988). Both approaches have flaws, however. Although the first clearly measures whether mechanisms are in place for citizen or businesses to have input, they do not measure the extent to which such mechanisms are actually used or with what levels of success. The second approach appears to address who wins, more than it explores actual expressions of input. It is clear that survey research has some inherent limitations. It is far easier to measure the existence of input mechanisms than to address actual influence. Because this research is based on both survey and case study methodology, it seems clear that some variables will be better measured with one approach than the other. For the most part, the survey employed additive indexes of avenues for citizen and business input, and the issue of use and real influence was left to the intensive case studies. Thus, the survey contained a number of different avenues for citizen, neighborhood, and business input, although questions asking for the responding officials to assess the influence of different components of the community were also included. In this manner, the survey, to the extent possible, measured both opportunities for input and perceptions of the success of such avenues.

Factor analysis of these questions indicates that community input and business input mechanisms represent two distinct concepts. The presence of elected neighborhood commissions for economic development, the existence of active pro-growth and no-growth groups, and an assessment by local officials that community groups had the primary role in determining economic development policies were included in a single index measuring community input into the economic development process. The business input index includes agreement that mostly pro-growth groups are represented in the city, that local and nonlocal business officials primarily determine development policies, and that intensive use is made of business needs surveys to develop policies.

An examination of the frequencies for the components of the community and business input indexes clearly suggests that the latter are more prevalent than the former. Cities are more likely to survey businesses than citizens when considering economic development policies; 53% of cities use formal businesses needs surveys. And local business leaders (although not nonlocal leaders) are more likely to have influence in decisions than community groups. This, of course, is what much of the literature on growth machines and development regimes would lead us to expect. However, it is also the case that there are as many com-

munities where pro-growth and no-growth groups are equally represented as there are cities where pro-growth groups predominate (17% in
each case). Obviously, local business leaders could be supporting
growth limitation or management agendas. Canadian and U.S. cities
are basically identical in their input structures; there are no significant
differences in their relative levels of community and business input.

Economic Development Structure

This is a much more narrow concern than the issues raised earlier and
focuses solely on how the economic development function is placed
within the local government. Even cities that have external corporations as the primary source of economic development policy and decision making typically have some internal body that either supervises or
more likely, acts as a liaison with, the external organization. Although
larger cities—those over 100,000—appear most likely to have independent line departments for economic development (Clarke and Gaile,
1992), this is not necessarily the case for smaller communities (Reese,
1997). The internal organization of economic development is an important factor in the interplay between locus, structure, and input for economic development. For example, placing the economic development
function within the office of the chief executive is an obvious reflection
of strong executive influence and largely ensures that such influence is
maintained. Placing economic development within a planning or community development department may reflect less emphasis and/or resources for economic development. Freestanding departments, on the
other hand, suggest that a community expects a larger role for development and sets the stage for greater influence by economic development
staff professionals. Such arrangements were measured by a question
that simply asked what form the structure of economic development
took in the city but was also explored by asking about the influence of
various actors within the city, principally the mayor versus the economic development director. Two indexes were created indicating the extent
of economic development functional independence as opposed to chief
executive locus. Locating economic development within the executive
office is most common (21% versus 17% with freestanding departments). However, the majority (50%) indicate that the economic

development director or professional is more likely to initiate policy than the mayor (16%). This provides somewhat of a mixed message between structure and locus issues. Thus, it appears that regardless of where economic development is placed (in its own department or in the mayor's office), the economic development professionals are more likely to initiate policies and programs than the chief executive. And of course, initiating policy says little about whose views are most likely to influence decisions at the end of the day. Very likely, in the chief executive arrangements, the development professional initiates policies although the mayor maintains decisional control. As indicated in past research, Canadian cities are significantly more likely to have independent economic development departments and less likely to place development within the office of the chief executive (Reese, 1997a).

Last, the resources devoted to economic development are an important part of the structural possibilities for development. Although a city devoting more resources to economic development may just be in the enviable position of having greater resources to allocate, more resources also may indicate a greater emphasis on the development enterprise, or indeed, even greater need for it. Resources, although simple in concept, are difficult to measure precisely. Respondents were asked to indicate the percentage of total general fund operating budget allocated to economic development activities. Although this provides a quantitative dollar measure of resources, it is limited to general fund sources. Clearly, cities may use a combination of monetary resources for economic development, including state and federal funds, special tax assessments, interest on investments, and so on. This makes it very difficult to assess financial resources, either from a survey or even by looking at local budgets. However, given these limitations, general operating budget allocations provide a reasonable measure of relative resource effort. In addition, respondents were asked to indicate the number of professional staff working solely or primarily (at least 70% of the time) on economic development activities. Both of these variables loaded on a single factor creating an index of economic development resources. On average, 9% of local general fund revenues are devoted to economic development, and two staff persons work solely or principally on economic development, including the director or department head.

Decision-Making Styles

Although *who* makes decisions is obviously critical, *how* economic development decisions are made is also an important component of the local civic culture. A recurring theme of past research has been the role that turbulence or uncertainty plays in determining how local officials perceive their environment and consequently approach development decision making. Feelings of lack of control over the environment, that job expectations exceed resources, and that few citizens or other officials understand the nature of the development task appear to reduce rational decision making and encourage "shooting at everything that flies," behaviors where all possible policies are pursued rather haphazardly (Rubin, 1988; Reese, 1993b, 1997a). In accordance with past methods, a series of survey questions related to how the environment was perceived and how decisions were made. Factor analysis was then employed leading to the identification of indexes measuring perceived turbulence in the environment, the extent of planning and evaluation supporting development decisions, the extent to which decisions are made rationally, and the extent to which development officials approach their task in an entrepreneurial or proactive manner.

Turbulence in the environment is indicated by the extent of agreement with the following statements: I have to spend too much of my time "firefighting" rather than on longer-term problems; People in this community too often judge my work on immediate results rather than on long-run progress; I undertake activities just to please constituents or other officials, even if I think these activities accomplish little; Cities emphasize showcase projects to distract from a lack of progress in solving more pressing problems; and Other city officials do not have a very good idea of what an economic development practitioner should do. In short, the index measures the extent to which local officials felt in control of their environment, that other actors understood what their jobs consisted of, and how often they had to engage in activity to please others that didn't really seem to be part of a long-term development strategy. In short, perceived turbulence creates an environment much like that described by Lipsky (1980) in relation to street-level bureaucrats. Under conditions of high job stress, such bureaucrats were likely to resort to coping mechanisms to both simplify their jobs, reduce cognitive dissonance between personal conceptions of a successful activity and reality, and to protect themselves in case of conflict.

Perceived turbulence seems quite high for local officials engaging in economic development. For example, numerous officials indicated that more time is spent reacting to emergencies than on planned activity (47%), that their work is judged on immediate rather than long-term results (56%), and that few other actors in the city really understand what a development practitioner should be doing (43%). These perceptions of uncertainty in the environment appear the same on both sides of the border; Canadian and U.S. local officials are not significantly different in their tendencies to perceive their environment as turbulent.

The next obvious question, then, is what difference these perceptions of turbulence make in the development decision process. Are decisions made rationally after careful analysis of the environment and the likely outcomes of policy options? Are economy development programs and incentives carefully evaluated after the fact to see if they have achieved local goals? Three indexes address these concerns. First, the survey asked officials to indicate which of a number of planning and evaluation methods they used in their community. These ranged from post hoc evaluation to cost/benefit analysis to economic forecasting. Seven different evaluation and analysis techniques loaded on one factor and compose the planning/evaluation index. Three other planning techniques—decision trees and PERT and GANTT charts—loaded on a separate factor, representing planning methods typically employed to model the steps that must be taken to implement policies as well as time and resource requirements (see Reese, 1997b for a more compete description of these methodologies). Three additional questions loaded on a separate factor and more closely address how decisions are made, as opposed to the use of particular planning tools. "Rational" decision making was indicated by the extent of agreement with the following statements: Forecasting of future jobs and other benefits is conducted for each prospective development project; The economic development plan guides decisions; and There is a great deal of direction and focus to economic development efforts.

Although a number of cities use strategic planning in their economic development policy efforts (60%), less than 50% use any of the other planning or forecasting techniques. Of these cost/benefit analysis

(48%) and economic forecasting (47%) are most frequently used. Far fewer cities use decision analysis techniques, with decision trees being the most common at 15%. These data represent a classic "is the glass half full or half empty" dilemma. On the one hand, close to half of the cities are using some form of planning methodology to support their economic development efforts. On the other, use of most techniques is below 48%, and only 32% of cities are evaluating their policies after implementation. Thus, even if a good number are using systematic planning, actual analysis to see if policies are doing what they intended or indeed, anything at all, is relatively rare.

The evaluation and planning data aside, most local officials *perceive* that their policy processes are rational and systematic. Of responding officials, 66% indicate that there is a great deal of focus and direction in their economic development efforts, and half say that their activities are guided by a development plan (57% of the cities have such plans) and that forecasting is done for all projects. Thus, it appears that officials are somewhat optimistic about the actual level of rationality in their decision-making efforts; however, again, there is a reasonable amount of planning taking place. It is interesting to note that there are no significant differences among cities in Canada and the U.S. in their propensity to use planning/evaluation, decision analysis, or rational processes in decision making. Although some past studies have indicated a stronger history and practice of urban planning in Canada (Rothblatt, 1994), other studies have not found this to be the case (Reese, 1997b).

A final decision-making index was constructed out of four questions that loaded on a single factor: The city offers all economic development incentives legally allowed; Any program increasing the number of jobs in the community is good; Incentives offered by other cities strongly influence local activities; and The city tries to implement policies used successfully in other cities in the region. The interpretation of this index requires a bit of explanation. In previous research (Reese, 1997a), a similar index was interpreted as indicating a city that was shooting at anything that flies.[1] In other words, the use of all legal techniques and the copying of policies used in other communities was taken to represent reactive, nonprogrammatic behavior. Using all legal policies suggested that a city was trying everything possible in a scattershot manner in the hope that something, *anything,* would lead to revitalization. Using policies employed elsewhere seemed to represent an effort to apply silver bullets with little consideration for local contingencies. However, based on further analysis and data collected in the case studies, it became apparent that reconsideration, and indeed, reconceptualization of this index was in order. Thus, whereas for some cities it may well be the case that using a number of different types of policies and attempting to borrow and refine techniques used successfully elsewhere represents a wanton attempt to try everything, it may also be the case that some cities exhibiting the same behaviors are actually being *entrepreneurial.* As is discussed later, several of the case cities were doing a wide variety of policies and programs and were making extensive use of all state and federal grant programs. However, these cities *also* were carefully planning and evaluating their efforts and had highly professionalized economic development staff. For these cities, taking what they felt was creative advantage of a number of program and funding options and scanning the environment to find new policies that could be adapted for local use actually represented creative, proactive, entrepreneurial behavior. In short, based on the case studies and further analysis of the survey data, it was concluded that this index more often represents entrepreneurial behavior than "shooting" behavior, and the interpretation of it as the latter represented a value judgement that does not seem to match well with the reality reflected in the responses.

Overall, levels of entrepreneurialism are mixed depending on the specific question in the index. Of the cities, 60% try to adapt and implement policies used successfully by other cities in their region. Almost half offer all economic development incentives legally allowed. Fewer respondents agreed that any program that might increase jobs was "good" (32%), and 35% agreed that the incentives offered by other cities strongly influenced their activities. There is no significant difference in the level of entrepreneurialism among cities in Canada and the U.S.

Local Economic Development Goals

Respondents were asked to indicate the importance of sixteen common development goals. Factor analysis was then employed to determine if there were conceptual commonalties among some of the goals, and four goal types were identified: traditional goals, alternative goals, Type II goals, and growth management goals. Traditional economic development goals revolve around diversification of the local economic base, attraction of new business, expansion/retention of existing business, and promotion of industrial growth. Alternative goals stress more entrepreneurial or demand-side perspectives and tend to focus on the creation of small local businesses rather than the attraction of large industrial facilities. The alternative goal index includes promotion of small business growth, promotion of service sector growth, and development of tourism/convention sectors. Respondents from cities emphasizing Type II goals identified the following as being important: promotion of social equity, development of minority businesses, and neighborhood/community development. Growth management goals include limiting economic growth and ensuring that any growth is properly managed.

Emphasis on traditional development goals is clearly the most widespread; 92% of the cities want to expand or retain existing business, and 84% view business attraction as their most prominent goal. Seventy-seven percent and 78% desire to promote industrial growth and diversify the economic base, respectively. Alternative goals are also important to most cities in the sample: 64% emphasize small business growth, 44% tourism and conventions, and 40% service sector growth. Although growth management is an important goal in many cities (46%), few want to go further to limit economic growth (only 3%). From 15% to 35% of the respondents said that the Type II goals of social equity, minority business, and neighborhood development were important outcomes of their development efforts. Respondents from Canadian cities were significantly more likely to identify alternative goals as being important, but there were no other significant differences in goal emphasis.

SUMMARY

Certainly, the economic development literature provides a rich theoretical and methodological foundation on which additional research and model building may occur. In this chapter, the beginnings of a comprehensive model of local decision making as it applies specifically to one policy arena—economic development—are developed. The goal is to integrate the various concepts and measurements of causality, building on previous studies of economic development specifically but of local policy making and civic culture in particular. The independent, explanatory variables were presented and then described in a variety of indexes covering environmental variables that focus on government structure, community spatial characteristics, internal demographics, local fiscal health, and interlocal competition. In addition, the various components of civic culture operationalized as including locus of power, economic development structure, decision-making styles, and economic development policy goals were presented. Together, these are the elements of a comprehensive explanatory model of local decision making.

It is interesting to begin to see the wide variation of local governments in North America as it pertains specifically to economic development decision making. The decentralization that comes with federalism provides a near-endless number of local government situations. Clearly, local environments vary tremendously in virtually every manner. There are few environmental variables for which there is little variance other than that most cities have nonpartisan elections and are not part of a multitiered governing arrangement. Beyond this, use of reform structures, central city versus satellite, economic need, strength and diversity of economic base, and perceptions of interlocal competition vary significantly across the cities. Although most local officials feel competitive pressures from other cities in their regions, the other environmental variables acting on local decisions are anything but uniform. Indeed, even the national boundary between the U.S. and Canada appears to have little uniform relationship with any of the other independent variables.

The diversity of communities is also seen in the framework of civic culture. The picture presented is one of diversity in locus of power, economic development structure, and decision-making styles. Together, these factors appear to result in a rich array of economic development goals, although a common emphasis on economic base diversification and business attraction and expansion is apparent. Intuitively, in an environment in which local governments are allowed to be creative and innovative, to grow healthy or to stagnate, and to be inclusive or exclusive, the challenge of understanding "who governs?" and "what difference does it make?" is extraordinary. This challenge is addressed in succeeding chapters as the analysis moves on to the development of a model of economic development policy process that focuses on local civic culture. This model, based on the survey data, is then assessed and fleshed out through the use of the case studies.

NOTE

1. The index used by Reese (1997a:111) included the following survey questions: The city pursues all incentives allowed by law; There is a strong demand for incentives by businesses; and The city grants all demands for incentives.

5

MODELING
LOCAL ECONOMIC
DEVELOPMENT POLICY

The purpose of this chapter is to explore the role local civic culture plays in economic development policy making. It proceeds by (a) examining the relationships among the various components of local civic culture, (b) modeling the relationships between environment and local civic culture, and (c) presenting a model depicting the effects of environment and culture on local economic development policies. The basic argument for this analysis was presented in Chapter 2. To recapitulate, the approach to economic development and the particular mix of policies and programs pursued in a particular community are products of the interaction between the environment of the community, its unique history, and the civic culture that develops from and then feeds back into these forces. The local civic culture encompasses, but is not limited to, what is currently understood to be the local governing regime. Thus, although an analysis of local culture considers the structure

of and relationships among groups and interests that coalesce to provide the resources to govern the locality and organize demands into
social outputs or production, it also includes those forces that bring the
regime into being and shape its standard operating or decisional procedures. The broader notion of civic culture also includes decision-
making styles, the nature and effects of the local vision and goals, and
how all of this is translated into public policy.

The models presented in this chapter are admittedly extremely complex. This remains the case even after a number of variables initially examined were dropped from further analysis. This is inherent in trying
to explore concepts as broad as the environment and culture of local
economic development. Modeling is essentially an exercise in simplifi-
cation. All aspects of the "real world" cannot be included because the
heuristic value of the model would be lost (i.e., the simplifying and explanatory power). The challenge is to encompass and portray the complexity present in reality and include those variables that are critically
important in understanding the milieu of local development while at
the same time keeping the presentation and discussion manageable.

This balancing challenge has been addressed here in several ways.
First, as just noted, many of the independent variables identified in the
previous chapter are deleted from the analysis as it progresses so that
the model finally presented is the most parsimonious possible. In short,
those independent variables that were not related to process or policy
later in the model or that were redundant in effect to other variables
were dropped. Second, although the relationships among the environmental variables were analyzed, that discussion is presented in the Ap-
pendix to this chapter to streamline the presentation. Many of the relationships between environmental variables, such as governmental
structure, are well addressed in the literature and do not need to be reex-
amined here. Third, the aspects of civic culture are examined separately
prior to modeling their relationships to economic development policies. This allows for description and examination of the interrelationships among the attributes of local civic culture. The relationships between civic culture and the environment are then presented and
discussed. The last section of the chapter presents policy models that include all of these relationships. Last, the case studies in subsequent
chapters permit the development and illustration of a number of the
key relationships in the models. Thus, what is minimized due to simpli-

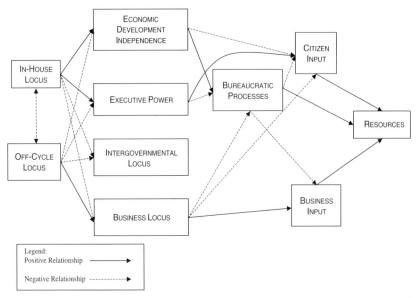

Figure 5.1. The Political Culture of Local Economic Development: Locus and Structure

fication or is overshadowed by the complexity of the whole is revisited in more detail within the case studies.

THE CIVIC CULTURE OF
LOCAL ECONOMIC DEVELOPMENT

At this point, the relationships between the aspects of local civic culture are explored. The presentation is organized around the major components of culture: locus of power, decision-making style, and development goals. Figure 5.1 portrays the expected or hypothesized relationships among the locus of power measures based on the determinants research presented in Chapter 1. Figure 5.2 shows the hypothesized relationships among the decision style and goals variables.

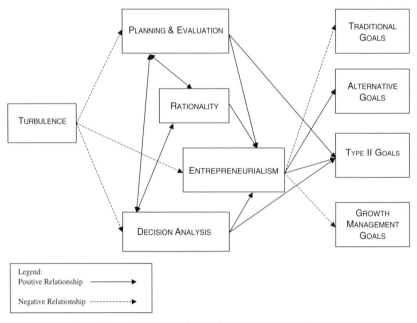

Figure 5.2. The Political Culture of Local Economic Development: Decision Style and Goals

Locus of Power

Hypothesized Relationships

Again, Figure 5.1 portrays expected relationships based on past research. Cities where economic development functions are kept primarily in-house will likely grant more power to either the economic development department or the office of the chief executive, depending on where that function is housed. In turn, such cities should grant less power to intergovernmental bodies and the business community. Conversely, cities that have chosen to place development decision making in an external commission or corporation are likely to evidence greater business influence and less emphasis on other governmental actors. It is also anticipated that the placement of the economic development function will have an impact on the nature and number of avenues for wider community input. Thus, locating economic development responsibilities in an independent department would reduce opportunities for citizen involvement, whereas locus in the mayor's office should increase it. Similarly, placing economic development functions within an external business-type organization should increase opportunities for business input at the expense of citizen input.

The use of bureaucratic procedures to make decisions should be greater where development activity is primarily the responsibility of an independent economic development department within the city government structure. Placement of economic development functions within the mayor's office is likely to increase "political" processes for decision making and reduce the reliance on bureaucratic staff and procedures. Given the literature suggesting that professionally administered cities are less open to community input, broadly defined, it is expected that cities that tend to make development decisions bureaucratically will be less inclusive. They will rely more on professional staff and seek less input from both the business community and neighborhood groups. Last, it is expected that many interests will be pressing for greater resources devoted to economic development. Although professional staff will obviously be pressing for more resources, the literature also suggests that voters and the business community generally will desire more active economic development efforts by the city. It should be noted that this model only represents relationships among the civic culture variables; environmental forces also affect available resource levels, and those relationships are considered later in the chapter.

Actual Relationships

Correlation analysis indicates that in-house and off-cycle locus of control for economic development decisions are indeed trade-offs; the indexes are significantly and negatively related (see Table 5.1). Cities that keep development in-house are more likely to grant authority to both an independent economic development department and the executive office, as expected. They are also less likely to give power to either intergovernmental agencies or to the business community. Cities where the locus of power is in an external agency do not necessarily grant more power to business groups, but they do tend to provide more avenues for business input. This emphasizes the fact that the *availability* of input mechanisms does not necessarily result in *influence*.

TABLE 5.1 Correlation Matrix—Locus of Control Variables

	In-House Locus	Off-Cycle Locus	Economic Development Independence	Executive Locus	Inter-governmental Locus	Business Locus	Bureaucrats	Citizen Input	Business Input	Resources
In-house locus	1.00	-.53*	.15*	.16*	-.24*	-.33*	-.03	-.08	-.23*	-.16*
Off-cycle locus	-.53*	1.00	-.31*	-.19*	-.04	-.04	.02	-.01	.23*	.12
Economic development independence	.15*	-.31*	1.00	-.44*	.01	-.17*	.27*	.02	-.06	.16*
Executive locus	.16*	-.19*	-.44*	1.00	-.11*	-.06	-.16*	.06	-.13*	-.13*
Intergovernmental locus	-.24*	-.04	.01	-.11*	1.00	.06	.00	-.02	.06	.02
Business locus	-.33*	-.04	-.17*	-.06	.06	1.00	-.16*	.10	.03	-.06
Bureaucrats	-.03	-.02	.27*	-.16*	.00	-.16*	1.00	-.04	-.03	.13*
Citizen input	-.04	-.01	.02	.06	-.02	.10	-.04	1.00	.33*	.13*
Business input	-.23	.23*	-.06	-.13*	.06	.03	-.03	.33*	1.00	.11
Resources	-.60*	.12	.16*	-.13*	.02	-.06	.13*	.13*	.11	1.00

*Significant at the .05 level

Although not portrayed in the Figure 5.1, in an effort to simplify presentation, the relationships among the various locus variables are largely as expected. Having an independent development department is a trade-off for locating economic development functions within the mayor's office. The presence of a development department also appears to reduce business influence; there is no relationship between the extent of reported business influence and chief executive control. However, having an independent development department has no effect on propensity to grant power to intergovernmental bodies, and chief executive control significantly reduces regional efforts. In short, it appears that placing economic development functions within the mayor's office will significantly reduce intergovernmental efforts at economic development, whereas having an independent development department reduces business influence.

As expected, an independent economic development department provides greater opportunity for professional influence although this is less likely when business groups drive economic development or where the locus of decision making resides in the mayor's office.

It is interesting to note that none of the locus issues portrayed in Figure 5.1 are significantly related to the number of avenues for citizen input into the development process. Thus, it appears that opportunities for citizen input are more likely to be affected by the environment than locus-of-control issues. This will be discussed more fully later in the chapter. Business input is increased when economic development functions are located in an external body and is decreased by locus with the chief executive. Business and community input are significantly and positively related to each other. This, too, is counterintuitive according to past arguments concerning elite or growth machine approaches. According to these theories, one would expect to find business input supplanting citizen input; indeed, businesses would be expected to want to keep citizens out of the process both to make procedures more predictable and to solidify their own power. Why these two variables appear to reinforce each other as opposed to being trade-offs is more fully illustrated in the case studies to come.

Finally, having an independent development department and granting power to bureaucratic professionals is related to increased resources. In reality, these forces are probably mutually reinforcing. Greater resources are necessary to support an independent department and hire staff. Once in place, those actors press for additional resources. Although business input is not related to resources, it appears that citizen pressure does enhance budget and staff devoted to economic development as expected. Last, cities with independent departments devote greater resources to economic development than those where it is part of the office of the chief executive. Again, this is likely due to the higher costs associated with a freestanding department.

This does raise an important issue about the path analysis that follows. As will be discussed more fully later, path analysis does not provide information on direction or causality. In other words, it will not tell us with any certainty whether structure leads to resources or resources lead to structure. That conclusion must be based on theory and reasoning. Because resources are affected by many variables in a community and because many factors influence structure of economic development besides resources, it seems more reasonable to place resource allocation later in the model. In other words, it is not as persuasive to argue that staff and budget allocation determine the structure of economic development. Rather, certain structural arrangements necessitate particular resource allocation. Creating an independent development department run by professional staff, for example, is a decision likely to perpetuate certain resource patterns.

It is clear from the foregoing narrative that many of the structural issues are really trade-offs: in-house versus off-cycle locus and internal economic development department versus external business organization, for example. Thus, to simplify further analysis, the extent to which a community keeps economic development under governmental control is used as a proxy for the off-cycle variables. In a similar manner, only the economic development independence and executive control variables are included in further analysis representing the main alternative internal structures. Because so few cities leave development decisions to intergovernmental bodies or business organizations and because these are trade-offs for the other two variables, only the internal options are used in further analysis. The proclivity to participate in intergovernmental arrangements for economic development and the use of business organizations will be explored more fully in the case study analyses. Again, the goal is to keep the statistical models as parsimonious as possible.

The relationships among the various locus-of-control measures can be summarized as follows:

Local government responsibility for economic development is primarily exercised either by an independent department or the chief executive's office.

Placement of economic development functions in the office of the chief executive reduces intergovernmental efforts, whereas an independent department appears to reduce business input and increase the role of professional bureaucrats.

Placement of development functions outside the city government is associated with greater resources devoted to economic development.

The extent of citizen input appears to be affected more by environmental forces than any particular structural arrangement.

Business and citizen input appear to reinforce rather than supplant one another. The presence of a large number of opportunities for business input does not preclude citizen or neighborhood input.

Citizen pressure in particular appears to increase the level of resources devoted to economic development. It is also likely that economic development professionals have a significant role in pressing for increased resources.

Decision-Making Style and Development Goals

Hypothesized Relationships

Figure 5.2 portrays the expected relationships among the remaining civic culture variables: decisional environment, decision style, and goals. Presumably, perceived environmental uncertainty and stress reduce deliberative action. In other words, quick decisions should replace those supported by planning, evaluation, and decision analysis. Similarly, such an environment should also lead to policy actions that are closely tied to past experience; new, innovative, or potentially risky activities will likely be avoided. In short, environmental turbulence should reduce entrepreneurialism on the part of local development officials.

The extent to which economic development is approached in an entrepreneurial manner should be manifest in the types of goals the city sets for economic development. Specifically, an entrepreneurial approach would be one where the public sector is actively involved in initiatives to support the development of businesses through such mechanisms as research and development or start-up loans, takes an active role in both property development and management, provides support to small businesses through incubator programs, and other activities that require active and innovative approaches to capital creation. Cities approaching economic development in such a manner should de-emphasize traditional industrial attraction and stress the development of new local businesses. Although some growth management efforts may be entrepreneurial, it is expected that entrepreneurial cities will more likely pursue growth as opposed to growth limitation. Cities with more entrepreneurial approaches should also be more open to Type II goals, which emphasize development of minority businesses and neighborhood development. Last, planning, evaluation, and decision analysis should lead to the kind of deliberative and future-oriented thinking that is a necessary prerequisite for Type II policy goals, because social equity and neighborhood development tend to be longer range outcomes. Other variables such as residential need will undoubt-edly contribute to social equity goals, but these relationships will be considered later.

Actual Relationships

The correlation analysis (see Table 5.2) does not support several of the expected relationships in Figure 5.2. For example, it does not appear to be the case that turbulence decreases planning/evaluation or entre-preneurialism; indeed, it is not significantly related to either variable. Instead, perceived turbulence in the environment appears to lead di-rectly to two of the goals: reducing both traditional and growth man-agement goals. Thus, it appears that regardless of entrepreneurialism, officials perceiving stress in their environments are less likely to pursue even the traditional goals of industrial attraction. Similarly, planning and evaluation appear to have no effect on entrepreneurialism; they, too, appear to affect goals directly. Here, planning and evaluation are significantly and positively related to all of the developmental goals. This relationship obviously needs further exploration because planning should permit officials to discriminate among goals rather than pur-suing them all. However, it could be the case that planning and evalua-tion simply allow officials to develop goals. In other words, they permit goal-directed behavior, regardless of the particular goals involved. This will be explored more fully in the case studies. Higher levels of entre-preneurialism do appear to be related to a greater emphasis on Type II goals, as expected. However, entrepreneurial approaches are also related to traditional rather than alternative goals.

Last, it should be noted that the three indexes measuring systematic forms of decision making—planning and evaluation, decision analysis, and rational decision making—are positively related to each other and related to the economic development goals in a similar manner. In later analyses examining decision-making style and economic development policy, it was also clear that the three indexes perform in the same manner. Thus, only one index is used in further analysis because they are basically proxies for each other. Because it contains more of the variables typically considered to constitute planning and evaluation, that index will remain in further analysis.

In summary, then, the following can be concluded about the style and goals components of civic culture:

> Turbulence in the environment appears to reduce risky, creative, or nontraditional economic development goals.
>
> Planning and evaluation appear to increase the ability of local officials to pursue goals of all types. In other words, it seems necessary for goal-directed behavior to occur although it does not appear to drive any particular type of development goal.
>
> An entrepreneurial approach to development appears associated with Type II goals. Officials viewing development in a more entrepreneurial manner are more likely to focus on social equity, minority business, and neighborhood development.
>
> An entrepreneurial approach to development is also associated with emphasis on traditional development goals. Thus, entrepreneurialism leads to the typical stress on industrial growth and attraction but appears to move beyond that to also heighten concern with Type II or social equity goals.

MODELING THE ENVIRONMENT AND CIVIC CULTURE OF LOCAL ECONOMIC DEVELOPMENT

Based on the relationships just discussed, path analysis was used to create an overall model portraying the relationships among the environmental and civic culture variables (thus, all of the environment variables are now depicted in the presentation). As such, it also includes all

TABLE 5.2 Correlation Matrix: Decision Style and Goals

	Turbulence	Planning and Evaluation	Decision Analysis	Rationality	Entrepre- neurialism	Traditional Goals	Alternative Goals	Type II Goals	Growth Goals
Turbulence	1.00	-.08	.06	-.36*	-.04	-.24*	-.10	-.04	-.16*
Planning and evaluation	-.08	1.00	.55*	.33*	.06	.31*	.26*	.33*	.17*
Decision analysis	.06	.55*	1.00	.30*	.17*	.18*	.16*	.41*	.28*
Rationality	-.36*	.33*	.30*	1.00	.35*	.40*	.32*	.35*	.24*
Entrepreneurialism	-.04	.06	.17*	.35*	1.00	.22*	.11	.17*	.02
Traditional goals	-.24*	.31*	.18*	.40*	.22*	1.00	.44*	.31*	.32*
Alternative goals	-.10	.26*	.16*	.32*	.11	.44*	1.00	.39*	.24*
Type II goals	-.04	.33*	.41*	.35*	.17*	.31*	.39*	1.00	.33*
Growth goals	-.16*	.17*	.28*	.24*	.02	.32*	.24*	.33*	1.00

*Significant at the .05 level

of the direct paths that were left out of the initial models to simplify analysis but portrays a reduced number of indexes based on the rationales provided. Path analysis "begins with a set of structural equations that represent the structure of interrelated hypotheses in a theory" and follows standard statistical procedures for tracing paths (Bohrnstedt, 1982: 441). Such analysis assumes that the error correlations for endogenous variables are zero, thus allowing the use of ordinary least squares regression to estimate the path coefficients (beta weights). It is also assumed that random disturbances are not correlated with each other or with exogenous variables.

It is important at the outset to be clear about what path analysis can and cannot do. Although it shows the relationships among variables within a system and allows the statistical development of a model, it will not determine lines of causality. In other words, it will not determine if structure leads to agency or whether the reverse is true; only theory based on previous literature will do that. Arguments about the effects of individual variables on economic development culture and policy have been presented in earlier chapters. The expected lines of causality have been portrayed in the initial models in this chapter. These serve as the basis for the model in Figure 5.3. None of the paths in the model are block recursive; in other words, each path is going in only one direction, creating an ordered system (Davis, 1985). Because of the added complexities of modeling block recursive paths, they have not been included in the path analysis. The overriding goal here is to provide as clear and simple (as possible) a picture of how the environment relates to local civic culture and how both in turn affect development policy. The case studies to follow allow for "unpacking" and further development of more complex relationships. It should also be made clear that the goal here is not to explain local civic culture nor, later on, economic development policy. Rather, the purpose is to explore the relationships among the environment and the various components of culture and to examine how these ultimately relate to different policy choices by communities. In short, concern with the paths and relationships among variables outweigh those with the ultimate explanatory power as measured by R^2 values. As suggested by King (1991), the point of the regression analysis here is to "estimate a causal effect" as opposed to "the unattainable (and unclear) goal of determining every possible cause" of economic development policies (1051).

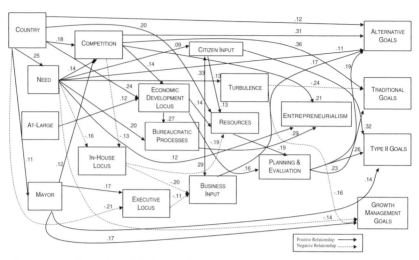

Figure 5.3. The Political Culture of Local Economic Development:
Comprehensive Model

Economic Development Goals

Paths are typically analyzed and discussed by working backwards
through the model from dependent to exogenous variables, and the discussion here follows that process. Table 5.3 provides complete data for
the path analysis in Figure 5.3. *Traditional industrial attraction goals* are
related to competition, planning and evaluation, and turbulence in the
environment. Cities with officials who perceive greater environmental
stress are less likely to pursue traditional development goals. In short,
traditional industrial attraction and retention goals are more likely to be
expressed where competition is high but other types of environmental
turbulence are low. Of the variables in the model, the best predictor of
traditional development goals is competition among cities for development. Looking across the different development goals, it appears that
competition enhances goal-directed behavior, especially when coupled
with planning and evaluation (particularly for traditional and alternative goals), whereas turbulence and uncertainty reduce the tendency to
emphasize particular development goals.

Alternative economic development goals, such as small business development, appear related to competition, residential need, location in

TABLE 5.3 Path Analysis: Environmental and Civic Culture Variables

Dependent Variable	b	BETA	Significance
Traditional goals ($R^2 = .26$)			
Competition	.36	.36	.00
Turbulence	−.24	−.24	.00
Planning/evaluation	.23	.23	.00
Constant	−1.9E-02		.69
Alternative goals ($R^2 = .27$)			
Country	.28	.12	.02
Residential need	.11	.11	.04
Competition	.31	.31	.00
Business input	.17	.17	.00
Planning/evaluation	.20	.19	.00
Constant	−.11		.07
Type II goals ($R^2 = .23$)			
Mayor	.15	.14	.01
Citizen input	.31	.32	.00
Planning/evaluation	.27	.26	.00
Constant	.35		.01
Growth-management goals ($R^2 = .08$)			
Mayor	.17	.17	.01
Turbulence	−.17	−.17	.01
Residential need	−.14	−.14	.02
Constant	.34		.01
Entrepreneurialism ($R^2 = .18$)			
Residential need	.12	.12	.03
Competition	.21	.21	.00
Bureaucrats	.29	.20	.00
Constant	−2.8E-03		.96
Planning/evaluation ($R^2 = .07$)			
ED independence	.15	.16	.01
Resources	.18	.19	.00
Constant	1.22E-02		.85
Turbulence ($R^2 = 02$)			
Residential need	.13	.13	.02
Constant	1.29E-02		.82
Bureaucrats ($R^2 = .11$)			
Residential need	.20	.20	.00
ED independence	.28	.27	.00
Constant	2.66E-02		.63

(Continued)

TABLE 5.3   (Continued)

Dependent Variable	b	BETA	Significance
Resources (R^2 = .12)			
Country	.45	.20	.00
In-house	−.20	−.19	.00
ED independence	.14	.14	.04
Citizen input	.14	.13	.05
Constant	−9.3E-02		.24
Citizen input (R^2 = .12)			
Residential need	9.06E-02	.09	.09
Business input	.33	.33	.00
Constant	.12E-02		.82
Business Input (R^2 = .15)			
In-house	−.20	−.20	.00
Executive locus	−.11	−.11	.05
Citizen input	.29	.29	.00
Constant	−8.6E-03		.87
Executive locus (R^2 = .07)			
Country	.47	.21	.00
Mayor	.17	.17	.00
Constant	.49		.00
ED department independence (R^2 = .11)			
Country	.53	.24	.00
At-large elections	.15	.12	.03
Competition	.13	.14	.02
Constant	−.41		.00
In-house locus (R^2 = .05)			
Residential need	−.16	−.16	.00
Competition	−.13	−.13	.02
Constant	1.30E-02		.81
Competition (R^2 = .08)			
Country	.40	.18	.00
Residential need	.14	.14	.02
Mayor	.13	.12	.03
Constant	.15		.25
Residential need (R^2 = .06)			
Country	.57	.25	.00
Constant	−.15		.02
Strong mayor (R^2 = .01)			
Country	.24	.11	.04
Constant	2.08		.00

Canada, planning and evaluation, and opportunities for business input (see Table 5.3). This suggests some complex interactions among the various measures of stress—competition, residential need, and turbulence. It appears that competition is related to industrial development goals when coupled with turbulence. However, if the situation is not perceived as being turbulent by local officials—even in the face of higher residential need—it appears that more nontraditional or even more entrepreneurial goals are pursued. Because greater business input avenues are also present in this model, it may be that the local business community is pushing for business development goals rather than a focus on industrial attraction. Residential need may also necessitate smaller investments that would help local residents more directly for both jobs and business development opportunities, as opposed to efforts to attract large industrial operations. Although competition among cities is almost a given (indeed, competition is the best predictor of alternative goals as well), perceptions by local officials that their jobs are not well understood and that they have little control over their environment lead to more traditional (or perhaps safe) economic development goals. On the other hand, input by the local business community and residential need appear to stimulate support for development of new, often smaller, local businesses.

Type II or *redistributive and equity goals* are related to planning and evaluation, community input, and a strong mayor. It is interesting to note what is not present in this path, specifically, signs of fiscal or environmental stress in the form of residential need, competition, or turbulence. It appears that having more inclusive politics, particularly giving citizens more avenues for input, absent a lot of environmental stress, is related to Type II goals. Thus, citizen pressure, absent economic stress, produces redistributive and social equity goals. Such stress pushes the city toward traditional goals as noted earlier. Citizen input is the best predictor of Type II goals, and the presence of a strong-mayor system facilitates the expression of community desires. Such a dynamic conforms to much of the structure literature, which has suggested that less-reformed systems (that is, those with strong mayors) facilitate political expressions.

Last, *growth management* or *limitation goals* are related to the presence of strong-mayor systems, an absence of turbulence, and low residential need. Clearly, growth-limitation goals are the result of a healthy economic environment. This is logical because it would be those communities already experiencing economic growth and its possible negative effects that would embrace limits on or management of growth. However, the presence of a strong mayor is the best predictor of growth-management goals. This suggests that such goals require strong executive leadership to be accepted and implemented within the community.

Decision-Making Styles

Entrepreneurial behavior is related to competition, leaving decisions to bureaucrats, and high residential need. It appears that stress in the environment, in the form of residential need and competition, may stimulate more entrepreneurial behavior by economic development professionals. Indeed, it is the extent to which bureaucrats have influence in decision making that is most strongly related to entrepreneurial perspectives. It was noted earlier that entrepreneurialism has no apparent effect on economic development goals, borne out in the path analysis.

Planning and evaluation behaviors appear related to placing the locus of economic development in a department and devoting more resources—budget and staff—to economic development. The independent department likely represents a greater commitment to economic development, which is enhanced by additional resource allocations. Of these two variables, resources are most strongly related to planning and evaluation. Thus, is seems clear that one way for communities to enhance systematic decision-making processes is to provide greater resources toward the overall development function.

Perceptions by local officials that the decision-making *environment is uncertain and turbulent* is not well explained by the variables at hand; only greater need remains significantly related to turbulence in multiple regression. Higher levels of residential need appear to contribute to perceptions by local officials that they have little control over their activities and that other actors do not really understand their roles in the community. This then leads to an emphasis on short-term actions rather than more long-term program goals.

Bureaucratic decision making is related to the placement of economic development in an independent department and greater residential need; structure is more strongly related. This simply confirms the fact that the various structural and locus variables are self-reinforcing. An initial decision to create an independent economic development department has implications for how decisions are made—in this case, bureaucratically.

Resource allocation to economic development is related to country, a free-standing economic development department, and citizen input. Cities in Canada with independent departments and greater citizen input have higher budgets and more staff devoted to economic development. Keeping the locus for economic development decisions within local government, however, tends to be related to lower resources. First, it is interesting to note that, with the exception of country, resources are not related directly to environmental factors, such as residential need or competition. Environmental stress thus seems to be related to resources only through structure and locus. Regardless of the particular environment of cities, then, it is citizen input and the decision to create an independent economic development department that appear critical in the decision to allocate greater resources toward economic development. Given that resources are related to the extent of planning and evaluation later in the model, these input and structure decisions are particularly important. That country is significantly related to resources suggests that Canadian cities give greater importance to economic development or at least are willing to devote greater resources to it. Although it is true that Canadian cities in the sample, as a whole, are larger and that larger population is positively related to economic development resources, resources and population size are not related in multiple regression. This suggests that country has an effect independent from simple population size.

Locus of Power and Economic Development Structure

Cities with more avenues for *citizen input* have higher levels of residential need.[1] Furthermore, the correlation between citizen and business input remains in the multiple regression analysis. Indeed, business input is the best predictor of citizen input. As noted earlier, business and citizen input do not appear to be mutually exclusive, as many of the regime studies would suggest. It is true that prototype caretaker regimes would include both neighborhood groups and small local businesses. However, the putatively more prevalent developmental regime would focus on business to the exclusion of citizen interests. The fact that all types of input mechanisms are related suggests that, whereas power may not necessarily be evenly distributed, the opportunities for public and private input are mutually reinforcing.

Greater *business input* is related to economic development structures involving external bodies. Clearly, retaining the primary locus of decision making in local government opens the development process to a wider range of interests than off-cycle arrangements. It is interesting to note that environmental forces are not directly related to the nature of input mechanisms in a community. Neither residential need nor competition serve to open or close the development decision-making process to either citizens or businesses directly; structure affects locus.

U.S. cities, and those with a strong mayor, are more likely to vest power over economic development in the *office of the chief executive.* Given a strong-mayor system, the tendency is for the mayor to maintain control of economic development. Location of the city in the United States is the strongest predictor of executive locus, partly because fewer U.S. cities have free-standing development departments.

Placing the locus for development decision making within a *free-standing economic development department* is related to being in Canada, having at-large elections, and higher levels of competition. This leads to speculation that competition may heighten the importance placed on economic development, leading to a decision to create an independent department. Furthermore, because independent departments are related to greater resources, more bureaucratically driven decisions, and more planning and evaluation, it appears likely that all of these are related to the more reformed governmental structures represented by at-large elections. Yet country of location is the most important predictor of both structural alternatives. This suggests that the organization of the economic development function is more the result of national environment, culture, or history.

The Environment of Economic Development

Higher levels of perceived competition are evident in strong-mayor systems, in Canadian cities, and in cities with higher residential need. Of these, country is the best predictor of competition. Strong-mayor cities are more likely in Canada, where residential need is higher. At-large structures are not related to the other environmental variables.

Summary of
Environmental and Civic Culture Paths

Path analysis is usually interpreted by working back through the model, with the discussion organized by dependent variable. Examining the effects of the independent variables in turn—in other words working forwards through the model—provides a useful summary. The following summary addresses the most important explanatory variables.

Country is quite important both in its direct and indirect effects. Canadian cities are more likely to have a mayor, their officials perceive more competition with other cities, and they have greater residential need. Canadian cities devote more resources to economic development and are more likely to vest decision making in the economic development director in an independent department. Although they are more likely to have strong-mayor structures, Canadian cities are less likely to give decision power to the chief executive. Canadian cities are more likely to emphasize alternative economic development goals, such as small business development or new business start-ups.

Having a *strong mayor* is also important. Cities with strong mayors are more likely to locate economic development responsibility in the office of the chief executive. Mayor cities reflect greater perceived competition (although this is likely the result of being Canadian). Mayor cities are also more likely to emphasize Type II and growth goals. Thus, it appears that Type II and growth goals are more politically motivated and perhaps require stronger executive leadership.

Residential need is a critical environmental variable. Officials in cities with higher levels of residential need perceive more competition. Cities with greater need are less likely to keep economic development functions in-house (perhaps, because they can't afford it). Later in the model, greater need leads to more avenues for citizen input, more decisions left to bureaucrats (in this case, in the external organizations), greater turbulence in the environment, more entrepreneurial approaches, and less emphasis on growth limitation. High-need cities are more likely to emphasize alternative goals, such as local small business development. Overall, a poor economic environment is related to greater stress as officials feel more competition and turbulence. Such cities apparently seek to deal with stress and the lack of resources by doing economic development off-cycle, leaving the locus to private organizations. This all relates to less growth-management goals and more alternative goals.

Competition for economic development is another critical environmental force. As with need, city officials feeling more competition are less likely to locate economic development internally. Perceived competition is related to external structures for carrying out economic development responsibilities. For those cities that keep economic development in-house, competition is related to an independent economic development department. Thus, cities where perceptions of competition are high appear to either shift locus outside the city or put the power into the hands of economic development professionals internally. Competition is also related to a more entrepreneurial approach to economic development and a greater stress on both traditional and alternative goals.

Placing economic development *in-house* is related to fewer avenues for business input and fewer resources devoted to economic development. Giving the *executive* the most power over economic development internally reduces avenues for business input. This may also partially explain the connection between strong mayors and both Type II and growth-management goals.

Giving power to economic development *professionals* within the city is related to more evaluation and more resources for economic development.

The pressure of multiple *citizen input* avenues is associated with more resources for economic development and greater emphasis on Type II goals. Although *business* and citizen input are related, they lead to different outcomes later in the model. Citizens press for redistribution and equity goals, whereas businesses press for local business development goals.

Having more resources for economic development is related to more planning and evaluation.

MODELING ECONOMIC
DEVELOPMENT POLICY OUTCOMES

Although important in understanding various aspects of the environment and civic culture of economic development, the foregoing analysis begs the question, "What difference does it make?" Is civic culture related to economic development policy outcomes? Do different types of cultures lead to different development policies? These questions are addressed in this section. In Chapter 3, ten economic development policy indexes were described. Although creating explanatory models for each of the ten policy types is a useful enterprise, the real purpose here is to determine the extent to which different civic cultures lead to substantially different development policies. To that end and to simplify analysis, explanatory models are presented for six policy indexes: loan; zoning; marketing, financial, demand-side, and focused Type II policies.[2] Path analysis is used to explore the relationships between the environment, civic culture, and economic development policies. The front end of all the policy models is the same as that portrayed in Figure 5.3 because the relationships between the environment and culture can be assumed to be stable across policy types. The discussion is organized by each of the six policy outcomes, and data are presented in Table 5.4.[3]

Profile of a High-Loan City

The loan index includes the following development techniques and was created based on factor analysis as described in Chapter 3: direct loans, small business loans, loan guarantees, start-up loans, and community development loans. Based on the data presented in Table 5.4, it appears that greater loan activity is stimulated by location in the United States, having ward-based or combination electoral systems, high residential need, high business input, an entrepreneurial approach toward economic development, and an emphasis on alternative economic development goals. Together, these variables explain 41% of the variation in loan activity; country and entrepreneurialism are the best predictors, respectively.

A high-loan city would be one with economic stress, as indicated by residential need, and relatively high levels of input into the political process emanating from the wards and the numerous avenues for business input. The approach to development is entrepreneurial, and the emphasis is on smaller, local business development. Given that most of the loans in the index are for small business development or business start-up, this model is perfectly logical. Local officials are pressed to take action, and the business input and an entrepreneurial perspective lead to an emphasis on economic development strategies that serve smaller local firms. Looking back through the paths, it appears that the inclusive input informs a professional decision-making process be-

TABLE 5.4 Path Analysis: Policy Outcomes

Policy Outcome	b	BETA	Significance
Loans (R^2 = .41)			
Country	1.17	.50	.00
Ward elections	.22	.17	.00
Residential need	.24	.23	.00
Business input	.11	.11	.02
Entrepreneurialism	.24	.24	.00
Alternative goals	.18	.18	.00
Constant	−2.1E-02		.86
Zoning (R^2 = .26)			
Residential Need	.16	.16	.01
Competition	.15	.15	.01
Bureaucrats	.15	.15	.01
Planning/evaluation	.18	.17	.00
Growth goals	.35	.34	.00
Constant	−5.8E-03		.92
Marketing (R^2 = .49)			
Country	.40	.18	.00
Competition	.42	.43	.00
ED independence	.20	.20	.00
Business input	.15	.14	.00
Traditional goals	.20	.20	.00
Constant	−.13		.01
Demand-side (R^2 = .31)			
Competition	.19	.19	.00
Resources	.35	.23	.00
Entrepreneurialism	.20	.19	.00
Type II goals	.29	.29	.00
Constant	7.39E-02		.22
Financial (R^2 = .29)			
Country	.91	.39	.00
Residential need	.19	.18	.00
Competition	.18	.05	.00
Bureaucrats	.10	.10	.05
Entrepreneurialism	.22	.22	.00
Planning/evaluation	.13	.13	.01
Constant	.28		.00
Focused Type II (R^2 = .05)			
At-large elections	2.9E-02	.13	.04
Type II goals	3.44E-02	.19	.00
Constant	.14		.00

cause alternative goals are also driven by planning and evaluation as well as bureaucratic decision-making processes.

Profile of a High-Zoning City

The zoning policy index includes the following: protected districts for manufacturing, growth-management zoning, and zoning variance provisions. Cities more likely to use zoning policies to either regulate or enhance economic development are those that have higher residential need, leave decisions to bureaucratic processes, use planning and evaluation, perceive high levels of competition, and express growth-management goals. Together, these variables explain 26% of the variation in use of zoning policies. Planning and evaluation and growth management are the strongest predictors of zoning policies. A high-zoning city is marked by fiscal stress and uncertainty due to the high levels of perceived competition. However, these cities reflect less political influence, particularly from the business community, and leave decisions to bureaucrats who are using extensive planning and evaluation. Looking back through the paths, there are few mechanisms for citizen input. Such cities emphasize growth management or controlled growth goals. Hence, it is logical that they approach economic development through changes in zoning processes, most of which limit rather than ease development. In this sense, the professionalism of those making economic development decisions appears to outweigh the high levels of citizen need that might otherwise push officials to avoid any limits or restrictions on potential development.

Profile of a High-Marketing City

The marketing index includes liaison committees, brochures, foreign-business attraction, visits to firms, trade shows, development of export markets, site promotion, and holding special events. Cities engaging more heavily in marketing are located in Canada, perceive greater competition, delegate economic development functions to an independent department, provide many opportunities for business input, and emphasize traditional goals (attract/expand industry, diversify economic base, and promote industrial growth). Together, these variables account for 49% of the variation in the use of marketing poli-

cies; competition, the presence of a freestanding economic development department, and traditional goals are the best predictors. The profile of a high-marketing city is one in Canada (likely because they are
more limited in the other types of economic development policies they
can pursue) and perceiving competition with other cities. This reflects
an environment involving competition but limited residential need.
Although there appears to be a number of avenues for business input,
the real locus of power is in an independent economic development
department and director. Traditional goals of industrial attraction and
retention are emphasized. In the face of competition, with limited economic development options, economic development officials appear
to respond to business pressure by marketing the city in fairly traditional ways, activity that does not require any special evaluation or
entrepreneurialism.

Profile of a High-Demand-Side-Policy City

The demand-side policy index includes the following individual policies: training/retraining activities, public/private research and development, business incubators, and sale lease-back arrangements. Cities
evidencing demand-side policies are those where higher levels of competition are perceived, with more resources devoted to economic development, with entrepreneurial approaches to economic development,
and where Type II goals are emphasized. These variables account for
31% of the variation in demand-side policies. Type II goals and resource
levels are the best predictors. The profile of a high-demand-side city
would be one where officials perceive competition, absent any pressures of residential need. Thus, officials are able to devote relatively
high resources to economic development. They emphasize social equity, minority development, and minority business growth goals—in
other words, "growing their own," which is the bedrock of demand-
side strategies. They are also very entrepreneurial in their approach to
economic development. Resources are also a critical factor, and cities
that look to the economic development director and department for decisions are more likely to devote resources to economic development.
Following the paths backwards, citizen input also enhances Type II
goals, so it is logical that the input in these cities is more likely to be
neighborhood based rather than from business.

Profile of a High-Financial-Incentive City

The financial-incentive index includes the use of tax abatements, tax deferments, employment tax credits, enterprise zones, and in-kind service provision. Cities are more likely to use financial incentives if they are located in the United States, have high levels of residential need, perceive competition with other cities, leave decisions to professional bureaucrats using high levels of planning and evaluation, and approach economic development in an entrepreneurial manner. These variables account for 29% of the variation in the use of financial incentives, and country and entrepreneurialism are the best predictors. Cities using financial incentives manifest high economic stress and perceived competition. They tend to be in the United States because state enabling legislation is more likely to allow the use of financial incentives by local government. The locus of power emphasizes bureaucratic decision making that tends to be based on planning and evaluation. Although some of the financial incentives are pretty standard (tax abatements and deferments), the use of enterprise zones or employment tax credits may indicate greater creativity than would at first be expected. Indeed, it may require the more entrepreneurial approach evident in these cities.

Looking back through the paths, these cities also tend to delegate development decisions to an economic development department, further strengthening bureaucratic processes. None of the goals are related to financial incentives, suggesting they constitute a type of development strategy pursued regardless of particular economic development goals. It is interesting to note that financial incentives and zoning are the only policies driven by both residential need and perceived competition. Residential need alone appears to lead to loans, if the city is more politicized. Competition alone leads to marketing and demand-side policies, if greater resources are devoted. But the combination of residential need and perceived competition appears to foster traditional financial techniques without specific growth-management goals that lead to zoning policies.

Profile of a Focused-Type-II City

The nature of cities focusing on policies that either redistribute the benefits of economic development or attempt to ensure that businesses "pay back" for benefits received was one initial theme of this analysis. Again, this variable represents a focus on Type II policies to the exclusion of other types of incentives to distinguish those cities focusing on such policies from those doing everything. A focus on Type II policies is related to having at-large elections and expressing goals that emphasize social equity and redistribution. These two variables are the only ones significantly correlated to focused Type II policies in multiple regression, and they account for only 5% of the variation. Of the two, Type II goals is a slightly better predictor. The profile, then, of a city focusing on Type II policies would be one that has a reformed governmental structure that emphasizes Type II goals. Looking back through the paths, because Type II goals are driven by citizen input and planning/evaluation, it could be posited that citizens are pressing for equity strategies, and professionals are selecting Type II policies based on planning and evaluation processes. The bottom line is that there remains much about Type II policy use that is not measured by the survey. Race may be one of these issues because that is not included for the Canadian cities. This link and other possible causes of Type II policies are explored more fully in the case studies.

SUMMARY

Several conclusions can be drawn from the path analysis leading to economic development policy outcomes. Across the six models, it can be observed that a combination of environmental and civic culture factors affect each policy type. Although country, residential need, perceived competition, and governmental structure are present in many cases, cultural forces, such as goals, decision-making style, locus of control, and political input, are present in every case. Thus, economic development policy is the result of a complex blending of environmental and cultural forces. In short, although "politics matters," so does the environment, particularly economic and national forces. Furthermore, among the components of civic culture in the equations, forces beyond regime are important. In other words, although such regime or locus variables as business input and bureaucratic versus executive locus are present in the equations, decision-making style and process, overall approach to development, and development goals are also critical components in attempting to explain development policy. Regime is a necessary but insufficient element in understanding local economic development policy making.

The explanatory power of the models varies widely by policy type. The explanatory power for loans and marketing is high, although for focused Type II and zoning policies, the regressions are more frail. Indeed, the interpretation of R^2 values can be fraught with complexities; "an R^2 adjusted of .35 may be high or low, depending on the ease with which Y yields itself up to explanation, the exactitude with which Y and the X's have been measured, and the X's conceptual propinquity to Y" (Luskin, 1991: 1043). Hence, because of the inexactitude in which economic development policies and their determinants have been measured in the past, as well as uncertainty about the relationships between environment, structure, locus, and culture, it is not surprising that the explanatory power of the regression analysis is wanting.

The analysis thus far provides a strong sense that "culture matters" and indicates to an extent how it matters. But clearly, much is left to be explored in the case studies, where forces can be examined in more depth and in a more contextually sensitive manner. In this sense, the case studies that follow allow for a search for the forces that might account for the variance left unexplained across the policy regression models. More important, the case study analysis affords a more contextual exploration of the local civic culture than is possible with cross-sectional survey data. Thus, the *quality* of the analysis shifts away from static correlations of placement of the economic development function and business input mechanisms, for example. Instead, a more nuanced examination of the history of economic development structures in a community as they change from internal to external control can be portrayed. Simple input mechanisms become a sense of the actual power of individual business leaders. A strong-mayor system becomes an individual with a particular approach to economic development. In this way, a local face is added to the cross-sectional data, and a better sense of what's really going on in the regression analyses can be gained.

NOTES

1. Although a significance level of .05 was used as the cut point in the other regression equations to determine if a particular variable should be included, residential need

is left in the citizen input model. Theoretically, greater need should increase citizen input. Furthermore, inclusion of this variable increases overall explanatory power.

2. Full path analysis results for all policy types are available from the authors.

3. The residuals from the regressions were saved and various diagnostics conducted. It appears that the assumptions of normal distribution and linearity are sound. Path residuals were significantly correlated in several cases although all correlations were below .22 except in the case of citizen and business input where the path residuals are correlated (positively) at .31 and for executive control and economic development independence correlated (negatively) at .41. Although this may tend to bias standard error estimates, Bohrnstedt and Carter (1971) suggest that unless the correlation is extreme, the bias is not prohibitively serious. Correlations under .50 would appear not to represent a significant problem.

APPENDIX TO CHAPTER 5:
THE ENVIRONMENT OF LOCAL ECONOMIC DEVELOPMENT

As noted in the chapter, there are a number of important and interesting relationships among the environmental variables. However, many of these have been well explored in the literature, and an extended discussion detracts from the focus on local civic culture. To keep the central discussion manageable, the relationships among the environmental variables are presented here.

Spatial Location

Basic correlation analysis on the components of the environment considered here revealed many interrelationships, some of which revolve around country of location (see Table 5.A). In short, country is a critical spatial variable and is significantly related to the other spatial measures. For example, Canadian cities are more likely to be core cities and to be located in the West and East regions. U.S. cities are more likely to be located in the West Central and Central regions. The only region not significantly related to country is the Great Lakes region. Regarding governmental structure, Canadian cities are significantly more likely to have mayors, less likely to have partisan elections, and are more likely to be part of a two-tier governing arrangement. Country is also related to several of the fiscal and demographic characteristics. For example, Canadian cities have significantly greater residential need, have had greater population growth over the past ten years, and have higher assessed property values. Officials in U.S. cities perceive greater levels of economic growth, however, and indicate that their cities are more likely to use taxes above and beyond the property tax. Last, officials in Canadian cities are more likely to feel that they are in competition with cities outside their region.

In addition to these relationships with national location, other spatial variables are interrelated. Regional governance arrangements, such as two-tier systems, are more common in the Great Lakes region (likely because of the inclusion of the Province of Ontario) and occur less frequently in the central region, and core cities are more likely to form part of such an arrangement than satellite cities or those more isolated from urban areas. Place in the urban hierarchy is affected by region; cities in the Great Lakes region are more likely to be core cities in their urban areas. Core cities have significantly less residential need and more economic growth. Respondents from core cities are also more likely to perceive regional competition. All of these relationships are intuitively logical, although there is cause for concern.

Country is related to all of the other spatial variables, a situation that was expected to create problems in the path analysis used to model civic culture and policy traits. Such relationships early in a model can cause problems because when independent variables in a regression are correlated with each other, explanatory power is overstated, and relationships among other independent variables become blurred. Indeed, many of the relationships noted earlier are likely the result of the country variable. Thus, country was used as a proxy measure for all of the other spatial variables in further analysis. For example, location in Canada is a proxy for being part of a two-tier structure and for being a core city as well as being located in the west and eastern regions of each country. This also makes sense theoretically; country should be the primary exogenous or driving variable. It is the most fixed of all the variables in the model and defines a set of other spatial, historical, and legal relationships that affect local government structure, fiscal health, taxing capacity, and even the parameters of interlocal competition.

In summary, the following are essential findings regarding environmental forces:

> Country acts as a proxy for region, place in the urban hierarchy, and regional governance arrangements.

TABLE 5.A Correlation Matrix: Environmental Variables

	Country	West	West Central	Central	Great Lakes	East	Core/Satellite	Tier	Executive	Election	Partisan	Need	Population Change	Growth	State Equalized Value	Nonresidential Base	Extra Taxes	Regional Competition	Extraregional Competition
Country	1.00	.16*	-.17*	-.22*	-.06	.32*	-.14*	.31*	-.11*	-.01	.13*	.25*	.19*	-.12*	.18*	-.03	-.14*	-.01	.20*
West	.16*	1.00	-.13*	-.22*	-.26*	-.17*	-.11*	-.04	-.05	-.23*	.16*	.15*	.17*	-.07	.23*	.02	.30*	-.08	.04
West Central	-.17*	-.13*	1.00	-.19*	-.23*	-.14*	.06	-.08	.16*	.03	.17*	-.17*	.04	.14*	-.02	.04	-.13*	.02	-.15*
Central	-.22*	-.22*	-.19*	1.00	-.37*	-.23*	.10	-.11*	-.09	.22*	-.07	-.22*	-.04	.23*	-.09	.14*	.15*	.03	.07
Great Lakes	-.06	-.26*	-.23*	-.37*	1.00	-.28*	.11*	.19*	-.02	-.06	-.07	.00	-.10	-.06	-.05	-.13*	-.31*	.05	.05
East	.32*	-.17*	-.14*	-.23*	-.28*	1.00	-.06	.04	.03	.04	-.08	.17*	.02	-.14*	-.01	-.15*	.04	.01	-.04
Core/satellite	-.14*	-.11*	.06	.10	.11*	-.06	1.00	.12*	.03	.07	-.04	.32*	.07	.16*	-.07	-.15*	.01	.16*	-.11*
Tier	.31*	-.04	-.08	-.11*	.19*	.04	.12*	1.00	.00	.06	.05	-.04	.09	-.06	.01	-.03	-.09	-.06	.05
Executive	-.11*	-.05	.16*	-.09	-.02	.03	.03	.00	1.00	-.18*	.20*	-.07	.03	-.05	.01	-.08	-.03	-.03	-.14*
Election	-.01	-.23*	.03	.22*	-.06	.04	.07	.06	-.18*	1.00	-.08	-.11*	.08	.03	-.04	.10	.10	.06	.08
Partisan	.13*	.16*	.17*	-.07	-.07	-.08	-.04	.05	.20*	-.08	1.00	-.12*	-.02	.05	-.08	-.01	-.07	-.11*	-.07
Need	.25*	.15*	-.17*	-.22*	.00	.17*	.32*	-.04	-.07	-.11*	-.12*	1.00	-.22*	-.17*	.05	.24*	.12*	.01	.17*
Population change	.19*	.17*	.04	-.04	-.10	.02	.07	.09	.03	.08	-.02	-.22*	1.00	.09	.41*	.01	-.04	.08	.06
Growth	-.12*	-.07	.14*	.23*	-.06	-.14*	.16*	-.06	-.05	.03	.05	-.17*	.09	1.00	-.04	.22*	.03	.28*	.15*
State equalized value	.18*	.23*	-.02	-.09	-.05	-.01	-.07	.01	.01	-.04	-.08	.05	.41*	-.04	1.00	-.08	.03	.02	.05
Nonresidential base	-.03	.02	.04	.14*	-.13*	-.15*	-.15*	-.03	-.08	.10	-.01	.24*	.01	.22*	-.08	1.00	.15*	-.01	.23*
Extra taxes	-.14*	.30*	-.13*	.15*	-.31*	.04	.01	-.09	-.02	.10	-.07	.12*	-.04	.03	.03	.15*	1.00	.04	-.02
Regional competition	-.01	-.08	.02	.03	.05	.01	.16*	-.06	-.03	.06	-.11*	.01	.08	.28*	.02	-.01	.04	1.00	.22*

*Significantly correlated at the .05 level.

Canadian cities, having larger populations, are more likely to be the core cities in their regions and are more likely to be involved in two-tier governing structures.

Canadian cities have experienced greater residential need and slower growth, but this does not appear to be reflected in lower property values.

Canadian officials are more likely to perceive competition from cities outside their regions.

U.S. cities are more likely to have city managers and partisan elections.

Government Structure

As already noted, the various indicators of what is known as reformed government structure are not necessarily related. In other words, although it might be expected that cities with city managers would also be more likely to have at-large and nonpartisan elections, this is not always the case. This results from several factors: (a) Canadian cities did not experience the urban reform movement in the same way as U.S. cities and thus have no history of transition from unreformed to reformed structures; (b) previous research on U.S. cities has indicated that the various elements of reform are often mixed (Reese, 1997a); and (c) a large majority of cities have nonpartisan elections, so this particular element of reformism is so widespread that it has no necessary relationship to the other aspects of reform. Indeed, in Ontario for example, provincial regulations require nonpartisan elections, but other elements of government structure vary according to local discretion.

Correlation analysis indicates that cities with at-large elections are significantly more likely to have city managers; these two aspects of reform are related. Furthermore, cities with city manager or commission forms of government are more likely to have nonpartisan elections. Form of government also appears related to how officials perceive interlocal competition. Those in cities with strong mayors are more likely to feel the effects of extraregional competition. In short,

Cities with manager forms of government are more likely to have nonpartisan and at-large elections.

The presence of a strong-mayor system, however, is not inherently related to other aspects of reformed governments.

Officials in strong-mayor systems perceive more competition in the
environment.

Demographic Characteristics

Higher levels of resident need are correlated with several other demographic and fiscal variables in a predictable pattern. Cities with high
need have experienced greater loss of population over a ten-year period
and have lower levels of overall economic growth. Officials in high-
need cities are also likely to perceive greater pressure due to extraregional competition. Thus, it appears that need and lack of growth
create the kind of environmental stress that heightens perceptions of
competition. Cities with greater population growth also have higher
assessed land values.

Fiscal Characteristics

Past and current economic-base growth is related both to competition and the nature of the local tax base. Cities with a growing economic
base are likely to be those with a larger proportion of nonresidential
land uses. And cities with more nonresidential land uses are more likely
to employ taxation policies that shift the burden from property taxes to
other revenue sources, such as sales and tourist taxes. Thus, it appears
that a complex dynamic is at work; nonresidential tax base is related
both to greater opportunities for taxation and greater economic growth.
Such growth is then related to less residential need.

Increased levels of growth are significantly and positively correlated
with both regional and extraregional competition. Officials in cities
with growing economies are more likely to feel in competition with
other communities. Although this is somewhat counterintuitive—one
might expect that growth would lead to a lesser need to compete—it is
also possible that both residential need and economic growth create tensions or instability in the environment that enhance perceptions of
intercity competition. Because of the interrelationships between many
of the demographic and fiscal variables and to simplify the models, residential need was used in the foregoing analysis as a proxy for population change and economic-base growth. Furthermore, because the tax
variables—assessed value and tax structure—did not correlate with

other variables further in the model, they were removed from the analysis.

To summarize the findings related to demographic and fiscal characteristics, then,

- Higher levels of residential need serves as a proxy for slower economic growth and population loss and greater relative residential tax base and is thus used to represent greater economic stress in communities.
- Residential need appears to increase perceived extraregional competition for development.

Intercity Competition

The correlates of both regional and extraregional competition have already been identified. To summarize, only economic growth appears to be related to regional competition positively. A number of other environmental factors appear related to extraregional competition. Specifically, it appears that perceptions of competition are increased by location in Canada, greater residential need, more rapid economic growth, and a larger nonresidential tax base. Regional and extra-regional competition are positively correlated. This last finding raised the question of whether both should remain in the analyses. Because perceptions of regional competition are more common, it can be argued that such competition is a normal part of the economic development reality in most cities. Therefore, it is not going to separate or identify those cities that feel competition most acutely. For this reason, and because it was related to more variables later in the model, extraregional competition is the sole measure of competition in the analysis.

6

CATEGORIES OF
LOCAL CIVIC CULTURE

The path analysis in the previous chapter was instructive in several respects. It identified the relationships within and between the environment, civic culture, and economic development policy. It also clearly indicated that although several environmental forces contribute directly to economic development policy, civic culture matters in the policy choices made by communities. And civic culture matters, independent of the influences of the environment. The analysis strongly suggested that there is more to local economic decision making than just regime structure—decision-making styles and community goals are also critical. However, the path analysis also indicated that there is more going on in communities with regard to policy choice than is included in the models. Thus, although several of the policy regression equations accounted for quite impressive amounts of variation in policy choice (loans and marketing, for example), low R^2 values for other equations (zoning and focused Type II) suggest that many important forces are being missed.

This highlights the power of analytical approaches that combine methodologies. Cross-sectional survey data are inherently limited in a number of respects. By definition, they ignore history and context; the number of questions are limited and cannot be formed to address variations in local conditions. Statistical analyses cannot easily address casual questions, and the theory driving it all is often incomplete or does not fully capture either local idiosyncrasies or help identify when those idiosyncrasies may actually be masking underlying patterns. Case study analysis can be employed to address many of these shortcomings, particularly when directed and informed by the larger data analysis. Through more in-depth case study of cities drawn from the larger set, the role of history in present conditions can be examined. Local idiosyncrasies can be addressed, and patterned idiosyncrasies hopefully can be identified. Differences between local structures and process on paper and in actual application can be explored and faces put on the actors behind the questionnaires. This chapter serves as a bridge between the survey and case study analyses. It begins by using cluster analysis to identify groups of cities, based on important variables identified in the earlier analysis. These larger groupings then form the basis for the organization of the nine case studies to follow. The case cities are introduced at the end of this chapter using the frame provided by the cluster analysis.

CLUSTER ANALYSIS

Methodological Issues

The rationale behind cluster analysis was described in Chapter 3. To reiterate, cluster analysis is used to identify whether cities can be grouped or clustered based on particular variables of interest. Hierarchical cluster analysis is a mathematical procedure that begins with the same number of clusters or groupings of cases (cities, in this case) as there are observations. It then groups similar cases until the final cluster contains all the cases. Groups are constructed by minimizing the variance of squared Euclidean distances for each variable between cities. The two most similar cases are joined first, and the algorithm continues one step at a time until all the cities are joined.

Although cluster analysis was performed on cities focusing on Type II policies to initially draw the case study sample (as described in Chapter 3), it was again used to examine the data set as a whole to see if generalized types of cities could be identified based on civic culture. To make this analysis meaningful, appropriate variables must be selected to serve as the basis for the clusters. In other words, "similar on what basis" must be defined before cases can be combined. For this analysis, the regression results drove the selection of clustering criteria. The starting point was to identify those independent—environmental and civic culture—variables most often related to development policies in the regression analyses. Looking across the policy regressions, it is clear that several environmental and cultural forces occur in the regressions most frequently: country, residential need, governmental structure, community input, entrepreneurialism, goals, competition, planning and evaluation, and the extent to which bureaucrats are involved in the decision-making process. Using these variables as cluster criteria, several different cluster analyses were run. Most were unsatisfactory in several respects.

One shortcoming of cluster analysis is that if an individual city is missing data on any variable selected for analysis, it will be excluded from the final cluster solution. Using a large number of variables for clustering purposes often results in a very small number of cases being included in the analysis. Ultimately, the optimal selection of variables will include those variables that are theoretically important but also include as complete a response set as possible. Second, the most desirable set of clustering variables will be those that make significant distinctions between cases. In other words, having a preponderance of cases within one cluster and none in another is not very informative. It simply says that the cases are indistinguishable on those particular variables. Depending on the composition of clustering variables, analyses often resulted in either very small numbers of cases or having the bulk of the cases situated in just one or two clusters.

Ultimately, it was determined that a subset of independent variables from the regression equations resulted in the "best" cluster analysis, one that included a reasonably large number of cities and distributed the cities among theoretically interesting groups. This subset included the extent of community and business input into the decision-making process, regional and extraregional competition, planning and evaluation, residential need, change in unemployment over a ten-year period,[1] and governmental structure (partisan versus nonpartisan elections, at-large versus ward elections, type of chief executive).

The cluster analysis was done in two stages. First, only the subset of variables just identified were used as the basis of clusters. Then, the economic development policies were included as well. Initial analysis indicated that although the first set of variables served to distinguish a number of different types of cities, once economic development policies were added, the large majority of cities grouped in one cluster. In other words, although there are many differences among cities in environment and culture, most are very similar when it comes to development policy. Both analyses are presented here.

Cluster Analysis

Environment and Civic Culture

Table 6.1 contains the partial agglomeration schedule for the cluster analysis using the environmental and civic culture variables. The first column lists the stage of the cluster solution and the second provides the number of clusters in that solution. The third column indicates the agglomeration coefficient, and the final column lists the difference in the value of the agglomeration coefficient from the prior stage. Typically, the agglomeration schedule showing change in the agglomeration coefficient is used as a guide for identifying the optimal solution (Everitt, 1993). Thus, a relatively large jump in the coefficients suggests that two heterogeneous clusters are being combined and that the appropriate solution is the one just prior. There are fairly large jumps in the agglomeration coefficient at the second, sixth, eight, eleventh, thirteenth, fourteenth, and sixteenth stages. The eleven-cluster solution was selected because it provided the largest number of clusters with at least several cities in each cluster; solutions beyond the eleventh included many clusters with only one city. In other words, the eleven-cluster solution seems to do the best job of actually making meaningful distinctions among groups.

The eleven-cluster solution results in seven clusters containing more than a single city; these will serve as the focus of discussion. Examining the characteristics of the seven groups (see descriptive data in Table 6.2)

TABLE 6.1 Partial Agglomeration Schedule: Environment and Civic Culture

Stage	Clusters in the Solution	Agglomeration Coefficient	Change in Coefficient
271	20	15.645	.06
272	19	15.748	.10
273	18	15.889	.14
274	17	16.242	.35
275	16	17.242	1.00
276	15	1.702	.46
277	14	1.420	.72
278	13	1.119	.70
279	12	19.421	.30
280	11	20.124	.70
281	10	20.395	.27
282	9	20.967	.57
283	8	21.680	.71
284	7	21.965	.29
285	6	24.029	2.06
286	5	24.666	.64
287	4	25.246	.58
288	3	26.198	.95
289	2	28.454	2.26
290	1	30.149	1.70

reveals four general types of communities: mayor-dominated systems, elite-dominated systems, externally dominated systems, and politically inclusive systems. Thus, the most robust clustering criteria included both environmental (residential need, change in unemployment, competition) and civic culture (business and community input, decision-making style) as well as government structure that mediates between those variables. However, the implicit assumption of the four-type characterization scheme is that governmental structure, input, and locus of power attributes form the dominant distinctions among cities. Such an interpretation is consistent with the casual ordering presented in the models in the proceeding chapter, where structure and locus lead to community visions and, ultimately, development policies. Although

TABLE 6.2 Characteristics of Clusters

	Inclusive Low Need (N = 37)	Elite Closed System (N = 207)	Inclusive High Need (N = 5)	Inclusive Reform (N = 20)	Economic Development Elite Business Input (N = 4)	Externally Driven (N = 10)	Mayor Driven (N = 4)
Percentage United States	65	7	60	75	75	70	75
Percentage West	16	13	0	35	0	20	25
Percentage West central	11	11	0	15	25	0	0
Percentage Central	35	25	0	0	25	10	25
Percentage Great Lakes	19	31	60	25	25	50	50
Percentage East	14	13	40	15	0	10	0
Percentage nonpartisan	92	71	00	95	100	100	100
Percentage at-large	3	47	40	90	75	80	75
Percentage strong mayor	65	42	40	15	25	50	50
Business input	.62	-.12	.47	.72	.84	-.56	-1.27
Citizen input	.90	-.35	.48	1.79	9.79e	-.22	-.84
Extraregional competition	.87	-.11	-.48	-.47	1.32	-.24	-.40

Regional competition	.27	-8.0e	-8.4e	-.30	1.35	-.48	-.54
Planning	.47	2.53e	.54	-.42	2.22	-.33	-8.1e
Need	1.65e	-.23	2.50	.13	.70	2.46	-2.3e
Unemployment change	-.70	-.90	4.40	-1.28	-1.56	3.48	-9.54
Percent white	91	92	.90	.90	.76	.68	.90
Percentage manager	27	43	20	85	75	30	25
1990 population	11,715	11,005	8,961	11,357	9,695	8,374	10,403
Traditional goals	.43	6.64E-04	-.65	-.45	.36	-.12	-.73
Alternative goals	.40	-9.4E-02	.48	-1.3E-03	1.01	-.22	-.48
Type II goals	.47	-.13	.28	.46	1.03	-.36	-.43
Growth goals	.57	-9.1E-02	-.48	.25	1.55E-04	1.55E-04	-.58
Bureaucracy	.13	-4.7E-02	-.21	-.46	.53	3.21E-03	-.44
Growth	.18	1.07E-02	5.37E-02	-.15	1.02	-.49	-.28
In-house	-.13	2.31E-02	-.38	2.82E-03	.57	-.32	.25
Economic development independence	.34	-4.6E-02	-.66	-.31	.12	.15	-.37
Executive control	-.22	1.54E-02	.72	4.27E-02	-.18	-.25	.56
Resource	.15	-6.6E-02	-.20	-.21	.60	.22	-.34
Entrepreneurialism	.31	-5.7E-02	-.15	-.24	.37	2.05E-02	-.44

the categorization scheme could rest on such environmental attributes as country or economy, such an approach would not capture the pivotal role of the civic culture attributes (as indicated in the path models). Nor do the environmental variables alone appear to distinguish meaningfully among groups of cities (as suggested by initial cluster analysis).

In short, the clustering solution reflects the pivotal cultural traits of each grouping of cities. The *mayor-dominated systems* represent cities where a strong chief executive maintains primary control over economic development decision making. Bureaucratic or professional staff discretion is limited and framed by the mayor, and both business and citizen input avenues are minimal. Cities *dominated by elites* leave economic development decisions to either professional staff or business elites. Input from citizens is typically more limited than business input, particularly in the business-dominated elite cities. Cities that are *externally dominated* have placed primary economic development responsibility in a body outside of the local government. Although some of these cities maintain an in-house economic development department or function, external bodies play an important role. And as is often the case with extragovernmental arrangements, avenues for community input are minimized. Last, *politically inclusive systems* exhibit numerous mechanisms for both public and private input. The locus of power rests not with a single actor nor with professional elites but reflects the community at large. Hence, there is no one group or interest that consistently dominates economic development decision making. Table 6.3 contains the primary civic culture traits of each of the four types of cities.

It should also be noted that the classification and subsequent profiles of each cluster are basically impressionistic. Because of the small number of cities in most of the groups, there has been no attempt to use statistical tests of difference or significance. The main purpose of this analysis is a heuristic effort to identify distinctive groupings of cities, provide a description of such groups—including both environmental and civic culture traits—and then describe how the case studies will further explore the role of civic culture in economic development decision making.

TABLE 6.3 Major Civic Culture Attributes

Civic Culture	Locus	Locus	Structure	Decision Style	Decision Style
	Locus	Input		Plan/ evaluation	Entrepre- neurialism
Mayor dominated	Mayor	Limited citizen input	Within the executive office	Generally low	Dependent on personality of mayor; generally low
Externally dominated	Members of external body	High business input, low citizen input	External body	Moderate	Moderately conservative approach to economic development
Politically inclusive	City council and bureau- crats	High citizen input, high business input	Free- standing or combined internal department	Generally high	Conservative approach to economic development
Elite dominated (bureaucrats or business)	Bureaucrats or bureau- crats and business leaders	Low citizen input, moderate business input	Internal free- standing department	Generally high	Entrepre- neurialism is high, active approach to economic development

Mayor-Dominated Systems

Environmental Characteristics: Overall, the mayor-dominated cities tend to be located in the Great Lakes region of both the United States and Canada. Again, emphasizing the fact that the various attributes of governmental reform do not necessarily go together in practice, partic- ularly in Canada, the mayor-dominated cities tend to have nonpartisan and at-large elections. Cities in the mayor-dominated group have healthy economies, and officials perceive little competition from other cities.

Civic Culture: The primary cultural trait of cities in this group is the presence of strong mayors and few formal mechanisms for broader input by businesses or citizens (see Table 6.3). These cities keep the responsibility for economic development in-house and are most likely to locate economic development responsibilities in the office of the chief executive. The decision-making style in such cities appears to be one that does not emphasize formal planning or evaluation, processes more common with professional staff. Rather, the style of decision making is dependent on the particular personality of the mayor; some may be very systematic in their analyses, others may employ more of a "seat of the pants" style. Because planning and evaluation are important to the creation of development goals in a community, it is not surprising that these cities tend not to identify any type of goals as being important. Similarly, the overall approach to economic development is not particularly entrepreneurial. Such cities appear to stick to traditional approaches to economic development that do not entail financial risk nor innovation on the part of the local government. As will become more clear in the case studies, this tends to be translated into development policies emphasizing traditional financial incentives and infrastructure investment.

Externally Dominated Systems

Environmental Characteristics: As with the mayor-dominated group, these cities tend to have nonpartisan and at-large elections and strong-mayor structures. Economic stress (high residential need, increased unemployment, and slow growth) is much more prevalent among these cities, however. It is also interesting to note that cities in this group are the most racially diverse of all the clusters (U.S. cities only). Race has not been included in the analysis to date due to the lack of data for Canadian cities, but the case study analysis allows for some exploration of the possible effects of race.

Civic Culture: The central trait of cities in this cluster is that they tend to place responsibility for economic development in an external body; they are more likely to have such an arrangement than cities in any other cluster. In this case, it appears that economic stress shifts the locus away from the mayor to an external body with potentially greater resource opportunities. Indeed, greater resources are devoted toward economic development in these cities, presumably supported by the private sector organizations. Although these cities often have strong-mayor structures on paper, economic stress may shift economic development functions to external bodies. Avenues for citizen input are low given this external arrangement. Although the cluster traits in Table 6.2 show that business input is also low in these cities (although not as low as in the mayor-dominated cities), theoretically, it would be reasonable to expect that the extent of business input will vary depending on the structure of the external organizations. Thus, in cities where businesses have institutional membership on those bodies, private-sector input should be much higher. This is borne out in the case studies to follow; the extent of business input depends on the nature of those external organizations. Decision making is not driven by planning and evaluation, and no particular goals are identified. Thus, it appears that external bodies do not necessarily guarantee more systematic decision making than governmental bodies. Indeed, the economic development approach here is not particularly entrepreneurial. It can be argued that the high levels of economic stress limit the possibilities for development policy in these cities and that the result is a reliance on more traditional, and perhaps less resource intensive, policies, such as marketing.

Politically Inclusive Cities

Although there are three subcategories of politically inclusive cities, the common feature is the broad array of input avenues for both residents and businesses. Whereas one subgroup clearly has reformed governmental structures, the other two include a mix of structural types. This suggests that no structural arrangement is inherently more open or closed to community input. The distinguishing feature of the other two subgroups is their differing economic-stress profiles; one cluster has very high levels of residential need, whereas the other shows an improving economic situation.

Inclusive Reformed Cities

Environmental Characteristics: Cities in this cluster tend to be located in the western region of both countries, have nonpartisan and at-large elections and, almost uniformly, city managers. Economically, they tend to have moderate levels of residential need and have had lower levels of economic growth than cities in other clusters. However, unemployment has dropped significantly over a ten-year period, suggesting some economic improvement.

Civic Culture: Even given the city manager form of government, levels of both citizen and business input are high. There is no particular pattern among such cities as to internal or external placement of economic development responsibilities, although they tend not to have independent economic development departments. Resources devoted to economic development tend to be low. Little planning and evaluation is used to make decisions, perhaps due to the lack of independent development departments. Officials in these cities identify both Type II and growth management goals as being important. Thus, it appears that the presence of some need in the context of an improving economy allows for a focus on equity issues but also increasing concern about managing growth. The high level of citizen input also likely increases the concern with Type II goals, as suggested in the path analysis.

Inclusive Healthy Cities

Environmental Characteristics: The primary difference between these cities and those in the previous cluster lies in their strong economies; residential need is low, unemployment decreasing, and the economic base is growing. Structurally, these cities tend to be more unreformed than those in other clusters, particularly in their tendency to have ward-based elections and strong mayors.

Civic Culture: As with the previous group of inclusive cities, avenues for both business and citizen input are numerous here. Relatively high levels of resources are devoted to economic development, and levels of planning and evaluation are also high. Development is approached in an entrepreneurial manner, and all types of development goals are pursued. Despite the putative strong mayor systems among these cities, the locus of control does not appear to remain in the mayor's office; these cities tend to place responsibility for economic development in independent departments. This tendency to leave decisions to professional bureaucrats within independent departments likely increases the levels of planning and evaluation as well as the innovative nature of the overall approach to development.

Inclusive Economically Stressed Cities

Environmental Characteristics: Structurally, these cities tend to be unreformed with partisan elections and ward-based councils. However, they are more likely to have city managers than mayors, a trait that separates them from the former group of inclusive cities. Other significant differences are the high levels of residential need, growing unemployment, and lack of growth in the economic base among these cities. They are clearly the most stressed of the inclusive type. Last, they tend to be located in Canada.

Civic Culture: As with the other two groups of inclusive cities, business and citizen input are high. Two structural tendencies are present in these cities; external locus for economic development or placement of development responsibilities in the office of the chief executive. Perhaps the high levels economic stress shift development functions outside the local government as was the case with the external-dominated cities. Regardless of whether economic development is placed internally or externally, decision making is supported by high levels of planning and evaluation, and alternative and Type II goals are emphasized.

Elite-Dominated Cities

There are two clusters of cities loosely identified as elite-dominated. In both cases, there are few avenues for citizen or neighborhood input into the economic development decision-making process. One of the clusters reflects numerous opportunities for business influence, considered "elite" input; the other is more closed.

Professional Elites with Business Input

Environmental Characteristics: Governmentally, these cities are very reformed, with nonpartisan and at-large elections and city managers.

Economically, the cities in this cluster have low levels of residential need and have experienced the highest levels of economic growth of all the clusters. It is also interesting to note that they also have a relatively large nonwhite population, an issue to be addressed in more detail in the case studies.

Civic Culture: Cities in this cluster tend to have certain identifiable groups dominating economic development decision making, specifically, economic development professionals and business elites. Economic development responsibilities are placed in an independent economic development department. Thus, decisions are left to bureaucrats, who use planning and evaluation and approach economic development in an entrepreneurial manner. All economic development goals are pursued, with particular emphasis on alternative and Type II goals. Cities in this cluster devote the highest levels of resources to economic development. Even given that the locus for decision making appears to rest with development professionals, there are a variety of mechanisms for business input into the process. However, the decision process appears closed to citizens, for the most part. In short, this cluster is characterized by professional elite domination with business input. And subsequent case study analysis indicates that the bureaucratic and business elites influencing the decision process in these cities tend to engage in high levels of planning and evaluation and take an innovative and entrepreneurial stance toward economic development. These patterns are not evident in the cluster discussed next.

Elite Closed Systems—Bureaucratic Domination

Environmental Characteristics: On the whole, the 207 cities in this cluster reflect low residential need, modest decline in unemployment, and stable economies. Because of the large number of cities in the cluster, many different structural and locus patterns are present, with no identifiable pattern for the cluster.[2] The group includes many partisan cities and is almost evenly divided between at-large and ward systems.

Civic Culture: Most cities in the data set provide few avenues for input on economic development, either for businesses or citizens, although these cites are less closed than either the mayor-dominated or externally dominated systems. Other than the limited avenues for input, no other patterns are present. The case studies clearly indicate that many of the cities in this cluster leave decision-making locus to economic development professionals, who tend to make extensive use of systematic planning and evaluation systems, although this is not clear from the cluster analysis.

The fact that so many cities fall into this cluster says much about the limitations of large data set analysis. Although it is theoretically possible that the large majority of cities in the set are basically similar in most cultural respects, this is not likely. Rather, it is more likely that subtle differences are present that are not being isolated in the statistical analysis nor perhaps even tapped by the survey. The case studies in the next chapters clearly identify important historical and cultural differences among cities even in the same cluster. To a large extent, surveys only provide a surface view of cities and their culture and politics.

Clusters of Civic Culture and Economic Development Policies

Subsequent to clustering cities based on environment and civic culture, a second analysis was run, including the ten categories of economic development policies. The purpose of this analysis was to identify clusters of cities using policy outputs as distinguishing variables. In this case, a five-stage solution seemed most appropriate due to the large jump in the agglomeration coefficients at that point (see Table 6.4). The five-cluster solution, however, includes only three clusters with more than one city. One overwhelming conclusion can be drawn from the analysis. Once economic development policies are added to the mix, cities become even more similar, at least on the surface. Although seven different clusters of civic culture can be identified, there are only three clusters, once economic development policies are included; 175 cities are together in one group, with only 15 and 6 in the other two clusters. In short, cities are much more similar to each other in terms of economic development policy than they are different, and cities of different types are likely to employ similar policies. Again, the caveat should be added that differences in the nature and intensity of policy choice and mix of policies pursued are not well measured by the survey.

TABLE 6.4 Partial Agglomeration Schedule: Environment, Civic Culture, and Economic Development Policies

Stage	Clusters in Solution	Agglomeration Coefficient	Change in Coefficient
185	20	34.239	.28
186	19	34.613	.37
187	18	34.932	.32
188	17	35.324	.39
189	16	36.370	1.05
190	15	36.946	.58
191	14	37.639	.69
192	13	38.376	.74
193	12	39.031	.66
194	11	40.400	1.37
195	10	41.713	1.31
196	9	43.984	2.27
197	8	45.782	1.80
198	7	46.708	.93
199	6	49.678	2.97
200	5	53.267	3.59
201	4	53.866	.60
202	3	54.627	.76
203	2	57.380	2.75
204	1	58.802	1.42

Overall, the cities within the three different clusters do vary somewhat in the types of economic development policies pursued (see Table 6.5). One cluster (15) clearly represents cities shooting at everything that flies. These cities employ fairly high levels of economic development techniques across the board. Cities in the most numerous cluster tend to focus their efforts on traditional infrastructure development and various types of loans. The third group of cities is most interesting in that they represent a clear focus on Type II economic development policies. They are low on all the policy indexes except for the Type II index, and

TABLE 6.5 Characteristics of Civic Culture Clusters and Economic
Development Policies

	Cluster 1 (N = 15)	Cluster 2 (N =175)	Cluster 3 (N = 6)
Percentage United States	79	87	33
Percentage West	14	7	50
Percentage West Central	11	7	0
Percentage Central	25	33	0
Percentage Great Lakes	30	33	17
Percentage East	13	13	17
Percentage nonpartisan	77	80	100
Percentage at-large	41	40	100
Percentage strong mayor	47	47	67
Business input	.10	.37	.57
Community input	-.10	1.40	7.86e
Extraregional competition	9.68e	.31	-.54
Regional competition	-2.5e	.29	-.78
Planning	.17	1.32	4.56e
Need	-.17	.97	8.09e
Unemployment change	-.86	.19	-4.05
Percentage white	92	74	90
Percentage manager	39	40	33
1990 population	41,376	12,072	20,418
Market	5.16e	.35	-.62
Finance	.10	1.63	-.51
Loan	.16	1.40	-.60
Site	.10	1.45	-.77
Infrastructure	.18	.69	-.67
Zoning	6.31e	1.17	-.68
Appearance	.10	.83	-.10
Type	6.90e	1.57	.86
Demand-side	-2.7e	2.18	-.41
Focused Type II	8.02e	.12	.9

they are significantly higher than the other groups on this index. The fact that a set of Type II cities can be identified through cluster analysis is significant.

Shooting Cities

The cities high on economic development policies across the board tend to have very open input systems, providing for both citizen and business input. Perhaps, this leads to more policy effort to meet the demands of various interests. There are no clear structural patterns among these cities, but there are high levels of planning and a perception of competition among local officials. Competition, too, is likely to drive the use of many different types of techniques. These cities also have relatively high levels of economic need. In short, there appears to be a clear dynamic among these cities: High fiscal stress, competitive pressures, and political demands drive the use of a broad array of economic development techniques. Efforts at planning and evaluation do not appear to affect this general dynamic. These cities are more likely to be located in the United States and tend to be in the central region of the country.

Traditional Economic Development Cities

These cities evidence no particular regional or national pattern. They have healthy economies and represent a mix of governmental structures—not surprising, given the large number of cities in the cluster. Businesses are more likely to have opportunities for input than citizens. There is some evidence of planning and evaluation but little perceived competition for economic development. On the whole, the cities in the cluster have relatively stable economies and evidence little innovation in their economic development policies, instead focusing on infrastructure development and loans. It would be reasonable to conclude that this is the case in medium and smaller communities across the two nations.

Focused Type II Cities

The very small number of cities in this group (six) are healthy economically and perceive little competition for economic development.

Thus, it appears they have the luxury to apply strings to their economic development incentives and programs. These cities are more likely to be in Canada and in the western and west central regions. They have reformed governmental structures but with strong mayors. They have very high levels of business input but very little citizen input. Business influence is clearly not inimical to Type II policies; indeed, it may foster them.

Summary

The foregoing analysis provides the basis for an overall categorization scheme based on civic culture. It also highlights the inherent limitations of cross-sectional survey research and attendant statistical analysis, clearly illustrating the importance and necessary contribution of case study analysis. To summarize,

Four general civic culture categories can be identified: (a) mayor-dominated systems, (b) externally driven systems, (c) politically inclusive systems, and (d) elite-dominated systems.

Mayor-dominated cities place the locus of economic development control in the office of the chief executive; few mechanisms exist for community input.

Externally driven cities place the main responsibility for economic development outside the government and provide few opportunities for community input. This is likely the result of high levels of economic stress in these communities.

Politically inclusive systems have a number of avenues for both citizen and business input. Inclusive cities can have a variety of structural forms, both generally and for economic development.

Elite-dominated cities have limited avenues for citizen input, although business input is often extensive. Decision-making elites can either be from the business community or professional bureaucrats within the local government.

When economic development policies are considered, cities become more similar than different; most focus on traditional infrastructure development and loans.

A group of cities focusing on Type II policies can be identified, and they tend to have relatively strong economies and reformed governments.

The fact that cluster analysis is unable to distinguish between large groups of cities suggests that more subtle differences are being masked by the survey methodology.

CASE CITY PROFILES

At this point, a brief introduction to each of the nine case study cities is presented, organized around the environmental and civic culture variables that served as the basis for selection. As noted in Chapter 3, three cities each were selected from the states of Michigan and Ohio and the province of Ontario. These include Allen Park, Cadillac, and Romulus in Michigan; Coshocton, Fairborn, and Kettering in Ohio; and Cornwall, Gloucester, and Oakville in Ontario.

Michigan Cities

Allen Park

The city of Allen Park is located to the southwest of the City of Detroit within the Detroit metropolitan statistical area (MSA). Incorporated in 1957, it is an older inner-ring suburb in the downriver portion of the metropolitan area. As its promotional material notes, Allen Park is "the gateway to southeast Michigan. . . . As visitors from all over the world leave Metro Airport, they pass one of the most recognizable structures in the country—the giant Uniroyal Tire, which is located in Allen Park."[3] It is a relatively small city, with a 1990 population of 31,092, down slightly from 34,196 in 1980. Population for 1999, calculated by the South Eastern Michigan Council of Governments, is estimated at 28,747, indicating that the pattern of population loss has continued. It has a weak-mayor form of government, with a city administrator. The mayor is independently elected and represents the city at large. The administrator is appointed by city council, as are the department heads. Thus, the primary locus for governing power lies with the city council, which is elected at large on nonpartisan ballots. Overall, the city's economic profile is one of a stable, middle-class, white community. Average incomes rose slightly between 1980 and 1990, from $15,300 to $17,013. Per capita income levels were stable at $10,163 in 1980 and $10,021 in 1990. Poverty was stable and low over the ten-year period, moving from only 2% to 3%. Similarly, unemployment was low and dropped between 1980 and 1990 from 9% to 6%. The population is 96% white. In 1990, 85% of the housing units were owner occupied, and the median housing value was $66,600; most homes were built in the 1950s. Only two new housing permits were granted in 1999, illustrating that the city is basically fully developed. Of the 16,543 jobs in the community in 1990, the majority (42%) were in services, followed by 26% in manufacturing and 15% in retail trade. Major employers include Ford Motor Company (with extensive operations in the city), Lear Corporation, Lockheed, Hewlett Packard, IBM, Alcoa, and APAC Papers and Packaging. The largest land use in the city is for single family residential (51%) followed by woodlands/wetlands (14%—the Rouge River runs through the community), transportation/communication/utilities (7%), commercial/office (7%), and industrial (6%). Not surprisingly, given the small size of the community, Allen Park has neither an independent economic development department nor a planning department. Planning is contracted out to a private planning firm, and the primary responsibility for economic development lies with the assistant city administrator. Other development functions, such as building and engineering, are housed in separate departments.

Cadillac

The city of Cadillac is located in central western Michigan. Situated on two lakes and a river (total shoreline in the city is 39,300 feet), the city represents both an industrial and recreational center.[4] This recreational focus and lake location have much to do with the city's slogan, "The Tree City," prominently displayed on the business cards of local officials. Cadillac is the largest community in Wexford County and serves as an employment and retail center in the region; marketing material indicates that Cadillac has a market area population of 60,000. The city itself has a small population that has been stable over the ten-year census period; 10,199 in 1980 and 10,194 in 1990. The projected population figure for 2000 is 10,654. These figures are augmented by seasonal residents and tourists, and the city estimates that there are an additional 2,500 residents at any given time. Economic census figures for the city illustrate the problems that can arise with using 1990 census data for case studies in 1999. According to the census, economic stress is high in this city; poverty rates were high and increasing: 13% in 1980 to 16% in 1990. Unemployment is stable but also very high: 12% in both censuses. Average income increased slightly from $10,859 to $11,241 between 1980 and 1990. Median household income in 1990 was $22,159. The city is 98% white. City data on unemployment at the time of the case study, however, indicate significant economic improvements since the 1990 census. Unemployment is currently 7%, and city officials indicate that they cannot, in good conscience, continue to market the city, due to a worker shortage. Indeed, they indicate that everyone in Cadillac who wishes to work is working. The gap between census figures and economic conditions at the time of the interviews was not as wide for any of the other cities in the study. Of the housing in the city, 60% is owner occupied, and 42% of the structures were built prior to 1959. Median housing value is $37,692. The primary land use in the city is Lake Cadillac (23%), vacant land (23%), streets (21%), and residential (18%). According to an analysis of total floor space in the city, manufacturing/industrial uses predominate, with 58% of floor space, followed by commercial uses (35%) and office space (7%). The largest employers in the city are Miejer, Transppo Group, Avon Rubber and Plastic, AAR Cadillac Manufacture, Four Winns (boats), Michigan Rubber, CMI Case Parts, and Mercey Health Services. The structure of the local government is a mix of reformed and unreformed; city council is elected by ward in nonpartisan elections, the chief executive is a city manager, and the mayor is elected at large and presides over council. There is no independent economic development department; rather, development responsibilities are vested in the city manager. The director of administrative services assists the manager in economic development functions.

Romulus

Like Allen Park, the city of Romulus lies to the southwest of the city of Detroit, in the downriver area. It is in the Detroit MSA, 17 miles southwest of Detroit's central business district and just to the west of Allen Park. It, too, is an older, inner-ring suburb. However, unlike Allen Park, Romulus did not fully develop and still has relatively large parcels of land available for both residential and industrial use. Indeed, between 1970 and 1980, Romulus added 1,600 new housing units. Small portions of the community remain semi-rural. Population in the city is stable, with some population loss between 1980 and 1990 (from 24,857 to 22,898) and a slight upturn by 1996, when the estimated population was 23,616. Most economic indicators suggest that the city experienced some growth between 1980 and 1990. Unemployment dropped significantly from 17% to 10%, although it remains relatively high. Although the percentage in poverty rose from 10% to 13%, average and per capita incomes also rose slightly, from $11,681 to $12,008 and from $6,892 to $7,554, respectively. Romulus has a relatively large nonwhite population; 76% of residents are white, 22% are African American, and 2% Hispanic. Of the housing stock, 65% is owner occupied, and the average price of a house sold is between $110,000 and $125,000.[5] The largest employer and one of the most distinctive features of the community is Detroit Metropolitan Airport. Indeed, the airport is completely surrounded by the city of Romulus and employs 11,110 people. The airport, the land it sits on, and a number of acres surrounding it belong to and are controlled by Wayne County. As discussed later in the case study, this creates interesting opportunities and challenges for the city. In addition to the airport, the city is bisected by two major freeways and five railroads, making transportation generally one of its most important industries. Other large employers in Romulus include Northwest Airlines (3,904), General Motors (2,317), Lear Seating (565), Romulus Schools (550), Federal Express (467), and Borg Warner (320). The largest employers tend to be related either to the auto industry or the airport. Like many of the cities in the data set, the government structure in Romulus represents a mix of reform characteristics. The city has a strong mayor with an at-large council; all elections are nonpartisan. Economic development is located in a larger community development department, and the mayor maintains primary control for development decision making. The city contracts for planning services.

Ohio Cities

Coshocton

The city of Coshocton is located in the Midwestern part of the state and is considered part of the Appalachian area (in the western foothills) for federal grant purposes. It lies in a rural area 72 miles northeast of

Columbus and 100 miles south of Cleveland. The city experienced a population loss between 1980 and 1990, from 13,405 to 12,193. Economic conditions were basically stable for the ten-year period, although poverty worsened somewhat. Average incomes went from $12,827 to $12,487, unemployment was stable and relatively low at 7%, but poverty increased from 10 to 13%. The community is 98% white. Median family income for Coshocton Country was $20,000 in 1990. Of the housing units in the city, 59% are valued at less than $50,000, and 66% are owner occupied. The government structure is primarily unreformed, with a strong mayor, a council combining at-large and ward seats, and partisan elections. Thus, Coshocton represents one of the most unreformed structures, at least on paper. Economic development responsibility is vested in an external, public/private body, Jobs Plus. The city has a mix of manufacturing, commercial, and agricultural enterprises, and the largest employers are Pretty Products (auto supply), Ansell Edmount Industries (synthetic industrial gloves), General Electric, Oscar Meyer, Kraft, and Stone Container (a large paper mill located downtown). Residents are primarily employed as machine operators (15%), administrative support (14%), service and sales (13%), and professional specialty (11%), according to the 1990 census. The city includes a historic district, Roscoe Village, that serves as a tourist attraction. The presence of a local basket crafter as well as many antique sites surrounding the city adds to its tourist business.

Fairborn

The city of Fairborn is a suburb of Dayton contiguous to the city on the southeast. Historically, the current city of Fairborn is a composite of two towns: Osborn, which was located in the Huffman Dam flood plain and was moved in 1922, and Fairfield, which was separated by one street from the relocated city of Osborn. The two consolidated in 1950 into the city of Fairborn. The city is home to Wright-Patterson Air Force Base, with over 32,000 military and civilian personnel, as well as Wright State University with 17,000 students. Fairborn's population increased slightly from 1980 to 1990, from 29,702 to 31,300. Fairborn was recently designated by the Office of Management and Budget as a "Central City," reflecting its development as a regional employment center in its own right. Although poverty rates are high and increasing (from 12 to

15%), unemployment dropped from 11% to 7% over the ten-year period. Average incomes rose from $10,638 to $13,053. Thus, although still
economically stressed, the city reflected improvement from 1980 to
1990. The city's population is 92% white. Much of the city's housing
stock is older, on small, often narrow lots.[6] Primarily because of the air
force base and the university, Fairborn has a very large percentage of
renters; only 50% of the housing stock is owner occupied. The city's
1991 master plan includes a land use profile indicating 29% vacant/
undeveloped/agricultural; 22% low-density residential; 18% infrastructure; 12% public; and 5% flood plain and high-density residential.
Commercial and industrial uses are a small but growing part of the
city's land use profile. The governmental structure is fully reformed,
with a city manager and at-large and nonpartisan elections. Economic
development is located in a larger community development department, along with building, zoning, and planning.

Kettering

The city of Kettering is also a suburb of Dayton, located five miles to
the south. Kettering is a medium-sized city and represents one of the
larger case cities; the 1980 population was 61,186, and the 1990 population was 60,569. It was incorporated as a city in 1955. The economy of
the city is strong; unemployment is low and dropped over the ten-year
period from 5% to 3%, and concomitantly, poverty rates are also low—
4% in both 1980 and 1990. Average incomes increased from $15,270 to
$18,988. The population of the city is 98% white. The city has 27,096
housing units and approximately 1,500 businesses and employers. Of
the housing units, 66% are owner occupied, and 63% of the units are valued between $50,000 and 99,000. The four top employers are Delphi
(General Motors), Bank One, Victoria Secret Catalogue, and the Kettering Medical Center. The largest percentages of residents are employed
in professional specialty occupations (20%), executive/administrative/
managerial and administrative support (16%), and sales occupations
(13%), according to the 1990 census. Much of the city's land is already
developed; only about 10% of the land area remains open for development. The governmental structure represents a mix of reforms: a
city manager, nonpartisan elections, and a mixed council with four
district and two at-large members. Economic development responsibil-

ities are vested in an independent economic development department. There are separate departments for planning, engineering, and housing rehabilitation.

Ontario Cities

Cornwall

The city of Cornwall is located in eastern Ontario, on the St. Lawrence River, roughly an hour away from both Montreal and Ottawa. It is also very accessible to the northeastern United States via the Seaway International Bridge. It was incorporated as a town in 1834 and as a city in 1945. As of 1999, seventy manufacturing industries were located in Cornwall, employing about 5,748 people.[7] The population has been basically stable, growing slightly from 46,425 to 46,905 from 1981 to 1991. The 1999 population is at 47,403. Both a technical college (St. Lawrence College) and a university (University of Ottawa, Cornwall Campus) are located in Cornwall, as is The NAV Canada Training Institute (air traffic control). Approximately half (48%) of the City's residents speak both English and French. Both poverty and unemployment rates are high but have dropped or remained stable (respectively) over a ten-year period. This is a common pattern in Ontario, which emerged from a recession in the early 1990s. Poverty rates declined from 21% to 17% and unemployment rose from 10% to 11% in the ten year period. City officials indicated that 1999 unemployment rates were between 6% and 8%. Per capita income also dropped over the ten-year period, however, from $17,883 to $15,072, and average wage rates are below the national average. Employment by sector is as follows: 41% service; 21% manufacturing; 19% trade; 6% government and construction; 5% transportation/communications; and 4% finance/real estate. The largest employers in the city are the public schools, the separate (private) schools, Domtar Papers, Hotel Dieu (health care), the hospital, the city, Robert Laframboise Mechanical, Morbern Inc. (fabrics), Satisfied Brake, and Ridgewood Industries (furniture). The city has a large industrial park with over 400 acres of land available for development. Average housing prices in the city are $89,730, well below the national average of $167,114 (for 1998). The city has a reformed governmental system, with a chief administrative officer (equivalent to a city manager) and at-large and nonpartisan elections. Economic development responsibilities are vested in an independent economic development department with planning and recreation services located together in a separate department.

Gloucester

The city of Gloucester is a contiguous suburb of Ottawa and was part of the Ottawa-Carleton Regional Government at of the time of the survey and case study interviews. As of January 2001, Gloucester and several other cities in the region (Cumberland, Vanier, Rockliffe, Nepean, and Kanata) and townships (Osgoode, Rideau, Goulbourn, and West-Carleton) became part of the city of Ottawa. Gloucester is located about ten minutes from Parliament Hill in downtown Ottawa. It was incorporated as a city in 1981. The population of the city has been growing steadily from 89,810 in 1981 to 101,485 in 1991. Poverty and unemployment were low and stable during this period, 8% and 6% respectively. Per capita income dropped from $31,334 to $20,905, over the same period, however. The Macdonald-Cartier International Airport serving Ottawa is located in Gloucester, although this does not seem to create the same challenges as it does for Romulus, Michigan, perhaps because of differences in scale. About 13,000 acres of the city are urban, whereas 73,000 are rural. The city also includes 7,700 hectares of the greenbelt that surrounds the city of Ottawa. Although 40% of the rural area is controlled by the federal government via the greenbelt, portions are designated for future development. The local workforce is 45% bilingual. The city is the location of 120 high tech firms, and for this reason, the city bills itself as the "Silicon Valley North-East Sector." The city has a commercial/industrial base of over 4,000 companies with some of the largest employers being Telesat Canada, MBNA Canada, Telemark, Canadian Security Intelligence Service, Dew Engineering and Development, Esso Aviation Services, Hudson General Aviation Service, ABB Power Generation Segment, and the Royal Canadian Mounted Police. The government structure represents a mix of reforms with a city manager and nonpartisan but ward-based council seats. Economic development responsibility is vested in an independent department. Because it is part of a regional government, there is some division of labor for economic development with the regional authority. At the time of the

interviews, the regional body was primarily responsible for regional
marketing and small business development, with the city carrying out
its own development efforts.

Oakville

The town of Oakville is a contiguous suburb of Toronto and is located
between Toronto and Hamilton on Lake Ontario. It is not included
within the Metropolitan Toronto Regional Government. As their marketing material indicates, "one quarter of Canada's population lives
within a 100 mile radius of Oakville." Although the population of
Oakville is large and growing (from 87,107 in 1981 to 114,840 in 1991), it
has chosen to retain the "town" designation. Current population figures, 132,000 in 1999, indicate that growth has continued. A 4% population growth rate is expected, and the 2001 projected population is over
155,000. In Ontario, town status in no way reduces taxing or service authority but allows the community to retain its image as "the biggest little town in Canada." Indeed, this "small town" has the largest population among the case study cities. To accommodate the population
growth, Oakville has been adding about 7,500 housing units per year;
about 77% of the total housing stock is owner occupied. Poverty and unemployment are low and stable; poverty declined from 6 to 5% and unemployment increased from 5 to 6% over a ten-year period (1996 rates
are at 5.6%). Average household income was $77,253 in the 1991 census
and $83,671 according to 1996 figures. This community, then, has one of
the heartiest economies of the case studies. The city has an economic
base of over 4,000 firms employing about 54,000 people. It is the location
of Sheridan College, which includes a premier school of animation. Employers are concentrated in the automotive, aerospace, high technology,
and pharmaceutical sectors. The largest employers in the city include
Ford Motor Company of Canada, Sheridan College, the Regional Municipality of Halton, Halton Healthcare Services, Lear Corporation, the
Town of Oakville, Menasco Aerospace, Halton Regional Police Service,
Canada Loyal Insurance, General Electric Canada, Procor Limited, and
TDL Group (all with over 400 employees). Over 202 companies have
their headquarters in Oakville. Oakville has a town manager, with partisan and ward-based elections. Although economic development used
to be conducted by an independent city department, this structure was

changed in 1999 with the creation of the external Economic Development Alliance Corporation. This nonprofit corporation is run by the former economic development department head.

Summary

   The cases range in population size from Cadillac, with 10,194 residents, to Oakville, with 114,840. All of the Canadian cities are among the largest: Oakville, Gloucester, Kettering, and Cornwall. Examining the various indicators of economic health—unemployment, poverty, and income—the healthiest cities appear to be Kettering, Oakville, Gloucester, and Allen Park. Coshocton and Fairborn are moderately healthy. Cornwall, Cadillac, and Romulus are the most economically stressed. It should be noted, however, that case study interviews indicate that the economy is on the upswing for the three most-stressed cities and that current unemployment and poverty rates are much lower than in the past census. Among the case cities, it appears that size is related to economic health: The larger cities are healthier than the smaller cities. The cases provide a wide range on both unemployment (from 3% to 12%) and poverty (from 3% to 17%). Average incomes range from $11,241 in Cadillac to $77,253 in Oakville. The case cities also provide structural variation both in general governmental structure and for economic development. The majority of the cities have city manager systems; only Romulus and Coshocton have strong-mayor systems. All of the cities have nonpartisan elections except Coshocton. Election methods for city council are more varied: Four cities have at-large systems, three have a combination of at-large and ward seats, and two have wards. Only the city of Coshocton has a completely unreformed structure, whereas Allen Park, Fairborn, and Cornwall are completely reformed. Economic development structures are also mixed. Three—Gloucester, Kettering, and Cornwall—have independent economic development departments. Two cities, Coshocton and Oakville, place responsibility for economic development in an external body. Fairborn and Romulus locate economic development within a larger community development department. Last, Allen Park and Cadillac vest primary responsibility for economic development in the office of the chief executive, both city managers.

In short, there is a good bit of variation on the basic variables of interest. The case study chapters to follow will obviously present more detailed descriptions of the civic culture of each community. This discussion will be organized around the major clusters of civic culture identified earlier in this chapter: mayor-dominated, externally driven, politically inclusive, business elite-dominated, and bureaucratic elite-dominated systems. Although the justification for categorization of the case studies will be made in subsequent chapters, their placement is summarized as follows:

> Mayor-dominated systems: Romulus
> Externally driven systems: Coshocton
> Politically inclusive systems: Oakville, Fairborn
> Business elite-dominated systems: Cadillac
> Bureaucratic elite-dominated systems:
>   Active: Kettering, Gloucester
>   Passive: Cornwall, Allen Park

A brief return to the issue of case study selection, discussed in Chapter 3, is important here. As is obvious from the earlier discussion, the cities selected based on their high-score Type II policy use also represent the basic cultural types identified in the foregoing cluster analysis using all cities in the data set. Why is this the case? Like past definitions of economic development policies discussed earlier, the answer is a good news/bad news story. First the bad news: Although the cities were selected because their surveys indicated they made extensive use of Type II economic development policies, this turned out not to be necessarily the case on case study analysis. Bluntly put, some of the survey forms indicated Type II policies that did not appear to be in actual use in the cities, based on discussion with local officials. Although it is possible that the cities could have been using Type II policies at the time of the survey but then stopped before the case studies, discussions about that possibility suggest that this was not the case. Thus, although the survey forms for several of the case cities appeared quite accurate regarding Type II policy use (Romulus, Coshocton, and Oakville, for example), this was not universally the case. The case cities ended up reflecting the regular spectrum of cities with some high and others low on Type II policies.

Second, the case cities were selected not only to represent cities high on Type II policy use but also to ensure that they reflected a variety of other environmental and structural features. Hence, the good news is that the cluster analysis of the Type II cities led to the selection of case cities that also represented the broader types of culture identified in the cluster analysis of all the cities. In short, a retrospective examination of the case cities leads to confidence that they indeed represent the major cultural types present in the population of cities.

Case Study Methodology

The methodology for the mailed survey and resultant indexes have been detailed in previous chapters as has the rationale for the selection of the nine cases. The case study analyses, the questions asked, the actors interviewed, and the documents gathered were framed by the civic culture attributes previously discussed. The overriding purpose of the case studies was to examine more closely the unique civic culture surrounding economic development in each community: the history behind that civic culture, the character of decision-making processes, the nature and intensity of economic development efforts, and a sense of the accuracy of the initial survey responses. As described to interviewees in each city, the goal was to make the survey data come alive, to put names and faces on the economic development effort. A uniform script of questions was asked in each of the nine cities, although particular order and emphasis varied by the exigencies of individual cases. A uniform set of groups or actors were also targeted for face-to-face interviews, although this too varied somewhat, depending on each city's economic development and governmental structure.

Questions Asked

The primary questions were organized around the major attributes of the environment and civic culture used in the foregoing analysis. Obviously, the case study format allowed for more in-depth examination of many of the variables, particularly those that related to community vision, local political history, the detail available on economic development policies and programs, the roles of individuals in communities, and so on.

Economic Health: Because the census data were drawn from 1990/1991, survey responses from 1995, and the case studies conducted in 1999/ 2000, it was obviously useful to obtain a more detailed sense of both past and current economic health of each city. This allowed for a comparison of how accurately the census data reflected current conditions and how economic health may drive development decision making. Basic health questions from the case studies related to current unemployment and poverty rates, perceptions of whether the economic base of the community had grown or declined over the past ten years, and comparative perceptions of economic health from different actors (business, government, community, for example).

History of Politics: Although form of local government is a critical environmental variable, it does not capture several realities of local governance. First, many local governments do not operate in the manner the charter would suggest. Local variations in history and individual personalities can affect how governmental systems operate in practice. Often, local history can shed light on many current practices that on the surface seem unexpected or even irrational. As the literature on path dependent policies suggests, past programs and activities strongly frame current realities (Woodlief, 1998). To this end, the following historical issues or questions were explored in each city: mayor/city manager changes (how often, why), council changes, any recent changes in formal governmental structure, does political party matter and what is the dominant party, where have most of the individuals running for and being elected to office come from, common recruiting practices, what have been the most contentious issues for the past several years, what groups were involved in these issues, who "won," are elections close?

Competition: Perceptions of competition among cities for economic development are a central component of the environment of local economic development. Although the survey asked general questions about competition, the case studies allowed for a more detailed exploration of exactly which and what types of cities were seen as competitors and how much effect that seemed to have on development policy choice. The following questions were explored in each city to gauge competition: How much in competition do they feel with other cities for eco-

nomic development, which cities exactly are seen as the greatest competitors (close by, regional, cross-border), does competition affect the
economic development policies they select, do respondents feel they
are in a good competitive position, does competition appear to lead to
copy-cat behavior or does it stimulate greater innovation?

Locus of Power: The case studies offer an opportunity to explore in more
detail what actors or interests actually exercise the most influence in
economic development decision making. Although the survey shed
light on such issues, gaining different perspectives within a single city
allowed for a much more accurate and nuanced picture of power systems. The following questions were explored to address locus of control: How are economic development policy decisions made, who has
the most influence in selecting policies, who initiates most economic development policies, where do the concepts for policies come from, how
much citizen interest and influence exists, have citizens fought any policies or developments, who is in the governing regime for economic
development?

Business Input: One of the major attributes of local systems of influence
includes the nature and extent of both business and citizen input. Large
surveys are usually unable to distinguish the finer points about what
types of businesses have input and how the input channels actually
work. For example, it has been noted that business input measures tend
to indicate avenues for input rather than actual influence. The case
study interviews were designed to examine this more carefully. The following questions were used to examine the nature of local business input: How much business input is there, through what avenues (formal,
informal), are local or nonlocal businesses most influential, what is the
nature of those businesses with input (size, sector, ownership structure), how diverse are businesses and business groups that are involved, how do businesses feel about business/government relationships in the city, how do they view the competition—business versus
citizen versus government—for power in economic development?

Citizen Input: The nature and influence of citizen input was a central
concern as well. Although many questions focused on citizen versus

business input, various attributes of citizen or neighborhood input were also explored, including what types of citizen or neighborhood groups are active in the city, does input come primarily from organized groups or individual citizens, is there a no-growth element to citizen concerns, what types of development projects are citizens likely to raise concerns about, what are the avenues for citizen input, how successful are citizen or neighborhood groups in achieving their ends?

Planning and Evaluation: Although the survey measured whether particular planning and evaluation practices were used by cities, it really could not assess the extent, regularity, and intensity of planning and evaluation techniques. Nor could it gauge whether such evaluation was actually integrated in subsequent policy decisions. The following questions were used in each city to assess systematic decision-making procedures: Are policies actually evaluated in a systematic fashion, what evaluation methodology is used, how is it used—does it inform future decisions (to select projects, to justify projects, to see if projects worked), who does evaluations, is there an economic development plan and does it influence decisions?

Nature and Effectiveness of Economic Development Policies: Surveys can only assess the use of particular economic development policies in a very static sense: has the community ever used a particular policy and to what extent. Even though the "to what extent" questions were included on the survey, it is still difficult to assess intensity of use. Thus, the case studies also focused on what techniques were being implemented and to what extent. Furthermore, perceived success or effectiveness of policies was also examined. The following questions were explored in each city: How effective have the city's economic development policies been, what have been the most serious problems/challenges related to economic development, how are programs organized, what funding arrangements have been used for particular policies, what kinds of Type II policies in particular have been used, how much of any positive change is due to economic development policies, what signs of economic development success can be identified, what are their perceptions of success?

Intergovernmental Relations: Although the survey included several basic questions about the locus for economic development (e.g., a regional or other higher level government), it did not explore in detail the extent and nature of intergovernmental arrangements for local economic development. In the case studies, then, the existence and use of intergovernmental bodies and arrangements was explicitly examined through the following questions: What type of state/provincial assistance is available and used for local economic development; does the city cooperate with a regional, county, or other areawide economic development body; what types of federal economic development grants have been used; what is the nature of relationships with county, state/provincial, federal governments; are there avenues for working with other neighboring governments on economic development?

Racial Diversity: As has been noted on several occasions, because the Canadian census does not include city-level racial data, it was not possible to include race as a variable in the aggregate analyses. Through the case studies, however, exploration of the racial diversity of a community and possible relationships between race and civic culture and economic development policy are possible. The following questions were examined in each community: What is the racial composition of the residents, what has been the racial makeup of local government officials, are there any perceived racial divisions or conflicts in the city, are the races spatially separated, are Type II policies race based?

Policy Orientation of Decision Makers: The survey did not attempt to explore the basic policy orientations of local decision makers. An important part of the local civic culture is the extent to which it is perceived as being acceptable or desirable to rely solely on market mechanisms to foster economic development or whether various market interventions or public sector entrepreneurialism is acceptable. To get at these issues, the following questions were used: What is the perceived proper role of government in economic development, how much should the government stimulate economic development, how entrepreneurial should the government be, to what extent should the public sector intervene in the private market?

Local Goals/Vision/Symbols: Although the survey included questions about specific economic development goals, it did not attempt to examine broader community visions. In other words, it did not provide a sense of where local officials and community actors see the community today, where they hope it will be in the future, what they think are particular strong points, and what might be perceived as the most pressing concerns, particularly concerns that need to, or can be, addressed by greater economic development. To examine these issues, the following types of questions were asked in each city: What are the most pressing economic development challenges in the city, what are your long-term goals for the city, how do you think the city appears to outsiders?

Other Documents

In addition to face-to-face interviews in each city, a number of documents were also acquired and examined. These included any tourist or economic development promotional material, materials explaining particular economic development programs, general fund budgets, the economic development and/or comprehensive plan in place in 1994, the organizational chart for the city, and any economic development ordinances.

Actors Interviewed

Although the specific individuals interviewed varied somewhat in each city due to differences in government and economic development structure, respondents were basically similar across the communities and included the following types of community leaders:

Chief executive (mayor and/or city manager/administrator)
The economic development director or individual responsible for economic development
Representatives from city council
Representatives from the planning and zoning board/commission
Planning director
Downtown development authority director

Chamber of commerce representatives
Regional/county economic development director

Anywhere from seven to ten individuals were interviewed in each of the nine cities, typically over a two-day period.

NOTES

1. The inclusion of unemployment change over the respective ten-year census period is the only variation from the path analyses previously discussed. Early correlation analysis indicated that this variable was significantly correlated with many of the policy indexes. It was left out of the subsequent regression analyses because the residential-need variable is serving as a proxy in an effort to reduce the complexity in the ultimate path models. In exploring the most robust combination of variables for the cluster analysis, it was included and found to be effective, along with need, in distinguishing among different types of cities.

2. It is useful to note that a number of additional cluster analyses were run on just the 207 cities in the largest cluster. The hope was that by adding additional criteria variables to the analysis, finer distinctions could be identified among the cities. Even with all of the variables from the path analysis in the cluster analysis, 132 cities remained grouped in one cluster (and the number of cases dropped to 158). The survey analysis (and the survey itself) is simply not identifying finer differences among cities.

3. Unless otherwise noted, all information on the nature of the case cities was drawn from the census noted, city web pages, and city promotional or tourist material.

4. All data other than that included in the census are from the City of Cadillac, Long Range Comprehensive Plan of 1994.

5. Noncensus data are drawn from the Romulus Web site and Master Land Use Plan of 1989.

6. Noncensus data are drawn from the Comprehensive Land Use Plan of 1991.

7. Noncensus data are from the City of Cornwall Community Profile, 1999.

7

THE "STRONG MAYOR" CASES
Romulus and Coshocton

In Romulus, Michigan, Mayor Oakley has his fingers on the pulse of the city. Assisted by his community development director, he is the central player in the city's economic development efforts. Located on the fringe of Detroit Metropolitan Airport, Romulus both benefits from the transportation-related and transportation-dependent industries—often branch plants—and is hurt by the negative externalities of noise and tax base loss. Economic development, framed by this "tumor in the community" and a still-powerful "fraternity" of multigenerational families, both black and white, provides an interesting backdrop for the role of strong mayoral leadership.

Coshocton, Ohio, presents a "classic" American small-town image: a historic downtown with well-kept homes surrounded by farmland rolling into the Appalachian foothills. It serves as an employment and shopping node for the surrounding area. Although having a strong-mayor system by charter, economic development in Coshocton is the purview of business leaders, institutionalized through an external public/private partnership. In Coshocton, local, traditionally homegrown business leaders

AUTHORS' NOTE: Many single words and phrases appear in quotation marks in Chapters 7 through 10; they are all direct quotes from the interviewees. The quotes are not generally attributed to specific individuals due to confidentiality concerns.

are expected to act in the best interests of the community; businesses "give back" in Coshocton. Economic development efforts in Coshocton are shaped by this business volunteerism ethic as well as the privatized nature of functional responsibility.

According to the cluster analysis in Chapter 6, there is one major type of strong-mayor city, one where the strong-mayor formal structure plays out as expected. The mayor dominates decision making in the city, keeping economic development closely within his/ her locus of control. Romulus represents such a case. City council has little direct involvement in development decision making, and there are few formal avenues for either citizen or business input into the process. *Formal* is the operative word, however, because the mayor is very present in the community at large and makes many informal contacts, particularly with members of the business community. In short, economic development is largely within the purview of the mayor.[1]

However, Coshocton also has a strong-mayor form of government, but responsibilities for economic development have been delegated to a private development organization, Jobs Plus. The individual occupying the mayor's office at the time of the case study was not a strong executive; the Safety Services Director was essentially in charge of all major city services (except for police services, which were provided by the county since 1981). Although the city has few avenues for citizen input into the economic development decision-making process, the placement of economic development in a private organization enhances responsiveness to business interests. Clearly, not all strong-mayor systems operate according to city charter.

The cluster analysis also pointed to potential differences between cities in the clusters represented by Romulus and Coshocton. It suggested what might account for a city such as Coshocton to shift from a strong-mayor system. Economic stress appears present in strong-mayor cities with externally driven economic development efforts. It is possible that higher levels of unemployment and poverty, lower median incomes, increasing unemployment, and slow economic-base growth mitigate to shift the locus for development to an external body that might be able to bring greater resources—both professional and monetary—to the table.

Coshocton and Romulus have very similar economic histories, however, so something beyond the economy is affecting present paths.

The correlation analysis and regression models already presented also speak to various dynamics that might be present in cities with strong executive control over the economic development decision process as opposed to those that have external development departments. For example, higher levels of residential need are associated with an external economic development function in multiple regression. Other environmental stresses, particularly in the form of competition, also appear to enhance this tendency. Greater business input and influence is associated with off-cycle locus, as would be expected; leaving economic development in the hands of the mayor appears to have just the opposite effect. And as suggested earlier, cities with external bodies for economic development devote more resources, budget and personnel, to the effort. Cities where economic development decisions rest with a strong chief executive are more likely to emphasize Type II and growth-management policy goals, suggesting that strong, political leadership may be important in efforts to pursue nontraditional or more controversial goals.

Can these dynamics be seen in Romulus and Coshocton? Are there other aspects of the civic culture in these two cities that are critical to economic development process and policy that are masked by the large survey analysis? Do the differing civic cultures and locus of power really matter? Do the two cities have substantially different approaches to economic development? And do different economic development policies result? These questions will be addressed in the rest of the chapter, which is organized by the essential traits of the environment and civic culture of the communities as presented in proceeding analyses.

THE CIVIC CULTURES
OF ROMULUS AND COSHOCTON

The Environment of
Local Economic Development

It has been argued in previous analysis that the critical factors shaping the environment of local economic development decision making include economic forces, local government structure, and the nature of intercity competition. All of these were explicitly explored in the case study analysis. Historical environmental conditions were also examined, including the unique political history in each community.

As presented in the preceding chapter, the economies of Romulus and Coshocton are quite similar; both reflect relatively high levels of economic stress, although both appear to be improving. Romulus is almost twice as large as Coshocton, but neither is large. Romulus had a 1990 population just under 23,000; Coshocton's population was just over 12,000. In both cities, the poverty rate is high and increased from 10% to 13% between the 1980 and 1990 census. However, unemployment improved considerably in Romulus (from 17% to 10%) and remained stable in Coshocton (at 7%). Median incomes are almost identical: Coshocton is slightly higher at $12,487, Romulus is at $12,008. Beyond these basic similarities, there are some demographic differences between the cities. Romulus has a significant African American population (22%), whereas Coshocton is predominantly white (98%). More important, the composition of the economic base and employer profiles are quite different.

The Romulus Economy

A large portion of the land in Romulus is devoted to Detroit Metropolitan Airport. The airport itself and the surrounding land that must remain vacant to meet federal noise and safety restrictions amounts to 36 square miles; in other words 1,100 acres of land within Romulus are officially off the local property tax roles. Another ring of land just beyond the noise barrier *could* be developed but is owned by Wayne County, which runs the airport. That land could be sold for transportation-related businesses thus putting it back on local tax rolls. However, the county appears to prefer to lease the land, which brings in no additional revenue for the city. The whole issue of airport land development and administration is a major source of contention between the city and the county. In this regard, city officials see the airport as both a benefit and a curse. Its presence has been the stimulus for a great deal of traffic through the city and has led to an economy largely based on the transportation industry. On the other hand, its presence represents a loss to the city tax revenue and reduces land values due to the disincentives of living near a major airport. The transportation-related businesses have also increased traffic in and around the city, placing additional burdens on infrastructure.

Obviously, because of the airport, many of the major employers in Romulus are transportation related. Other employers are tied to the automobile industry because the city is in metropolitan Detroit. The economic base of the community includes Northwest Airlines, General Motors, the airport itself, Lear Seating, Federal Express, Borg Warner, and the local school district. In short, although auto suppliers and transportation firms are well represented, "you can't buy a shirt in Romulus." There are no shopping malls or even significant retail operations. The city has long been trying to attract a developer for 311 acres of land near a major freeway, I-94. Indeed, during the previous mayor's administration, an off-ramp was built, funded by the city, and significant infrastructure put in place to support a major outlet mall (it was estimated that 15% of the city budget was devoted to these efforts). Because that "deal" fell through, what remains is a large, prominently marked exit leading to a boulevard that goes nowhere and is home to nothing. The city is currently negotiating with a developer to locate an office/hotel project on this land. Although obviously desirable to the city, such a development would not address the need for additional retail and the goal of making Romulus a destination rather than a pass-through to the airport.

Downtown Romulus visually demonstrates the imbalance between industrial and transportation land uses and retail development. The most prominent structure houses the Landing Strip, named both for its proximity to the airport and the activities that take place therein. Although the exterior of the historic building is attractive, there is no escaping the fact that a strip club is one of the most well-known downtown tenants. However, the city has used community development block grant (CDBG) funds effectively to implement a streetscape project, and the downtown now has attractive sidewalks, trees, and banners. A ubiquitous so-called big-box drug store is also moving downtown, suggesting that some development is taking place that might, perhaps, work to address the retail deficit. It is interesting to note that, whereas many cities are not excited about gaining big-box business and do not offer financial incentives for them, Romulus did and is very happy to have it. Clearly, the nature of the particular local economy has much to say about economic development priorities.

It is also interesting to describe the visual impressions of each city in an effort to provide a feel for the places. This would include those traits that are noticeable to moderately casual observers. Although downtown Romulus lacks significant retail, it is identifiable in that there is a clearly distinct downtown with a number of historic buildings. The remaining land use in the city is mixed. There is a good deal of vacant land in the city ripe for both residential and commercial development. In the more rural areas of the city, one finds the typical juxtaposition of old, poorly maintained houses on both small and large tracts of land, large and very expensive estates, some working farms, and a variety of commercial and industrial uses, all in relatively close proximity. Land surrounding the airport has the expected mix of commercial, transportation, hotel, parking, and strip-shopping uses. There are a number of nice older neighborhoods in the city with primarily lower- to middle-class housing; the average price of a house recently sold in the city ranges from $110,000 to $125,000. However, the city is also now beginning to benefit from relatively low land prices. Although formerly agricultural land has given way to expensive subdivisions in many surrounding communities, this is just starting to take place in Romulus. Officials expect that housing development will increase in coming years, another reason for the emphasis on retail development.

The Coshocton Economy

Coshocton offers a contrasting employment mix as well as a very different visual picture to visitors of the community. The economic base is more diverse, with agriculture, industry, commercial uses, and tourism development. The city has many firms that were originally locally owned but have since been sold to outside investors; to "big brother," as local officials put it. However, the original owners remain in the city ("rather than go to Florida and die there"), and the firms still have relatively strong local ties. Large employers include Stone Container (a large paper mill located just outside of the central business district), Petty Products (auto supply), Ansell Edmount Industries (synthetic industrial gloves), General Electric, Oscar Meyer (bacon plant), Kraft, and Longenberger baskets (a specialty company that sells homemade baskets via retail and home parties). Although smaller than Romulus, the economy in Coshocton is more diverse.

Visually, the city is charming. The surrounding areas are primarily rural with a very small town every so often. There are clearly no shopping centers or significant places of employment near here; Coshocton serves as the employment locus for the immediate area. Despite the odorous and not very aesthetic paper mill located within walking distance of the downtown, there is very nice older housing within the city limits and some very large new housing in the hills surrounding the city. The higher- and lower-end housing is divided geographically, and this is quite visible. Housing near the mill is on the lower end, and there are trailer parks mixed with single-family housing relatively near the mill. A bit farther from downtown, there is extremely nice older housing with a great deal of character. Homes are very well kept, and preserving the historic image of the city appears important even when the houses are not historical; electric candles in windows are common.

There are many retail and commercial establishments, including the almost obligatory Wal-Mart, Rite Aid, and CVS drug stores and fast food stores but also several restaurants (including Chinese and Mexican), some small-town clothing stores, and a Quality Feed Store. The big-box businesses developed here without public incentives and are not universally welcomed. Overall, there appears to be enough retail and commercial shopping that basic needs can be met within the city. Just inside the city limits is Roscoe Village, a regional tourist site composed of small specialty shops, historic buildings, a small players' guild, basket makers, and a hotel. It was developed by a local businessman and is one of the top 20 historical sites documenting the 1840s to 1860s, when the Ohio Erie Canal was the major means of transportation. There are also many Amish restaurants and antique stores in the areas around the city, so although somewhat isolated, Coshocton has a significant tourist base. There are several additional hotels just outside the downtown area.

Coshocton has an identifiable and attractive downtown with a historic court house. There is visible evidence of infrastructure improvements, including the typical streetscape with trees and brick pavers, banners, benches, and lights. This gives the central business district (CBD) a uniform appearance. Newer strip developments with the franchises and so on are located just outside the CBD.

Local Government Structures and Politics

As noted earlier, both Romulus and Coshocton have a strong-mayor form of government. In Romulus, other aspects of the structure are more reformed: Elections are nonpartisan, and the council is elected at-large. Coshocton has a more traditional unreformed structure, with partisan elections and a council composed of both district and at-large seats. How have these structural attributes played out historically?

Politics in Romulus has been somewhat mixed; there have been long periods where most officials have run unopposed interspersed with intense electoral competition. The current mayor had actually served three terms before being unseated by a female opponent. "The lady" (as the current mayor referred to her) was in office for six terms with little opposition until the current mayor ran again in opposition. This latter conflict appeared to be primarily issue related and revolved around the prior mayor's support of the freeway interchange project and a well project that raised concerns about toxic waste. The election was extremely close; the current mayor won by only six votes (or four, depending on the respondent). The current mayor's policy is to limit the extent of public money for private interests for economic development unless a significant benefit to the city is likely to result. However, because a planning commission member indicated that the former mayor lost because she did not sufficiently cater to the needs of the "old boys network," it is possible that other factors were at play.

Membership on the city council had been quite stable until just recently, although interactions were also quite contentious. It appears that one very long-time council member (on since 1958) was a bit fractious, and a more cooperative spirit has been developed since he retired. The deputy mayor (the highest vote "getter" in council elections) has been on council since 1987 and in that position over the past two mayoral administrations. Indeed, he pointed out that his vote totals have exceeded those of the mayoral candidates. The council is still divided, however, with a four-member voting block of new members, Republicans, and a three-member block of old timers who are Democrats. It appears, how-

ever, that the normal "bickering" does not extend to economic development decisions; they are typically made with little dissension. Various
quirks should be noted here—the city is nonpartisan, but the voting
blocks on council are distinctly partisan. Although the at-large council
base may dilute minority voting strength in the city, the highest vote
getter across recent elections is an African American. The only thing
that operates completely as expected here is that, with the strong-mayor
structure, the mayor retains control over economic development decision making.

Historically, politics in Coshocton have been much more consensual.
The unreformed structure of the city belies a general calm; partisan elections do not appear to lead to partisan politics, and ward-based elections do not seem to produce geographic divisions. Indeed, the culture
appears to be such that when officials attempt to play partisan politics,
the community reacts negatively. For example, the mayor has had a
long career with the city, serving on council and as the safety services director prior to his run for office. He was fired from that position by the
previous mayor, a Republican, because he is a Democrat. The voters reacted negatively to that display of partisan politics and possible ageism
(the fired director and current mayor is likely in his 80s) and strongly
supported the former director in his run for mayor. Indeed, in the words
of one city official, the current mayor "whipped his butt."

Actors external to the city in regional government also indicated that
in Coshocton, "officials work across party lines." County officials, too,
appear to cooperate in a bipartisan manner. In short, although it appears that some tensions arise from the partisan nature of local elections, the voters do not react well to such divisions, and elected officials
appear to work well across party lines. The main point of contention in
Coshocton appears related to the mayor's office. In the election following the case study, the elderly mayor was also defeated.

Intercity Competition for Development

Competition for economic development is viewed somewhat differently in the two communities. In Romulus, local actors provided differing perspectives on the extent of intercity competition. For example, the
director of planning and community development indicated that the
city was in competition with others in Ohio, Indiana, and even North

Carolina. Because Romulus is near the Ohio border, perceived competition with cities in that state was most acute. Within the state, other downriver communities, such as Taylor and Huron Township, were mentioned as well as the rapidly growing northern suburb of Novi.

Most of the competition appears to be mediated by land brokers because of the extent of developable land in the city. Otherwise, the development director felt that the city competed mostly by being "business friendly" and "flexible." The mayor, on the other hand, perceived no particular competition with downriver neighbors. Although he recognizes that Romulus is "in competition" because the city has land that other area communities lack, he does not really see other cities as being "competitors." A member of the planning commission summarized the mixed feelings about competition well: On one hand, Romulus is getting development without having to compete, getting the "run-off" development from the almost fully developed northern suburbs. On the other, there is a recognition that if the city does not "get along" with developers, they will lose the development to other places that are more often out of state.

Competitive pressures seem more strongly felt in Coshocton and are more uniformly perceived among respondents. Local officials view intercity competition as one of their more significant challenges, and they feel in competition with everyone. The strongest competitive pressures appear to come from cities close by, some of which are perceived as giving benefits away to business. Relative to many of the surrounding communities, Coshocton lacks available land for development, which limits their ability to compete fully. They also feel intense competition with cities across Ohio and believe that state activities exacerbate this (such feelings were evident in other Ohio cities as well). State development officials bring "leads" around to many cities and provide cities with required specifications so that competition actually escalates. This process was characterized as a constant fight, "like selling cars or real estate." On the other hand, officials indicated that such competition does not completely drive local economic development policy and that they don't want any business just for the sake of having it. Rather, they pay attention to the number and types of jobs that are likely to develop as well as the "fit" between the business and the nature of the community. They have a very good sense of the difference between "good" and "bad" jobs. If the jobs are "good," they will actively compete.

Racial Issues

One of the significant limitations of the large data analysis is the lack of racial data for Canadian cities. Clearly, no examination of economic development policy, let alone urban politics more generally, is complete without consideration of race. Questions about race, racial relations, and possible relationships between race and economic development were a specific focus of interviews. As noted previously, Romulus is notable in both the survey data set and among the case study cities for its relatively significant African American population. The racial makeup of interviewees in Romulus was evenly divided. The deputy mayor and the director of planning and community development are African American, whereas the mayor and planning commission member are white. Responses about racial diversity were relatively uniform, although some interesting inconsistencies arose. The mayor indicated that there were no racial problems in the city; the only racial problems related to "kids fighting in school." At the same time, he related a story about a racial conflict involving city council, where the police had to be called. Similarly, the planning commission member said that although there are external perceptions that the city is segregated and has racial problems, this is not reality; race relations were good. However, his wife then mentioned that several years ago, a neighbor had a cross burned on their lawn.

The latter incident in particular seems to belie somewhat the picture of racial harmony portrayed by all of the actors interviewed. The economic development director took a more analytical approach to the question, perhaps because he is not a resident of the city, noting that African Americans are geographically concentrated "by choice" and appear to be more middle class generally than most of the rest of the population in the city. He also said that there is little racial tension, particularly in comparison to the city where he last worked. The deputy mayor characterized racial relations as "good" but then noted that there is "no utopia" and that there have been complaints from young black men about police harassment. More to the point, he noted that African Americans as a whole are left out of economic development decisions in the community. There are no black developers coming before the planning commission, and they are not particularly "encouraged." Overall, most areas are integrated, and black professionals appear to be moving

into the community to live. The council member perceived no city service distinctions based on race of neighborhoods, noting that many city
employees providing the services are African American and ensure
high quality services to all areas. Last, residents of the city clearly vote
across racial lines, evidenced not only by the fact that the deputy mayor
is African American but also in that Jesse Jackson won the presidential
primary in that city in the early 1990s. In short, either officials are loathe
to mention racial conflict or local history reflects a generally positive situation, with some areas of concern.

Coshocton has almost no racial diversity; census figures from 1990
indicate that it is 98% white. Minority residents appear to be largely Hispanic, specifically Mexican Americans. Local officials indicate no particular racial tensions, although they admitted that there may be some
isolated problems or concerns of which they were not aware.

Civic Culture

Local Traditions

Each city has its own unique feel produced by a number of impressions and discussions with individuals. The collective local traditions
include what groups have been historically influential, local images—
how officials and residents see themselves and the community—tolerance for conflict, views about appropriate levels of volunteerism, and so
on. All lead to a very complex character profile for each city. And although it is not possible to fully capture those profiles, it is useful to present a very condensed description of some of the main characteristics of
such local traditions.

Several things stand out in Romulus. First, historical development
patterns in the city play a large role in defining current development
and shaping how residents and officials see themselves. Romulus was
originally a rural farming community and still retains large tracts of un-
developed land. There are many residents in the community (although
their numbers are declining) whose families have lived there for generations, at least five generations in some cases. Indeed, the mayor is a fifth-
generation resident of the city. These "generational families" were identified by some of the respondents as a "fraternity" of long-time, largely
Polish residents who neither trust nor want to let "newcomers" into the

circle. Indeed, it was said that "there are folks here for 25 years that *think* they are old-timers," but they are not. Other respondents made reference to a "breakfast club" of long-term residents and other prominent interests. These ties are strengthened by the fact that many of these residents attend the same Catholic parish. Indeed, it appears that many city officials are members of the parish. Thus, there are some overlapping cleavages in the city covering ethnicity, religion, and length of residence.

To some extent, these "calling cards" have an important role in who attains power within the community. However, because of the declining numbers of long-term residents (currently about 5%), the historical relationships appear to be producing a balancing of development and maintenance interests. Although some of the long-term residents want to "keep the city like it was in the 1800s, not acknowledging that we are past the horse and buggy days," local officials and newer residents strongly feel the need for greater development. Furthermore, it is also important to remember that there is a significant minority population in Romulus, including a number of generational African American families. This all appears to lead to a practical situation where the interests of development and growth management are balanced and where development is accompanied by policies that attempt to ensure that local and minority residents will share in the benefits of development. Last, it was also noted by a local official that the presence of generational families and other long-term residents of Romulus promoted a sense of "ownership of the community." Although such a situation can lead to a closed political system, it can also provide the roots necessary for future community solidarity and commitment.

Three attributes stand out about Coshocton. First is the very high— perhaps even uncommonly high—level of regional cooperation in economic development that appears to exist. Second is the extensive and institutionalized role of businesses in not only economic development but the whole community—it is clearly part of the culture that businesses and business leaders will volunteer, be active in, and give back to the community. Third is a strong commitment to preservation of the community's historic and rural character. The first two traits will become evident in the discussion to follow. The third was clear not only in the case study but in simple observation of the community. Historic buildings are carefully preserved; maintaining the uniform historic character of the downtown is important. Residents clearly share this ethos in the up-keep of their homes and in the preservation of the general historic character. Perhaps because of its small size and rural history and nature, there is a strong sense that the private sector should be left to function as it deems best. But there is also the expectation that the private sector will participate actively and act in the best interests of the community and participate for the community good. This perception appears to play out effectively in strong volunteerism by the private sector, participation in and support of local schools (each school has been "adopted" by a business), and is translated into the use of private money for public ends, such as downtown infrastructure maintenance. There appears to be little political conflict in the city; cooperation at all levels (private/public, local/regional, Democratic/Republican) appears to be a strong part of the culture.

Locus of Power

Questions about locus of power for economic development in each community relate to how economic development is structured, who has primary control over decision making, and the balance of power between elected and administrative/appointed officials. It also incorporates the composition of the broader governing regime, including business and community input.

Everyone interviewed in the city of Romulus agreed that the mayor was the main locus of power for economic development decision making. As he put it, he and the director of planning and community development are the key decision makers, with the latter acting as filter or gatekeeper. Businesses or developers will typically contact the director, and the "live ones" are brought to the mayor. Although the mayor gives city council some credit for development initiatives, he also notes that he's sure of their reactions before he brings anything to them, clearly pointing to the real power locus. The city council member did not give council as much credit as the mayor, suggesting that the comment was as much a magnanimous or political statement than reality. There do appear to have been some cases in which the mayor requested a twelve-year tax abatement for a particular firm and council only approved a six-year abatement, but such situations do not seem to be common. The director of planning and development also pointed out that the mayor is a building contractor by profession and has long-standing ties to the local business community. The mayor is very much "hands-on" and is very visible in the community, permitting close contact with business interests quite apart from his department administrators.

Reactions were mixed regarding the "power" of other actors—some felt the planning commission had a role because they did not always approve the mayor's initiatives (usually, but not always). The development director indicated that the commission had nine "very active, very serious members." However, the commissioner interviewed indicated varying levels of expertise among the members: Some are very diligent and visit sites, whereas others do not really "understand the development process" and get "hung up" on tangential issues, such as retention-pond design and exterior brick color. Sometimes, he noted, the planning commission is "a barrier to development." The city contracts planning services with a private firm, and they have a role in development decisions to the extent that the commission typically supports their recommendations, and then, council usually approves. It is interesting to note that direct communication also occurs between members of the city council and the planning commission. Council members regularly attend commission meetings and speak directly with commissioners about their positions on policy.

In summary, the basic process for decision making in Romulus is that the director of planning and community development initially interacts with developers, but everything is then done in close conjunction with the mayor. The mayor brings initiatives to planning consultants, the planning commission typically recommends what the planners have suggested, and then the city council approves the recommendations of the commission. The mayor is pivotal at various points; he initiates development policies and projects, he communicates directly with members of the planning commission (or at least the member interviewed) prior to decision making, and he communicates directly with council members. "He comes to council prior to meetings, brings the issues, and works things out." Thus, it appears that the mayor does considerable informal legwork with various city actors to ensure that things go smoothly and, in the process, solidifies control over the development process.

The power structure for economic development is quite different in Coshocton; power is more diffuse and tends to be delegated to off-cycle organizations, typically, privately controlled and often at the regional or county level. There is no internal economic development department, and the current mayor has little role in development. The safety services director, who acts as a city manager, appears very aware of economic development activities, but primary authority for initiation and implementation lies with Jobs Plus, an external organization. This is a city/ county organization receiving funds from the city and county as well as the chamber of commerce and the Community Investment Corporation (CIC), which acts as a pass-through for the county funding, and all of these actors have representatives on the Jobs Plus board. Legally, Jobs Plus is an arm of the chamber; however, over two thirds of their budget comes from public sources. The director of Jobs Plus has been running the organization since its inception in 1993 and has a law degree with a sales background.

Although Jobs Plus seems to be the main institutional locus for economic development decisions, there are many other actors that have a role. The Tourist and Convention Bureau is active in promoting the city through marketing campaigns and in conducting special events; its efforts are supported by a local tourism tax (bed tax). The Town Center Association implements most of the downtown activities and programs, such as streetscape maintenance, business and marketing surveys, festivals, holiday lights, and so on. The CIC was created as a result of state legislation in 1963 authorizing nongovernmental entities to buy and sell property and make use of low-cost loans. Although they have been involved in some land acquisition and the development of an industrial park, they do not appear to be particularly aggressive or innovative in economic development more generally. The Coshocton Foundation is also active in local development. Currently run by a retired banker, it has had a significant role in the development of a large regional park with a state-of-the-art aquatic center. The Ohio Regional Development Corporation (ORDC), a privately held, areawide organization, primarily engages in grant writing and administration for constituent governments. Related to economic development, it has been involved in applications for and administration of CBDG, parks and recreation, infrastructure, housing assistance and rehabilitation, public safety, prison, drug prevention, and state capital improvement grants. As one county official noted, the head of Jobs Plus is the "salesman," and the head of ORDC is the "banker." The Central Ohio Rural Consortium has a major role, along with a multicounty Private Industry Council, in job training. All of the local and regional actors agreed that there is not a single initiator or power locus for economic development. Activities are shared, and all of the various actors appear to work well together.

It should be noted that this general culture of cooperation, private-sector involvement, and aversion to conflict can have an unanticipated down side. To put it gently, some local officials (both public and private) appear "past their prime." Some influential members of the various boards are retired owners of major businesses, and it appears that other actors have been loathe or unable to remove them. As a result, some of the organizations are not as active or innovative as other community leaders would like; the CIC was mentioned several times as an example of this. In short, there are great benefits of a local leadership that remains in the community and continues to be active and committed to volunteerism. However, this can also result in limited turnover to bring in new blood and ideas. Some of the economic development organizations in Coshocton seem to be suffering from this, perhaps reducing their effectiveness.

It should also be noted that local officials did indicate that there is some disagreement among the various actors and organizations in Coshocton, but this is kept outside the economic development realm. Furthermore, there are some that don't completely trust the director of the ORDC—the grant agency—and local officials provide differing views about how important he is in economic development. County officials say he's critical, although local actors outside his organization don't mention him much. It was suggested that there is general local distrust about grants—residents and business leaders would prefer no grants and a tax reduction from state/federal governments instead.

Role of Professionals Versus Elected Officials

Although the mayor of Romulus listens to the advice of and works closely with such professionals as the planning firm and the economic development director, it is always clear who is "in charge." The balance of power rests with elected rather than appointed officials. In Coshocton, the locus for economic development is much more fragmented and lies with the heads and boards of external, regional, or business organizations. Clearly, local elected officials have only a very minor role. "Professionals" run economic development in the city albeit external to the local government.

Business and Community Input

Citizen groups are clearly not part of the governing regime in Romulus. There is some citizen input to government, however, so it should not be concluded that citizens are passive and uninformed. Rather, they tend to use traditional formal channels for input, such as attending city council and planning commission hearings and writing letters or making phone calls. The city makes no particular efforts beyond this to solicit citizen opinion. Because of this, citizen input is not organized, and it reflects individuals concerned with a particular development project. And most of the concern has taken the form of opposition to proposed developments, particularly those that are perceived as being too dense. Such opposition is dealt with by "educating citizens" regarding why and how development benefits the city or through attempts to balance the needs of the developer by giving something back to the city (this will be discussed more fully later).

Business input takes place in quite a different manner in Romulus. Again, there are few institutionalized channels for business input, and the city does little to formally solicit business "opinion." The bulk of formal input appears to come through the various boards and commissions. Members of the TIFA, DDA and Brownfield Group have natural access to city officials. The chamber of commerce also invites the planning and community development director to attend meetings and keeps members informed of development initiatives in the city. Both small and large and local and nonlocal business representatives appear to be included on these boards. Board input includes support of local hiring requirements and oversight of the point system for awarding tax abatements. In other words, current businesses keep an eye on the incentives offered to prospective businesses.

More informally, the mayor travels the city regularly, stops and asks what is going on, speaks with members of the business community directly, and has contact with other businesspersons through his professional contracting work. Although citizens must make a positive effort to inform the city of their opinions, businesses have more direct contact through the mayor. It should also be noted that the mayor's "travels" around the city also benefit citizens and the community at large. For example, if he comes across anyone who needs something addressed by the city, he will act as "fixer" and put them in touch with the required parties. He also told a story about his involvement in a dispute with the county over its removal of rose bushes on a parcel of city-owned land near the airport. Seeing the "demolition" in progress, the mayor got out of his car and directly addressed the issue with the contractors doing the work. Very little escapes the mayor's notice in Romulus.

However, it is unlikely that such direct contacts permit access to all businesses and all businesses equally. Indeed, the mayor indicated that there is no formal or "organized" business pressure in the city nor is there a consistent set of developers that keep coming before the city or the planning commission. In short, although businesses and citizens have a "voice" in the city through different mechanisms, it does not appear that either group is a regular or institutionalized part of the governing regime. Instead, this is very much a mayor-run show.

Businesses have much more direct input in Coshocton, primarily through the various formal organizations active in economic development. In this manner, businesses are completely integrated into the decision-making structure. There is a separate Plaza Association for businesses located outside the downtown in the strip-shopping areas. The chamber of commerce primarily represents industrial firms (a historic tradition in the city). Retail businesses have direct power over downtown initiatives through their participation in the Town Center Association. Business leaders meet with prospective firms, marketing the city to both local and nonlocal interests. Members of the chamber of commerce sit on the boards of Jobs Plus and the CIC.

Like Romulus, there is little formal input by citizens in Coshocton, and residents appear to make less use of traditional options, such as planning commission or council hearings. Although there are always a couple of citizens ready to fight city hall, there has been little conflict over growth, zoning, tax abatements, and the like. This does not appear to be an environment where citizens regularly come to public hearings to express their views. Indeed, the fragmented structure of economic development functions and the private sector locus is not likely to enhance opportunities for citizen input. Such off-cycle arrangements often produce "invisible" policy making, which is sometimes the intent. It should also be noted that there is a relatively high level of "interlocking directorates" in Coshocton. Thus, although there are a number of different boards and organizations involved in different aspects of economic development, the same actors show up in board membership. For example, the Tax Incentives Board includes the safety services director, county commissioners, and three area school superintendents; the Jobs Plus Board includes the president of city council, county commissioners, and chamber members; the CIC board includes past prominent business leaders; the director of ORDC is also the head of the County Planning Commission and is on the Board of Health. The director of ORDC was even unwilling to identify the members of his board. Most local organizations, then, have common county and business representatives.

Regime Status

Based on the forgoing descriptions of locus of decision making and business and community input, what can be said about the nature of the governing regimes in Romulus and Coshocton? In Romulus, there basically is no regime, based on the regime criteria presented in Chapter 2. The business community is not sufficiently involved in governing and does not have any ongoing institutional presence. The mayor-dominated nature of the civic culture precludes the development of a broader governing regime. And because Romulus is a small city and politics are both familial and familiar, a mayor does not need to marshal other resources either to be elected or to govern. Coshocton, on the other hand, has institutionalized, stable roles for business leaders in decision making. The resources of the private sector are used in many ways both for social production—the ability to govern—and for more direct subsidization of the costs of services and infrastructure. Thus, Coshocton represents a developmental regime by virtue of its component parts, its participants. But as will become apparent when policies are discussed, the coherent policy agenda that results is not one traditionally predicted by the prototype developmental regime.

Intergovernmental Relations

All the actors are unified in Romulus about their almost fierce dislike of Wayne County. It is almost as if they were discussing the deeds of an "evil empire." The airport was described as a "tumor" in the community and a "walled prison." The owner and operator of the airport, Wayne County, does not fare much better. The situation with the airport seems designed to breed discontent and makes it difficult for the city and county to work cooperatively on almost any project, including economic development. If regional cooperation is going to take place here, it can not be centered at the county level. Complaints and concerns about the County are broad: tax dollars lost to the airport and ring land, the condemnation of 200 homes for airport development (in a city that needs more housing), poor information and communication flows, speculation on other land around the airport, and poor management of the airport generally leading to reduced development in the surrounding area. To be fair, local officials did note that one cooperative project with the County and other area communities, the development of a ring road, has gone well. The problems surrounding the airport also appear to affect relations with the federal government. Although federal relationships regarding CDBG funds are smooth, those related to the airport are not; local officials express concern over federal regulations regarding the ring land around the airport. It was also noted that the congressional representative has not done much for the city, manifested most directly by the fact that a neighboring city got a new post office, and Romulus did not.

Relations with the state and other downriver communities involved in the Downriver Community Conference (DCC) are almost uniformly positive, however. Thus, regional cooperation occurs; it simply does not take place at the county level. State representatives are perceived as working hard for the city, and returns have included a TIFA exemption to capture school taxes, cooperative visits to firms with representatives from the state Economic Development Corporation, state support of road projects, and state funding for brownfield revitalization. Through the DCC, Romulus cooperates with neighboring communities in lobbying state and federal officials, business attraction and retention efforts, and job training and search services.

Intergovernmental relations, particularly those between the city and county, are as good in Coshocton as they are contentious in Romulus. The city and county work together formally through several bodies, including Jobs Plus, and the city works with other communities through the ORDC. The city has consciously decided to work with the county on job training, and this appears to be going smoothly. Both local and regional officials appear in agreement that county and regional relations are very good, despite partisan differences (city officials are Democrat and county officials are Republican). Although local officials in Coshocton have very little interaction with the federal government (there is some interaction with the Federal Aviation Administration regarding the airport, but CBDG funds are administered through the ORCD), they did note that there have been some problems with the Army Corp of Engineers over the definition of wetlands: Apparently, a hole was dug in the industrial park to acquire fill dirt; when it filled with water, federal officials declared it a wetlands. Relations with state officials appear very positive. State programs are used for research and development, tax abatements, and job training, and city officials have direct contacts with state economic development officials.

Planning and Evaluation

Across the interviews in Romulus, a consistent picture emerged regarding planning for, and evaluation of, development policies and programs. There is little systematic or formal assessment. There is no formal economic development plan, although the 1989 Master Plan includes some development goals and objectives. The planning and community development director conducts his own "evaluations," which consist of determining what incentives other communities are offering firms and then ensuring that Romulus' package is competitive. Evaluation is interpreted as assessing the land costs and availability in the city and surrounding communities to be sure that the city is competitive in that regard as well. The mayor responded that formal evaluation is really unnecessary in the city; a great deal of development is occurring, so their policies must be "good." When specifically asked to assess the effectiveness of the city's economic development policies, the community development director indicated that they had been quite successful. He did note the confounding effects of the generally good economy, the availability of inexpensive land, and the mayor's connections in the business community. The development director pointed out that the need to measure development "success" was really quite new to the city because their economy has been expanding only recently. Absent formal evaluation, he was unable to distinguish the reasons for their success. And success was seen as increased investment as well as a "business friendly environment" and "positive perceptions of the city," relatively soft indicators. The planning commissioner noted that there is really no coherent plan or pattern for economic development in the city. Thus, what evaluation there is, is primarily geared toward ensuring that the city remains competitive, and as long as there is demand for development in the city, this is unlikely to change.

Although Coshocton also does not have an economic development plan (and not much of a master plan), a number of evaluations of various aspects of their economic development efforts are done. Given the largely rural nature of the area surrounding Coshocton, there is a great deal of historic opposition to planning, in general. Formal zoning in the city only began in 1962, a fact evident by the location of a mobile home park very close to city hall, for example. Residents in the rural areas do not want zoning and do not like to be told what they can do with their land. The city planning commission controls the city and exercises extraterritorial jurisdiction three miles beyond the city border. But beyond that, there is no planning nor any body to complain to if problems arise; the county can only control zoning within subdivisions. Evaluation is conducted by the separate, typically private, organizations that implement economic development policy. Jobs Plus assesses job creation or loss, whereas the Town Center Association surveys businesses about current and future needs, assesses space in the downtown, evaluates the best use of retail space, and had conducted a business retention survey. The CIC evaluates job figures as well as land use and business success in the industrial park, and the ORDC conducts evaluations mandated by federal and state grants. And although there is no overall coordinating agency for these evaluations, it is clear that they do not overlap. The various organizations appear to communicate well with each other and are very much aware of each other's activities.

Local officials' assessment of the success of economic development activities in Coshocton was quite positive, with the notable exception of the activities of the CIC. It appears that the industrial park, although full, does not have the uniformly desired industrial tenants (there is a large warehouse, for example, that employs few people), and the one building they developed on spec is still vacant. Others note that the CIC has performed poorly, is not aggressive enough in land acquisition, and gets too tied up in small legal issues, such as oil and gas rights. It also appears to be too passive and staid in its development approach, according to several local officials.

Views About the Role of the Government in the Economy

On the surface, there is a great deal of business-friendly rhetoric among local officials in Romulus. When asked about local policies or local views about business, they indicate that they are business friendly, or as the mayor said, "we just try to be sociable." However, underneath, there appears to be an orientation toward business that includes strong sensibilities toward balanced growth and balancing business and community needs. At the same time that they take a sociable stand toward business and are willing to grant incentives to businesses they really want, they also talk about the scale of developments, protecting green space, limiting truck traffic, expecting businesses to give back to the community in the form of donations to charity, and imposing claw-backs and hiring goals on tax abatements. Thus, whereas at times, the planning commission is "embarrassed" by how much the mayor and council are willing to give away to secure *desired* development, the incentives are not universal nor without some at least implicit "strings." Nor are they used indiscriminately for all types of development. The mayor clearly expressed the opinion that as a general rule, he does not like to spend public money on private development. Again, a balanced approach to the private sector seems to be the rule in Romulus.

There are much closer ties between public and private sectors in Coshocton; it is more difficult to distinguish the boundaries between the two, almost to the point that the public role vanishes. Indeed, economic development is mostly a private affair here. Local officials feel strongly that the private sector should be "left alone" to conduct business, and the city has only a very limited role in economic development. Although the streetscape development was supported by general obligation bonds, it is maintained with private funds. Local officials express the view that the private sector is the best judge of what it needs for training and development. In short, the culture is almost entirely one of hands off the private sector, with almost complete delegation of economic development responsibility to private organizations.

Entrepreneurialism

The overall approach to economic development in Romulus is traditional, with some notable exceptions. They do not appear to be particularly risky but rather employ typical strategies, such as tax abatements, TIFAs, business visitation, infrastructure development, and a variety of red-tape-reduction efforts. None of the financing or organizational arrangements are particularly novel. On the other hand, Romulus is one of the most active cities with respect to Type II policies, discussed more fully in the next section. They have been willing to explore hiring goals for businesses receiving abatements, use an abatement formula that includes an assessment of both the number and quality of new jobs, and pursue reparations from businesses that leave before the end of their tax abatement period. So although not particularly entrepreneurial, the city is innovative in its experimentation with Type II policies.

Coshocton is both similar and dissimilar in the level of entrepreneurialism. The economic development policies themselves are not particularly innovative nor unusual; traditional marketing, infrastructure, and downtown development activities predominate. However, unlike most cities, they too are experimenting with Type II policies, such as claw-backs and a tax abatement formula that includes consideration of the number and nature of prospective jobs. Coshocton differs from Romulus in *how* these policies are implemented. The almost exclusive reliance on the private sector for all aspects of economic development activity and the very limited use of public resources is relatively unique among cities in the data set. But whether this results from an entrepreneurial perspective about economic development or from a combination of local culture and limited public sector resources is questionable.

Goals and Visions

It is interesting to note that although there is little formal planning and evaluation in Romulus, all respondents pointed to similar things when asked about development goals for the city. Clearly, everyone is "on the same page," even if there is no formal script. Officials in Romulus agree on the following goals: increased retail/commercial development to provide shopping opportunities for local residents; increased residential uses, particularly on the moderate and higher end ("we need more roofs," several officials noted); industrial attraction with an emphasis beyond transportation in an effort to diversify the economic base; and office development. Officials are also very clear on what they don't want for the city: go-go bars, massage parlors, and more transportation development, particularly trucking firms. More housing was stressed emphatically as a goal as was the desire for shopping alternatives within the city. Although there is a good bit of developer interest in housing development in the city, these projects tend to involve manufactured homes—"houses on wheels"—thus, the desire for higher-end housing alternatives. It should also be mentioned that although local officials share the same development goals, there is some division in the community about the balance between growth and maintaining the nature of the community. Romulus is an old community with a number of multi-generational families, as noted before. Many of these individuals want to limit growth and preserve the rural nature of the city. This seems to be the impetus for much of the citizen attendance at planning commission and council meetings, and citizens have been successful at getting modifications to projects, requiring less density.

Local officials in Coshocton are also in agreement on goals. Although they want to expand the industrial base, they also want to preserve the rural nature of their community. They are very aware of the costs of large industrial development in terms of the increase in demand for local services as well as the impacts on quality of life more generally. As the director of Jobs Plus said, "I would resign and fight it if there were a movement to bring something like a Honda plant here. Five thousand new jobs would change the character of the area for the worse." Thus, officials see attraction of modestly sized industry as a goal along with diversifying the economic base. They want to avoid being tied to one or two large employers. In addition to diversifying the industrial base, local officials are also pursuing retail and commercial development. Specifically, they want to ensure that retail space continues to be available at reasonable rates and that the downtown is well integrated with the strip-shopping areas just outside it. More specifically, they want to develop a new industrial park on about fifty acres of land near the local airport. This land is currently part of the county, but Coshocton is hoping to annex it in the future.

ECONOMIC DEVELOPMENT
POLICIES IN ROMULUS AND COSHOCTON

It is useful to remember that one of the initial foci of this research was to examine cities that made extensive use of Type II economic development policies. Although the surveys indicated that all of the case study cities employed moderate efforts at Type II policies, it became clear in the case studies that, in some cases, the surveys were not completely accurate in this regard. As a methodological note, surveys were quite accurate in capturing all other kinds of economic development polices and programs. Thus, it could be the case that respondents sensed that saying they used Type II policies was the expected response and so overrated their actual efforts. At any rate, because of the particular interest in *why* cities employ Type II policies, they will be discussed separately from the general economic development policies pursued in each city.

Overall Policies

The economic development policies in Romulus are fairly traditional. The director of planning and community development identified six overall economic development programs: business attraction/ retention, tax abatements, brownfield redevelopment, a TIFA, a DDA, and expedited development processes. The mayor also noted that the city issued zoning waivers and had new ordinances to regulate growth. Under the business-attraction-and-retention program, the city works with the state jobs commission to visit all employers with over 100 employees. These visits are designed to help them identify job training funding; make them aware of local incentives, such as tax abatements; and develop relationships through which other needs can be identified and transmitted to local government. Although the city grants tax abatements, they use a point system in evaluating requests that considers the nature of the business, the number of jobs to be created (based on data presented by the firms), the percentage of local hires likely to occur, conformance with the master plan, and whether the firm in question has had a good reputation in other locations. The brownfield redevelopment program is a state-funded effort to clean and redevelop "dirty" sites and includes efforts to cooperate with the state Department of Environmental Quality to clean up and convert an old landfill to a golf course. About two thirds of the land area in the city is included in the TIFA, and the TIFA board also uses a point system for awarding incentives. Expedited development processes include efforts to reduce red tape, and the planning and community development staff act as ombudspersons for businesses to help them navigate the local system for zoning variances and offer other technical assistance in preparing applications going before the planning commission. This includes pre-planning committee meetings, where the development director discusses potential projects with commission members. Zoning waivers are typically granted in conjunction with highly desired development in the DDA. For example, the city has granted waivers for the number of required parking spaces in the downtown area. In other cases, the city is becoming more active in regulating growth. For example, greater attention is being given to tree ordinances, design requirements, sidewalk requirements even in industrial areas, and a preference for retention versus detention ponds, all to ensure that development is more pleasant and to enhance the long-run desirability of the city.

Although structured and implemented quite differently, the actual policies employed in Romulus and Coshocton are quite similar. Coshocton tends to use traditional types of economic development programs and strategies. They have an industrial park that is full (although one building is still vacant), and they are currently developing a second park. They give tax abatements, but here also a formula is used, and there is a Tax Incentive Board, including representatives of the school systems, that determines allocations. The city does not have a formal TIFA or DDA; however, development activities in the downtown area are similar to most cities, including a very attractive streetscape. The

difference in Coshocton is that all downtown association activity is conducted through completely voluntary private-sector organizations
funded through member dues and a property owners assessment. The
downtown associations have been active in events in addition to the
streetscape and are now moving into storefront development, business
attraction efforts, and education on building restoration and upkeep.
All the typical activities of a DDA are occurring here, though organized
on a private basis. The Community Investment Corporation is autho-
rized by Ohio law to buy, sell, and accept land for redevelopment projects. This organization developed the industrial park but has also engaged in some speculative development of buildings. The city is also
active in job training initiatives, although most are implemented at the
county level through the Central Ohio Rural Consortium. Such efforts
include job training, welfare-to-work programs, a one-stop employment and training resource shop, preemployment training, and summer internships for at-risk youth. The city explicitly has decided to stay
out of training and participates in regional efforts.

Type II Policies

Romulus clearly is willing to at least experiment with Type II policies. Although they do not have local or minority hiring *requirements,* for
example, they do have "targets" that are part of the formula for granting
tax abatements (typically, the goal is 20% resident hires). Most local officials indicated that hiring *requirements* were simply not feasible due to
labor market shortages in the area, particularly for high-skill jobs, and
may perhaps even be illegal. It should be noted, however, that absent
any systematic evaluation system, local officials have no way of determining if firms have met hiring targets. Even the presence of an abatement formula, however, is relatively unique, because many cities tend
to offer tax relief indiscriminately or whenever asked. The city also
"suggests" that firms use local venders in purchasing decisions. And although not specifically a Type II policy, the city has also recently experimented with more direct roles in hiring new workers. For at least one
business, city officials conducted the job screening and application
process at city hall.

In addition to hiring and purchasing targets, the city also requires
firms to return their tax abatement savings to the city if they relocate be-

fore the end of the abatement period. As the mayor noted, one prominent firm had to "give the city a big check." The mayor also noted that if
you give something to a firm, it just makes simple fiscal sense to ensure
that the city is going to benefit in some way. In short, to him, it is just
good business sense to get something back for public money spent and
to attempt to add some performance guarantees. It does not appear that
there is strong public pressure for these kinds of Type II policies, although the mayor notes that there are times when the city council is
looking to limit development. Instead, much of the impetus for Type II
policies appears to be coming from the mayor, a long-time businessman, who just seems to feel that such policies are a prudent investment
move for the city. There also appears to be little business resistance to
the Type II efforts, because, as the mayor says, "they understand that
they are asking for something from the city."

Coshocton also evidences a relatively high emphasis on Type II policies. As in Romulus, they feel that requiring firms to hire local workers
in return for tax abatements would be "illegal." However, their abatement formula includes consideration of whether the prospective jobs
pay a living wage, whether the company is stable, and how likely it is
that the company will remain in the community. Claw-backs have just
recently been used: Firms have to pay reparations to the city if they
leave before the abatement or contractual period ends. As local officials
say, the company "will have to make the amends" in Coshocton. And although not specifically a Type II policy, the city is very aware that quality-of-life issues are an important economic development tool. "Not
only do you sell land and infrastructure, you're selling the community,"
said one local official. To this end, they are very aware of such issues as
the quality of their schools, low crime rates, good services, and low
housing prices, and they market these attributes.

Coshocton County is also involved in the use of Type II policies. For
example, a county tax abatement was granted for the development of a
new hotel in Coshocton, but local contractors and suppliers had to have
a chance to bid on the project and be involved in development. The
county also gave a tax abatement to a small railroad that runs through
the area and were then able to pressure the firm into improving the
safety of eleven crossings. It was made clear that in return for the abatement, they were expected to be "good citizens."

CULTURE, PROCESS, AND POLICY

A number of questions were posed at the beginning of this chapter:

Do higher levels of fiscal stress lead to an emphasis on external organizations?

To what extent are perceptions of intercity competition for development associated with an off-cycle locus?

Do different kinds of economic development policies result when the locus of power rests with an external, often business-led, body?

Are there distinctly different civic cultures in Romulus and Coshocton?

Do the different cultures lead to substantially different approaches to, or processes for, economic development?

Do the different civic cultures lead to different kinds of economic development policies?

These questions implicitly focus attention on three central variables. First, cities vary in their local civic culture. That variation, then, affects both how economic development is conducted and what policies result (Table 7.1 provides a summary of these differences). Very clear differences are evident in the civic culture of Romulus and Coshocton as well as in how they approach economic development, how decision making is structured, and in the locus of power for development decisions. There are more subtle differences in what they are doing—that is, the economic development policies that result.

The Environment

Romulus and Coshocton have almost identical residential-need profiles; both are moderately stressed economically. Although both are relatively small cities, the former is twice as large. Romulus is a formerly rural area, rapidly losing that basic character, and is part of a large metropolitan area. Coshocton is a relatively isolated small city in a rural area, and this is unlikely to change. Officials in Romulus perceive little competition from other cities, primarily because they have low-cost vacant land, and others in the area do not. Coshocton feels in strong competition with other cities in the area for exactly that reason: They

TABLE 7.1   Comparison of Romulus and Coshocton: Environment, Culture, and Policies

Romulus	Coshocton
Environment	
Moderate residential need	Moderate residential need
Low perceived competition	High perceived competition
Formal structure: strong mayor, at-large, nonpartisan	Formal structure: strong mayor, combination, partisan
Actual structure: strong mayor, partisan	Actual structure: city administrator, nonpartisan
Racial diversity	Racially homogeneous
Culture	
Contentious politics	Little politics
Old-timers versus pro-growth	Consensus on culture maintenance
Informal business input	Institutional business input
Few avenues for citizens but moderate input	Few avenues for citizens and low input
Mayor locus of power	External locus of power
Public-sector locus	Private-sector locus
Very negative relations with county	Very cooperative relations with county
Locus of power concentrated	Locus of power dispersed
Little business volunteerism	High levels of business volunteerism
Low planning, low evaluation	Low planning, high evaluation
No governing regime	Development regime
Policies	
Little marketing	High marketing
No industrial parks	Industrial parks
Infrastructure development	Infrastructure development
Tax abatement with formula	Tax abatement with formula
DDA	Voluntary downtown association
TIFA	No TIFA
Streetscape	Streetscape
Little tourism development	Strong tourism efforts—tourist tax
Business visitation	Business needs surveys
Hiring goals	No explicit goals
Claw-backs	Just starting claw-backs
Regional training	County training
Brownfield redevelopment	No brownfield redevelopment
Zoning variances	Little zoning policy

have little available land within the city for "easy" development. The governmental structure of Romulus is strong mayor and nonpartisan; actual operating patterns are strong mayor but with visible partisan voting patterns. Coshocton has a strong-mayor form of government with partisan elections, but in reality, the city operates much like a city administrator system, and partisan differences are largely unimportant.

The Culture

The overall culture of Romulus can be summarized as follows:

A strong-mayor locus of control

Relatively high levels of political contention

The presence of an "old-timers" clique that opposes development within a general framework of support for development

Informal, face-to-face political interaction

City both supports and regulates business

Some regional cooperation but extremely contentious relations with the county

Informal business input into the development process

Little effort on the part of the city to increase avenues for citizen input, but formal methods are actively used

Little planning and evaluation of economic development efforts

Primary economic development goals are housing, retail, and base diversification

The culture in Coshocton is quite different:

Strong emphasis on private-sector independence

Low levels of political conflict

Strong regional and county cooperation

Consensus to maintain small-town character and limit growth

Little to no public role in private development

Off-cycle/private locus of development decision making

Many institutionalized avenues for business input

Few avenues for citizen input and little use of the formal processes available

Little planning but relatively extensive evaluation of economic development policies

Primary economic development goals are industrial expansion while preserving the small-town nature of the community

The Policies

Economic development policies are fairly traditional in Romulus
and primarily include infrastructure provision; business retention; zoning variances; abatement formula, including hiring goals; DDA; TIFA;
streetscape, and training at the regional level. Type II policies include
hiring goals and claw-backs. Policies in Coshocton include marketing,
industrial parks, infrastructure provision, tourism promotion, abatements with formula, streetscape, regional training programs, and business surveys. Type II policies are present in the very recent claw-backs
and an expectation that business will give back to the community.

SUMMARY

The questions posed at the beginning of this section can now be
addressed based on consideration of the essential traits summarized in
Table 7.1. First, higher levels of fiscal stress do not appear to lead to use
of external organizations. Stress may be a necessary but insufficient
condition for the development of off-cycle decision making for economic development. Perceptions of competition are higher in Coshocton,
however, suggesting that such environmental stress may have more of
an effect than residential need on the structure of local decision making.
The residential-need profiles in Romulus and Coshocton are basically
identical, yet processes for development decisions are very different. It
appears that the external locus of control of economic development in
Coshocton results from *cultural* factors. The mayor in Coshocton at the
time of the case study was elderly and did not appear to have a significant leadership role in economic development. Although this could be
posed as an explanation of the off-cycle structure, this would be a mis-
take. The idiosyncratic situation with the current mayor was temporary,
and the external structure of economic development predated him by at
least six years. Rather, the civic culture of business volunteerism and a
hands-off stance toward the private sector predisposes Coshocton to external, private economic development decision-making structures. In

short, it is the culture, not the economy, that sets the parameters for both decision-making structure and locus of control. And although other environmental variables are different in the two cities, particularly racial diversity and perceived intercity competition, they appear to have little visible impact on either how decisions are made or the policies ultimately pursued.

Second, there are distinctly different civic cultures in the two cities. The two cultures are different in several key ways: internal versus external placement of economic development responsibilities, a relatively activist versus a laissez-faire posture by local government toward the private sector; mayoral versus private sector locus of power, concentrated versus dispersed power structure, informal versus institutionalized business input, and moderate contention over growth versus agreement on local-character maintenance (with Romulus and Coshocton portrayed respectively). Last, Coshocton has a governing regime—developmental—whereas Romulus does not.

These different cultures appear to produce different economic development processes. Economic development decisions in Romulus are tightly controlled by the mayor, and little is left to chance. Businesses have informal input if they have contact with the mayor—citizens, only if they attend public meetings or engage in contacting behavior. Decisions are made with little formal planning or evaluation; rather, they are based on what the mayor considers to make good business sense for the city. Economic development in Coshocton is implemented by a variety of external bodies, both local and regional. Authority is dispersed with little public-sector involvement. Many actors have a role in economic development, but the business community is prominent because of institutional memberships in many of the important organizations. Although there is little history or acceptance of formal planning, each group involved in development evaluates their own activities. Resources brought to the table tend to come from state or private sources.

The role of business in economic development in Coshocton raises an important concern about causality, relating back to the pivotal role of civic culture. The path models in Chapter 5 suggest that off-cycle economic development structures will lead to or enhance business input into the decision-making process. But correlation is not causation. Do the off-cycle structures facilitate business input, or are off-cycle structures created in communities where business influence is already high?

Although there is no way to unpack the causal links in multiple regression, the case studies are another matter. In Coshocton, it seems clear that the local culture of private-sector independence and business activism predated the economic development decision-making structures. Hence, a structure was chosen to match the existing cultural milieu. It would have run counter to the local civic culture to have a strong governmental role in economic development, and the aversion to conflictual or partisan politics maintains the fragmented, external, and largely private structure.

Last, does internal versus external locus for economic development make a difference in policy? Do the different cultures in the two cities produce different policy choices? The answer to this last question would be a qualified yes. There are some modest differences in development policy in the two cities. Romulus does not actively market the city nor does it have an industrial park, activities common in most cities. They use other common tools, however, such as a DDA and infrastructure development. What is particularly unique about Romulus is the extent of Type II policies. Although Coshocton appears to employ a broader and more traditional array of development strategies, they do not have a formal DDA. All of the customary activities of a DDA are conducted through the voluntary business associations. They make less use of Type II policies and are just recently experimenting with clawback provisions. Ensuring that businesses pay back to the community is more a matter of cultural expectation than a guarantee codified informal policy. In short, whereas the internal, mayor-led development efforts in Romulus may be more limited in scope, they are more creative in their experimentation with Type II policies. The business-led external bodies in Coshocton are more active across the board in economic development, although they tend to focus on relatively traditional activities. Clearly, more is done with less public effort and expense in Coshocton.

This last issue is interesting and brings the focus back to the role of regimes in local governance. Several points are important. First, the developmental regime in Coshocton does not lead to policies that benefit businesses to the exclusion of the community at large. The civic culture in Coshocton, expecting businesses to be good local citizens, leads to private-sector subsidization of public services and infrastructure with claw-backs placed on firms that don't end up being good enough citi-

zens. This is not what the theory of development regimes would predict. This brings up the most critical point: Regime analysis without
consideration of the larger civic culture is simply incomplete. Romulus
doesn't have a regime; indeed, a regime is not really necessary. Exploration of civic cultures provides an understanding of communities that
do not have regimes. The development regime in Coshocton does not
have the policy agenda normally associated with a development regime
due to the city's particular civic culture. How the issue of regime plays
out in the other case cities and will be explored explicitly in the succeeding chapters.

What are the critical forces that led these cities to do what they do and
structure how they do it? In Romulus, the mayor is strong, both structurally and as an individual, affecting how decisions are made as well as
the level of Type II policies employed. Government structure as well as
individual actors are important. The extent of land availability—an environmental feature—affects economic growth prospects as well as
what is possible as far as economic development. However, the relatively contentious politics, often partisan despite the putative
nonpartisanship, and the need to balance old-timer and growth interests are the cultural forces or "necessary conditions" that mediate between structure, the economy, and local development policies. The
Type II policies in particular (hiring goals, abatement formula, claw-
backs, and growth management policies) reflect the cultural imperatives in Romulus.

In Coshocton, the economy and the competitive pressures, although
more strongly felt than in Romulus, appear to have had little impact on
either process or policy. The environmental factor—limited land available for development—constrains to an extent what is possible in economic development or, more to the point, the ease with which development can occur. Thus, "land-poor" Coshocton is still planning a second
industrial park, though it will require annexation. The environment
may add more steps or make things harder, but again, it is not a sufficient explanation of either process or outcome. The critical *determinants*
of locus of control, decision-making processes, and economic development policies are the business volunteer ethic, a private-sector emphasis, regional collaboration, nonpartisan cooperation (again in a partisan
environment), and consensus on maintaining a shared community vision. These are all civic culture variables.

Although these cases clearly suggest that culture is more important than economics or structure in framing economic development process and policy, they also raise more questions for further analysis. Is the presence of a strong, political chief executive a prerequisite for Type II policies? Are externally driven private organizations more likely to emphasize evaluation and pursue a broader array of development activities? Does a culture of business volunteerism always produce benefits for the larger community? When citizens have more input, do different policies result? These questions will be addressed in the case studies to come.

NOTE

1. Although many of the findings from the interviews are attributed to specific actors, background information and other descriptive data are not always identified by source. It is useful, then, to indicate the specific actors interviewed in each community. In Romulus, the following actors were interviewed: director of planning and community development (at several different times), the mayor, a member of the Planning Commission, and a city council member who is also the deputy mayor. In Coshocton, the following were interviewed: mayor, safety service director, director of Jobs Plus, director of the Town Center Association, chair of the Coshocton County Commission, and the director of the Ohio Regional Development Corporation.

CHAPTER 8

THE INCLUSIVE CASES

Oakville and Fairborn

Oakville bills itself as the "biggest small town" in the province of Ontario. With a 1999 population of 132,000 and its retention of "town" status, that certainly appears to be true. As an upscale suburb of Toronto, Oakville has attempted to slow development through complex zoning and land use processes and policies and limited public provision of infrastructure. And true to its small-town image, the political system is open to all comers, citizens and business leaders alike. Recently, an increasing desire for a more diversified tax base, including "clean industry," has created cross-pressures with the historic no-growth stance. To date, relations between the city council that primarily sets economic development policy and the newly formed external public/private body that implements it have been smooth. But it is possible that future pro-growth and no-growth battles will play out between these bodies.

Fairborn, Ohio, is home to both Wright State University and Wright-Patterson Air Force Base. This creates a highly transient population best illustrated by the city's 50% rental housing stock. Voters have not approved a millage increase or bond issue in years. Although development of affordable housing and moving renters to ownership are goals in the city's long-range plan, residents have risen in opposition to a planned housing development. The long-term city manager's efforts to increase citizen participation in Fairborn may be beginning to bear some fruit, but

NIMBY (not in my back yard) opposition in the community may well be getting in the way of building on the military and high-tech base that local administrative officials desire.

            This chapter focuses on the two cities that have the most politically inclusive systems—Oakville, Ontario, and Fairborn, Ohio. The primary characteristics of these cities is that decision-making processes are open to a variety of interests in the community, citizens as well as businesses. As a result, politics tend to be somewhat conflictual, characterized by a greater amount of input, debate, and concern with accommodating multiple interests. As the cluster analysis indicated, there are three types of inclusive cities within the data set: (a) those with completely reformed governmental structures, (b) economically robust cities with mixed governing structures, and (c) more fiscally stressed cities with mixed structures. Oakville represents cities that have a mix of reformed and unreformed structural features and healthy economies, whereas Fairborn has a reformed structure. Among the case cities, Fairborn represents a moderate level of economic stress.

There are some differences between the types of inclusive cities suggested by the cluster analysis presented in Chapter 6. For example, inclusive reformed cities tend to have moderate levels of residential need and lower levels of economic growth, both certainly the case in Fairborn. Planning and evaluation appeared to be relatively low in such cities and an emphasis was placed on Type II and growth management goals. The latter may be the result of recent drops in unemployment in these cities, signaling at least some economic growth. In contrast, the healthy inclusive cities have very strong economies. Oakville is a good example of this because it has one of the fastest growing economies among the case cities. Cities in this cluster also had higher levels of planning and evaluation and, not surprisingly, greater resources devoted to economic development. These cities are most likely to have ward-based council structures—also the case in Oakville. Economic development tends to be the responsibility of independent departments and even given the politically inclusive atmosphere, professional bureaucrats have a major decision-making role.

The correlation and regression models in Chapter 5 also point to some important relationships between citizen and business input and other process and policy variables. Again, because the main trait of inclusive cities is the high level of input opportunities for both businesses and citizens, it is useful to highlight other variables correlated with input. For example, higher levels of business input are associated with more loan and marketing activity. Business input is also associated with a greater emphasis on alternative development goals, whereas more citizen input is related to a focus on Type II goals. Citizen input appears to be related to greater resources devoted to economic development. Last, the fact that business and citizen input mechanisms are positively related clearly demonstrates the existence of politically inclusive cities where a diversity of groups and interests have input into decision-making processes.

The reformed structures present in one cluster of inclusive cities are related to focused Type II policies and independent economic development departments. The healthy economies and ward-based council, present in Oakville, are associated with greater loan activity, fewer financial incentives, and less of a tendency to vest economic development authority in an independent, in-house organization.

How different, then, are cities with politically inclusive systems? Do Fairborn and Oakville conform to the traits indicated in the foregoing analyses? Are there other cultural forces present that distinguish between process and policy in inclusive cities? Last, how important are the differing economic profiles of the two types of inclusive cities?

THE CIVIC CULTURES OF OAKVILLE AND FAIRBORN

The Environment of Local Economic Development

The brief city summaries in Chapter 6 indicated that the economies of Oakville and Fairborn are rather different, as are the sizes. Oakville is the largest case city, with a 1991 population of 114,840. Average income was $77,253, unemployment at 6%, and poverty at 5%, according to the 1991 census. Fairborn, on the other hand, had a 1990 population of 31,300, average income of $13,053, unemployment at 7%, and 15% of the population in poverty. Oakville has been experiencing strong population growth and demand for development. Poverty and unemployment have been low and steady. Fairborn's population is basically stable, and although unemployment dropped from 11% in 1980, poverty increased from 12%. Thus, the cities are also different in their growth trajectory, with Oakville booming and Fairborn basically stable with recent modest growth, according to the case study interviews.[1] Obviously, given this and the size disparity, the two cities have very different economic bases, as described in the sections to follow.

The Oakville Economy

The economy in Oakville and the surrounding region is extremely healthy. As one Town publication notes, "Oakville is now one of the fastest growing commercial and industrial hot spots in southern Ontario." Thus, growth management and base diversification concerns outweigh any efforts to generate or attract development. The Town of Oakville is home to over 4,000 employers with a labor force of over 70,000 and at least 200 corporate headquarters. Significant employment clusters include automotive, knowledge-based, business service, aerospace, and pharmaceutical sectors. The largest employers in the city reflect this mix of sectors and include Ford Motor Company of Canada, Sheridan College, the Regional Municipality of Halton, Halton Healthcare Services, Lear Corporation, the Town of Oakville, Menasco Aerospace, Halton Regional Police Service, Canada Loyal Insurance, General Electric Canada, Procor Limited, and TDL Group. In short, the economic base of the town is healthy, growing, and diverse. Construction activity also manifests this fact. According to Town reports, record levels of new industrial and commercial construction took place during 1998; total building permit value was over $400 million (CD), a 21% increase, and new industrial construction was up 22%. Again, the emphasis on growth management is not surprising.

Juxtaposed with this significant growth is the Town's "image." As the 1999 Community Profile notes, "The Town of Oakville provides all the advantages of a well-serviced urban center, yet prides itself on having small town ambiance." At the core of the town in the downtown area are many nineteenth-century buildings, hearkening back to the town's founding in 1827, that house a variety of shops, services, and restaurants. The downtown is lovely and clearly identifiable, with a streetscape that includes period lighting, banners, and brick paving.

The shops are diverse and primarily upscale. The desirability of the downtown area also contributes to tourist activity in the town. Tourism is a $50 million industry in Oakville, and primary attractions include the town's proximity to Toronto as well as local shopping, parks, two natural harbors on Lake Ontario, golfing, and a variety of festivals, theaters, and galleries.

This mixture of high-tech industrial development and business headquarters with the small-town "vision" and tendency for the community to be viewed as a "bedroom community" for Toronto (daily out-migration is 15,000 workers), both in perception and fact, leads to interesting cross-pressures for economic development professionals, which will be discussed more later. The "conflict" between the location and economic growth of the town and its historic and persisting image is at the root of many aspects of both policy and process in this community.

Housing near the downtown and on the Lake Ontario waterfront is also diverse, high end, and very attractive. Homes are nestled in and around the lake, with many historic houses mixing in with newer, more contemporary structures. The mix of styles "works" aesthetically. The most desirable housing in the town lies closer to the downtown area and by extension, the lake. Housing moving away from the downtown area includes a traditional mix of newer ranch homes, suburban "mansions," and multifamily housing. There are no low-income areas in the town, but there are housing options for blue-collar workers along with some rural housing that is dispersed (25% of all housing development must be "affordable" by law). However, respondents indicated that there are different residential interests in the town based on geographic location; the older downtown area—old Oakville—where the primary concern is growth limitation, the newer northern area—uptown—"where the newcomers live" and growth is more acceptable, and areas slated for possible development beyond uptown. It is expected that the completion of a new toll road (an extension of highway 407) to be completed in 2001 will put additional growth pressure on these more "remote" areas.

The Fairborn Economy

With a 1990 population of 31,000, Fairborn is considerably smaller than Oakville. Of the nine cities examined, Fairborn is in the middle on

most demographic indicators. It has relatively moderate unemployment (7%) and average income levels ($13,053). Only when it comes to
poverty levels is it near the top, with 15% of its residents in poverty. Two
economic features stand out in Fairborn. Wright-Patterson Air Force
Base, with over 32,000 civilian and military employees, is located just
outside the city limits in the township. Wright State University, with
17,000 students, is located within the city. Thus, among the residents of
Fairborn are many college students with typically low incomes and en-
listed military personnel (officers with higher incomes tend to live in
the surrounding townships). Poverty figures are likely inflated due particularly to the high student population. Over 50% of the housing in
Fairborn is rental property. Thus, the city houses two major employers
with relatively transient residents/workers. Local officials also noted
that the city had recently annexed some very-low-income, relatively
rural areas that have affected the city's overall poverty levels. The economy has been on the up-swing in recent years, however, with both single family and business growth. The public works director said that he
had been with the city during "austere" times and that the current situation is very good. Census figures support this view; although poverty has been increasing, unemployment dropped from 11% to 7% between 1980 and 1990, and average incomes rose by $3,000 over the same
period.

Other major employers in the city include Handyman Home Centers
(headquarters, distribution, and outlets), Miami Valley Publishing
(printing), Southwestern Portland Cement, Ali Industries, and Stadco
automatics. Overall, the economic base represents a mix of some high-
tech development tied to the base and university, distribution- and
transportation-related firms (due to the city's location on several major
highways), and heavy industry. As their publicity materials note,
Dayton/Fairborn is the nation's tenth largest "90-minute" land market
(more than 5.6 million people live within a 90-minute commute radius)
and the largest "second-morning" land service area (area that can be
reached by truck in a day and a half). In summary, Fairborn is an older,
inner-ring suburb of Dayton. It has a fairly diversified economy but is
uniquely affected by the location of the university and the Air Force
base.

Fairborn has a distinct downtown area that distinguishes it from the
newer Dayton suburbs, such as Kettering, to be discussed in Chapter 9.

Because it has just been designated by the federal government as a "central city," Fairborn has only recently become eligible for CDBG funds that could be used for downtown development. They are currently working on a downtown strategy but to this point have had limited funds to invest. Visually, the downtown presents a rather mixed picture. On the one hand, it has a clearly identifiable downtown with a mix of older and newer buildings. Banners further delineate the area. There are historic homes located near the downtown, and although mostly small, they are nice. There are a few restaurants and a modest variety of shopping opportunities and services. On the other hand, there is also a large and unmistakably vacant cement plant located right outside the central business district. There are also a number of "low-rent" motels, tattoo parlors, and the like, that presumably serve a military clientele. Fairborn is also fairly well known in the area for a number of costume/novelty stores located in the downtown. These, too, are a dual-edged sword. The city capitalizes on these with a marketing emphasis at Halloween; they hold a parade, for example. Yet having several costume shops in a small downtown lends a somewhat odd flavor to the area. The bottom line is that there is a great deal of potential to the downtown area, but there are particular distractions, and the full potential is not yet realized.

As noted in Chapter 6, Fairborn is actually composed of two historically separate towns, Osborn and Fairfield. The houses from Osborn were moved next to Fairfield in 1922 when the two towns were separated by just one street; they were joined in 1950, creating the only city of Fairborn in the country (according to local promotional materials). Many of the homes moved from Osborn lie just outside the central business district. These are varied, and many are very quaint. However, upkeep is variable, again likely due to the high proportion of rental housing. Beyond the downtown, the city has a variety of housing options, from modest subdivisions to some higher-end housing (over $170,000) on the township borders.

Near Wright State University, there is a good bit of new hotel/restaurant/strip-mall development, and the area is prosperous. Closer to the downtown, however, there are several strip malls with obvious vacancies. Fairborn's marketing materials characterize the city as having "small-town flavor, country air, and metropolitan zest." This is actually quite an accurate characterization. It is clearly an inner-ring suburb of Dayton, yet it has its own employment base. The older downtown and downtown housing do give it a small-town feel. Last, like many urban areas, the city boundaries meet up with township areas that still maintain some rural flavor although this appears to be rapidly disappearing. Beaver Creek, in particular—a contiguous township—is known for its high-end housing, shopping mall, and many high-tech industrial parks.

A final important point about the general economy of Fairborn relates to the issue of millages. This city relies more on income than property tax and, with the large number of renters and older residents (the "free-lunch bunch," as one official characterized them), has been unable to pass a millage since 1991, particularly a school millage (the city income tax is 1% with an additional .5% school income tax). One respondent indicated that it has been twenty years since the city was able to pass a dedicated tax levy. This revenue "stress" has led to problems funding both school and infrastructure that have affected the city's image both among its residents and in the Dayton area more generally. Thus, although the city promotes the low tax rate as a benefit to potential businesses, that too cuts in two directions. Costs but also service levels are low. This has several effects on economic development that will be discussed in later sections.

Local Government Structures and Politics

The governmental structures of the two cities differ somewhat. Oakville has a weak town manager, with nonpartisan but ward-based elections. Hence, it represents a mixture of reformed elements. Fairborn, on the other hand, is fully reformed: city manager, nonpartisan, and at-large elections. This clearly suggests that there is no one structure that is likely to lead to the inclusion of a variety of interests in decision making. Reformed cities can be just as inclusive as unreformed—the critical difference is the history of how things are done and cultural expectations regarding the relationship between interests and the city. This may have much to say about the conflicting findings of the government reform literature that have indicated both reformed and unreformed cities as more responsive. Although the governmental structures in the two cities in the previous chapter did not necessarily function as expected on paper, Fairborn operates in a basically reformed manner, and the wards in Oakville have geographic impacts on the decision-making process. In these cases, the formal and informal structures match.

Politics in Oakville appear to be fairly unstable, though not in a negative sense. Council members and mayors have changed in recent years, and these changes have affected the development stance of the town. And it seems likely that further electoral changes could change policy in different directions. It might be safe to say that Oakville is in a period of flux reflecting the difference of opinion between growth and anti-growth interests. The new faces on council have tended to result from retirements rather than defeats, yet the pattern has been for anti-growth members to be replaced by pro-growth ones. The majority of the council is now pro-growth, although there is still a consensus that they want to preserve the small-town image.

Town elections are nonpartisan, and there are "no overt party affiliations" among local officials. The conflicts that are clearly present revolve around the extent and nature of growth, not partisan politics. The ward-based elections come into play here. For example, there was strong residential opposition to the proposed expansion of a Gillette warehouse located near a residential area. There was concern over the likely increase in truck traffic, and the expansion was "killed" by council, based primarily on the votes of the council members coming from the two affected wards. The ward system also seems to be operating in a current conflict over the possible expansion of the local mall, with the proximate ward representatives predictably opposing it.

The town manager has been in office for almost fifteen years, providing leadership continuity. However, he is somewhat limited in his powers due to the decentralized nature of the administrative structure. Operations are departmentalized, with the heads of operations, planning, finance, and corporate/administrative services reporting to the manager. Two deputy managers, one for administration and one for operations, also report to the manager. The current manager tends to focus primarily on financial issues ("he's a finance person"), whereas policy leadership comes from the mayor (elected independently and at-large) and council. Indeed, it was noted that the mayor is a very strong leader with a consensus style of operation.

The current mayor has been in office for about twelve years. She is pro-growth and replaced a strongly anti-growth mayor. Council also reflects a pro-growth majority. It should be made clear at this point that "pro-growth" in Oakville does not necessarily mean the same thing as it does in many other communities, a point that will be clarified later. Suffice it to say that pro-growth, in at least one case, meant zoning land for industrial purposes—not buying it, developing it, or selling it—just changing the zoning to *allow* it. Growth promotion in Oakville is defined in a very "limited" context. This is a good example of the adage that "everything is relative."

As noted at the outset of this section, the governmental structure of Fairborn is fully reformed, with nonpartisan and at-large council elections and a city manager. Economic development is conducted in-house with primary responsibility vested in a community development department that handles economic development, building and zoning, and planning. The assistant city manager is responsible for support services; the head of community development reports directly to the manager.

Political conflict is difficult to assess in Fairborn based on turnover in elected positions. Both the mayor and council are term limited, so the community has a history of periodic changes among elected officials. The term limits were adopted in 1971, long before they become popular across the country, and prior to that time, there tended to be just a very few long-term mayors. It appears that many elected officials were formerly on the planning board, and at least one current member was planning a run for mayor. Although the mayor is independently elected, the position is clearly part-time and ceremonial: the mayor is paid $3,000 a year by the city. The current mayor characterizes his job as a "citizen volunteer."

Professional staff in the city appear fairly stable. The city manager has been in that position since 1985 and prior to that was assistant city manager and assistant finance director. In all, he has been with the city of Fairborn for twenty-five years. The community development director is newer, serving in that capacity for three years. The public works director has been with the city for twenty years. Overall, it appears that the "politics" of Fairborn are more stable than in Oakville. There are no obvious factions with different views about the direction of the city (pro-growth versus anti-growth, for example). Although there is regular turnover among elected officials, that is primarily due to term limits rather than differences on substantive issues. Professional staff maintain continuity. It should be noted that stable electoral politics does not mean that there are no contentious issues in Fairborn, it is just that they do not appear to play out in the electoral arena. Individual development projects have caused a good deal of controversy, and those will be discussed shortly.

Intercity Competition for Development

Competition is perceived rather differently in the two communities. The perceptions of competition differ *within* Oakville itself, depending on which side of the growth debate a particular individual is on. All of the respondents agreed that there are no feelings of residential competition. Oakville is growing so rapidly and developers are so interested in residential development that there is general consensus that they have no competition in that area. Indeed, most feel that residential growth needs to be limited. When it comes to commercial/industrial competition, the differences appear. Those officials interested in expanding, particularly in industrial development, feel that they are in competition with Missassagua, Burlington, and Milton in the Toronto area and regionally with cities like Buffalo and "in reality" all over North America. Atlanta was even mentioned as being in competition with the town by the executive of the chamber of commerce. "Competitive" actions appear to take the form of "looking as attractive and accommodating as possible" and streamlining the permitting process. Both of these areas have been problematic for those who support growth in the community because Oakville has historically been perceived from outside as being a "difficult" place to do business. It was also noted that the competitive position of the town for industrial development is inherently limited by transportation problems—primarily, those stemming from traffic congestion. Those opposing growth obviously are less concerned with "competition" because avoiding growth is the ultimate goal.

Officials in Fairborn, on the other hand, are much more attuned to competitive pressures. Greater perceptions of competition here appear to be a rational response to the city's much more precarious economic position and its location in an older metropolitan region. It is clearly different being a small suburb of Dayton than a large suburb of Toronto. However, there are other factors in Ohio than tend to exacerbate competitive pressures.

Local officials in Fairborn indicate that there is "absolutely regional competition" in the Dayton-Miami region. The area is very fragmented, and "we're all singing off different sheets of music." Indeed, they indicated that there is too much competition to put together unified packages to attract businesses to the area. Beaver Creek was frequently mentioned as the "problem city" as far as competition. They appear to be willing to offer most anything to attract development, and the older cities simply can't keep up. There are regional development efforts (by the Miami Valley Economic Development Coalition, for example), but this seems to increase rather than reduce competitive pressure, much the same way as it did in Coshocton. Thus, the *Site Seeker Report* lists business needs and is sent to all communities in a way that actually increases head-to-head competition. Outside of the region, less competitive pressure is felt; local officials do not feel that they are being played off other cities in other states. Other officials noted that although they felt competitive pressures and knew they were in competition with other cities for a General Motors facility, for example, they did not feel that in reality they were in a very good position to be competitive. "It's a mighty big corporation, and we're a mighty little city." Only the chamber of commerce official did not appear to perceive these competitive pressures. He noted that the chamber works closely and well with the county chamber, and both organizations support development anywhere in the county. This suggests higher levels of business than governmental cooperation at the regional level.

Racial Issues

Neither Oakville nor Fairborn have significant minority populations. There are some historically "ethnic" areas near the downtown in Oakville that tend to be Portuguese and Italian. Local officials indicate that there are no ethnic nor racial problems in the city. The lack of diversity and relative homogeneity in incomes suggests that this is the case. There is more racial diversity in Fairborn, where about 8% of the population is nonwhite. Local officials indicate no racial problems and noted that several owners of the largest businesses in the city were minorities; these are local resident owners. The living areas in the city are relatively integrated, and respondents indicated that segregation tended to be more by income than race, although this is presumed to overlap. Visually, there are a number of ethic restaurants and stores in Fairborn—mostly Korean—so there is some ethnic diversity as well.

Civic Culture

Local Traditions

Three cultural features stand out from the discussions in Oakville: growth management, the small town vision, and fiscal conservatism. First, the strong tradition of growth management is critical to understanding city policy and process. Although the number of elected and appointed officials in the "keep it as it was" group have diminished, there is still a very strong anti-growth sentiment in the community at large and even among some of the remaining council members. The deputy mayor has been pushing council to embrace a more pro-growth agenda for some time but is still viewed as "a lone wolf." There are many anti-growth interests among citizen groups, and it was noted that there were more organized, registered, and participative "rate-payer" groups in Oakville than anywhere else in the province. Although the balance of power has shifted to the pro-growth interests, the issue of growth is still very much in contention. One respondent noted that opposition to growth in the community is almost ironic, in that many of the most vociferously anti-growth residents are top executives in firms in Toronto. Thus, "they are capitalists by day but socialists by night" in their desire to press for growth management where they live but not where they work.

The issue of growth is intricately tied to the image that many residents and officials hold of the town. It is no accident that Oakville remains a town rather than a city. The town Web site bills Oakville as "the biggest small town in Ontario." Retaining the small-town image is critically important to many in the community. Indeed, it was noted that many former residents of the Montreal area have relocated to Oakville because it reminds them of the "small towns" back home.

The third leg of this cultural stool in Oakville is that many residents and officials are strong fiscal conservatives. The town has always maintained a "pay as you go" approach, not only to development but to services and infrastructure more generally. The concept of local debt is not acceptable or even considered. As a result, the town is seriously lacking in infrastructure, particularly in the form of roads, because officials have been unwilling to use prospective development fee revenues to pay for infrastructure. To leverage those funds in this way implies that growth not only be acknowledged but planned for. This has simply not been politically or culturally acceptable in Oakville, and little has changed in this respect. Indeed, one official noted that it has been almost impossible to even plan for new road development in the town and that even mundane city services, such as snowplowing, do not come close to meeting the "just in time" shipment needs of local businesses. Residential growth has almost no support, and industrial development is palatable only if residents "can't see, smell, or hear it." The local Ford plant had to be hidden behind trees to cover the "blight" of the facility.

There are several forces that appear to shape the local civic culture in Fairborn. The most prominent is a commitment on the part of local officials that all stakeholders in the community should have input into the decision-making process generally. This gets played out in close face-to-face relationships with private-sector leaders composed mostly of small locally owned firms and in proactive governmental efforts to solicit community input. Whereas the business sector has taken greater advantage of city offers for input, citizens still remain largely disinterested ("apathetic," some less charitable respondents said).

Two environmental forces and one historical force are also critical in understanding the city. First, residents are proud of the unique history of their city, composed of the combination of two older communities, and the fact that one, Osborn, actually moved, lock, stock, and barrel, to its present site. As in Romulus, there are a number of third- and fourth-generation families in Fairborn. Children tend to grow up and stay in the city if they can find a job. Many of the business leaders in the community are from these generational families.

The two environmental forces are the presence of Wright State University and Wright-Patterson Air Force Base. The former populates the city with large numbers of students and the rental housing that typically occurs in college towns. The university also provides a resource for local government that appears well-used and a technology base for economic development that is just being explored. Many cities are college towns, however. The presence of the Air Force base creates some additional interesting dynamics. First, the base adds to the transient population. Second, although students and military personnel clearly live in the city, both the base and the university provide almost isolated social-organization systems. This means, for the city, that although the people associated with these institutions are physically there, they are not necessarily well integrated into the community. They affect the housing market, the poverty rate, the types of businesses in the downtown, and the difficulty of passing a school millage, but they tend not to be active participants in the larger community.

It should not be assumed that no one associated with the base is involved in the city, however. Of the officials interviewed in the city, the mayor, both members of the planning board, and the director of the chamber of commerce were all retired military or civilian employees of the military who have decided to remain in the community. The exact impact of this type of resident mix—old-time residents and military in particular—could be the focus of an interesting study but is probably beyond the depth of this case study. However, it is clear that the military presence affects the local culture. And it was the retired military that were most negative regarding the health of the community.

This last point says something else important about the local culture. There are widely differing views among local officials regarding the nature, health, and future of Fairborn. Indeed, in some cases, it felt like officials were talking about completely different cities. Some portrayed the economy as growing and the downtown as healthy, diversified, and one of the strengths of the community. These respondents tended to be long-time, nonmilitary residents and city staff. Other respondents portrayed the downtown area as a "fossil" and saw the diversity of businesses as lacking cohesiveness and coherence. Indeed, two respondents explicitly described how Fairborn was viewed by those outside the community: lower income, older population, economic stagnation, poverty, renters, poor schools, property is a poor investment, some very undesirable areas. These respondents were all former military and were outside governmental office.

Thus, there are some rather significant cleavages in attitudes in the city, and these fault lines appear to divide along military versus nonmilitary, city staff versus board members, and even north versus south. The north end of the city includes the downtown and older subdivisions, whereas the land to the south has significant portions that remain rural. To the extent that the military respondents were all retired, there may also be a generational dynamic operating, but career military often tend to retire early, at younger ages. Suffice it to say that although input from all stakeholders is very much encouraged in the city, there is a significant diversity of opinion.

Locus of Power

Despite the town manager system of government in Oakville, most respondents agreed that the mayor and council were the primary policy makers for economic development. The evolution of the external economic development organization, the Oakville Economic Development Alliance (OEDA), is instructive in several respects. It highlights the locus of decision making but also suggests a shift in that locus over time. In short, during 1995-1996, the town sponsored an economic development strategic review (conducted by an outside contractor) that led to the adoption of an economic development strategy in 1997. At that time, a separate department for economic development was created (it had been part of planning) although it was not granted the status of other major town departments. The goals of the strategy included the creation of a public/private partnership for economic development in the third year of the plan. In 1999, the OEDA was formally created, though not without controversy. It remained the last part of the strategy to be adopted by the council. The town contracts with OEDA to implement the economic development strategy and retains oversight and budgetary primacy.

The adoption of a rather proactive economic development strategy and creation of a public/private partnership were relatively radical departures for a community that had basically been committed to a growth management stance with a culture that favored no governmental role in development. The impetus for the change appears to have come from elected officials supportive of growth, with strong backing from the business community that was dissatisfied with the lack of town activity in economic development. That business would support greater economic development activities is not surprising, though it is important to examine the motivation for that support. Although direct benefits in the form of incentives are always a possibility, officials and business leaders in Oakville were primarily concerned with tax base diversity. If the town were to remain primarily a residential bedroom community for Toronto, the number of jobs for local residents would be limited, and the tax burden would fall primarily on homeowners. The push for economic development stemmed from a desire to increase the industrial and commercial tax base, enabling the town to enhance public services. These goals were shared by local officials and businesses alike so that the impetus did not appear to be uniquely a business effort to gain particularized benefits. The various actors interviewed agreed that the mayor and council remain the initiators of economic development based on business *and* citizen pressure. Respondents indicated that the mayor and council "pushed" the change in economic development direction toward an external body and that the whole process was a collaboration between political and administrative actors.

Among the administrative actors, it is the OEDA that has the primary role in development policy implementation. *Implementation* is the operative word here, because "policy" was basically set out in the strategic plan that the OEDA is under contract to implement. Although economic development efforts are being undertaken by an external body, it is driven by goals developed by local officials, and as with any other contract, the town has the option of removing economic development from OEDA if officials are not satisfied. In short, elected officials are "holding the cards." This arrangement differs from that described in the last chapter in Coshocton, where an external body basically organizes and implements development policy with little governmental intervention. In Oakville, the director of the OEDA acts as "adviser to the town" on economic development, attends council and senior management meetings, and receives about 60% to 70% of his budget from the town through the contract for services. These constitute very direct connections.

Relations between the OEDA and other municipal departments, such as planning, appear smooth, although the relationship is still developing. Planning officials indicated that they did not "feel pressured" by OEDA to reduce planning and zoning standards and noted that they feel less pressured now than in the past. Several respondents mentioned the very high levels of credibility that the director of the OEDA enjoys in the city ("he walks on water," said one respondent), and the planners respect the fact that he doesn't press for every and any development. Current planning activities are still geared to managing residential growth while attempting to promote and protect industrial areas to keep the economy diversified. It was noted that the current land use plan was not developed to allow much industrial development, so inevitable conflicts occur between OEDA activities and the plan itself. In short, it appears that both the OEDA and the town planning department have central roles in policy implementation.

The locus of power for economic development in Fairborn appears to rest with professional staff within the city. The community development director has primary responsibility for economic development and is the typical development contact (although some leads come to the city manager first). He and the city manager confer, with the manager acting as "fixer" to ensure that the necessary things happen in the city. There are close positive working relationships between the city manager and development director. The public works director is also involved in the process because he acts as "the infrastructure guy." He serves as both a "gazer" and a "fixer"; he looks into the future to determine the infrastructure needs associated with proposed development and ensures that water and sewers are adequate for projects.

City council is kept fully informed of development efforts as well as staff activity more generally. The city manager's office prepares a staff presentation for every council meeting that includes formal presentations by all staff offices. The mayor and city manager also meet regularly, and the mayor sees no reason to object to the development efforts of city staff as long as it "meets city codes and they keep the sex stuff out of the downtown," and zoning is maintained to keep telecommunications towers from "popping up all over the place."

The planning board also seems to have a significant role in development decision making. Council relies on the recommendations of the planning board, and there is an attempt to work out any controversial issues before reaching council; "they are not always successful in this, but they try." There appears to be some level of conflict between city staff and the planning board. This was mentioned directly by the director of the chamber of commerce. It appears that their policy recommendations do "not always agree." Several relevant examples were mentioned in interviews with different actors. One project involved a combination gas station and fast food restaurant. Because the project met all zoning requirements, the city staff recommended approval. The planning board then recommended the opposite, due to concern about the development's proximity to a school, condominiums, and a park. There was concern that traffic would pose a hazard, particularly to chil-

dren. The council voted to deny a permit for the project, the city was
sued, and ultimately, the denial was upheld.

There are several points worth noting about this case. First, it is an example where the planning board and city staff recommended two different things, and the planning board "won." Second, although city
staff mentioned the project in interviews, it was used as an example of
"citizen opinion" prompting a decision to deny approval for a project.
There was no mention that staff had initially supported it. Third, it is interesting to remember that candidates for mayor and council typically
come from the planning board. Last, planning board members were
consistently more negative about the city, the health of the city, and city
administration than others interviewed. This suggests that although
city staff and the planning board are the most "powerful" actors in economic development decision making in Fairborn, they do not always
agree and may actually be in some competition with each other.

Role of Professionals Versus Elected Officials

As the foregoing discussion makes clear, elected officials in Oakville
are primary policy makers for economic development. As one official
noted, "each stage of the strategic planning process reflected the political will of the community." Having clearly set the policies and goals in
the strategic plan (to be discussed in more detail later), professional economic developers then implement those strategies. Locus of power,
then, appears to be comfortably shared in Oakville among elected officials and development professions in a manner much akin to that described in the politics/administration dichotomy discussion of old. Although much maligned as not matching reality, the dichotomy appears
to work fairly well in Oakville.

Local economic development in Fairborn is much more the purview
of professional staff. There appears to be less "political" direction than
is the case in Oakville. In Fairborn, the elected officials primarily stay
out of economic development. As the mayor noted, he doesn't "stick his
nose" into staff issues because that is not his proper role. Administrative
staff agree that the elected officials "keep their hands off" staff issues
and that this culture is "refreshing." It was also noted that some citizens
may think that the relationships between council and the city manager's office are too collegial and that council simply acts as a "rubber

stamp" to the manager. It is interesting that this concern was raised by an administrative rather than elected official. Thus, even though the economic development decision-making processes in both cities are relatively inclusive, they reflect a different balance of power with regard to elected and appointed officials. Although the culture favors policy direction by political actors in Oakville, the culture in Fairborn views economic development as the purview of professional staff, despite the recent case where city council voted against the recommendations of city staff, seemingly based on political pressure from citizens. Business and community input are also manifest in different ways in the two cities, likely affecting the policy roles of elected and appointed officials.

Business and Community Input

Because they have been defined as inclusive communities, both Oakville and Fairborn demonstrate considerable opportunity for business and citizen input into the decision-making process. The primary distinction between the two cities is how the input is realized and to what extent it occurs at the prompting of local government or emerges from the community itself. At the outset, it is important to note that neither of the local governments are adverse to community input—the difference lies in the extent to which they seek it.

In Oakville, it appears that business input is more institutionalized and perhaps more desired, whereas citizen input comes spontaneously and vigorously from outside the local government. This explicitly raises the value of the distinction between input mechanisms and actual input. Oakville businesses probably have more institutional access, but citizens clearly still have input. Businesses are formally represented on the governing board of the OEDA, for example. Indeed, they hold the majority of the seats: of the ten-person board, three are appointed by council, three by the chamber of commerce, and the rest represent businesses at large. In Oakville, the chamber tends to represent smaller, local firms and those related to tourism. Ford is a member, for example, but their "interests are not well represented," according to a local official. The at-large seats on the board obviously address this issue. The political strength of businesses may be limited somewhat not only because of the division between small/local firms and larger branch plants and headquarters but because the chamber organization itself appears decentralized. For example, it is run by twelve committees—rather than being controlled from the top, ideas percolate up from the bottom. This seems to mirror the operation of the local government, incidentally.

Aside from this institutional presence, no respondent in Oakville or in the region gave the impression that businesses "control" or drive the development decision-making process. Business leaders were obviously involved in pressuring elected officials to begin the strategic planning process, and business focus groups were part of that effort. However, there does not seem to be an identifiable business elite pulling the strings nor even exerting particular effort; as one official noted, business leaders "are lobbying but not controlling, they are not in the political machinery." Businesses do not support candidates for office, and there is no fear that businesses will try and take over decisions. Rather, it appears that although government officials are responsive to business, the strong culture of growth management and sense that developers should pay for development mitigate against a strong business elite here. Thus, it was noted that "the culture does not support the notion of a business elite even if they are moving to accept the need for some industrial development." It should be noted that business-government relations are smoother now than in the past, when there was open conflict between the chamber and the government at council meetings as well as in the local press. The creation of the OEDA and a more institutionalized role for business appears to have smoothed relationships quite a bit.

Despite this, all of the respondents indicated that citizen or rate payer groups were much more directly involved in governmental decision making. It was also noted that the government encourages an open economic development environment and that there are more citizen groups active in Oakville than in most other communities in the area. It appears that citizen input spreads across the board. For example, although much of it takes the form of opposition to specific development projects, other interests represent environmental concerns more broadly defined. And unlike many other cities, the input is not simply individual citizens fighting projects in the neighborhood but rather comes from organized, on-going groups.

Local officials were able to identify a number of development projects that have been successfully "fought" by citizens. These included denial of a permit for construction of a Home Depot because residents did not approve of the site, opposition to the Gillette warehouse expansion, and current strong opposition to the expansion of a shopping mall. It is useful to note that the town council and administrative staff also were opposed to the Home Depot on that particular site; thus, citizen opposition does not necessarily mean that they are at odds with the local government. Indeed, given the general commitment to growth management, citizens and governmental officials are very much in accord, sometimes in opposition to business leaders. In the case of the Gillette expansion, feelings on council were mixed, with representatives from the affected wards voting against it.

In Fairborn, both business and citizen input are actively sought by local officials. There are close institutional ties between business and the local government. At the same time, the city makes active efforts to solicit greater levels of both citizen opinion and participation in decision making. Although it appears that gaining business input has been more successful than citizen input, this does not appear to be from any lack of effort on the part of local officials.

Most of the business input in Fairborn emanates from the local chamber of commerce, although there appears to be a competing institution in the form of a downtown business association that may not be as well connected with the city. The city manager and mayor have direct contact with the chamber, typically by attending meetings; chamber members, on the other hand, attend council meetings and meetings of the planning board. The chamber is asked to nominate members to sit on any local committees that involve changes in city ordinances. The head of the chamber and the community development director write articles together for the chamber newsletter, distributed to about 600 local businesses. The chamber in Fairborn includes retail, industrial, and developer interests and thus represents a broad base of the private sector.

It is no surprise that business satisfaction with local government appears rather high; indeed, the impetus for the Vision 2005 plan (discussed later) came from local business leaders working with the community development staff. Various respondents noted that there is always some "friction" between the public and private sectors, however, because business tends to view government as a hurdle to overcome and perceives lack of support for infrastructure by the local government. There is agreement, however, that the city goes out of its way to expedite decisions, holding special council meetings if necessary. All of this is perceived by business as creating a "good business climate" in the city. In short, the business "word on the street" typically reaches city staff long before issues get to council and become a problem. Both private and public leaders feel that there is a positive and open partnership between the city and the chamber. Business input is direct, and there is "no political sugarcoating;" business leaders are very open about raising concerns or pointing out opportunities but tend to do so behind closed doors. Thus, although a chamber representative is always present at council meetings, they do not typically participate. And in the rare case where council's decision is at odds with the chamber, the chamber has not taken an official position. As the director of the chamber noted, "like in the military, if the council says OK to something, we go along and salute."

Citizen input is much less forthcoming in this community. Indeed, the mayor claimed that he had not received more than eight phone calls from citizens in almost two years. Given the large transient population, it is difficult to create and maintain citizen input. Group input certainly does not arise spontaneously as it does in Oakville. Most citizen input takes the form of individual or neighborhood opposition to a specific development project rather than from organized, institutionalized groups. The city is actively trying to create more organized citizen input, however. For example, the city manager has developed a very elaborate tracking system for all citizen contacts with the city. Using a computerized tracking system, every contact is assigned a number and sent to the proper department for resolution. The citizen is contacted, the resolution recorded, and at the end of the process, citizens are contacted again to record their satisfaction level. Beyond this, city staff must show that they have contacted all relevant elements of the community (all stakeholders) prior to bringing an issue to city council. All neighborhood associations receive the planning board agendas, and everyone within 250 feet of a proposed development is notified. There is also a "City Source" column in the local Monday paper (the Monday edition goes to all residents free of charge) providing updates on city activities. Seeking input is thus a required and expected part of the process; more to the point, one local official noted that they are trying to get citizens together "before there is a CVS [drugstore] in their backyards."

Much citizen input still takes the form of residents attending planning board meetings to voice opposition to particular projects. Organized neighborhood associations were characterized as "sleeping giants" that are only now starting to awaken, perhaps as a result of some of the governmental efforts. Significant citizen opposition has been raised to several development projects, including the combination gas station/restaurant noted previously. Residents close to the new CVS did not want it, although that opposition was geographically limited. There was environmental opposition to a plan to burn tires at a hazardous waste facility and opposition to the location of a yard waste drop-off site.

A larger problem has occurred surrounding the development of a "low-income" housing project on the border between Fairborn and the township (housing is to be priced from $100,000 to $125,000). Much of the opposition has come from township residents living near the proposed site. City residents have participated in petition drives with the township residents against the project (in Ohio, city residents are also residents of their townships but not vise versa; township residents have no formal representative in city government). It should also be noted that some citizens have lobbied for the scattered-site housing, so citizen opinion is by no means unanimous. The main problem with the current low-income housing development appears that, because it is located in a primarily rural area, residents are concerned with the density of the proposed development or, ideally, want no development at all. These concerns are being voiced as a desire for a "higher-end" housing development, however.

In short, although local officials are very open to and interested in both business and citizen input into decision making in Fairborn, business leaders are better able to take advantage of this. Due to the high percentage of transient residents, most citizen input has been tied to particular projects. Institutionalized citizen input in Fairborn remains a potential rather than an actual force, and planning board respondents noted that some of the citizen input is not necessarily completely productive for the city. "There is a penchant in Fairborn to create issues that make us look like boobs on the other side." Obviously, there seems to be some disagreement on how citizen input is viewed by city staff and planning board officials.

Regime Status

Oakville's very open political system provides avenues for many voices in the community to be heard. Unlike the other case cities, both business *and* citizen input is organized and institutionalized in Oakville. Business leaders are clearly involved in the governing regime through their majority position on the board of the external public/private partnership. However, citizen or rate payer groups are also represented on other local boards and are clearly heard at city council meetings. Thus, the governing regime in Oakville is composed of government, business, and citizen leaders. To date, this has resulted in a stable development policy agenda emphasizing growth management and a "business pays" attitude. Based on Stone's 1993 typology, Oakville has a middle-class progressive regime. In this higher-income community, citizen and business groups pressure government for regulations to manage growth and ensure a "fit" with the historic small-town image that is central to the civic culture. The emphasis on having the private sector pay for its own development is another aspect of the middle-class progressive regime, where regime actors monitor elites to guarantee that public goals are being considered.

Fairborn, on the other hand, has the prototypical maintenance or caretaker regime. Here, smaller, primarily local business owners are institutionally involved in the governing process. Although less organized, citizens also are active in the economic development process, primarily through opposition voiced at planning board hearings. The net result is a stable policy agenda that has led to limited governmental services and minimal support for private development. Pressures for low tax rates and the defeat of bond and millage proposals have ensured that the city will be frugal and limited in its public service levels.

Intergovernmental Relations

Oakville is part of the Halton region but is not part of a regional or metropolitan government; at this point, it is freestanding. It also does not appear that any consolidations or amalgamations are imminent, although local leaders did see the possibility for such in the future. Unlike the case of Gloucester, discussed later, this is likely to take the form of

adding surrounding areas and rural land to Oakville rather than folding
it into the metropolitan Toronto system. Likely because of this relative
freedom from concern about amalgamation, relations between Oakville
and the region are fairly smooth. The lines of responsibility are established and clear, though the recent creation of the OEDA may create
some duplication, a concern at least in the eyes of regional development
officials.

The Greater Toronto Marketing Alliance (GTMA) takes responsibility for promoting the entire region nationally and internationally. This
is a relatively new (two to three years old) public/private body composed of the boards of trade and the various cities in the region and financed by both the public and private sectors. The Halton regional
government tends to focus on a specific "package" of development activities perceived as more effectively conducted at a regional scale:
small business development, some business retention, transportation
infrastructure, labor force development, research and information services for businesses, and social assistance work placement, for example.
Planning activities are cooperative, with zoning and land use policy recently devolved downward to the local level. All of these relationships
seem functional and uncomplicated. Oakville officials did not raise any
particular problems about working with the region.

Regional officials, for their part, indicated that relations with Oakville were "medium to good" and that many other places have greater
intergovernmental problems. Most of the current interaction between
the region and town appears to revolve around clarification of respective roles, stemming from the change in the organization of development in Oakville. New personalities and mechanisms require new
relationships.

Because it has yet to become the focus of metropolitan reorganization, the province of Ontario has played a limited role in Oakville's economic development. Provincial officials make some corporate calls in
cooperation with local officials and are responsible for workforce development (often implemented at the regional level). There are five regions
in the greater Toronto area, with no formal governmental body to link
them together, although the Greater Toronto Service Board provides
some linkages. The GTMA also provides some coordination, at least in
the area of marketing. The federal government is not particularly involved in economic development aside from industrial and technology

transfer programs; national officials rarely participate in any incentive programs at this time. It may be the case here that intergovernmental relations are smooth because they are relatively limited and not too much cooperation is demanded of anyone.

Fairborn also has relatively calm relations with other units of local government, again largely because they are rather limited. In the same manner that the constant interaction with the county over the airport has created problems in Romulus, the relatively limited interactions between Fairborn and superior units of government appear to reduce problems. Fairborn officials seem to work well with the county on a limited number of issues. The county will direct potential businesses to the city, and the community development director speaks regularly with county counterparts. However, only "occasionally do they provide an actual development lead." The county has been involved in some joint land use studies, a study of older shopping centers, auditing, and providing support for small business loans and microenterprise development.

Economic development interactions with the state primarily involve funding for major infrastructure projects and small business administration loans. There is some limited dialogue with the state regarding enterprise zones that appears to be more reactive than proactive, and the city must provide the state with an annual report on all tax abatements. This appears to be the extent of state-level interaction. Last, interactions with the federal government are primarily directed to the census bureau and HUD. Fairborn receives about $500,000 annually in CDBG money, and these relationships do not appear to be problematic.

Fairborn appears to be beginning to explore the possibilities of some regional cooperation in the form of a "visioning" effort with Bath Township and Greene County. Because of this effort, Fairborn Area 2005, is still ongoing, it is difficult to assess its success. However, it does appear promising. A consultant was hired to develop a "shared community vision" for economic and community development among the city of Fairborn, the chamber of commerce, Fairborn city schools, Bath Township, Greene County, and the Fairborn DDA. The goal of the effort is to develop a strategic assessment and implementation strategy for marketing, infrastructure development, industrial development, education, community building, improved services, and better use of the Air Force base and the university.

In short, neither Oakville nor Fairborn have very extensive relationships with county, state/provincial, or federal levels of government. Although this keeps such relations smooth, it is clear that neither is making creative or proactive use of potential cooperative arrangements, although Fairborn appears to be moving in that direction with the Vision 2005.

Planning and Evaluation

A great deal of planning and evaluation take place in both these inclusive cities. Significant levels of planning were devoted to creating the development strategy and establishing the new structural arrangements in Oakville. Business and citizen focus groups, surveys of employers, and two public meetings were conducted as part of the planning process. The economic development strategy documents seven key objectives, development strategies, sector strategies, planning and land use strategies, marketing activities, and implementation steps. The service contract with OEDA includes explicit performance measurements; if goals are not met, the town can cancel the contract with the alliance. To track performance, the OEDA uses a computerized client tracking system that includes all business contacts. Weights are then used to indicate the extent of influence the OEDA has had on a project (the weights are established through consultation with businesses).

Each completed project by Oakville economic development staff is listed, and the total impact as far as new jobs, square feet, and property taxes paid is recorded. The level of involvement by economic development staff in each project varies and is shown as the "OEDA factor." This figure is then used to attribute a portion of the overall impact to the work of staff (OEDA Activity Report, Summer 1999).

The 1999 Summer Report includes data on economic development inquiries, completed projects, tourism levels, marketing activities, start-up projects, grants awarded to the town for economic development, partnership projects, and various studies and analyses of economic data and land use studies. The director of the OEDA indicated that he was not "afraid" of performance measures, that they are necessary to obtain political support, and that both business and community actors wanted an approach that included accountability on specific targets. Again, reflecting the extent of community involvement in Oakville, he concludes that "we have to be open to public scrutiny."

Planning and evaluation is also relatively common in Fairborn, although it tends to be conducted in a more diffuse manner, and there is no formal development plan. The city retained consultants to develop both its downtown revitalization plan and the Fairborn Area 2005 vision and strategy. Both of these efforts involved significant business and community involvement via focus groups and public forums. The latter plan explicitly includes a "community involvement system" calling for sponsors, a governing board, and seven community task forces. Again, the effort to involve residents is obvious. And the Vision 2005 includes clear objectives and strategies for economic development, so it could certainly be considered the city's development "plan." Furthermore, there is a five-year capital plan for the city that is updated every year. This identifies both capital project needs and grant funding possibilities.

Beyond these broad planning efforts, local officials in Fairborn evaluate projects by a variety of means. First, the tracking system for contacts with the local government explicitly includes satisfaction measures as well as how each concern was addressed. The Vision 2005 plan includes thirteen "community benchmarks for success," ranging from improved graduation rates, to reducing residents living in poverty, to increasing the number of technology-based companies. The city also has an ongoing evaluation system via a citizen satisfaction survey conducted every two years by Wright State University. About five or six "waves" of the survey have been completed. It seems clear that although the economic stress levels in Fairborn are relatively high, the city is blessed with very good city staff and management. If they do not have the resources to do the necessary planning and evaluation "in-house," officials are quick to use outside consultants or university resources. And in both cities, the relative openness to both citizen and business involvement is evident in how planning and evaluation processes are conducted.

Views About the Role of the Government in the Economy

In Oakville, the overriding view remains that the private sector needs to pay for its own development. Even given the new emphasis on industrial development efforts related primarily to marketing and governmental "red tape" issues, there remains a basic consensus that public funds should not be used to support private development. The growth management and pay-as-you-go mentality is still very much alive and well in the town at large.

Although not as emphatically tied to a pay-as-you-go mindset nor as interested in growth management, the overall expectation in Fairborn is that the private sector should pay for its own development. However, this stance is clearly more driven by the fact that there are simply not enough local resources here to support development. This is most evident with respect to infrastructure development and supporting millages. Citizens in Fairborn have not approved a millage, bond issuance, or special assessment for either infrastructure improvement or schools since 1991. Local officials attribute this to several factors, primarily the large renter base and a large population of "seniors." In the case of infrastructure, the city manager noted that businesses would probably like the city to provide more and better infrastructure, but "we don't subsidize development." Citizens and local officials also prefer to have the state fund infrastructure improvements. And when incentives are used, "it is up to the body politic to identify where exceptions should occur." There is an expectation that business should pay for itself in Fairborn, and limited resources are available to support development incentives.

Entrepreneurialism

Related to these perspectives on public support of private investment, it is not surprising that the approach to economic development in Oakville is very traditional and hence not particularly entrepreneurial. Extensive marketing efforts and facilitating development through one-stop shops and streamlined zoning and permitting processes are not particularly novel approaches to development. The director of the OEDA said "they try to make the environment conducive to development and that municipalities can only influence the process and do marketing." Oakville does not even engage in land development, a common strategy among Ontario cities that are limited in their ability to offer financial incentives. Even with the new efforts and external organization structure for development, the overall approach is conservative. And given the desire for growth management, entrepreneurial or risky policies are simply not needed.

Development strategies in Fairborn are equally traditional. Neither of these cities are particularly entrepreneurial in their approaches to economic development. For Oakville, a strong economy and a culture opposed to providing public benefits to private firms drives the conservative development approach. In Fairborn, the culture also opposes business subsidies. Even if this were not the case, the city simply does not have the resources to offer much in the way of business incentives. Policies in Fairborn pretty much revolve around downtown development, red-tape reduction, and limited tax abatements. Thus, both strong and weak economies produce limited and traditional economic development policies. In neither case does the culture support active entrepreneurial incentives. The other similarity in the two communities is, of course, the inclusive nature of the local politics.

Goals and Visions

Given the development of the new economic development plan in Oakville, specific goals and expectations are very clear. It should be remembered, however, that the historical and persistent goal for development in this town is "limitation," and the prevailing "vision" of the community is of a small town. Within this framework, the goals for the new OEDA include increasing marketing; integrating tourism into economic development efforts; making land use, zoning, and permitting policies more "user-friendly;" increasing public-private partnerships in the town; and improving infrastructure. These are very specific, almost mechanistic, goals, however, and many of them relate to reducing the perception that Oakville is a difficult place in which to do business. Overall, it seems clear that the desire to diversify the economic base, thereby reducing the reliance on residential taxes and providing local jobs, is the underlying goal for current economic development efforts. Growth management, particularly for residential development, and diversification of the economic base within that general management framework are the driving goals in Oakville.

Interview data suggest that the most important goal for economic development in Fairborn is economic base diversification—creating a good mix of residential, commercial, and *light* industrial uses but also a mix that more effectively builds on the high-technology infrastructure at the university and the Air Force base. There is also an emphasis on downtown development and balancing downtown with strip development. With respect to housing development, there is a strong desire to "transition" residents from rental housing to home ownership, and creating more low-end housing is explicitly addressed in the Vision 2005. Last, there is an emphasis on job creation, both to retain younger residents and because of the growing role of Fairborn as an employment center vis-a-vis the region, best illustrated by its new designation as a HUD entitlement city. Fairborn Vision 2005 includes a range of goals from quality public services to culture and the arts. In economic development, the "vision" emphasizes "balanced economic development," including "development of new sites for technology-based companies which focus on attracting privatized functions to Wright-Patterson Air Force Base."

ECONOMIC DEVELOPMENT
POLICIES IN OAKVILLE AND FAIRBORN

Overall Policies

Economic development policies in Oakville are traditional and very conservative. All of the Ontario cities are more limited in their abilities to use financial incentives, so development efforts must be concentrated in other areas. Even given this, activity in Oakville is limited. The town's efforts focus on regulations and marketing. One of the central goals of the OEDA is to help the town reform planning, zoning, and development fee structures. Currently, there are as many as nine industrial zoning categories that primarily appear to work to limit the ability of the town to approve industrial facilities. The goal is to reduce these to three. Because the town had done little marketing in the anti-growth period, one of the primary activities of the OEDA is to launch a marketing campaign. Initial efforts in this direction included regional presentations about the town and other trade show presentations, the development of a multimedia promotion for the town, and new brochures.

The 1999 Activity Report indicated a number of other economic development activities initiated by the OEDA. These included providing information and demographic statistics to prospective businesses, securing zoning variances to aid development projects, and producing a local business directory in cooperation with the chamber of commerce.

There are no industrial parks in Oakville, a rather unique situation. Because this is one of the activities localities have been allowed to do in Ontario, most communities are active in land development. There has been so much growth in the Toronto area that parks have not really been necessary, and there is little political support for industrial park development in the town because of the general view that developers should pay for all development. Indeed, even the private sector has shown little support for land development. The town is currently involved in the development of a technical park in conjunction with the animation program at Sheraton College, "the Harvard of animation." The goal of this effort would be to attract more animation-related "industries" to the community.

Workforce policies are primarily conducted at the regional or provincial level. Indeed, most of these efforts are funded by the latter and implemented by the former. As noted previously, the Halton region is responsible for small business support and development, job placement programs, business retention and attraction (although the town is getting involved in this as well), transportation infrastructure development (currently they are working with the province on a new high speed toll road and also conduct transportation studies), labor force infrastructure, business education and information seminars, and research for businesses, including regional business directories and GIS mapping of business information. In short, because of the town's history of growth management and eschewing of economic development, most traditional development activities, particularly the more entrepreneurial or innovative ones, are conducted at the regional level. The extent to which this changes with the new development strategy in Oakville remains to be seen. Obviously, regional officials believe that this is still in flux.

Because of the more liberal enabling legislation in Ohio than Ontario, Fairborn is able to employ a wider array of development incentives.

Given this, however, their economic development "arsenal" remains relatively traditional and conservative. Much of their efforts revolve around establishing "developer-friendly policies," such as one-stop building inspections, land use proposals, and zoning permits. City staff prereview all development proposals and use presubmittal conferences to address roadblocks before proposals go to the planning board or city council. City planning staff provide up-front assistance to small businesses.

The next most relied-on "incentive" in Fairborn is the availability and cost of local services and infrastructure. Local officials "advertise" that the city has the "lowest cost of government services" in the area. This is a classic example of "spin doctoring" because costs are low because voters have been unwilling to fully fund infrastructure improvement and maintenance. Service costs are low but so is service quality in some respects. Fairborn has basic infrastructure already in place, and this too is used for marketing purposes. There is a highway corridor around the city, and Fairborn operates its own water treatment plant. Other local services, such as building inspection, are all done "in-house," and this is marketed to developers as a means of shortening development time frames and cutting red tape.

Local officials also operate a business retention and expansion program and have visited fifty targeted businesses (major employers) to assess needs and identify problems. Marketing materials for the community are very professional and highlight development incentives (tax abatements, the enterprise zone, infrastructure); available industrial and commercial sites; market accessibility; and local history, lifestyles, and culture.

The city offers tax abatements, but officials are quick to indicate that they are more conservative than surrounding communities. Tax abatements are granted for five-year periods, whereas state law allows them for fifteen. The entire city is an enterprise zone where up to 75% of state taxes can be abated. The city has not engaged in much loan activity other than employing some state economic development grants. Job training is done at the county level. To date, there has been little land development, such as an industrial park, although officials note that Fairborn is one of the few cities in the area with land available for development. It is likely that both lack of resources and public attitudes against funding developers have stood in the way of such activities.

The most focused development activity recently has revolved around the downtown revitalization plan. They have been saving their recently designated CBDG funds to invest in a streetscape effort and currently have a grant program for facade improvement. The streetscape development includes streetlights, underground wiring, parking improvements, and general aesthetic improvements.

Type II Policies

Narrowly defined, there are basically no explicit Type II policies currently employed in Oakville. There is a requirement that housing developers provide at least 25% of their units as "affordable" housing; however, this is a provincial policy, not a local one. Development fees are charged in Oakville as they are across Canada. Typically, those fees are used to support infrastructure and other development costs in the locality. Their hesitancy in investing fees in infrastructure is a function of the desire to manage growth. The town does place demands on developers to provide certain limited amenities, such as sidewalks. The growth management culture in Oakville has served to limit not only traditional but Type II policies as well. A current push to reduce development fees to facilitate industrial development may suggest that Type II policies will receive even less emphasis. At the same time, the community has very few residents with low incomes, reducing the need to ensure that benefits of development are allocated to those in greatest need. There has simply been a lot of development here and low levels of residential need.

Fairborn, too, makes only very limited use of Type II policies, although they have explored them a bit more than Oakville. If developers receive governmental assistance, they are required in a contract to assist with schools and target local workers for hiring. The "patrons of education" program fosters cooperation between the school district and businesses and provides goods and services to the schools and employment opportunities for local graduates. To date, the city has not had to rescind any tax abatements due to nonperformance, but they have pulled incentives because firms have not met site plan requirements. As one local official noted, although they will facilitate development, the city "will not roll over for developers." Business appears to accept these restrictions because none have refused to come into the city due to them.

CULTURE, PROCESS, AND POLICY

See Table 8.1 for summaries and comparisons of Fairborn's and Oakville's environments, culture, and policies.

The Environment

Oakville and Fairborn have radically different residential-need and fiscal-health profiles. Oakville is a wealthy community, and the high demand for residential development means that growth limitation rather than stimulation is the overriding concern. Fairborn, although not the most stressed of the case studies, certainly has higher residential need, illustrated particularly by high poverty and low homeownership levels. The tax base in Fairborn does not sustain the level of services provided in Oakville, and the schools suffer from insufficient millage support. It is interesting to note that officials and business leaders in both communities express concerns about poor and/or insufficient infrastructure, a situation caused in Oakville by resistance to using development fees to support growth and in Fairborn by lack of resources. Officials in Fairborn perceive greater competitive pressures, particularly within the region. The difference in perceived competition is due both to the disparities in economic fortunes of the two cities but also because of more open regional competition among Ohio cities. In Ohio, cities have greater development policy options, and regional bodies appear to increase competition rather than induce cooperation (this was the case in Coshocton, as well). Although both cities are run by town/city managers and have nonpartisan elections, the district-based council elections in Oakville appear to create geographic divisions that are not present in Fairborn.

The Culture

The overall culture of Oakville can be summarized as follows:

High levels of input from both business leaders and organized citizen groups
Local government acceptance of community input
Strong and historical commitment to growth management

TABLE 8.1   Comparison of Oakville and Fairborn: Environment, Culture, and Policies

Oakville	Fairborn
Environment	
Low residential need	Moderate residential need—high poverty
Low perceived competition	Perceived regional competition
Formal structure: town manager, ward, nonpartisan elections	Formal structure: city manager, at-large, nonpartisan elections
Formal and actual structure match	Formal and actual structure match
Little racial diversity	Little racial diversity
Culture	
Open and active politics	Open and active politics
Institutionalized business input	Institutionalized business input
Organized citizen input	City attempts to stimulate citizen input; individual citizens active
Strong anti-growth sentiment, some old-timer versus pro-growth divisions	Residential mix of old-timers, military, and students
Council locus of power	Staff and citizen board locus of power
Public-sector locus	Public-sector locus
Economic development in an external public/private organization	Economic development within community development department
Cooperative, limited intergovernmental relations	Cooperative, limited intergovernmental relations
High planning and evaluation	High planning and evaluation
Low support for public subsidies	Low support for public subsidies
Progressive regime	Caretaker regime
Policies	
High marketing	High marketing
Regulatory facilitation	Regulatory facilitation
No industrial parks	No industrial parks
No financial incentives	No loans, limited tax abatements with strings
No enterprise zones	Entire city is an enterprise zone
Workforce development at regional level	Workforce development at county level
Business retention program with region	Business retention program with county
No Type II	Voluntary hiring goals and educational partnership

Historical opposition to public subsidy of private development

Decision-making locus rests with elected officials

Economic development authority vested in an external public/private body

Cooperative but limited intergovernmental relations

Strong planning and evaluation emphasis

Primary economic development goals: growth management and economic base diversification

The civic culture in Fairborn is quite similar even though most outer appearances would suggest that the two cities are very different:

High levels of input from business leaders and citizens, though the latter is not institutionalized like the former

Affirmative local government efforts to increase community input, particularly among residents

Historical opposition to public subsidy of private development

Resident base composed of generational families, retired military, and more transient residents, such as students and military personnel

Decision-making locus rests with administrative staff and volunteer planning board

Economic development authority located in a community development department

Cooperative but limited intergovernmental relations

Strong planning and evaluation emphasis

Primary economic development goals: economic base diversification, downtown revitalization, and increased home ownership

The Policies

Economic development policies are quite traditional in both Oakville and Fairborn. Both cities focus primarily on marketing and eased regulations or governmental processes to create a "business-friendly" environment. Neither city has developed industrial parks, and for both, workforce development is conducted at the regional level. Whereas Oakville does not offer loans or tax abatements due to provincial prohibitions, Fairborn is allowed to by state law but offers no loans and only limited tax abatements. The only significant difference between the two communities is in their use of Type II policies. Where Oakville has not experimented with them, Fairborn ties local hiring goals and partnerships with schools to their tax abatements. The "required" nature of these remains open to question, however, because different local officials indicated that they were both voluntary and mandatory. Suffice it to say that neither city evidences significant use of Type II policies. Oakville differs from Fairborn only in its strong tradition of growth management policies; this difference largely stems from its more robust growth rates.

SUMMARY

The last chapter described two cities where, despite similarities in many environmental respects—fiscal health and governmental structure—the civic cultures were quite different. Oakville and Fairborn, on the other hand, represent very different environmental profiles with similar civic cultures. An overriding lesson, one that will be repeated in the other cases, is that there is no inherent connection between environment and civic culture. Economic health, growth rates, and even governmental structure are not determinative of either culture or economic development process or policy.

The economic profiles of the two communities are very different. What effects does this seem to have on decision-making processes and outcomes? Because both communities have inclusive political environments, it clearly does not affect the basic parameters of decision making. There are several differences in locus of control and structure of economic development, however. In Oakville, the inclusive political framework appears to vest primary policy-making locus with city council. Although the recent creation of an external public/private organization for economic development may be a reaction to this—in short, an effort to remove some of the "politics" from the decision-making process—it does not yet seem to have had that effect. It appears that public expectations will continue to vest primary control in the hands of elected officials even if implementation responsibilities lie in an external organization. In Fairborn, economic development is placed within a community development department, and primary policy initiation appears to come from administrative staff. However, the planning board, composed of citizen volunteers, appears to have a consid-

erable role in economic development and has gone against the recommendations of city staff. And at times, city council appears to side with
the planning board, reacting in large part to citizen pressure. Politics,
representing and reconciling both community and business interests, is
alive and well in both communities and appears to be the driving force
behind not only what is acceptable policy but also how decisions are
made. It's not the economy but the civic culture that matters here. Similarly, the structure of economic development also appears to have little
role.

Although the governmental structures differ, given the ward-based
nature of council elections in Oakville, this also appears to have mar-
ginal effects. Council votes appear to break along ward lines only when
there is citizen opposition to particular economic development projects.
Geographic "fault lines" are also present in Fairborn where residents
near proposed projects are often in opposition. Their voices appear to be
strongly heard even absent a district-based election system.

With different environmental conditions and structural arrangements, the civic culture in the two communities is rather similar. Both
have many "old-time" residents with preferences for growth limitation,
although the long-term residents of Fairborn are supportive of economic development if it leads to job growth that will allow their children to
live in the community. Residents in both communities are generally opposed to spending public money on private development, preferring
that developers (or, in Fairborn, the state) support the costs. Residents
of both communities are reluctant to support infrastructure development. The reason in Oakville appears to be an aversion to growth,
whereas in Fairborn, it relates to resistance to increased taxes. And these
cultural similarities lead to a similar approach to economic development, one that is basically conservative and traditional and focuses on
marketing and streamlining governmental regulations, both relatively
low-cost and low-risk activities.

A final striking similarity in economic development decision making
in the two communities is the heavy emphasis on planning and evaluation. Why this is the case is open to speculation and will be considered
more fully in later chapters. However, two possibilities stand out. First,
both cities are run by long-term, professional city/town managers. It is
very possible that the general emphasis on planning and evaluation are
"tones" set by professional administrators. Second, the correlation be-

tween inclusive politics and planning and evaluation is intriguing. It is possible that, given the very open and sometimes conflictual politics in both communities, local officials use planning and evaluation to gain community support, channel participation, and perhaps, support desired policy options.

Given these very striking similarities, it should be noted that there are some important differences in the environment of the two communities that influence economic development process and policy. First, the low levels of economic development policy activity in Fairborn are related to the weaker economic base. The strong economy in Oakville leads to growth management efforts, whereas the weak economy limits development options in Fairborn. Second, the presence of the Air Force base and university in Fairborn affects the poverty rate, tax base, and homeownership levels. The high proportion of renters was pointed to in particular by many respondents as a reason for low levels of organized citizen effort. This creates a possible imbalance between business and resident input. The city has tried to address this by stimulating citizen input and organizing neighborhood groups. To the extent that this has still not been fully successful, residents are more disadvantaged in their political input in Fairborn than in Oakville, where they have more organizational resources. Still, citizen opposition does appear to be heard by the Fairborn city council. Last, although both cities appear to have stable governing regimes, they are of different types—middle-class progressive in Oakville and caretaker in Fairborn.

Do these differences affect policies or do the similarities in process and input have more of an impact? Based on the very similar economic development policies in the two communities, it could be argued that the similar cultures are more important than the economic differences. But because in some cases the effects of the economy and culture overlap, it is difficult to distinguish the relative impacts with complete certainty. Both cities employ traditional and conservative development techniques. In Oakville, a growing economy and a culture that expects businesses to support themselves reinforce one another. In Fairborn, a weak economy and local tax base limit the policy possibilities, but residents do not support public subsidies of development in any event. Even the modest flirtation in Fairborn with Type II policies confounds efforts to disentangle the effects of environment and culture. The fact that the strings attached to tax abatements are related to support of schools is likely the result of a weak tax base and the unwillingness of renters and older residents to support millages. On the other hand, the fact that Type II policies exist at all likely reflects strong citizen input and the cultural expectation that businesses give something back to the community. It does not appear that the different regime structures have a strong impact on policy aside from the growth management emphasis in Oakville. But even there, it is the small-town vision and pay-as-you-go culture that leads to an emphasis by regime actors on the regulation of growth. In both these cities, shared views of "acceptable" economic development policies color the particular regime structures.

In Romulus and Coshocton, the same governmental structures and economies produced different economic development processes and policies as a result of differences in the civic culture. In Oakville and Fairborn, similar civic cultures stressing political inclusion lead to similar processes and policies, even given radically different economic environments. In short, civic culture is critical.

NOTE

1. In Oakville, the following actors were interviewed: Director, Oakville Economic Development Alliance; Planning Services Director; Deputy Town Manager for Administrative Services; Director, Access Halton and Business Development Halton Regional Municipality; Executive Vice President, Oakville Chamber of Commerce. In Fairborn, the following actors were interviewed: Director, Community Development; Assistant Director of Community Development; City Manager; Mayor; Executive Director, Fairborn Area Chamber of Commerce; Public Works Director; Planning Board members.

9

THE ACTIVE-ELITE CASES

Cadillac, Kettering, and Gloucester

Cadillac is a small, relatively isolated city located on several lakes in central Michigan. Although Cadillac had high unemployment in the early 1990s, the economy has strengthened considerably. The city promotes its recreation and tourism "industries" and balances environmental concerns with its status as a regional employment and shopping node. "Civic volunteerism" is the watchword here, and business leaders and city staff cooperate closely and apparently seamlessly in economic development. "Politics" are disdained, and a strong sense of professionalism pervades staff and business activity. Economic development policies are characterized by complex and creative funding arrangements, typically using state money, and programs that emphasize the "business-friendly" stance of the city as well as efforts to increase population through worker attraction and housing development.

Kettering, Ohio, is an economically healthy inner-ring suburb of Dayton. Lacking a traditional downtown, like many newer communities, Kettering has developed a government, arts, and recreation center to serve as its focal point. City staff are the leaders in economic development planning and implementation in an environment that emphasizes professionalism and avoids "politics." Hit by military base closings, the city has taken a proactive approach toward redevelopment of its industrial base. Citizen and business leaders appear largely satisfied with the city's economic development policies and take little advantage of staff efforts to increase input, particularly business input. Local development policies revolve around arts development as well as traditional financial incentives and very creative industrial reuse projects.

Gloucester, Ontario, is a healthy and growing suburb of Ottawa. An independent city at the time of the interviews, Gloucester becomes a part of the Ottawa megacity in 2001, and the consolidation figured prominently in the minds of local officials. As an independent city, Gloucester has little citizen or business input into economic development decision making; policies are based on a strong platform of planning and evaluation. With the economic development department operating as a "profit center," achievement benchmarks in place, and accountability "embraced" by city staff, it is clear that "professionalism" is emphasized over "politics." In the face of provincial restrictions on financial bonusing, the local economic development program in Gloucester is focused on an active and innovative business development, retention, and expansion effort.

This chapter focuses on the two cities where bureaucratic elites have the greatest influence over and discretion in economic development decision making: Kettering, Ohio, and Gloucester, Ontario.[1] The third city, Cadillac, Michigan, has a decision-making process where both business and bureaucratic elites dominate in relatively equal measure. What the three cities share is an active, entrepreneurial, and innovative approach to economic development that is largely driven by local elites. The systems are relatively closed to groups beyond business and local officials, in the case of Cadillac, and largely limited to local officials in Kettering and Gloucester. In all three cities, "politics" is regarded as a dirty word, whereas cooperation and professional competence are emphasized. It is not surprising that political conflict is limited in all three cities. The cluster analysis in Chapter 6 indicated that there were two types of elite-dominated cities: those where bureaucratic elites alone dominated and those where there was a combination of professional elites and high business involvement. Thus, the three cities here cover these two clusters of cities.

Cadillac represents cities where bureaucrats and business elites dominate decision making. Like the majority of cities in the cluster, it has a primarily reformed governmental structure (although with ward elections) and has experienced high levels of economic growth over the past ten years. Unlike the other cities in the cluster, Cadillac still had relatively high levels of residential need, according to the 1990 census. Unemployment was particularly high, although officials indicated that it had dropped dramatically during the 1990s. As is characteristic of cities in this cluster, Cadillac evidences high levels of planning and evaluation and an entrepreneurial approach to economic development.

Kettering and Gloucester represent those cities where bureaucratic elites dominate economic decision making—the largest cluster, identified with 207 cities. As with the majority of cities in this group, residential need is low in these two cities, and input mechanisms for both citizens and businesses are limited. There was no particular governmental pattern to cities in this cluster because of the wide variety of cities in the group. This is evident with the two case cities—both have city managers and nonpartisan elections. Kettering has a council with a combination of ward and at-large seats; Gloucester has wards. Thus, Kettering and Gloucester represent a mix of reform elements.

Because the main trait of these cities is a decision-making process closed to citizens in all cases and businesses in two, along with an active approach toward economic development, it is useful to reiterate the findings of the multiple regression analysis regarding these issues. As suggested by the cluster analysis, leaving decisions to bureaucrats tends to increase both entrepreneurialism in approach to economic development and the extent of so-called professional behaviors, such as planning and evaluation. Giving greater power to bureaucrats appears to increase the use of zoning and financial incentives. Greater entrepreneurialism is associated with more loan, demand-side, and financial incentives. Last, planning and evaluation appear to stimulate development of a broader array of economic development goals.

The findings of the cluster and regression analyses are borne out in these three case cities. Although representing different states and countries, these three cities share strong cultural similarities, and their approaches toward economic development and the resulting policies are clearly more similar than different. This provides clear evidence of how local civic culture transcends state and national borders as well as population size and residential fiscal health.

THE CIVIC CULTURES OF
CADILLAC, KETTERING, AND GLOUCESTER

The Environment of Local Economic Development

The brief city summaries in Chapter 6 indicated reasonably wide variation in the environments of the three cities. Population varies from Cadillac with 10,194, to Kettering with 60,569, to Gloucester with 101,485. Cadillac struggled economically in the early 1990s but has improved considerably since then. In 1990, average income was $11,241, unemployment at 12%, and poverty at 16%. Kettering and Gloucester were much better off. Kettering had an average income of $18,988, with unemployment at just 3% and poverty at 4%. Gloucester had a high average income, $20,905, and unemployment and poverty rates were 6%. Whereas population growth rates were basically stable in Cadillac and Kettering, Gloucester grew by over 10,000 residents between 1981 and 1991. Thus, Kettering and Gloucester have similar economic profiles and population sizes, whereas Cadillac is smaller, with a higher level of residential need. The other major environmental difference between the three cities is that Kettering and Gloucester are located in large metropolitan areas, whereas Cadillac is the main employment center for a large rural area.

The Cadillac Economy

Though a small city, Cadillac serves as a retail and employment center and has a market area population of 60,000. It is the commercial and employment node for a large section of central western Michigan. Located on two lakes and a river, it is also a recreational center that caters to a larger market. Although even the 1990 census figures indicate high levels of economic stress—unemployment at 12% and poverty at 16%—economic forces since then have been much more positive, according to local officials. At the time of the interviews in the summer of 1999, unemployment had dropped to under 7%, and local officials were much more concerned about a labor shortage than with unemployment. As they indicated, "everyone who wants to work is working," and they were developing a promotional campaign to attract more workers to the area. Indeed, at the point of the interviews, local officials indicated that they could not, in good conscience, work to attract more businesses to the area because they simply did not have the available workforce. The city's marketing materials in the late 1990s indicated that over the past thirty months, there had been a 17% increase in employment and over $100 million in new private industrial development.

The city's status as a regional employment center is illustrated in the mix of employment opportunities. They have a diverse (typically, small and local) industrial base along with commercial and recreational employment. Firms have historically been locally owned, although in recent years, several have been purchased by external, in some cases, foreign, concerns. Operations remain relatively small, however, and foreign managers appear to make their homes in the community for the long term. As one business leader noted, "there is still a home-grown flavor to businesses in the city," even in the face of changes in ownership. Local leaders feel that there is a difference between having a local firm bought out and having a branch plant of a foreign firm; the former is believed to maintain a greater local commitment. The largest employers show the diversity of the economic base: Meijer (retail/grocery), Transppo Group, Avon Rubber and Plastic, AAR Cadillac Manufacture (pallets/containers), Four Winns (boats), Michigan Rubber, CMI Case Parts, and Mercy Health systems.

The mix of housing in the city is very broad. Around the lake areas, there is the kind of variety that is often found in recreational communities: small cabins alongside elaborate vacation homes and a mixture of second homes and full-time residences. The downtown is readily identifiable and very quaint; as their promotional material notes, Cadillac has "downtown vitality, lakefront allure." Cadillac has a traditional historic downtown area. The housing near the downtown also tends to be older, with a variety of styles and sizes. Everything is very well kept. As one moves away from the lake areas and the downtown, land use begins to be more rural, with single family homes on large lots. The downtown shopping district has a variety of stores with few vacancies and a streetscape project, including brick paving, trees, and banners. The only detriment to the downtown area is the presence of a large amount of commercial/truck traffic. A highway by-pass is currently being built, but until that is finished, a major state highway runs right through downtown Cadillac. Despite the efforts of local officials to make Cadillac a tourist destination, existing commercial facilities serve primarily a local consumer base. There is a theater, bank, small department store, and just a few restaurants: nothing particularly "up-scale." City Hall is located just behind the main commercial street on lakefront property and next to a small park where summer concerts are held. The city has done a good job of ensuring public access to the lake downtown, enhancing the overall atmosphere. The commercial area extends out from the downtown for several miles, with strip development and big-box chains serving the regional market. Thus, whereas the downtown and larger commercial districts are thriving, they provide goods and services for the local market area. This presents no particular problem except that it does not conform to the statewide recreational "product" that local business and city officials envision.

The Kettering Economy

Kettering is a much larger city, and the economy is much stronger than Cadillac's. It is a contiguous suburb of Dayton and has relatively close ties to the city. Incorporated in 1955, it is also one of the newer cities among the cases, and the housing and infrastructure illustrate that fact. The city is almost fully developed: Only 10% of the land area is vacant— redevelopment rather than development is the main goal in Kettering. Population has been stable at just over 60,000, and employment and poverty rates are very low. With average incomes increasing, the city's economy is stable and healthy. The largest employers represent a mix of traditional manufacturing (Delphi—a division of General Motors), services (Kettering Medical Center, Bank One), and commercial (Victoria's Secret Catalogue). The majority of residents are employed in white collar occupations—professional specialties, managerial, and sales.

Like many suburbs, the city does not have an identifiable "downtown." The most visible downtown area contains the city offices, a large park with a pool, an outdoor amphitheater that serves as a concert and event venue for the region, and an art facility. This area is set off by landscaping, banners, and streetscape, and it is very lovely. This, then, represents a cultural rather than a commercial downtown for Kettering. The commercial interests in the city are primarily located in strip shopping areas. Housing is relatively new, owner occupied, and moderately priced (the majority of houses are valued between $50,000 and $99,000). The quality of housing seems to be geographically organized, with lower-end housing (many containing the "decorative grillwork" often used to thwart criminal activity) located on the borders of the city and higher-end housing nearer the city center and theater area. Indeed, a number of very expensive multifamily and single-family units are under construction in the area right around the cultural facilities.

The Gloucester Economy

Visually, Gloucester looks very similar to Kettering. It is a relatively new (incorporated in 1981) contiguous suburb of Ottawa and also lacks a readily identifiable downtown area. As with Kettering, the city center is the location of local offices along with a large mall and several office towers. Population growth has been strong and unemployment and poverty stable at 8% and 6%, respectively. Given the economic downturn in Ontario in the 1980s, Gloucester's economy has done well. Between 1994 and 1997, the federal government downsized its workforce, affecting about 3500 residents of Gloucester. Despite this, the economic base is currently expanding as high-tech information firms discover that it is a relatively low-cost location within the Ottawa metropolitan area. The bilingual population fuels this economic development. The largest employers are the airport, serving the capital, and several airport-related firms, such as Esso Aviation Services and Hudson General Aviation Service. There are also a number of high-tech firms, including Telesat Canada, Telemark, and Dew Engineering and Development. Indeed, the city calls itself "Silicon Valley North-East," highlighting the fact that 120 high-tech firms are located there. Gloucester is also home to several federal departments, including the Royal Canadian Mounted Police and the Canadian Security Intelligence Service; over 30% of the residents are federal employees. Thus, the city benefits from its proximity to the capital as well as the location of the airport. It was clear from the interviews that having an airport in the city does not generate the kinds of problems it does for the city of Romulus, perhaps because of the smaller scale. However, like Romulus, Gloucester does not appear to have fully realized the economic development potential of the airport.

Housing in Gloucester includes a mix of multifamily and middle-income single-family units, often in close proximity to each other. Indeed, residential growth rates are likely to continue because the housing stock in Gloucester is cheaper than in neighboring suburbs on the west side of Ottawa. Currently, the demand for housing in Gloucester is strong. Although 73,000 acres of the city remain rural, 40% of that is controlled by the federal government in the green belt surrounding Ottawa. Still, the city has a reasonable amount of land available for both commercial and residential development. Although commercial development is spread through the city in strip fashion, there is a large upscale shopping mall located near the municipal center along with a large sports complex. Traffic is a major concern in this central area, and it takes a great deal of time to navigate around it during rush hour. The timing of traffic lights is a political concern. Although Gloucester certainly serves as a bedroom community for Ottawa, it is a commercial and employment center in its own right. Its status is much more that of an edge city than a traditional residential suburb.

Local Government Structure and Politics

All three elite-dominated cities have similar governmental structures, with a city manager and nonpartisan and ward-based or a combination of ward and at-large council elections. Cadillac and Gloucester have only ward seats, whereas Kettering has both at-large and ward representation. Cadillac does not have an economic development department, likely due to its small size; economic development responsibility is located in the manager's office and conducted by the manager and his staff. In the other two cities, there are free-standing economic development departments, common in cities where bureaucratic elites dominate development decision making.

Elected and appointed officials have been relatively stable in all three communities. In Cadillac, the mayor has been in office for ten years, and the city manager has worked with the city for twelve (four as city manager, eight as assistant city manager). There has been no change of personnel on city council since 1994 when one person lost because of their support for a planned unit development in the face of neighborhood opposition. Although the development was not to be located in the ward of the member in question, many from the affected ward went to the councilperson's church. Cadillac, thus, is a small town, with consensual politics based on familiarity. Although reflecting very different environments, there is also a striking lack of political conflict in the other two cities (at least, internal conflict). There has been more turnover in the

mayor and council in Kettering, but this had been the result of term limits that have since been repealed. Successful mayoral candidates have
tended to come from city council. In both communities, council votes
tend to be unanimous despite the ward divisions. There has been little
change in administrative officials in Kettering; the city manager has
been in his position for nine years and prior to that was a city planner.
The planning commissioner interviewed had been on the commission
for 25 years. In Gloucester, the current mayor had been in office since
1991. A new city manager and economic development director were recruited and hired within the past five years as the city embarked on a
more active economic development initiative. Both were selected to
more aggressively pursue economic development. The decision appears to reflect consensus on a desirable direction rather than the result
of conflict over leadership.

In short, there has been little political conflict in the three cities and a
general stability in elected and administrative personnel. It should be
noted that there did appear to be some political conflict in Gloucester in
the past, centered around some divisions between the mayor and council. Once the opposing members of council either did not run or were
not reelected, this disappeared. Apparently, the mayor also had some
conflicts with the previous city manager regarding their respective
roles. The mayor in Gloucester appears to be a strong individual and
clearly has had an effect on the general direction of policy in the city.
Currently, she appears to have a management team working in the same
direction as she is, and the basis for conflict is gone. The city manager
now runs the city with little direct political oversight.

Although all three cities have ward council systems, none appear to
have significant geographic divisions or conflicts based on the wards. In
Cadillac, a ward issue seemed to be important in only one election for
one councilperson in recent history. In Kettering and Gloucester, officials indicated that votes were usually unanimous, and any divisions
are worked out through consensus building. Cooperation rather than
conflict is the watchword in these three cities.

A caveat about Gloucester is warranted at this point. As noted in the
brief introduction, Gloucester was an independent city at the time of
the interviews in the fall of 1999. However, by the end of the year, the
provincial government decided that Gloucester and nine other cities
and townships would be consolidated into the regional government
of Ottawa. This was to take place in January of 2001. Thus, the "case" of

Gloucester is being reported as it was at the time of the interviews, real-
izing that at the time of publication of this book, it will no longer exist as
an independent entity. The "politics" of this reorganization were primary in the minds of all of the local actors interviewed in Gloucester,
who were, not surprisingly, strongly opposed, as well as the regional
officials interviewed, who were more supportive.

Intercity Competition for Development

The cities evidence differing perspectives on and levels of competition with other cities, apparently related to their place in the urban "hierarchy." Thus, officials in the more isolated Cadillac feel little competitive pressure from other cities in the region and only modest levels with
cities in other states. Those in Kettering and Gloucester feel strongly in
competition with cities near them in their metropolitan areas. Local officials in Cadillac felt little to no competitive pressure from other cities in
the state or even within the region. What competition they felt was with
cities in other states: Oklahoma, North and South Carolina, Ohio, and
Indiana. This competition was more related to the location decisions of
particular firms than a more generalized competition. And although
their tourism marketing is focused on the Midwest region, this again
has more to do with market area than specific competition. The competitive environment is quite different in the other two cities.

Officials in Kettering noted that they felt strong competition from
other cities in their region and with the city of Dayton. Dayton, however, presents a special case. Kettering officials are strongly committed
to regional cooperation, particularly with Dayton, and make affirmative efforts to reduce competition with Dayton so that the inner-city economic base is not further eroded. Several officials provided a telling
story about the relocation of Bank One headquarters from Dayton to
Kettering. Kettering did not try and "lure" Bank One, and when the firm
decided to move, Kettering voluntarily paid back the income tax loss to
the city of Dayton. Although some officials noted that this altruistic ges-
ture was made to "maintain good relations" with Dayton, others said
that it was to keep Dayton from "creating political hell" for Kettering
(Ohio requires a waiver from the city losing the firm only if a tax abatement was involved, which was not the case here). The mayor suggested
that the desire to work with and support Dayton comes from the fact

that many residents and local officials in Kettering have roots in Dayton. Whatever the motive, it appears that Kettering tries to avoid head-to-head competition with Dayton. And the Bank One situation does not appear to be an isolated case. Kettering officials also developed a voluntary metropolitan program where the suburbs contribute a dollar per resident for development in downtown Dayton. Kettering does not avoid competition with other suburban communities, however, and has been unable to match some of the deals offered by other cities or townships with more available land and/or a greater willingness to offer tax incentives.

Officials in Gloucester indicated that they felt strong competition with other cities in the Ottawa region, particularly those on the west side that have been the traditional location of the high-tech investment that the city desires. The city tries not to compete with other east-side communities and works in cooperation with them to get businesses to locate east rather than west of Ottawa. There is a clear regional divide in the Ottawa area. Gloucester officials also feel competitive pressure from cities in Quebec, where the province allows more discretion in the types of development incentives offered. It is interesting to note that officials in Gloucester were careful to point out that they felt more "energized and challenged" by this competition than stressed. This suggests that competition can have both positive and negative effects on cities. On the one hand, it can pressure officials to adopt expensive incentives in order to "keep up." On the other, it may lead local officials to explore more creative and innovative approaches to development, and this appears to be the dynamic in Gloucester. The effects of this on local policies will be discussed shortly.

In short, for none of these three cities is competition a negative force. But how officials interpret and address competition is quite different. In the relatively isolated Cadillac, competitive pressures are simply not salient. Officials in Kettering are openly and actively competitive with other cities in the Dayton area and larger region, but they emphasize cooperation with the city of Dayton itself. Last, officials in Gloucester compete with other cities on the west side of Ottawa and with cities in Quebec but try and cooperate with other east-side suburbs. Furthermore, they feel stimulated rather than threatened by these competitive pressures and react to them with more creative development policies.

Racial Issues

Racial diversity is not a central issue for any of these cities because they lack significant diversity or else the minority population is diverse. Cadillac is in the former category. Local officials indicate that the city is largely homogeneous, with some minimal ethnic rather than racial diversity. The largest ethnic groups are Vietnamese and Swedish. Kettering is still mostly white, though there has been a gradual increase in diversity as African American residents move into the community from Dayton. Thus, there are "one or two" neighborhoods that have increasingly diverse populations. Kettering has a range of housing options—from about $50,000 to three million dollars—along with a highly regarded school district, making it a desirable location for those with a range of family incomes. And although local officials indicate that there have been no racial problems in Kettering, there have been some conflicts that appear to have been more "personal" than racial in nature. If the diversity continues to increase in this city, racial issues may become much more central in the political life of the community than they were at the time of the interviews. Last, Gloucester's population is moderately diverse, but residents of color tend to be from Africa or the Caribbean; the largest immigrant group is Somali. Thus, although there is a moderately sized minority population, it contains a high level of internal diversity. Perhaps for this reason, local officials indicated that there have been no racial tensions in the community, and the immigrant groups have blended with other groups, including a substantial francophone population. In short, racial issues do not appear to be a significant part of the local culture, although Kettering may need to begin dealing with the challenges that increasing diversity is likely to present.

Civic Culture

Local Traditions

There are several critical features to the local civic culture in Cadillac. Literally, Cadillac is a small town, but it is also consciously viewed as a small town. Interactions are personal, face-to-face, and largely cooperative and consensual. The business cards of city staff and local officials include their home phone numbers, for example. Working cooperatively and the importance of volunteerism by both citizens and business leaders were emphasized in *every* interview in the city: "Tourism and industry work together," "the city is a joy to work with," "the city manager runs great government," "there is a community participation ethic in Cadillac," the city is small enough that "residents can be individually important and can contribute individually." The personal, cooperative, and volunteer ethics are very strong here. A final theme in Cadillac is the desire to appear "business friendly" and to facilitate business development. But although increasing the tax base is an obviously desired outcome, the goal most frequently mentioned was having enough jobs so that the children of Cadillac could stay there as adults; "it is a personal thing, as natives of Cadillac," "for the pride of having good jobs for our children and grandchildren."

There are three central elements of local tradition in Kettering: consensual decision making, aversion to anything "political," and an emphasis on professional leadership. The preference for consensus was mentioned by all of the local government officials interviewed, most typically in the context of city council deliberations. For example, the mayor indicated that "when there are disagreements on council, they eventually agree to disagree and then come to a consensus." Others noted that even though the council is elected by ward, this does not create divisions at this time; decisions are made by consensus. Closely related to this is a strong aversion to "politics." One respondent spoke to this directly, indicating that if a potential candidate for office "tried to stir things up," they were not going to get elected. "If it starts getting political, it just isn't going to get done." And although there are some partisan divisions at other levels of government, "we don't worry about that in Kettering." There are no political divisions because "we are a great city," indicated the mayor. Last, consensual decision making rests on the leadership of professional staff. Before each council meeting, the manager prepares a briefing book of staff reports so council never "has any surprises." In this way, the professional staff sets the parameters of debate, and the consensus develops around the reports because the elected officials don't "micro manage" professional staff.

The cultural attributes that stand out in Gloucester are very similar to those in Kettering, with an even greater emphasis on "businesslike" behavior on the part of the city. The general approach to governance is to "run the city like a business." For economic development, this is translated into a structure as a profit center, where operating funds are generated from increases in land assessments and sales. Hence, it is assumed that the activities of the department will pay for themselves. Consistent with this is an expectation that government officials will be "account-able." This means not only in a broad sense, as in fulfilling the mandates of the voters, but also in a more evaluative or outcome-oriented sense. Thus, it is expected that departments will set goals, establish benchmarks, evaluate themselves, and be held accountable. There is a very strong culture of professionalism in Gloucester, defined in a per-formance-oriented sense. The other theme in all the interviews revolved around the issue of governance or the debates about metropolitan con-solidation. To say that local officials were consumed by this would be an overstatement because they were clearly still going about the "busi-ness" of local government. Still, it was at the forefront of every discus-sion. This is not surprising because the very existence of the city (and the future of local officials) was in question.

In short form, the debate revolved around the implementation of the province's conservative government platform to achieve a 30% de-crease in taxes through a reduction in municipal units. The three op-tions being considered by a special provincial committee were (a) one megacity consolidating a number of municipalities; (b) a hybrid system where three cities (including Gloucester) would remain independent and the others would be consolidated, with some services moving to the regional level; and (c) no change. No one seemed to think the latter would occur. Although Gloucester officials agreed that residents were "overgoverned" in the area and that it "was high time" for some provin-cial reorganization, they obviously preferred the option that would leave Gloucester intact. The importance of this issue was so great at the time of the interviews that it raised intergovernmental relations and governance to the forefront of local discourse. Parenthetically, it was the megacity option that was chosen by the province, a result clearly ex-pected but not desired by local officials. The apparent irony for Glou-cester is that the local culture clearly emphasized professional deci-sion making and creative policy approaches, now in question with the consolidation.

Locus of Power

It is quite clear that in two of these cities—Kettering and Glouces-ter—the locus of power in economic development decision making lies with administrative officials, primarily the city manager and economic development director. The situation in Cadillac is a bit different; local administrators and business leaders share power in economic development decision making, apparently without conflict. In all three cities, there is little role for elected or "political" officials, and there is significant business involvement in Cadillac but not in the other two cities.

Cadillac is unique among all five case cities in the extent of cooperation between business and bureaucratic elites in economic development. All of the local respondents agreed that *within* the city, the manager and the director of administrative services (essentially the assistant manager) were left to conduct economic development without micromanagement by council or other elected officials. But it was also clear that external actors, primarily from the business community, had a significant role. It appears that economic development initiatives can come either from the city or the business community, depending on the particular project or where a contact is first made. All respondents outside the city agreed that there is "tremendous support from the city" for business projects and activities. Business leaders also acknowledge that the city "has it limits" in how cooperative they can be (zoning requirements have to be upheld, for example, but even when projects run up against ordinances, the manager acts as "troubleshooter") or in the amount of resources they can devote. Within those limits, however, they provide "excellent staff support" to the efforts of the several external business organizations. In short, all of the respondents appeared to agree that the locus of power runs "both ways" between city staff and external economic development organizations; "sometimes they lead, sometimes they follow" said one business leader of the city staff role in economic development. Or in the words of another, "everybody participates, the city manager is active, council is receptive, and major industry heads are interested in what's best for the city." In a nutshell, this statement appears to summarize the high level of cooperation between governmental and business professionals in the city.

The locus for economic development decision making in Kettering clearly lies with the city manager and economic development staff. As will be discussed shortly, there is very little business input in the city, and what there is tends to be initiated by city staff. Although the mayor indicated that at times she or the council initiated economic development projects, when pressed, she was unable to point to any examples and could also not think of an instance where the council had "vetoed" any of the manager's initiatives. The mayor's role in economic development appears to be primarily ceremonial, although she also sits on a number of advisory committees to foster regional cooperation. Here, too, policy ideas are brought back to the manager and council.

The situation is similar in Gloucester, where the city manager appears to be the main locus of development decision making. The explicit goal of the last city manager search five years before was to hire an individual who had a very strong background in economic development and who could take the city in a much more active and innovative direction; the current city manager fulfills this role. This effort was the direct result of the downturn in the economy between 1994 and 1997 and the downsizing of the federal workforce that negatively affected citizens and businesses in Gloucester. Early on, the manager helped the city create an Economic Adjustment Program and since then has been instrumental in implementing an active development strategy. The manager selected the economic development director, who is responsible for marketing. Although there is an active and cooperative chamber of commerce in Gloucester, they do not take a proactive role in economic development. The mayor participates in the initiatives and programs developed by city staff and acts as a "spark plug," sending ideas to the city manager. Still, the primary locus of power rests with the manager.

In short, the central characteristic of cities in the active-bureaucratic elite cluster is that central decision making and implementation initiative rests with the city managers and professional economic development staff. Unlike Fairborn, for example, there appears to be little role in economic development for other public bodies, such as the planning commission. Although they hold citizen hearings and are obviously part of the project approval process, they do not appear particularly powerful nor are their activities contentious in any of the cities. Although there is a significant business role in Cadillac and the mayor generates ideas and is an active participant in development programs in Gloucester, the locus of power rests with bureaucratic officials in all cases.

Role of Professionals Versus Elected Officials

In all three of these cities, the power balance between elected and appointed officials clearly swings in the direction of professionals. The only minor exception to this is that the mayor in Gloucester appears to play a leadership role and works in conjunction with the city manager and development director; she at least is involved in decisions about overall direction and goals. Beyond that, local appointed officials clearly take the lead in developing and implementing policy in all three cities. For example, Cadillac officials indicated that the city council basically told the city manager, "go out and get growth" and then stood back to let city staff do it. As another respondent put it, "the city manager is active, the city council receptive." Similarly in Kettering, local officials indicated that the council hired the city manager and stays out of his way. Very rarely do they "get into the sandbox and play." The city manager and economic development director are the central players in economic development decision making. The mayor agreed that she and the council largely reacted to staff reports produced by the city manager and that the council reached consensus based on these reports. In short, when respondents in Kettering were asked what actors had the most significant roles in economic development, the answers were, the city manager, economic development department, the planner and planning commission, and the engineering and transportation departments. All are local administrative units. The situation is similar in Gloucester. Although the mayor is available and willing to attend economic development "gigs" and participate as a booster in business visitation programs, the city manager and economic development director are the central players in economic development decision making and were explicitly hired to fulfill that role. It was indicated that the manager has "more ideas than he has time to implement" regarding development policy, suggesting that he is the main driver, with the economic development director implementing his agenda and taking the lead in marketing. In short, in all three cities, administrative rather than elected officials take the lead both in policy development and implementation.

Business and Community Input

There are high levels of business input in Cadillac but not in the other two cities. All three cities have in common the fact that there is little apparent citizen input. Although none of the local officials in any of the cities indicated an aversion to citizen input, and expressed desire for and described efforts to solicit input, little appears to have been forthcoming.

The business community in Cadillac is integral to the economic development effort and, indeed, many aspects of life in the community. There are three primary institutional sources of business activity: the Industrial Fund, the Downtown Fund, and the chamber of commerce. The Industrial Fund has a board made up of industrial and banking leaders and acts as a catalyst for industrial development through development and leasing of buildings, facilitation of relocation and expansion in Cadillac, and business retention efforts. Although clearly influential and active in economic development, leaders of the Industrial Fund were not willing to provide a great deal of detail on what activities the fund actually did other than these broad functions. Leaders feel that it makes sense for a private industrial organization to be doing retention and facilitation because the owners of industrial concerns feel more comfortable working with others in industry, and they have the personal contacts to assist development. All of the local officials agreed that having a lot of business participation increases the "business-friendly" image of the city. It should also be noted that the members of the board of the Fund have their own contacts in Lansing (the state capital) and lobby on behalf of the city. In addition to assistance in securing additional state funds for the city, local Fund leaders also mentioned an instance where personal contacts at the state level facilitated an industrial expansion through direct assistance in obtaining an air permit: "It was handled the way it should have been handled," personally and quickly.

The Downtown Fund is a spin-off of the older Industrial Fund and was created because top candidates for jobs were not coming to the city because "their wives didn't want to live in Cadillac" and because commercial leaders were interested in fending off the chain stores that were coming into the community. The Downtown Fund board includes bankers, realtors, and downtown commercial owners, as well as some manufacturing interests. The Downtown Fund provides one-stop assistance to those interested in locating or expanding a business in the downtown area, but they also extend their efforts outside the downtown to the northern commercial strip and even have assisted in the development of a ski lodge. Leaders in both organizations indicate that they prefer to work behind the scenes, "not many people know we exist," and let city officials take public credit for their accomplishments. As the chair of the Fund noted, the Downtown Fund "is able to make things happen, to know the people you need to talk to, within a structure behind the scenes."

The chamber of commerce is also active in development and represents a mix of retail and industrial businesses. Currently, they are emphasizing a stronger retail movement in the city, although they have a "very integral role" in all sectors of the economy. As with the Funds, the director of the chamber also has direct personal ties with the governor's office in Lansing as well as with the state jobs commission. The remaining central industry, tourism, is represented by a very active Visitor's Bureau; downtown merchants are also involved in this organization. Although these various organizations could get in each other's way, like other aspects of the development effort in Cadillac, they seem to work in coordination and are careful not to duplicate activities. In short, large aspects of economic development, such as the one-stop permitting, business retention, tourism, and downtown marketing, and even site and financial assistance, are provided by external, business-oriented organizations. There is another important by-product of this: Much of the economic development efforts are also financed, at least in part, by these organizations. It should be noted that this high level of input has continued even as some major employers have shifted from local to external ownership. Although most of the business actors involved in the two Funds are local, it was noted that even foreign managers are becoming integrated into the community.

There is much less citizen involvement in economic development in Cadillac. This is not to suggest that citizens are apathetic. Rather, the culture in Cadillac supports citizen (and business) volunteer activities, but these are directed toward the larger civic community goals rather than efforts to affect policy. More generally, there is little citizen opposition to development. Residents want more jobs in the community so that their children can stay. Those who want to limit growth tend to be newcomers from larger cities (such as Detroit and Chicago) who have vacation homes or have retired there—sort of a "pull up the drawbridge after they have gotten in" phenomenon. There are certainly no organized anti-growth movements in the city and, unlike many of the other case cities, little mention of citizen opposition to specific projects, even of a NIMBY nature. There are organized environmental or "green" groups in Cadillac, however, and they have opposed specific projects if they have potential negative environmental impacts. For example, a groundwater treatment system was opposed because fifty trees would have been removed. Citizens also attend zoning board meetings where projects are explained in detail, and it appears that city officials make affirmative efforts to provide such project information. The general culture of respect for opposing views and aversion to open conflict appears to extend to citizen interactions with government. Citizen opposition appears to be limited to multifamily housing proposals at this time; single-family housing seems uniformly desired. Opposition to multifamily housing appears to be the most contentious development issue in the city. In fact, the previous mayor lost his position because of his support for rezoning to allow a planned unit development.

Kettering appears to have little institutionalized business or citizen input. Although local officials acknowledge that there may be some "back channel" communication between business leaders and governmental officials, most business input appears to be the result of outreach efforts by the city. Local officials pointed to a number of business input mechanisms but indicated that businesses weren't really using them. Indeed, local officials noted that there was little to no business input or reaction even when the city revised the zoning and sign codes. It could well be that the external ownership of corporations and the branch plant nature of many firms limits the extent of interest or participation in local affairs. Even the areawide chamber of commerce serving three cities tends to focus on member services rather than governmental or policy issues.

Similarly, there appears to be little organized citizen input. The city has tried to involve citizens in the policy process without much success. All city employees must attend customer service courses, but generally, there is a low level of citizen complaints to be addressed. Input only appears to arise over specific projects or land use disputes. Unlike Romulus, for example, where the city is encouraging the development of big-box commercial enterprises, the city of Kettering is holding strictly to codes and zoning ordinances in an effort to restrict such development as much as possible, to preserve the older commercial districts. Indeed, there have been some complaints by potential business that Kettering is "difficult to work with" because they tend to hold strictly to ordinances and zoning standards. Citizen groups appear to support these efforts and perceive them as the city ensuring that development is the "best use" for a given neighborhood. Indeed, this support also seems to extend to existing businesses that feel that the standards ensure a nicer community appearance. The issue of older commercial districts most often engenders citizen input. At the time of the interviews, the city had received a petition with about 400 signatures from citizens wanting the city to assist in the redevelopment of an older strip shopping district (it should be noted that the city also desired to be more active in this area, but the district was involved in nonrelated litigation). Thus, it appears that a combination of a nonlocal business base and an agreement between citizen and governmental goals leads to limited business and citizen input in development.

The city of Gloucester has established a number of institutional relationships with the business community in an effort to stimulate greater business input. Yet local officials indicate that the chamber of commerce remains "inward looking" and that business leaders are not as proactive as the city would like them to be. The city established a memorandum of understanding with the chamber regarding their respective development activities, and the mayor has a monthly "business forum" to solicit feedback on business needs. The city has also organized breakfast meetings with the real estate community to assist them in marketing the city. Still, city staff say that they lead the business community "where we want to lead them" and that there is little pressure from business leaders. Business contacts appear to revolve around zoning requests or traffic issues. Local officials did note that there may be more direct business pressure at the regional level, although this was not mentioned by regional officials.

Similarly, there does not appear to be active and/or organized citizen input for economic development decision making. There are designated neighborhood commissions that are consulted in the general planning process, but these are not involved in economic development per se. Indeed, there are a number of citizen commissions, but they are activity based—parks and recreation, arts, sports—and have input in their respective areas. There is no commission for economic development. There has been little citizen opposition to development and broad general support for commercial development. Residents want to be able to "shop at home" and have taken an "it's about time" attitude regarding commercial development. It was suggested that because of the city's strong use of land use planning, citizens and developers know in advance where development will occur, so there is little controversy when it happens. Any development concerns involve traffic, and there are some environmental concerns about sprawl past the green belt surrounding Ottawa in the still-rural areas of Gloucester. On the whole, the city is trying to limit residential development because it is not "self-supporting."

Regime Status

The nature of the governing regime in each of these cities is fairly clear. Kettering and Gloucester do not have governing regimes according to a definition that requires stable business involvement. Although local officials in both of these cities have made affirmative efforts to involve the business community more directly and consistently in development decision making, business leaders have not been active as yet. Only in Cadillac is there a traditional development regime. In that city, there are very strong ties between business and city leaders, and business leaders are directly and institutionally involved in many aspects of economic development policy making and implementation. Much of the city's economic development effort is conducted, and in some cases financed, by external business organizations. Relations between these business groups and city leaders are close; the city manager sits on the boards of both the Industrial and Downtown Funds as an ex officio member. It is also interesting to note that the external boards tend to have interlocking directorships or "position overlap." For example, the brother of the chair of the Downtown Fund is on the board of the Industrial Fund, and the Downtown Fund was chartered with five of nine members of the Industrial Fund on its board.

Intergovernmental Relations

Intergovernmental relations are positive and relatively extensive in the two U.S. cities. Intergovernmental relations in Gloucester are intricately colored by the metropolitan consolidation debate and so were viewed much more negatively by local officials. Although Cadillac does not have significant relations with neighboring cities (because there are none nearby) nor with the county (the resources and capacities of rural northern Michigan counties are very limited), relations and ties to the state are numerous and uniformly positive. The creative funding options that local officials have been able to put together with significant contributions of state money are directly related to the innovative and very active approach toward economic development in the city. Cadillac is in the home region of Governor Engler ("Cadillac is Engler territory," noted one respondent), and its conservative representatives have supported close cooperation between the city and the state. Local officials also note that their good relations with the state are supported by the city's positive past track record with grants; "city officials have proven that they are creative problem-solvers who are able to create win-win situations for all parties, including the state," indicated the president of the chamber of commerce. This illustrates the unique blend of state political connections that open doors along with highly professionalized performance in Cadillac that keeps them open. The various private development funds have their own direct relationships with state government but also stress that this is as much the result of positive past projects as it is of "politics." Such discussions are further evidence of the unwillingness of respondents in Cadillac to acknowledge that *anything* is political, preferring to emphasize the professional accomplishments and cooperation among officials. On the other hand, it should be made clear that the ties between Cadillac and the state are also very personal. Relations with the federal government are minimal, perhaps because they are largely unnecessary. The county government is basically "written off" by Cadillac officials as having weak leadership and being largely "ineffectual," in the words of a respondent outside the local government. There does seem to be some active conflict between county and local officials, evidenced by a current lawsuit involving water/sewer access to the city's waste treatment facility for township residents.

Kettering appears to have positive working relationships with all levels of government, county, state, and federal. They work closely with the county on county-funded programs, but beyond this, interactions are minimal. As the largest suburb in the county, Kettering tends to run its own development programs. Relations with the state and federal governments are similar. They interact with the federal government regarding the CDBG program, and such relations are not problematic. They are also involved in some state programs but have had no conflicts there, either.

Intergovernmental relations are much more complex for Gloucester but need to be separated from recent problems related to the consolidation process (still under discussion at the time of the interviews) and the more regularized regional relationship that had been in place prior to the consolidation. Separate from the consolidation, relations between Gloucester and the regional government had been relatively smooth as far as economic development. The Ottawa Economic Development Corporation serves the Ottawa/Carleton region through a memorandum of understanding that outlines what the region will be doing for the city and vice versa. The region primarily focuses on marketing externally and entrepreneurship development. Although the region markets the whole area, cities are active in individual site development. Regional officials acknowledged that local/regional relationships were still "new and evolving" and that past relations were mostly project specific. Organizationally, there are several regional bodies with economic development responsibilities, although it seemed apparent that their roles and responsibilities would likely change in the wake of the consolidation. At the time of the interviews, the regional bodies involved in economic development included the following, overseen and largely funded by the Regional Municipality of Ottawa-Carleton:

Ottawa Economic Development Corporation: emphasizes marketing efforts

Ottawa Center for Research: provides a link between education, federal and provincial research initiatives, and businesses; provides networking activities among these interests, including a "smart capital" initiative, professional development programs for high-tech firms, operates an exchange program for government employees to do research and development in the summer

Ottawa Life Science Council: a small entity that focuses on agricultural issues and abandoned farm land

Ottawa Tourism and Convention Authority: receives provincial funds and then leverages those for regional tourism initiatives

The Ottawa Partners: composed of the heads of the other organizations and education and business leaders, their mandate is to coordinate all regional economic development activities and advise the regional council

Even prior to the conflict over consolidation, there were some conflicts between the regional and local bodies, however. Local representation on the regional council had recently been eliminated so that city officials were no longer able to appoint representatives. A regional Municipal Advisory Board with local representation had also been disbanded. All of this strongly suggests that the province was quite clear that the consolidation was coming, although local officials had not given up on some form of independence at the time of the interviews in the late fall of 1999. Obviously, relations between the city and the province have been totally colored by the fight over consolidation and the larger issue of off-loading of provincial activities to cities without corresponding funding. Thus, an interesting juxtaposition occurs whereby local officials feel "overgoverned" by the province at the same time that they are struggling with greater responsibility without the concomitant resources. In short, regional and provincial relations were in a significant state of flux at the time of the case study, and the decision in December to consolidate Gloucester into Ottawa could not have been a surprise, given the political and organizational environment. It should also be noted that very different pictures emerged from local and regional officials regarding the nature of local economic development efforts. Although regional officials tended to be condescending regarding the quality of local leadership and efforts and indicated that local discretion in development was limited, whereas regional activity was great, evidence at the local level belied that. Local efforts appeared active and creative and indeed had won national recognition. Suffice it to say that there appeared to be little love lost between local and regional officials in the wake of the "megacity" debate. Whatever positive working relationship and division of labor they had had in the past was no longer operative. It did appear clear that the city and regional body cooperated on marketing the Ottawa region as a whole. Local officials attended trade shows on behalf of the regional organization, and local officials agree that, to the outside world, they strive to present Ottawa as one community.

Planning and Evaluation

High levels of planning and evaluation are evident in all of these cities. This conforms to the regression analysis that indicated that giving development professionals within the city more discretion in decision making tends to be related to more planning and evaluation. The exact nature of planning and evaluation takes different forms across the cities, however, and tends to be related to the slightly different organization of economic development. In Cadillac, because of the role of external, private-sector bodies in decision making, planning and evaluation tend to be conducted by each organization or unit, as opposed to an overall plan for the city as a whole. Although this could lead to fragmentation of activities or uncoordinated efforts, this does not appear to be the case. It seems that the high level of cooperation and dialogue between the various institutional actors, as well as the overlapping memberships, ensures coordinated action even absent an overall plan. So the DDA has its own plan, the Brownfield development group has its own plan, the visitor's bureau has done strategic planning with the interests it represents, and so on. Again, the high level of dialogue between elites in these organizations and elites within city government limits duplication of effort and provides coordination among the groups.

Planning and evaluation in Kettering and Gloucester are very much the purview of city staff because they do not have the kinds of external involvement present in Cadillac. In both cases, a great deal of time and effort went into master economic development plans that are fairly recent in origin. Kettering contracted with a consulting firm from Texas to assist them in a strategic-planning process that culminated in a citywide economic development plan in 1999. Focus groups were conducted with city staff, businesses, and citizens. The plan contains explicit goals for each department involved in economic development. The city council instigated this process following the closing of an air force base, stimulated by a desire to be more proactive in future development efforts. Although local officials say there is no "formal" evaluation system, they monitor specific projects and track numbers of firms and jobs within the city. During the city budget process, they examine these figures and compare them to economic development goals. "Self-evaluation is part of the budget process," they note. At the same time, one official indicated that this budget evaluation is also somewhat "haphazard," suggesting that the budget review operates more in the nature of a "mixed scanning" approach where only particular areas are examined in depth each year. Still, the city has put a lot of effort into the development of a master economic development plan and makes significant efforts to include some evaluation of projects in the process. Several of their future goals relate to increasing the focus in their development efforts, better identification of priorities and evaluation of options, better prioritization for commercial strip redevelopment, and refinement of action plans for strategic goals. Clearly, officials in this city view the planning efforts as ongoing.

In Gloucester, the Economic Adjustment Program is the master economic development planning document developed by the new city manager. This set the agenda for a five-year program, identifying goals and strategies in five areas: business retention, marketing, industrial/commercial development, creation of a profit center for the economic development department, and community development. The last goal has been dropped from the plan, however, because they decided it would be more effective to work on community development through other actors in the city. The profit center goal relates to the organization of the economic development department as a "profit center," with all activity financed through the industrial reserve account supported by assessment increases and land sales. In addition to this citywide plan, the economic development department has an annual business plan that includes very concrete goals and performance measures. Furthermore, the city has conducted an office space study to gauge capacity, compiles statistics on the volume of traffic on the main highway through the city center to provide businesses with basic marketing and planning information, and has done a technological "hardware" analysis of the city and region. On the evaluation side, the benchmarks in the development plan allow for systematic assessment of development efforts. As the city manager notes, "we embrace accountability." This means that they try, to the best of their ability, to pinpoint what development city activities have affected and separate it out from what would have happened anyway. They are very aware of the difficulties involved in this exercise as well as the need to consider what would have happened without their efforts. Local officials also realize that they are somewhat unique in this focus on accountability, indicating that "most cities don't care *why* economic development happens, only that they can take credit." In Gloucester, it appears that local officials really want to *know*.

Views About the Role
of the Government in the Economy

Neither the local respondents nor the apparent local cultures in these three cities appear in opposition to relatively active government intervention in the economy, although the nature of that intervention takes different forms across the cities. In short, it appears that an acceptance of government intervention in the economy may be a prerequisite for an activist stance toward economic development.

Although there are strong expectations in Cadillac that businesses will support the community through volunteerism and will help subsidize many of their own economic development efforts, it is accepted that the local government will also be an active participant. City government freely gives tax abatements, is active in obtaining funding from the state, and is involved in many quite complex projects. There is little opposition to any of this. Being "business friendly" in Cadillac means that government and the private sector share active roles in the economy.

In Kettering, the desire to be proactive in development and generalized support of governmental efforts by businesses and citizens illustrates broad support for governmental efforts in addressing economic problems. Similarly in Gloucester, local officials, with apparent citizen and business support, have implemented a proactive program of business development. The award-winning business retention and development program defines government as a central business development resource. Furthermore, local officials take an active role in organizing and stimulating private-sector input as well as facilitating private development projects. In short, active public intervention in the private sector is an accepted part of the local cultures in Cadillac, Kettering, and Gloucester.

Entrepreneurialism

As implied earlier and inherent in the nature of active-elite cities, local officials take an active, innovative, and entrepreneurial stance toward economic development. In Cadillac, this can be seen in the very creative and complex use of project funding sources and in the effective interface between city and private economic development efforts. Although the government appears to be the central force in putting financing and projects together, each of the various external bodies are doing their own creative programming, from tourism marketing, to one-stop downtown development assistance, to community leadership development.

Kettering's redevelopment of a former air force base is probably the most significant visual evidence of their creativity in economic development. From the outside, this "business park" looks nothing like the air force facility it once was. Careful inspection of the "new" business park buildings reveals the curved airplane hangers behind new glass facades. Furthermore, Kettering's emphasis on the arts as economic development places them on the more innovative end of the policy spectrum.

It should be remembered that local economic development policy options are much more limited in Ontario. Most financial arrangements are not available to cities. Those proactive in economic development are going to emphasize marketing, land use, and business development efforts. Gloucester has taken an active role in the latter. The prize-winning Business Success Program includes mentorship, financial services, technical assistance, marketing assistance, evaluation services, relocation assistance, and more. Thus, the city government in Gloucester has basically taken on the role of business incubator and entrepreneurial stimulator.

Goals and Visions

Because these three cities have economic development plans—citywide for Kettering and Gloucester, within diverse organizations in Cadillac—local officials are very clear on their economic development goals and their desired vision for the future of their communities. For Cadillac, with their strong recent economic growth, the central goal is the attraction of workers with the skills necessary to support new businesses. Local officials noted that the city was about 400 workers short at the time of the interviews, and they were concerned about losing industry because of the worker shortage. A related goal is the "capture" of workers currently commuting into the city, trying to develop the housing base so that they become residents rather than commuters. In addition to the worker shortage, there is also a housing shortage in Cadillac; local officials indicate that the tri-county area needs about 1,700 more housing units. Several local leaders mentioned the desire that their children be able to remain and live and work in Cadillac. Although the city has sufficient low-income housing, they need more units in the $50,000 to $70,000 range. Builders in the area are also extremely busy, and this is hampering the development of additional housing. Once this need is addressed, the city would like to continue to expand the industrial base with a particular focus on existing and smaller businesses. Local business and governmental leaders are very clear that they do not want large manufacturers that are likely to change the nature of the community or that may do economic damage if they happen to close down, as was the case with a Goodrich plant. Although business leaders and city officials agree on goals, the former also indicated that another goal is the redevelopment of a local corporate leadership base. Many locally owned firms in Cadillac have been bought out by external, in some cases, international, owners. There is a desire to redevelop a culture of corporate civic involvement among the new employees and managers of these firms who are now making Cadillac their home. In all, most of the goals in Cadillac are tied to appropriate reactions to their relative success—making better corporate citizens of their new business owners, finding more workers for existing jobs, and creating housing for those workers. In the area of tourism, there are some specific additional goals. Local officials would like to see Cadillac become more of a vacation destination and would like to expand their recreation "product" to a more year-round industry. Despite the lake location, much of Cadillac's tourism takes place in the winter and is focused on snow-related sports, such as skiing and snowmobiling. They are currently trying to expand golf options, increase the length of tourist stays, and conduct internal marketing to make local residents more aware of the tourist advantages of Cadillac.

Goals in the other two cities are more traditional and less related to growth pressure than in Cadillac. Local officials in Kettering indicate that their central goals are the attraction and expansion of higher-density employers (in terms of number of jobs) and the attraction and retention of high-paying jobs. Essentially, they are more concerned about the quality than quantity of jobs in the community. Redevelopment and reuse rather than development are the keys here because 98% of the city is already developed. This redevelopment also specifically includes the need to revitalize older commercial areas in the city, perhaps into new uses. Local officials also noted a need to update zoning policies to shift the focus from "cornfield" development to the more current issues related to redevelopment. Other broader issues that officials in Kettering plan to address in the coming years include achieving greater regional cooperation for economic development, particularly with Dayton, and an emphasis on containing sprawl as businesses and residents move from Kettering to the outer-ring "exurbs" (this term was used by the economic development director, clearly indicating both an academic and practical awareness of this situation). Last, local officials in Kettering made an interesting point that all "development" in the city is not necessarily viewed as positive "economic development." In other words, the city has no particular desire for more "big-box" drug stores and makes no efforts to attract them. However, they have such development because zoning laws can not be used to keep them out. Thus, all development is clearly not seen as being equal in the eyes of local officials in Kettering, perhaps because they have the luxury of a relatively strong economy.

The goals in Gloucester revolve around business retention, increased office space, increased hotel capacity, selective development on the east side of the city (where they want the development of an agglomeration of high-tech firms), emphasis on high-tech and financial service or "value-added employment," and developing creative linkages for the town center area (government offices, golf course, entertainment area) that is divided from other parts of the city by the major highway. They were clear about the fact that retail or commercial development does not really help the tax base of the city. Furthermore, the ultimate goal of the economic development efforts is to relieve pressure on the residential tax base by increasing revenues from the industrial sector. Residential development is not seen as self-supporting and with the highest housing starts in the region, local officials allow residential development to occur without either assistance or hindrance.

ECONOMIC DEVELOPMENT POLICIES IN CADILLAC, KETTERING, AND GLOUCESTER

Overall Policies

The discussion of economic development policies in Cadillac took up the better part of the interview time with city staff. Cadillac has a very active and complex economic development agenda, with most projects having a variety of funding sources/arrangements. In addition, each of the several external organizations conducts pieces of the city's overall economic development activity. The city is primarily responsible for tax abatements, business visitation, worker attraction, administration of the DDA and TIFA, land development, infrastructure improvement, job training, facade loans, and brownfield redevelopment. Tax abatements are given to any firm that requests them, at 50% for the full twelve years possible. Local officials feel that an open door for tax abatements promotes the business-friendly atmosphere, and they would rather have "50% of something than 100% of nothing." The mayor and city manager visit large employers annually to assess business needs, provide technical resources, and show that they are business friendly. The city is currently developing a marketing program to attract workers and uses state CDBG funds for some retraining of those already employed. The business leadership is considering a larger training role, however, to better meet actual skill needs. To this end, business organizations are funding an individual to assess employer needs. The DDA program appears to be thriving; there is less than a 3% vacancy rate downtown. The TIFA was started in 1993 and by 1995 had a sufficient tax capture to finance a $60,000 streetscape in conjunction with state grant money and a special assessment. The city also provided significant infrastructure and service enhancement in the downtown (code changes, buried utility lines, paved parking), are connecting hotels with green space, and are currently developing a sports park. The city has also been involved in property development downtown financed through the DDA, general revenue, the community development fund, and CBDG capture. This is an example of their ability to package project funding from a variety of sources. Another example of creative project packaging is the development of a property for a state Department of Environmental Quality building. The state initiated the project, and the city purchased and cleaned a contaminated site (an interesting irony, having an environmental quality facility on formerly contaminated land) using state brownfield money. The city also sold bonds for the project and now leases the building back to the state. There was also an agreement that the state would not close the facility without an act of the legislature— more evidence of the close relationship between Cadillac and Lansing. Last, the city uses state CDBG funds to support industrial development initiatives, and a brownfield redevelopment authority covers the entire city. Local officials indicate they like contaminated sites because they

are eligible for state infrastructure and remediation grants. Several industrial sites in the city have been redeveloped by the authority.

As noted previously, the external organizations deal with other aspects of the total economic development effort, and rather than being duplicative, they seem to have an effective division of labor. The
major external players and their economic development activities are as
follows:

> *Industrial Fund:* Development and leasing of industrial properties; assis-
> tance in facilitation of industrial development; business retention calls;
> beginning a housing development initiative
>
> *Downtown Fund:* One-stop assistance for those interested in a downtown
> location; ombudsperson between business and government
>
> *Chamber of Commerce:* Auto-affiliated job training; retention calls; CEO
> Forum to develop business leadership; community leadership develop-
> ment program; one-stop web information for prospective residents;
> high school and junior high leadership programs
>
> *Visitors Bureau:* Community arts and concerts; marketing for tourism; com-
> munity holiday celebrations; sales of city logo merchandise

Kettering's economic development activities are somewhat less extensive but equally as creative in concept if not in financing. The most
interesting project is the business park previously mentioned. Visually,
the modern facades on airplane hangers and standard military buildings is extremely effective. The city has made an informational video
about this project, which they present as a model for other cities. The
city also does land development aside from the business park, including demolition and site preparation, and a new research and development park supported by a combination of state and foundation funds is
currently in progress. It is a bit unclear about the extent of the city role
in this latter project because the land is held and sold by the private
foundation. The city has a business retention/expansion program targeting medium and small businesses, including door-to-door discussions and surveys. The city offers tax abatements, but officials indicate
that they do this only rarely and have a self-imposed standard of a 20-
25 job minimum for a firm to receive an abatement. The city also participates in a number of intergovernmental programs, including small
business loans using CDBG funds, a county-linked deposit program,
county equity grants for site development and infrastructure, and the

state enterprise zone program. Last, city officials are very aware that investments in culture and their community arts facility are also economic development policies. These quality-of-life issues are explicitly a part of their economic development agenda. It should be noted that not all of these activities are entirely "produced" by the city because they employ external consultants when the need arises. Thus, consultants helped them with their strategic planning process and have been used to assist in marketing and in environmental reviews.

Because of provincial restrictions on financial bonuses, Gloucester has focused it efforts on business retention and development. The Economic Adjustment Program was instituted by the new city manager and emphasized continuous adjustment to economic change. Initial program efforts involved targeting 2,000 companies for personal visits. The whole city staff was asked to volunteer; 47 individuals in addition to the manager, economic development director, mayor, and council members were trained to make business contacts. Business leaders were asked what they liked about the city, what they needed from the city, what they needed to prosper more generally, and so on. Out of this, the rest of the businesses retention and support effort—The Business Success Program—evolved. This program, recipient of a provincial prize in 1996, includes

Business mentorship program

Financial services program

Technical evaluations for businesses

Quick Fix Program (where small city problems standing in the way of development are identified and addressed)

Marketing assistance

Beyond the Success Program, the city extensively markets its high-quality and bilingual workforce. They have also engaged in some property development, assisted in the conversion of an old movie theater into a performing arts center, and have helped find tenants for buildings along the major highway. Last, the city provides new employees/residents with welcome packages and business relocation assistance.

Type II Policies

Type II or progressive policies are very limited in these three cities. Although the economic development efforts are creative and innovative, they do not necessarily include Type II efforts. In Cadillac, the only program of a Type II nature is their parking linkage program where developers receiving incentives must leave land open for downtown parking. Kettering uses local hiring *goals* as part of their incentive decision; firms with more local content are favored. Local officials emphasized that although there is no written policy, they may adopt such hiring linkages on a case-by-case review. Last, Gloucester has a "buy Gloucester" program; a business directory of contact information for purchasing personnel to let them know what services and products are available in the city is distributed in an effort to increase local sales. They have just begun to experiment with linkage programs in the form of allowing a cellular relay tower to be located on top of the municipal building in return for a donation from the company, which was used to purchase a bus for senior citizens. In short, these are not "high" Type II cities.

CULTURE, PROCESS, AND POLICY

Table 9.1 compares the environment, culture, and policies of Cadillac, Kettering, and Gloucester. These are discussed in more detail in the sections to follow.

The Environment

The economic environments in Kettering and Gloucester are very similar; both are healthy communities with low levels of residential need, unemployment, and poverty. Indeed, they are the healthiest of all the case cities on most indicators. The historic profile in Cadillac has been very different, with the highest 1980 unemployment levels, high poverty, and the lowest median incomes among all the cities. On the surface, then, Cadillac's economy is the weakest of the group. However,

TABLE 9.1 Comparison of Cadillac, Kettering, and Gloucester:
            Environment, Culture, and Policies

Cadillac	*Kettering*	*Gloucester*
Environment		
Moderate to high residential need, dropping after 1990	Low residential need	Low residential need
Moderate perceived competition	Moderate to high perceived competition	Moderate to high perceived competition
Formal structure: city manager, nonpartisan, ward	Formal structure: city manager, nonpartisan, ward and at-large	Formal structure: city manager, nonpartisan, ward
Wards matter little	Wards matter little	Wards matter little
Little racial diversity	Little racial diversity but increasing	Little racial diversity
Culture		
Low levels of politics	Low levels of politics	Low levels of politics
Institutionalized business input	Little business input	Little business input
Little citizen input	Little citizen input	Little citizen input
Strong city/business cooperation	Disdain for politics, professional planning ethic	Disdain for politics, professional planning ethic
Volunteer ethic	City staff locus	City staff locus
Business/city share power	Public-sector locus	Public-sector locus
Economic development in manager's office plus external private organizations	Independent development department	Independent development department
Cooperative extensive relations with state, poor relations with county	Cooperative, moderate intergovernmental relations	Negative intergovernmental relations (consolidation issues)
Strong support for public subsidies with expectation for private subsidy	Strong support for public subsidies	Moderate/strong support for public subsidy given provincial restrictions
Moderate to high planning and evaluation	High levels of planning and evaluation	High levels of planning and evaluation
Development regime	No regime	No regime

TABLE 9.1   (Continued)

Cadillac	Kettering	Gloucester
Policies		
Moderate to high marketing	Moderate marketing	High marketing
Regulatory facilitation/ one-stops	No regulatory facilitation	Regulatory facilitation, quick-fix program
Industrial parks	Industrial/business parks	No financial incentives
High financial incentives	Modest financial incentives	Extensive business retention/ development
Business retention	Business retention/ expansion	No DDA
Infrastructure development	TIFA, enterprise zones	Land development
Worker attraction, job training	Land development	Business incubator services
DDA, TIFA	Fine arts development	Cellular tower linkage
Brownfield redevelopment	Considers jobs when granting abatements	
Land development, lease back		
Tourism development		
Parking linkage program		

Cadillac experienced significant economic growth during the 1990s and has current unemployment and poverty levels much more in line with the other cities. It is clear that Cadillac has been dealing with a more challenging economic environment than the other two cities, however. The governmental structure is similar in the three cities; all have city managers and nonpartisan elections. Cadillac and Gloucester have ward-based councils, whereas Kettering has a mix of ward and at-large seats. Likely due to their location in large metropolitan areas, officials in Kettering and Gloucester perceive high levels of competition with cities in their immediate region. In the more isolated Cadillac, perceptions of competition appear more modest and are mostly in relation to other parts of the country, perhaps making those pressures seem more remote.

The Culture

The overall culture of Cadillac may be summarized as follows:

High institutionalized input from the business community with low residential input

Emphasis on cooperation, consensual decision making, and disdain for "politics"

High levels of cooperation between the public and private sectors

Strong professional ethic

Strong community volunteer ethic

Moderate planning and evaluation emphasis, although somewhat fragmented in implementation

Extensive and positive relationships with the state, limited and negative county relations

Decision-making locus is shared by city staff and business leaders

Development regime

Economic development authority is shared between governmental and external business bodies

Primary economic development goals are worker attraction, tourism diversification, small/medium-sized business development, community leadership development

The civic culture in Kettering is somewhat similar, but there is a very different relationship between the public and private sectors. In Kettering, city staff are clearly in control, with little overt business input. The culture in Kettering is as follows:

Low levels of business and citizen input, although the city has tried to increase both

Emphasis on consensual decision making and aversion to "politics"

Emphasis on leaving decisions to professional staff

Strong planning and evaluation

Modest levels of intergovernmental cooperation, yet relationships appear good, particularly with Dayton

Decision-making locus rests with city staff

Primary economic development goals are development of arts and culture, development and expansion of medium-sized businesses, increase in high-quality jobs, and reuse of older industrial and commercial sites

Even though they are located in different countries, the civic cultures in Kettering and Gloucester are almost identical. The culture in Gloucester can be summarized as follows:

Low levels of both business and citizen input, although the city has tried to increase both

Emphasis on consensual decision making and aversion to "politics"

Emphasis on leaving decisions to professional staff

Strong planning and evaluation

Government should operate like a business and economic development as a profit center

Strong emphasis on accountability of city staff as measured by outcomes

Low levels of intergovernmental cooperation; the whole issue clouded by the consolidation debate

Decision-making locus rests with city staff

Primary economic development goals are business development and retention, emphasis on high-tech attraction, relieving pressure on the residential tax base, and integrating the city center with the rest of the community

The Policies

Economic development policies are entrepreneurial, creative, and very active in all three cities, even though the particular policies employed vary. Indeed, each city has crafted an economic development agenda that appears to match their respective local needs, goals, and situations. Cadillac has the broadest array of activities, perhaps because efforts are conducted and financed by both the private and public sectors. Complex financing arrangements blend a great deal of state money along with local resources. Kettering has been extremely innovative in the development of business parks, turning what might have been a shattering economic loss (the closure of a military base) into an economic development gain. Traditional development policies, such as tax abatements and land development, are used in innovative ways, showing that the policy itself may not be as important as the overall approach of which it is a part. Including arts and culture as an explicit part of their economic development effort is also innovative. Last, without financial incentives, the city of Gloucester has created an innovative business development and retention program that places the city government in the role of entrepreneur. Type II policies are almost totally absent in these cities, clearly indicating that there is no inherent relationship between creative and/or entrepreneurial policies and more progressive policies that would redistribute the benefits of development more broadly.

SUMMARY

Several "lessons" about local civic culture stand out in this chapter. First, as has been noted previously, the economy is clearly not the determining force in either culture or approach to economic development. The economic environment has been very different in Cadillac than in the other two healthy cities. Yet very similar civic cultures are evident, emphasizing consensual decision making, aversion to politics, and professional planning and evaluation. Even with different environments, similar cultures lead to similar entrepreneurial approaches to economic development.

It should also be noted that the regime status of the three cities is different. There is a classic development regime in Cadillac, whereas there is no apparent regime in the other two cities because of the lack of significant business input. What does this say about the role of regime within the culture of economic development? First, it seems clear that businesses do not need to be involved in a regime for the city to pursue a business-friendly stance toward economic development. Policies in Kettering and Gloucester are clearly focused on assisting business, even absent institutionalized business input. Second, it is also apparent that having a development regime with a strong business role does not preclude private-sector subsidization of economic development. Indeed, in Cadillac, not only do businesses finance many economic development activities, the ethic of volunteerism in the community ensures that business leaders are active in many wider community projects and efforts. Development regimes do not a priori mean that businesses will take advantage of the community. In short, the nature of the regime appears to have little to do with the approach toward economic development; civic culture is a mediating force.

These case studies also indicate that there may be a set of complex interactions between several of the variables explored. It appears that the civic culture in the three cities—emphasizing cooperation, consensus, and aversion to politics—is related to a strong emphasis on planning and evaluation, leaving primary decision making with city staff (or staff in combination with business leaders), which in turn produces an entrepreneurial and active approach toward economic development. Placing the economic development power locus with staff is related to high levels of planning and evaluation and active and innovative policies. It seems just as clear that these cultural forces do not lead to Type II policies. Perhaps, the lack of political input from the larger community and the aversion to the political give and take necessary for a diversity of demands to come before the public agenda limits the opportunity, or perhaps the ferment, necessary for Type II or progressive policies to develop. A weak economy clearly does not appear sufficient to necessitate Type II policies, or they would be more evident in Cadillac. Rather, it may be that a relatively closed, bureaucratically driven process may not provide a congenial forum for progressive policy making.

Along the lines noted, it is important to distinguish innovative or entrepreneurial policies from progressive policies. They are obviously not the same things nor do they occur together in the same cities. Local policies can be creative and the stance toward economic development entrepreneurial without any necessary connection to efforts to redistribute the benefits of economic development. It is also important to note that the overall approach toward economic development is more important than the particular individual policies pursued. Thus, the civic cultures in Cadillac, Kettering, and Gloucester appear to lead to an entrepreneurial stance toward economic development with the local government taking an active role in private-sector development. However, the particular policies used in each city are different and designed to match particular local conditions and needs. Again, this is just what one would expect of decision making based on high levels of planning and evaluation, a relatively good match of local conditions and goals to actual policies. This appears to be the case in these three cities.

NOTE

1. The officials interviewed in Cadillac included City Manager; Director of Administrative Services; President of the Chamber of Commerce; Mayor; Executive Director, Cadillac Area Visitor's Bureau; Chair, Cadillac Downtown Fund; Chair Cadillac Industrial Fund; two Industrial Fund members. Respondents interviewed in Kettering included: Mayor; Law Director; Chair, Planning Commission; Community and Economic Development Director. Officials interviewed in Gloucester included: City Manager; Manager, Economic Affairs; Marketing Projects Coordinator, Ottawa Economic Development Corporation; Executive Director and Research Fellow, Ottawa Centre for Research and Innovation; City council member; Manager, Economic Affairs, Regional Municipality of Ottawa-Carleton.

10

THE PASSIVE-ELITE CASES

Cornwall and Allen Park

Team Cornwall is a voluntary association of local businesses whose main purpose is to be a city booster, to help market their city to potential businesses, and to be ambassadors to keep the public aware of the good local industry. The group was created to open up a dialogue about business in Cornwall. Team Cornwall members had baseball cards made up with their names, photos, and brief business biographies. They distribute these at trade shows and are very proud of their role. They keep their eye on the Economic Development Department, but see the city as being "insular." One Team Cornwall member said, "They just are not aggressive enough," and he offered an example of Team Cornwall placing its logo on a number of private trucks that travel throughout the region. The city decided that it would be better to use the city's own logo, and Team Cornwall conceded. But the conclusion has been that the city has moved too slowly in following through. This passive, perhaps hesitant, approach to economic development seems to characterize the city's efforts. But elected officials do not appear to be unhappy with the role their staff plays.

Allen Park has its share of conflict over local policy. The last mayor served for one term and was defeated. Although unusual, it also appears that city council regularly overrules the recommendations of its professional staff and consulting planners. The mayor is part time and not in city hall on a regular basis. City hall is a converted church, and there is interest in building a new civic center complex, but its location is another source of conflict. Downtown business interests want it located down-town, whereas city officials are looking at an outlying site. The chamber of commerce president is unhappy with the city's deaf ear to their con-cerns. There is a dialogue, just not much response. They are currently pressing the city to have a more open input system for both private citi-zens and business interests.

     The two cities profiled in this chapter fall into the same larger cluster as Kettering and Gloucester. Thus, they, too, represent cit-ies where bureaucratic elites dominate the economic development deci-sion-making process, and there is little business or citizen input. Beyond this, however, Cornwall and Allen Park differ from the cities in the previous chapter in several important respects. First, Cornwall and Allen Park have not experienced the levels of economic growth present in either Kettering or Gloucester. Whereas Allen Park has been stable economically, Cornwall faced significant economic stress during the 1980s. Thus, the environments of the two groups of cities have been rather different.

     Second, general acceptance of things "political" is broader in Cornwall and Allen Park. Whereas political debate in the former is quite civil, there is a good bit of open conflict in the latter. In neither city was there the type of open and uniform aversion to "politics" so characteris-tic of Kettering and Gloucester.

     A third significant difference between the cities profiled in the pre-vious chapter and Cornwall and Allen Park is their very different stance toward economic development. The hallmark of cities in the last chap-ter was their active, entrepreneurial, and innovative approaches to eco-nomic development. Officials in Cornwall and Allen Park are signifi-cantly more reactive or passive in their economic development efforts. They are business friendly when approached but do not go out of their way to either attract or foster new investment. And predictably, their economic development policies are more traditional and limited, par-ticularly in Allen Park.

     There were 207 cities in the elite-dominated cluster, and it should not be surprising that cities with different situations and approaches to economic development should be included. Cornwall and Allen Park differ somewhat from the majority of cities in the cluster in their relatively weaker economies, less planning and evaluation, and a less active approach toward economic development.

Although regression analysis indicated that cities with little business or citizen input and a high reliance on bureaucrats are more likely to use planning and evaluation and have an entrepreneurial approach to economic development, this was not the case in Cornwall and Allen Park. Here, leaving decisions to bureaucrats has resulted in little planning and evaluation and a generally passive and traditional economic development effort. Why is this the case? What appears to cause Cornwall and Allen Park to have very different approaches to economic development than Kettering and Gloucester? Are differing economic forces all to "blame," or are there aspects of the civic culture in Cornwall and Allen Park that mitigate against a more active stance? These questions are addressed in this chapter.

THE CIVIC CULTURE OF CORNWALL AND ALLEN PARK

The Environment of Local Economic Development

The economic settings of Cornwall and Allen Park are very different, as are their size and location relative to other communities. Cornwall is a free-standing city of an estimated 47,403 in 1999, whereas Allen Park is an older inner-ring suburb of 28,148 (estimated 2000). Although Cornwall has struggled with economic transformations since the significant Canadian recession of the 1980s, its population has held steady, and recently, its unemployment rate dropped to the 6% to 8% range. Yet it has a high level of poverty and a declining per capita income. Cornwall's average housing prices are well below the national average for Canada. Allen Park is a stable, middle-class, homogeneous, white suburb of Detroit that is half the size of Cornwall. Although its population has dropped 16% since 1980, this is due in part to the aging of residents. Per capita income levels have been stable, and poverty has been both low and stable over the past decades. Likewise, unemployment is low and dropped substantially between 1980 and 1990. Clearly, these two cities have faced very different economic challenges and opportunities.

The Cornwall Economy

Historically, Cornwall's strategic location between Ottawa and Montreal, adjacent to Highway 401 on the St. Lawrence River near the United States border, made it an attractive site for business and industrial development. The location is competitive—within a day of many places, including Detroit, Chicago, New York, and Ottawa. But with the opening of free trade with the United States, industrial reorganizations, and the severe 1980s recession in Canada, the city and the immediate region suffered tremendous job loss. Population held steady, however, between 1981 and 1991. But during this time period, the per capita income dropped significantly, from $17,893 to $15,072. Likewise, poverty rates hovered in the 17% to 21% range, and unemployment was stuck in the 10% to 11% range. Clearly, the 1980s were not particularly kind to Cornwall.

By 1999, however, the economic condition of Cornwall had begun to change, and some of its problems were touted as developmental advantages. Average housing costs in Cornwall are $89,730, well below the national average of $167,114 (for 1998). Average industrial land prices are an impressive 5% of those in Montreal, 3% of those in Toronto, and 16% of the average for Ontario. Relatively high unemployment rates translate into available work force. Low wages and a stable population translate into high workforce retention and wage advantages. These developmental advantages are opportunities for a struggling community. On the other hand, they are also characteristics of a community in severe economic distress.

Cornwall sells itself as a manufacturing community; "We make things and ship them all over the world."[1] Cornwall is home to seventy manufacturing industries employing approximately 5,748 people. Textiles, pulp, and paper were the traditional foci, but most recently, the city has attracted plastics, electrical, high-tech, furniture, and chemical industries. The city's largest employers are Domtar Papers (pulp and paper, with 1000 employees), Morbern (fabrics, 400), Satisfied Brake (375), Ridgewood Industries (furniture, 225), Lightolier (lighting, 130), Lilly (plastics, 117), Marimac (bedding, 111), Richelieu Hosiery (clothing, 110), and Canadian Technical Tape (tape, 92). In 1998, Supply Chain Management, handling distribution for Wal-Mart Canada, invested $55 million in a state-of-the-art distribution center. In all, 1998 saw $150 million in new investment in Cornwall. The economic base of the town is relatively diverse and growing at last.

One of the city's current initiatives is called Smart City, designed to increase and update its telecommunications infrastructure and thereby compete for some of the new high-tech jobs. With these improvements, Cornwall has been identified as one of Ontario's preferred locations for call centers because close to 50% of the population is bilingual. In addition, Cornwall owns a 1,600-acre fully serviced industrial park with ample room for future businesses.

Another significant Cornwall advantage currently is derived from the decision earlier in the 1990s to sell the city-owned Cornwall Electric, as a part of the general Ontario deregulation process. The city made $68 million on the sale, and the money was placed in a fund to pay off all city capital debts as they come due, with a balance of $24 million going into an endowment-type fund for community capital projects. Citizens were given a tax cut after the sale, rates were frozen for three years, and Cornwall's electric rates are still lower than those of Ottawa and Toronto.

Cornwall also has the advantage of an identifiable downtown, with a variety of generalized and specialty stores, including the obligatory coffee bars. Even though currently lacking a DDA, the shopping district has a nice streetscape with banners and historic lighting. There is an area of historical houses just outside of the central business district that is also very lovely. A bit removed from the CBD is another shopping district that, although known as a French business district, currently has a relatively varied mix of shopping and service alternatives. The city's location on the St. Lawrence also affords a scenic waterfront area that is the location of parks and the city's recreation and convention complex.

The Allen Park Economy

The population of Allen Park was 31,092 in 1990 and is projected to have declined almost 10% to 28,148 by 2000. Yet the number of households actually rose by around 100. This is a typical pattern for an older suburb (it was incorporated as a city in 1957) and one in which most of the housing was built in the 1950s and 1960s. The population is aging, but the neighborhoods are retaining their grace and family focus. Total annual births are less than annual deaths, and in the last four years, there have been fewer than three annual new housing permits. But like Cornwall and so many other cities, its location is crucial.

Occupying only 68 square acres, Allen Park is centrally located between the Detroit Metropolitan Airport and the City of Detroit at the intersection of Interstate 94 (Chicago to Detroit) and State Highway 39 (the Southfield Expressway). On I-94 in Allen Park is a widely recognized symbol of Detroit and the auto industry, the giant Uniroyal Tire. But most important, Allen Park is near the city of Dearborn, the home of Ford Motor Company. At one point, Henry Ford owned one-third of the land in what is now Allen Park. The city is home to seven Ford plants; Fairlane Business Park, developed by Ford Land Development, which houses several major suppliers for Ford; and Ford-family-owned Detroit Lions' about-to-be-constructed practice fields and training camp. Clearly, the city's location and its strong industrial base tied to Ford Motor Company has enabled its neighborhoods to age graciously and to maintain their attractiveness to a new generation.

Housing values declined dramatically throughout much of the Detroit area in the 1980s, and Allen Park was not spared. Allen Park's median housing value declined from $76,296 in 1980 to $66,600 in 1990. In 1980, it was well above the outside-Detroit county average of $63,767, whereas in 1990, it was below the outside-Detroit county average of $67,900. The 1990s were much more kind to the Detroit metropolitan area than the 1980s, and this is seen in Allen Park's substantial growth of median home sale prices between 1985 and 1997, from $47,610 to $103,189.

Following the housing pattern in Allen Park, average incomes rose only slightly between 1980 and 1990, from $15,300 to $17,013. Per capita income levels were stable: $10,163 in 1980 and $10,021 in 1990. Poverty was stable and low over the ten-year period, moving only from 2% to 3%. Similarly, unemployment was low and dropped from 1980 to 1990 from 9% to 6%. But again, the 1990s were kinder to Allen Park, and by 1996, the average unemployment was only 1.8%, well below the metropolitan average in the 3.0% to 4.0% range. Although more recent per capita income data are not available for Allen Park, Detroit primary metropolitan statistical area per capita income grew from $21,316 in 1990 to

$30,118 in 1998. There is every reason to believe that Allen Park's per ca-
pita income rose significantly in the 1990s, given its low unemployment
rate and its significant increase in housing prices. Unlike Cornwall, Allen Park weathered a severe area recession in the 1980s without much
long-term impact on housing, wages, or employment.

Allen Park is Ford territory, and whereas 29% of its workforce is employed in manufacturing work, 45% is in service jobs, much of it related
to the automobile industry. Ford suppliers predominate, many in the
(Ford) Fairlane Business Park, including Lear Corporation, Lockheed,
Hewlett-Packard, IBM, and Alcoa. Recently, Danou Enterprises developed an 83-acre tract in Allen Park that houses other Ford suppliers as
well as Sverdrup Corporation, which constructed wind tunnels for
Ford to test cars in simulated climactic conditions from around the
world. Other national companies are also located in Allen Park, including a Frito-Lay plant, United Distilleries and Vintners, APAC Papers
and Packaging, Roush Corporation, and Ameritech. In 1998 alone, Allen Park had over $150 million in large-project investment, including
$100 million for the wind tunnel project. Thus, unlike Cornwall, the eco-
nomic base of Allen Park is disproportionately concentrated on a single
industry (autos), but like Cornwall, it is currently in a substantial
growth mode.

Although Allen Park has benefited from its location in many ways,
this has not extended to its downtown area. On the whole, the central
business district is outdated and rather dilapidated looking. Although
there is an identifiable shopping area and the city has made an attempt
to set this off through the use of banners, many storefronts are vacant.
One of the respondents noted that many city residents go to surrounding communities to shop, and there are few non-fast-food restaurants in
the downtown area. Primary downtown businesses provide services
rather than goods. All of this makes the city's emphasis on downtown
redevelopment discussed later quite understandable. In large part, city
officials view economic development in Allen Park as "downtown
development."

Local Government Structure and Politics

The government structure of Cornwall is reformed—city administrator, nonpartisan elections, and ten city council members elected at large.

Allen Park has a weak-mayor form, with a city administrator, several appointed department heads, and an independently elected clerk and treasurer. But Allen Park also has nonpartisan elections and an at-large council of six. Allen Park operates essentially as a council/manager form of government, even though there are numerous positions in the city that are independent of the Chief Administrative Officer (CAO).

Politics in Cornwall are active and polite, whereas they are active and rather conflictual in Allen Park. In the last mayoral election in Cornwall, there was no incumbent, five "high profile" candidates, and the race was not seen as contentious. At the same time, four new city council members were elected as a result of both retirements and defeats. The city council represents diverse points of view and has had a period of adjustment where new council members are learning the ropes and coming together. Divided 6/4 votes are not unusual, although it appears that there is little if any conflict over economic development policies. Diverse points of view seem to come together on economic development.

In the last election in Allen Park, the incumbent one-term mayor was defeated, purportedly because the new mayor, who had served on the council, ran a better campaign with a strong grassroots door-to-door effort. However, the incumbent mayor had been subject to a recall campaign, sued the recall supporters for slander, and won. Still, all respondents agreed that there were no substantive issues involved in the election, but rather merely a popularity contest. A chamber member noted, "These little towns can get really vicious. Very small town politics can be nasty." Previous mayors served long terms in office. In the prior election, all incumbent council members were reelected, and one new council member was chosen. The fact that a council member ran against the incumbent mayor suggests that there is underlying political rancor here despite protestations to the contrary. Chamber members observe that the current mayor and the council are in frequent conflict, even though the mayor is only one of seven voting members of the city council.

The mayor of Cornwall presents himself as a hands-on leader who ran on an economic development platform. He appears to be very influential on the Smart City initiative, sort of his pet project. He is polished and handsome, making a very good external spokesperson. It also appears that he is not fully involved in much of the actual implementation of economic development. But he provides focus for the city, such as the high-tech, Smart City initiative. The vision comes from the mayor's office.

As in Cornwall, the mayor of Allen Park is just one of several votes on city council. The position is largely symbolic and dependent on the personality of the office holder. It is a part-time position, and the mayor is not in city hall very often. There is little evidence that the mayor of Allen Park is a central player in setting policy direction in general or in economic development in particular.

Although the mayor of Cornwall has a vision, he is merely a member of city council and cannot really go anywhere without its support. Council membership in both communities is a part-time position; there is neither sufficient time nor money for members to do their own information gathering. Thus, they largely accept staff information and recommendations. Both councils have smooth relationships with their CAOs. But the fact that the Cornwall CAO was stepping down suggests that there was some unhappiness with his performance. The Cornwall council functions in a nonpartisan manner although some of the members have open party affiliations or have held provincial office with party affiliation. There are two strong Liberals and two strong Tories on council, but that does not always get in the way. One council member indicated that he believed that the lack of wards helped council function better.

The CAO of Cornwall grew up there and had been with the city for 32 years in various capacities. He concurrently held the position of city clerk. The mayor indicated that the CAO was "retiring," although in reality he was going back to holding only the clerk's position. The CAO said that it was time to make this change so that the city could get new blood and ideas. The styles of the young, smooth new mayor and the older, low-key CAO appear to be rather different.

The CAO of Allen Park had retired from a position in the private sector and consequently had no fear of losing his job. He had a strong professional demeanor and was previously involved in a variety of city boards. The prior two CAOs held their jobs for many years, suggesting that the position tends to be stable, unlike many city management jobs. He was very business oriented and liked working with Ford and other business people. A chamber member referred to the CAO as the city's "godfather." Allen Park also employs an assistant city administrator with the economic development portfolio. Responsibility for staffing the DDA and most other economic development functions lies with this individual and is not focused in a formal economic development department. The DDA itself is largely dominated by its small staff. Planning is contracted out, and the planning function is staffed by the city engineer. In most areas, it appears that the administrative staff is in charge in Allen Park; relations with city council are good because the latter seems to avoid micromanagement. Yet the planning commission and its staff complain that council regularly ignores its recommendations. This conflict appears to be related in part to an outdated zoning ordinance that directs the planners' actions but not city council's.

The administrative staff in charge of economic development in Allen Park has a traditional outlook as evidenced by the limited array of economic development policies. Chamber members suggested that the individual assigned to the DDA is not really qualified to be out front selling the city.

In addition to the conflict noted earlier between the planning commission and the city council in Allen Park, there appears to be some rancor between the DDA board, the city council, and city administration related to the location of a new municipal complex. A planning official pointed out that the city has had some trouble getting the "gears to mesh" between the mayor, council, planning commission, and DDA. Apparently, neither the current nor previous mayor have been strong enough to be proactive, so most participants look to the city administration for guidance.

Cornwall's administrative staff, including the CAO, appear to be professional and in charge. The CAO presents a very traditional perspective on his responsibilities in the area of economic development: to understand council's direction and then support them with information and recommendations on what is necessary to retain and attract business. Of course, the nature of that information can easily shape council's direction, so his role may be more substantial. A business leader suggests that the administrative staff is very conservative but *in control*. He complained that they were in need of more direction from elected officials who were largely "scared of the administration." He felt the CAO needed to be more aggressive in economic development policy. Being CAO and city clerk was just too much for one person, for he needs to be out there selling the city. He complained that the Director of Economic Development (a city department), although professional and competent, with a background in international trade at the federal government level, had settled into a style that lacked passion.

Intercity Competition for Development

Neither Cornwall nor Allen Park appear terribly concerned about competing against other communities for economic development investment, although both are more than willing to respond to opportunities that present themselves. Both communities rely on their locational advantages to attract sufficient investment without needing to be terribly aggressive. Having said that, Cornwall's recent and to some extent current economic difficulties and its status as an independent city require that it be more assertive in marketing itself to the outside world.

Cornwall's location on the U.S. border, on the St. Lawrence River, on Highway 401, and one hour away from Ottawa and Montreal has traditionally given the city locational advantage. It is deep in their history and very much taken for granted. But the Economic Development Department contracted with consulting firm KPMG to outline their business costs in comparison to other cities in North America and Europe. This analysis, "The Competitive Alternative," outlines Cornwall's advantages in location and business costs and makes an especially strong case. With this history and this outside analysis in mind, the mayor is somewhat sanguine about intercity competition. "I'm not a big believer in incentives, they pit community against community" and "at the end of the day, buying businesses is not the way to go." This is an unusual attitude for a city with significant job losses, high poverty, high unemployment, and declining incomes. The mayor notes that Cornwall is in competition with other cities in North America generally and other sites in eastern Ontario because of the regional component of location decisions.

Other local officials in Cornwall are equally sanguine about the need to compete. The CAO points out that they are receiving a fair amount of interest from businesses that might invest in Quebec. These businesses are somewhat nervous about Quebec's conflict over separation and find that Cornwall's location nearby in Ontario allows investments that build on Quebec's economy without the risk of becoming entangled in uncertain politics. "Cornwall is close but safer as a location." Economic development officials are looking for "anything Quebec" to attract business that is afraid of the Quebec "situation." Economic development officials note that they are not feeling pressured because development is just coming to them due to the proximity to Quebec and the fact that the city is bilingual. Thus, even though officials are aware of the need for comparative analyses with other communities in order to compete, they are not terribly concerned about competition, for they expect their advantages ultimately to pay off. And by the late 1990s, they were beginning to reap the fruits of their location.

Allen Park's location in the middle of the Detroit metropolitan area and near Ford Motor Company's Dearborn headquarters and manufacturing facilities has meant that the city has never needed to compete to thrive. From its incorporation as a city in the 1950s, its location has been a major asset enabling it to largely ignore the very concept of competition. You can only compete if you are out there aggressively looking for new development, which Allen Park is not. But when business opportunities land on Allen Park's doorstep, they are willing to compete, much like Cornwall. A recent example of this is when Ford came to local officials with an interest in locating its new wind tunnels in Allen Park. Ford was also looking at other local communities. They wanted a full 15-year tax abatement on personal property, assistance with planning and zoning, and help brokering the land deal. They were given everything they asked.

When it comes to Allen Park's commercial areas, there is a greater sense of competition though little evidence of an aggressively competitive strategy. With the development of enclosed regional malls nearby and the reemergence and renovation of neighboring downtowns, Allen Park's central shopping area began to struggle. Local officials and local chamber members are keenly aware of the surrounding patterns and the need to be competitive to survive. Although they created a DDA in the early 1990s for this purpose, they have not moved rapidly to keep up with the needs or the competition.

Racial Issues

Neither Cornwall nor Allen Park have any significant minority groups, although Cornwall does have a substantial French population and a traditionally French downtown area. There is little indication that race plays a role in local politics or in economic development policy decisions in either community. Although Allen Park is located in Wayne County, Michigan, where there is a substantial African American population, individual cities continue to be heavily segregated, as in Allen Park.

Civic Culture

Local Traditions

Environmental factors are important in shaping local traditions and approaches to economic development in Cornwall. It is an old city, dating back to 1784, that evolved into an administrative center for eastern Ontario and a manufacturing community that ships its products throughout the world. Its fortuitous location made it possible for development to occur with little effort by local leaders. Business located in Cornwall due to its locational advantages. Just as business came to Cornwall without urging from city officials, during the 1980s, it left when the external economic environment began to change. Cornwall took an especially hard "hit" from the deep Canadian recession, and its citizens and leaders continue to feel the repercussions. As a result, there is a pervasive attitude that both good and bad happen to the city over which it has little control; city officials are waiting for private decisions to occur. This rather passive acquiescence to economic fortunes has an obvious impact on the culture surrounding economic development.

A second aspect of Cornwall's local tradition is derived from its city manager form of government and the largely hands-off attitude of elected officials toward their own responsibilities as well as those of city administrators. Politicians don't get involved in the day-to-day operations of economic development or, for that matter, much of city affairs. Although the mayor has his Smart City initiative, he does not appear to be a dynamic player in the city's services or policy initiatives. City council tends to function without much public conflict and with little visibility. City administrators are competent and professional but not aggressive. The city administrator sees his job as an analyst, not an innovator or initiator. Indeed, he indicated that during the period of economic downturn, his primary economic development function was to "assess the city's losses." Specialized administrators, such as those in the economic development department, appear to respond appropriately to requests brought to them by businesses, but they are not out front aggressively recruiting new business opportunities for Cornwall. The result of this passive administrative style is that some in the business community complain about a lack of leadership in the city.

The concern about passive leadership appears to shape another significant aspect of local tradition in Cornwall: a somewhat troubled public/private relationship with suspicions in both directions. Key city officials complain about the politics of the chamber: "Business sometimes shoots off without full information." Another pointed out that businesses tend to fight among themselves over commercial development "because it's a question of dividing up the pie." But industrial development appears to be left to city administrators without much disagreement from business. Last, although the chamber meets with officials from the economic development department almost daily, one Team Cornwall official would like his group to play a larger advisory role. He laments that city officials are not interested. This business leader's view of elected officials and staff is not particularly positive: Elected officials "need to be stronger and more assertive in wrestling power from bureaucrats;" administrative officials "don't have enough passion for what they do and therefore move too slowly."

Allen Park does not have the historic base of Cornwall; it is a relatively new city, and most of its development dates from the 1950s. But the giant Uniroyal tire off Interstate 94 speaks loudly to the primary economic factor that frames Allen Park's civic culture—the automobile industry. The other major attributes of local traditions are the small-town culture of schools and sports and the generally conservative outlook of citizens and government officials.

Allen Park's location near Ford's Dearborn has defined its economic outlook. The city is comfortably middle class and jobs at "Ford's" (i.e., Mr. Ford's place) are plentiful and reasonably secure. Economic growth and stability are not conditions that city fathers must pursue; rather, they have always been a part of Allen Park's existence. From the development of manufacturing facilities, to the Fairlane Business Park, to the Sverdrup-owned wind tunnel facilities for Ford Motor Company, to the practice facilities for the Ford-family-owned Detroit Lions, Allen Park has not had to seek out economic opportunities—they arrive on their own. City officials are overwhelmingly business friendly but not aggressive in seeking out business opportunities; there is simply no need.

Its status as a "company town" is coupled with a civic culture built on a generally conservative small-town outlook. As other surrounding communities condemned and demolished cinder block buildings from the 1950s to make way for new developments, Allen Park was resistant to change and confiscating private property. The city watched as neighboring Lincoln Park and Taylor substantially redeveloped portions of their communities, tearing down public housing and reinventing their commercial areas. Past school millage elections and community bond elections for a new city hall, a recreation complex, and school construction failed on their first attempts, so officials are gun-shy of large new activities and want to do all planning for any major development before the public or anyone else is involved. Discussions throughout Allen Park are sprinkled with references to lifelong Allen Parkers. There are many multigenerational residents, and the politics is definitely one in which everyone knows each other. The city has an identity distinct from that of newer, growing suburbs, a pride in its stability, and a resistance to change even as its age begins to show.

Locus of Power

Although the city manager system of government in Cornwall should allow city council policy leadership with the CAO or city manager following their direction, the locus of power over policy is somewhat unclear. It is almost as if local officials are loathe to indicate that they take the initiative in economic development. One exception is the mayor, who sees himself as being hands on. However, none of the other interviews suggested that he was, in reality, heavily involved in economic development issues. Rather, he seems to be a front man or salesman for the city. The manager suggested that he takes his lead from council, but council is part-time with little remuneration and heavily dependent on staff. Economic development staff suggest that policy initiation is diffuse, shared among staff, council, and business. As a result of this diffusion, it appears that little policy initiation occurs. Ultimately, a planning staff member may have captured the situation best when he observed that council sometimes makes bad decisions, so staff is particularly sensitive to how it provides information to council to achieve a preferred outcome: "Council is part-time and not paid well enough to do their own information gathering—they accept what staff gives them." Thus, within an overall diffuse locus of power, it appears that staff play a key role in guiding city council through policy development but does so hesitatingly and most often in response to the particular needs of business as they arise.

Two specific examples of how the locus of power operates in Cornwall are illustrative. One involves the recent development of a large Wal-Mart distribution center at the city-owned industrial park. The company sought infrastructure improvements (water and sewer lines), land at a competitive rate, and a new road for access to the nearby highway. The economic development staff were supportive, as was the city manager, and ultimately city council, and there was little controversy or conflict, public or behind closed doors, and the development proceeded smoothly. No clear locus was identifiable in this development. The other example is somewhat less straightforward: the sale of the municipal electric company, Cornwall Electric. In response to an Ontario deregulation process, this was the first municipal utility privatized in the Province. Utility board members and city staff first became aware of the opportunity to sell the utility and moved rapidly to construct a deal. The negotiations occurred behind closed doors, and when citizens first learned of the imminent sale, there was initial resistance for fear of rate increases. There was no evidence that the mayor played a major role in these negotiations but substantial evidence that staff helped construct the plan. This strongly suggests that administrators play a central role in Cornwall. And within that administrative framework, it appears that development locus is shared by the economic development director and the city administrator. To wit, one respondent indicated that 99% of the time, projects or firms come to the economic development director who then brings them to the city administrator. Relations between planning and economic development staff appear cordial, again with the latter taking the lead.

The locus of power in Allen Park for economic development decisions is officially in the hands of the city council but is shared with the city administrator and the DDA staff. Policy making is minimal and reactive. When business comes calling, Allen Park responds favorably, with all actors in agreement. The DDA initiative appears to have originated from a prior city administrator, supporting the notion that the staff basically run the show in Allen Park.

Currently, Allen Park is looking at the possibility of relocating its city hall from a remodeled church to a new facility. The decision making here captures many aspects of the city's locus of power and style over such actions. The DDA would like to see the new facility downtown, per its master plan, whereas other city officials are interested in an outlying site in a new industrial area. They feel they would not be taking up valuable business land downtown and have an opportunity to swap a downtown city parking lot for the outlying land for the civic center. Clearly, the city administrator is not interested in discussing the project in public until the deal is done, and chamber of commerce officials are not particularly happy with this approach. Currently, they are organizing among themselves to make a bid for more influence in city hall but are pursuing a somewhat confrontational approach.

The city planning commission appears to have some role in economic development, but internal conflict limits its power vis-à-vis city staff. The commissioners are prone to "rowdy" meetings where they fight among themselves, and council tends to override "everything" they recommend. This pattern in the area of planning, along with the conflict between the DDA and the city and the chamber and the city over the location of city hall seems to point to the city administrator as a key actor dominating policy but in an atmosphere of at least underlying small-town conflict.

Because there is no economic development department per se—the assistant city administrator is responsible for the development function—the central internal locus for development decisions rests with the city administrator's office. However, there is some external competition for power between the city and the DDA. City officials indicate that there are some strong personalities on the DDA board, and there have been conflicts between the DDA and the city over policy issues extending beyond the location of city hall. As one official noted, the DDA is clearly not a "rubber stamp" for city policies and often takes the initiative in development related to the commercial district. In short, city staff are the main locus of power for economic development in Allen Park with the exception of downtown development where there is some competition with a strong DDA board.

Role of Professionals Versus Elected Officials

The foregoing discussion makes clear that staff dominates elected officials in development decision making in both cities. To the extent that anyone dominates economic development policy in Cornwall, it seems evident that professional staff is in charge. As one businessman concluded, "elected officials need to be more dictatorial, but they are scared of the administration." The role of administrators versus elected officials in Allen Park is remarkably similar. Department heads refer to the city administrator as the "godfather," and all policies seem to point in his direction.

Business and Community Input

Obviously, one of the main traits of elite cities is the limited nature of business and community input. "As far as economic development is concerned, the city is working in a vacuum!" observed a Cornwall businessman. Team Cornwall was created to open up a dialogue between the city and the business community, but it remains far from acting in an official advisory capacity. Both the mayor and city council members suggest that business has some input, but much of it is behind the scenes—informal, low-key, and personal. And to date, this input has not necessarily been productive. A planning official observed that the chamber of commerce "likes to direct policy without sitting at the table. Business sometimes shoots off without full information."

Cornwall used to have two business improvement associations— one for the main downtown area and a second for the French business area. But with a new provincial law prohibiting tax increment financing, these organizations disappeared. It appears that there is only an inactive hotel/motel association, and no local advisory group dedicated to promoting local tourism. Tourism in Cornwall is handled primarily by a regional body. This apparent paucity of official avenues for business input results in the informal and somewhat sporadic input system currently operating.

The situation for individual citizen or neighborhood input in Cornwall is similar. Most officials indicate that citizens are involved but only on specific issues. There are no ongoing neighborhood groups, although some more specialized interests have emerged expressing a concern with reducing the traffic and speed on the main historic residential street and some opposition to industrial location on the east side of the city. Several officials observed that Cornwall has its "hot potato" issues, but the public is generally unaware of them because economic development discussions on city council are usually closed and sometimes "secretive." The sale of Cornwall Electric was one of those hot potato exceptions where citizens were heard in crafting the final deal. There was no indication, however, that citizens were involved in planning the sale and use of the proceeds. Rather, they were heard once the initial decisions were made. Clearly, Cornwall is not open to citizen input except in extraordinary circumstances.

Allen Park's commercial business community voiced complaints very similar to those heard in Cornwall about limited input avenues. Although working relations are generally good regardless of who the mayor is, formal input is not solicited, and little is done with the input that is obtained. The mayor and the administrator are on the chamber board and give short reports at each meeting, but the dialogue is slim. Traditionally, the chamber has operated as a "service club," staying out of city affairs, although in the past few years, they have become increasingly active. They are just finding their voice as a watchdog over government, and chamber officials had recently sent a letter to the city complaining about the lack of both business and citizen input processes for the municipal complex debate.

It is important to distinguish between input from different kinds of businesses in Allen Park, however. The active chamber primarily reflects the interests of locally run and owned enterprises. They are focused disproportionately on local commercial activities and are frustrated at the lack of sufficient input into city decisions or direction coming from the city, particularly as it relates to the downtown area. But Allen Park is home to a large number of nationally owned manufacturing enterprises, which, like Ford, seem to get most of what they need and want from city officials to continue to operate and to expand selectively. However, although local officials respond to the needs of large firms on a case-by-case basis, their input does not appear to be institutionalized.

As in Cornwall, the lack of input in Allen Park applies to citizens as well. Individual citizens who serve on the planning commission complain that they are too often overruled. City officials deal with citizens individually and directly. There is no anti-growth sentiment, few citizens ever attend planning commission meetings, and there are no identifiable neighborhood associations and few city advisory boards. Any citizen opposition to development is related to specific projects, typically revolving around noise and traffic concerns (or odor, in the case of a current conflict over the venting of sewer "stink pipes") and the desire to save trees. In fact, there is substantially more citizen involvement in local schools and school sports in Allen Park than in city business; this is part of the small-town culture. As one official noted, the greatest input from citizens "are requests for block party permits in the summer."

Regime Status

Both Cornwall and Allen Park display very closed political systems, providing few avenues for outside voices to be heard. Unlike many other cities, neither business nor citizen input is organized or institutionalized in these communities. There are precious few official or nonofficial advisory boards for business or citizens. Cornwall has an extensive set of city hall Internet Web pages, including descriptions of each department and tremendous detail about their economic development function and marketing. Yet there is not a single mention of any kind of citizen or business advisory function. Allen Park has no Web page and turned down an offer from the chamber of commerce to share the cost of creating one. In Cornwall, there were few references to informal behind-the-scenes business influence other than the mayor's observation that the city and the chamber of commerce are "partners." The specifics of such partnerships were never identified by the mayor, chamber members, or other elected or administrative officials. On the contrary, business leaders are dissatisfied with elected officials and administrative staff due to the lack of aggressiveness in providing leadership.

In Allen Park, business leaders have been largely reticent about becoming actively involved in city affairs, and now that there is some budding interest, they are not satisfied with the opportunities that exist. In both Cornwall and Allen Park, "governing" is heavily dominated by professional administrators who are business friendly but very low keyed. With good times in Cornwall, administrators are prepared to respond, albeit somewhat passively, to economic development needs; likewise, when bad times predominated, they were equally passive in their response. Similarly, in Allen Park, administrators are prepared to respond to potential developments, such as the wind tunnel project, but see little reason to aggressively foster such relationships. Administrative officials observed that elected officials should be making decisions; they don't really need citizen input. And of course, these same administrators are keenly aware of the part-time nature of elected officials and their dependence on administrative staff for information and guidance. In both Cornwall and Allen Park, regimes are absent altogether.

Intergovernmental Relations

Cornwall is a separated city with a county providing services only to the surrounding rural area. Although the province has given great attention to governance issues in the larger urbanized areas, such as Toronto and Ottawa, these are not primary issues for a smaller, free-standing community like Cornwall. But that is not to say that provincial policies have not been felt at the local level. Changes in tax laws, who collects taxes, and off-loading of services (social services, social housing, and ambulance services) have created pressures on cities, particularly because money has not followed these delegated services. Apparently, the province is expecting the various local levels to sort out their own relationships, and in Cornwall, this has led to some underlying conflict. The CAO suggested that the province does nothing for the city in the area of economic development, and in the rare cases they do get involved, they hurt more than help, and development ends up being steered to Toronto. He was not particularly optimistic about the province's support for urban areas.

Cornwall's surrounding consolidated tri-county area has its own economic development department, merged with a federally funded nonprofit community development corporation. This organization provides venture capital and loans for small businesses within Cornwall (and outside), but otherwise, its role is equivalent to Cornwall's own economic development department for businesses located outside of the city. No one in Cornwall mentioned the potentially competing role of the county or the Community Development Corporation. The Community Development Corporation played no role in attracting or supporting the new Wal-Mart distribution facility or in any other major development project in the city in the prior two years. The staff of the two organizations clearly complement each other rather than compete. This is another example of the passive domination by bureaucrats in Cornwall in general and in economic development in particular.

The city also participates in a variety of small federal initiatives. Examples include the federally funded, chamber-initiated study of Cornwall's business costs, the federal business facade program, and some aspects of the Smart City initiative.

Allen Park's intergovernmental relationships appear to be harmonious though not extensive. The county (Wayne) played a major role in constructing a "super sewer" several years ago and managed to satisfy a variety of local concerns without problems. City officials know state administrators and always receive the support they request—for example, paving roads leading to the downtown and permits to do rail grade level crossings. Relationships with federal officials appear to be limited to work on the CDBG program, and most of that is through Wayne County. The county also runs several job training and brownfield redevelopment programs, but these are not of great importance to fiscally healthy Allen Park. Last, relationships with other "downriver" communities are characterized by high levels of cooperation, including a Rouge River Partnership that is attempting to revitalize areas around the river. Thus, Allen Park's intergovernmental relationships are smooth but relatively limited.

Planning and Evaluation

There is little planning and evaluation taking place in the passive bureaucratic-dominated communities of Cornwall and Allen Park. In Cornwall, the city council is the planning board, and conflict is narrowly defined and minimal. There are no ongoing mechanisms for business or citizen involvement in the planning process except on a project-by-project basis, and this is rare. Planning staff give professional advice and dominate the decision making. Both council members and staff acknowledge and accept this pattern.

Allen Park's planning commission is a citizens' body that has difficulty attracting volunteers. Although the relationship between the commission and their staff and consultants appears to be favorable, the city council is ready and willing to overrule professional planning recommendations.

Cornwall's current master plan is undergoing provincial review, a five-year requirement. Provincial approval is required if substantial changes are proposed, and the province is looking to extricate itself from this level of micromanagement. In the meantime, however, Cornwall's plan has some issues relating to commercial development that appear to be controversial, reflecting the polarization among different commercial interests in the city—downtown, the French quarters, and the outlying strip developments. A working group of city staff and chamber representatives developed the new master plan, but chamber members were divided among themselves between existing and new developments. Real estate interests saw the new master plan as being too complex for commercial development. Economic development staff are more heavily involved in industrial/manufacturing development and the industrial park, areas in which there do not appear to be any "land mines." This may explain some of the chamber members' dissatisfaction with the economic development director—too heavily focused on industrial at the expense of commercial development, and little ability to reconcile the conflict between different commercial interests within the community.

Planning officials in Cornwall observe that the secretive nature of economic development makes planning difficult to implement. There is no master economic development plan for Cornwall, and there is a minimal amount of monitoring of activities, limited to contacts files, Web hits, permits issued, and the like.

Allen Park also does little planning and systematic evaluation, although there is a downtown development plan prepared by a consultant. Evaluation occurs only implicitly within the annual budget process. The assistant city administrator in charge of economic development does no central planning. The DDA informally looks for a ratio of 2:1 for business/DDA funding of projects, but beyond this, there is no systematic evaluation.

Views About the Role of the Government in the Economy

In passive cities, such as Cornwall and Allen Park, it is not really clear that there is an overriding "view." You just do what you've got to do when asked. Certainly, there is no clear opposition to assisting private business with public funds. In Cornwall, the Wal-Mart Distribution Center was facilitated by the sale of city-owned industrial land at a "competitive" rate, with substantial infrastructure improvements. There was no apparent opposition to these actions. Yet Cornwall's actions on the city-owned electric company suggest that local officials are sensitive to a balance in the government's role in the economy. Likewise in Allen Park, there was no evidence of opposition to the huge tax abatement for the Ford wind tunnel project. Yet officials are hesitant to condemn private property in the downtown area for redevelopment. In summary, both Cornwall and Allen Park may be characterized as business friendly but clearly not aggressive in their approach to economic development. A conservative stance toward government intervention in the economy is part of the local culture in these two cities.

Entrepreneurialism

One would be hard pressed to describe Cornwall's economic development strategy as entrepreneurial. Municipal services are limited though adequate in good economic times. Their marketing activities are substantial but not unusual. There is no clear-cut program to streamline development, but there is certainly a business or development friendly atmosphere. There is no clear downtown development strategy currently, and relationships with the chamber of commerce are limited if not strained. But in a strong economy and with a good location, economic growth is occurring without resistance. The memories of bad times continue to resonate and support a pro-growth atmosphere. If government activities ran against local expectations, who knows if there would be resistance. Economic development is not a particularly public enterprise in Cornwall, so it is largely dependent on the initiative of business and the response of local bureaucrats.

The picture in Allen Park is very similar, although the primary focus of the city's effort is responding to development requests (such as the wind tunnel) and activities centered around the downtown commercial area through the DDA. Allen Park is not particularly entrepreneurial in its economic development approach and policies. It does not own an industrial park, which would require some marketing to develop as in Cornwall. Rather, Allen Park's industrial park is privately owned, marketed, and managed. The lack of entrepreneurialism in Allen Park may

be a result of the city having few funds to spend. With money beginning to come into the DDA through tax increment financing, this may
change.

Goals and Visions

Cornwall's vision appears to be simple: economic growth. Their extensive marketing materials don't make much distinction among different types of business, although their central location and their bilingual
population suggest particular opportunities. There is some emphasis
on general manufacturing, particularly in plastics, and "anything Quebec" to attract business afraid of the potentially unstable Quebec situation. The mayor's "smart community" initiative has a high-tech focus,
and there are a variety of activities taking place with the support of federal and/or provincial governments to build the needed technology infrastructure in Cornwall and attract call centers and high-tech firms.
The mayor also spoke of business retention, but there is no clear downtown development focus. The Small Business Self Help Office, however,
is there to respond to business inquiries.

In 1997, a chamber group, Connection Cornwall, obtained federal
funding for the KPMG marketing study that presented a very favorable
position for the city. The report has been the foundation of a substantial
general city-run marketing effort with a very broad focus on industrial
development. But there is little emphasis on tourism, downtown development, or workforce training, all very common economic development goals in other more aggressive communities.

Allen Park's economic development goals are very limited; the only
"problem" area appears to be the downtown. Thus, downtown development is their primary goal, although they also speak to the need to
maintain a good business climate to make businesses want to locate
there. The downtown is "old and ready to die." They note that neighboring Lincoln Park has done a lot of condemnation to get rid of old
buildings so they can develop anew, but Allen Park has been hesitant to
do this. They have a lot of older buildings that are not historically interesting. Trying to fix facades in Allen Park is like "putting lipstick on a
pig," says the city engineer. The city is going to have to deal with the
cost/benefits of the condemnation issue and are looking at other
downtowns as models. They expect to work with the DDA to create a

downtown master plan and to coordinate the city's master planning effort.

The mayor and city administrator also spoke about the need for greater centralization within the city economic development function. Planning is divorced from economic development. Although the DDA is within the purview of the assistant city administrator, the norm is for the city to set policy and the DDA to govern itself. This leaves city officials outside of any action, if there is any action.

There are other needs in Allen Park related to an aging infrastructure. Citizens are passing school millages, although it usually takes a few votes, but they are not passing bond issues to improve infrastructure. They have problems with water and sewer lines as well as roads and parking, all of which need investment. Allen Park has only a very broad vision (to be business friendly) for economic development and few focused goals.

ECONOMIC DEVELOPMENT POLICIES

Overall Policies

The policy framework for economic development in Cornwall is somewhat limited in vision (like Allen Park) although in implementation, a broad array of policies are used (unlike Allen Park). The limited vision may be due to the constraints placed on local governments by the provincial government, and some of it results from structural fragmentation at the local level. A major focus in Cornwall is a substantial marketing program that includes an Internet Web site with comprehensive information on the area, marketing brochures, selected advertisements, dissemination of the results of the KPMG comparison study of local business costs, and attendance at trade shows. The marketing program emphasizes quality of life in the community, although there was some criticism of the quality of the product from individuals within the city's business community.

Other economic development policies include a major industrial park with substantial available land. The city has been ready to make infrastructure improvements (water, sewer, and roads) at the site when opportunities arise, such as the Wal-Mart Distribution Center. To sweeten the deal, it is Cornwall's policy *not* to impose any development charges. City-owned land in the industrial park has been sold at competitive rates and even below cost when necessary to close a deal. Working with the county's nonprofit community development corporation, small business loans and venture capital funds are available, although these were not brought up by city officials. Also, working with the county, Cornwall was in the process of hiring an export development officer to help area industries develop export potential. The "smart community" initiative to increase the telecommunications infrastructure and high-tech employment base is one of the mayor's main policies, and some provincial funds are available to support this effort. Last, the economic development staff act as facilitators for existing and potential businesses in dealing with problems with other levels of government and getting through bureaucratic red tape.

Although there are no focused downtown or commercial development policies, the city does participate in a federal facade program that pays for the labor to reconstruct business fronts. Also, there is a business visitation program run by the economic development department in which the mayor participates.

Tourism is not a focus of the economic development department or the city generally, but this is primarily a result of centralizing those responsibilities in a regional body to build on the regional facilities. The city supports a civic center with convention facilities, a marina and hockey rink, and a variety of festivals and carnivals. But these are not thought of by local economic development and elected officials as economic development, even though there is a variety of such components in operation. The sole exception to this limited view of tourism is held by the city's head of planning who also has responsibility for recreational facilities.

In summary, on close examination, Cornwall's economic development strategies appear to be rather extensive, although not necessarily comprehensive or innovative. Individual discussions with local business leaders, city council members, and even administrative officials did not reveal the full breadth of available policies. It is almost as if no single player is aware of, or responsible for, the full scope of policies. This appears to be a result of the "behind-the-scenes" approach to economic development, the lack of consistent and open input from business or citizen groups, the limited direct involvement of city council members, and the fragmentation of responsibilities among several governmental bodies.

The centerpiece of Allen Park's economic development policy framework is its Downtown Development Authority, created in the early 1990s. A master commercial design plan was created in 1992, along with a Tax Increment Financing Authority. Public funds have been used for parking, streetscape improvements, a recently created facade improvement program, and a building purchase and renovation program. The DDA purchased three buildings for sale or lease at favorable rates and hopes to attract a microbrewery to the area. Currently, Allen Park is working on a new master plan for the downtown and some adjacent commercial areas and with additional TIFA funds coming in, considering a broader scope of activities. In addition, DDA staff serve as ombudsmen between businesses and city departments. The DDA no longer operates an unsuccessful commercial loan program, a referral system to private loan providers with little subsidy.

Industrial development policies include substantial tax abatements. The mayor pointed out that the city has to use tax abatements because the competition is using them. The city strongly feels that abated development is better than none. The city has also worked with state government to enhance the road system serving industrial and commercial developments. There was one example of the city working with the county government to develop a brownfield site, but there does not appear to be any consistent effort at brownfield development in Allen Park.

Although Allen Park has a major industrial park, it is owned and operated by Ford Land Development. The city has little role in this major development except supporting some adjacent road construction activities.

Although not specifically and directly economic development, the desire to move the Allen Park city hall into new facilities has had an indirect economic development impact. Chamber officials want the new city hall downtown to help reinvigorate the area. City officials prefer an outlying site in an industrial park to make space downtown available for commercial development.

Allen Park does not have a business visitation and retention program, any marketing activities whatsoever, including a Web site, a city-owned industrial park, or a workforce development program. The last category is provided by the county government but appears to be

totally off Allen Park officials' radar screen. Some of these potential policies are rather simple to operate, whereas others require a major con-
certed effort. Allen Park's economy has not really struggled, and the
presence of Ford Motor Company facilities has meant that they have not
needed an aggressive set of economic development tools.

Type II Policies

Cornwall and Allen Park fall at the bottom of the case study cities in
terms of Type II policies. In Cornwall, the one exception occurred in the
sale of the city-owned Cornwall Electric Company. The sale garnered
$68 million Canadian, and the funds were used to retire all upcoming
municipal debt, making Cornwall one of a handful of debt-free cities,
and to create a permanent endowment-type $24 million fund whose
proceeds are used for community improvement projects, such as a new
municipal swimming pool. Utility workers were guaranteed continued
employment and rates were frozen for three years. Otherwise, there are
no examples of municipally imposed development fees, private infrastructure requirements, local hiring, housing or the like. The memory of
extraordinarily bad economic times in the city makes it difficult for such
policies to emerge. But Cornwall is essentially a business-friendly environment in which there is little expressed interest in trying to squeeze
additional direct benefits from economic development activities for the
community.

Allen Park has no Type II activities whatsoever. Tax abatements are
given without any quid pro quo. There is no growth management
movement in the city, and the level of growth is not threatening. Consequently, there are no extraordinary public benefit expectations of developments coming into the city.

CULTURE, PROCESS, AND POLICY

Table 10.1 gives a comparison of the environments, culture, and policies of Cornwall and Allen Park.

TABLE 10.1 Comparison of Cornwall and Allen Park: Environment, Culture, and Policies

Cornwall	Allen Park
Environment	
High residential need	Low residential need
Moderate perceived competition	Low perceived competition
Formal structure: council/manager, at-large, nonpartisan	Formal structure: weak mayor, council, chief administrative officer, at-large, nonpartisan
Actual structure: council/manager, some partisan divides	Actual structure: weak mayor, CAO, some partisan divides
Racially homogeneous, bilingual	Racially homogeneous
Culture	
Little politics	Contentious small-town politics
Low-key professional bureaucracy with mild business unhappiness	Low-key bureaucracy with mild business unhappiness
Few avenues for business input but simmering discontent	Few avenues for business input but simmering discontent
Few avenues for citizens, with low input	Few avenues for citizens, with low input
Locus of power shared between bureaucracy and council	Locus of power shared between bureaucracy and council
Public-sector locus	Public-sector locus
Limited intergovernmental relations and conflict over changes from province	Cooperative, limited intergovernmental relations
Locus of power dispersed	Locus of power concentrated
Moderate to high business volunteerism	Low business volunteerism
Economic development in an internal department	Economic development in a combined internal department
Business friendly but passively so	Business friendly but passively so
Moderate planning, low evaluation	Moderate planning, low evaluation
Policies	
Moderate marketing	No marketing
Industrial parks	No public industrial parks
Infrastructure development	Infrastructure development
No tax abatements but below-cost land sales and no development fees	Tax abatements without formula
Voluntary downtown association	DDA
No TIFA	TIFA
Streetscape from previous era	Streetscape from previous era

TABLE 10.1 (Continued)

Cornwall	Allen Park
Modest tourism development by independent body	No tourism development
Business visitation and small business self-help center	No business visitation; informal ombudsman role
No hiring goals	No hiring goals
Type II limited to one major project	No Type II
Provincial training in theory only	Regional training
No brownfield development	Limited brownfield development
Little zoning policy	Little zoning policy

The Environment

Cornwall and Allen Park have very different experiences and needs in terms of the local economy. Although the economy is doing well today in Cornwall, the deep Canadian recession of the 1980s continues to be felt. Its population is stable, but the community suffers from a high poverty rate, high unemployment, low and declining per capita income, and low housing values. And yet for the past few years, business investment in the city has risen substantially. In contrast, the 1950s Detroit suburb of Allen Park is aging and losing population as a result. But it is basically a stable middle-class community. Although earlier recessions led to lower housing values, the 1990s have been very kind to Allen Park—very low unemployment, substantially rising per capita income, and zooming housing values. Currently, both communities have locational advantages that permit a passive approach to economic development. As a result, officials in both communities are not terribly worried about competition with other cities. Cornwall is aware of its locational advantage for companies doing business in Quebec that are nervous about its unstable political environment. Likewise, Allen Park is aware of its long-term locational advantage from Ford Motor Company and businesses associated with Ford. By being responsive to these companies, Allen Park receives a reasonable share of economic development and does not have to worry about competition. Both cities are essentially run by professional administrators, although the symbolic

mayor of Cornwall appears to have more opportunities to provide policy leadership on the council than the weak mayor of Allen Park.

The Culture

The civic culture of Cornwall and Allen Park are remarkably similar
in many aspects related to input and structure:

Low levels of input from business and citizen groups
Low-key and passive bureaucracy, mayor, and business community
Informal business input but simmering discontent
Decision-making locus rests with bureaucracy and council
Economic development in an internal department
Business friendly but passive
Public-sector locus

The unique aspects of Cornwall's civic culture point to

Little politics and largely cooperative behind-the-scenes actions
Limited but somewhat conflicted intergovernmental relations
Locus of power dispersed among various bureaucracies
Moderate business volunteerism
Moderate planning, low evaluation
Emphasis on general manufacturing, high technology, and anything
    Quebec

The unique aspects of Allen Park's civic culture include the following:

Contentious small-town politics
Limited but cooperative intergovernmental relations
Locus of power concentrated in city administrator's office
Low business volunteerism
Low planning, low evaluation
Emphasis on keeping Ford Motor Company happy

The Policies

Economic development policies are limited and traditional in both Cornwall and Allen Park, and one is hard pressed to identify much creative or proactive policy in either community. Within this similar framework, there are some differences, some of which are explained by state or provincial laws constraining a variety of policies. Both cities do limited infrastructure development and have completed downtown streetscapes. Neither city has hiring goals or Type II policies, and both rely on other government bodies to do job training. These similarities reflect limited and traditional approaches. Cornwall has an extensive marketing program, operates a substantial industrial park, and has a regular business visitation process and a small business self-help center. Allen Park does none of these. It has no marketing, no public industrial park, and no business visitation program. All are allowable in Michigan and considered rather traditional and common. But Allen Park provides tax abatements without a guiding formula and has a DDA and a TIFA. Provincial law prohibits all three in Cornwall. Last, Cornwall does modest tourism development by an independent governing body, whereas Allen Park does nothing related to tourism. Allen Park has a limited brownfield development effort through intergovernmental programs and makes limited use of zoning policy for economic development, whereas Cornwall pays little attention to these areas. Although the differences are real, the policies themselves are very traditional and passive.

SUMMARY

These cases present a somewhat mixed picture regarding the effects of the environment—specifically, the economy—on local economic development process and policy. First, it is clear that process and policy are basically similar in these two cities: Local administrative officials pursue a passive or reactive economic development agenda with traditional and conservative policies. On the one hand, it appears, then, that objective economic conditions have little effect. Allen Park has been quite stable economically, whereas Cornwall has suffered. Yet process and policies are similar. On the other hand, both cities have significant locational advantages and are home to a good bit of investment from large corporations. These locational advantages have allowed both cities to maintain and indeed, even improve, their economies while pursuing a modest and reactive development program. Thus, it is clear that for these cities, the economy plays a role in the overall approach to economic development. But is this the only force at work? Will cities with locational advantages necessarily have a passive approach to economic development? Gloucester suggests that this is not the case. It is located in a booming metropolitan area and enjoys the same land cost and housing price advantages as Cornwall. It also operates under the same provincial restrictions on financial incentives. Yet Gloucester has a proactive and entrepreneurial approach, whereas Cornwall does not. Obviously, more than location is at work.

The active- and passive-elite cities share a decision locus profile where city administrators/bureaucrats have the central role in development decision making. Yet policies in Kettering and Gloucester are active, and in Cornwall and Allen Park, they are not. What else, then, may be operating within the local civic culture that makes the difference? A glance at the cultural summaries for Kettering/Gloucester and Cornwall/Allen Park reveals significant and important differences. In the former two cities, there is an extreme aversion to political conflict; an emphasis on professional behaviors, including extensive planning and evaluation; and an emphasis on alternative economic development goals, such as culture and the arts, business development rather than recruitment, and creative reuse of property. These same conditions are quite different in Cornwall and Allen Park. For example, there is no particular aversion to politics and there are visible partisan differences in both communities and a good bit of political conflict in Allen Park. Although decisions are left to city staff, there wasn't the consistent mention of professional values across actors in the city; levels of planning and evaluation are low in both cases. Economic development goals are very traditional in Cornwall and Allen Park: increase manufacturing investment, downtown redevelopment in Allen Park, and an emphasis on pleasing big business.

Another significant cultural difference lies in the relationship between citizen and business leaders and the city. In Gloucester and Kettering, local officials welcome input and have sought to solicit it. Thus, it appears that the lack of citizen and business input is the result of basic agreement and satisfaction with the city agenda. This does not appear to be the case in Cornwall and Allen Park, where local officials appear more interested in making economic development decisions behind closed doors and make no affirmative efforts to secure broader input. Furthermore, it appears that business groups, and perhaps citizens, in these cities would like a larger voice and are becoming increasingly dissatisfied with the historically passive economic development approach.

From these differences in local civic culture, several tentative connections can be drawn between culture and approach to economic development. It was concluded in the last chapter that consensual decision making, aversion to politics, an emphasis on professional behavior, and very high levels of planning allowed administrative officials to pursue an active and creative approach to economic development. Generally, community consensus on the appropriate role of local government in the economy (an active one) and on goals gives local officials the legitimacy and "space" to experiment with creative and perhaps risky economic development options. Local officials were open and solicitous of business and citizen input; there was no fear of negative reactions. Thus, the stance of local administrators toward their economic development task was professional, confident, and energized.

The overall civic culture is very different for local officials in Cornwall and Allen Park. Particularly in the latter, local politics has been conflictual. In neither city are administrative officials actively seeking input from the larger community—indeed, they avoid it. In Cornwall, that appears to stem from a desire to keep things polite and perhaps allow staff to go about their jobs with as little diversion as possible. But in Allen Park, it is the direct result of having been "burned" by the media and by citizens refusing to approve funding for city projects. The festering conflict over the location of the new municipal complex suggests that this reaction is not irrational. At the same time, it seems clear that local business leaders and citizens are not necessarily happy with the existing economic development approach and would like more input. Couple this with an administrative culture that appears to be very cautious and conservative and where little forward-thinking takes place and it is no surprise that the economic development approach is basically traditional and passive. Indeed, the local culture and administrative culture reinforce each other. If the larger environment is uncertain, planning becomes a very uncertain enterprise and caution the only reasonable approach. Where the cultural milieu is more uncertain, the best bet is to play it safe. Combine this general cultural picture with the locational advantages of Cornwall and Allen Park, and a reactive and passive approach to economic development is almost a given. Again, the environment sets the larger framework for economic development, but the local civic culture mediates, and in this case, compounds, its effects.

NOTE

1. Respondents interviewed in Cornwall included chief administrative officer; manager, Planning and Recreation; manager, Community Development Corporation; mayor; city council member; senior development officer, Economic Development Department; and Team Cornwall member. Respondents interviewed in Allen Park included president, past-president, and executive director, Chamber of Commerce; assistant city manager responsible for economic development; DDA grant coordinator; mayor; city administrator; city engineer; and planning commission member.

11

COMPARING CATEGORIES OF CIVIC CULTURE

Linking the Methodologies

This chapter summarizes the case studies and examines the connections between the survey and case study analyses. Both exercises are essential and provide different lenses through which local civic culture can be viewed. First, although the nine cases have been grouped into the six general categories—mayor dominated, externally driven, politically inclusive, bureaucratic elite-dominated passive, bureaucratic elite-dominated active, business/governmental elite-dominated—it is useful to examine patterns in either process or policy that cross categories and perhaps organize the cities in different ways. Second, it has been argued that the combination of survey and case study methodologies employed here allows a more complete analysis—both in breadth and depth—of local economic development, specifically, and civic culture more generally. Thus, it is useful to explicitly revisit what both the path analyses and case studies have to say about the civic culture of economic development. Are the two methodologies providing consistent findings? How do they complement each other to provide a more complete picture of the cultural dynamics of local economic development? In the final analysis, both methodologies point to the primacy of civic culture in economic development process and policy. The path analyses and case studies highlight a similar set of cultural forces that appear central in understanding how cities approach economic development and in the policies they pursue. Although the case studies allow for a more nuanced examination of culture, the two methodologies reinforce and complement each other in interesting ways. This chapter begins with a summary of the case studies and then examines local civic culture as expressed in the two methodologies.

THE CASE STUDIES

Mayor-Dominated Systems

Romulus represents cities with strong-mayor systems of government, where the mayor dominates development decision making. Environmentally, it has moderate levels of residential need as indicated by unemployment, poverty, and median income and is racially diverse. In Romulus, the politics are relatively contentious, and the locus of decision-making power lies with the mayor; decision making overall is centralized. There is little formal business or citizen input, although the mayor, a local contractor, has close ties to the business community. There is no governing regime in the true sense of the term because the private sector has no consistent role in governing, and power is so centralized in the mayor. A number of multigenerational families still wield influence within the community, however, both socially and politically. Indeed, the mayor comes from one such family. Problematic relations with the county and the federal government over issues related to Detroit Metropolitan Airport permeate the political environment, limiting the energy and resources devoted to economic development. Although few formal planning and evaluation methodologies are used in decision making, the mayor has a keen business sense and is loathe to provide incentives to business without guarantees that the city will benefit. Economic development policies *overall* are traditional and conservative. However, the unique feature of development policy in Romulus is the use of several Type II strategies, including a formula for tax abatements that includes the number and quality of jobs generated, local hiring goals, and clawbacks. It appears that the use of Type II policies results from a mayor with a strong sense that any development policies should benefit the city and not be a "give-away," a need to balance diverse interests in a community with sometimes fractious politics and a racially diverse population, and a historical tendency to leave development decisions to the mayor.

Externally Driven Systems

Coshocton represents cities where the locus of control for economic development lies in a body external to the local government. Indeed, this is the case even though the city has a strong-mayor form of government. Like Romulus, Coshocton has moderate levels of unemployment, poverty, and median incomes, but it is racially homogeneous. The political background in Coshocton is very different, however; partisan divisions and conflicts are disdained, and cooperation is the watchword between governmental actors, among levels of government, and between the public and private sectors. Economic development decisions are made by an external body controlled almost totally by business. Various business organizations operate in the city and conduct (and fund) different aspects of development policy, such as downtown development. The locus of power is dispersed, although clearly resting within the private sector. The public sector tends to be less involved in economic development, and the expectations are that businesses will pay for their own needs.

As a result, development policies tend to be limited and quite traditional: marketing, industrial parks, and limited infrastructure investment. Coshocton, too, has recently begun to experiment with Type II policies, most notably, clawbacks tied to a development formula for allocating tax abatements. Thus, although the city has a development regime, policies promulgated by regime members are not what would traditionally be expected. The willingness of local business leaders to push for performance guarantees and clawbacks may seem surprising on the surface. It is important to remember that Coshocton's business base is composed primarily of smaller, locally owned businesses, although some have recently changed to absentee owners. Nevertheless, business leaders controlling economic development policy feel that new firms coming into the city should be required to "pay back" to the community in cases of nonperformance. They are very aware that the future of the city lies in the continued diversification and growth of small firms and do not wish to engage in development policies that would support the attraction of investment that does not conform to existing community visions.

Politically Inclusive Systems

Oakville and Fairborn represent cities that have open political systems, both to business and citizen interests. Environmentally, the two cities are very different. Oakville has a strong and growing economy, whereas Fairborn has high poverty and unemployment. Although both have city manager forms of government, Oakville has ward-based council elections, whereas Fairborn's are at-large. These environmental differences aside, the two cities have very similar civic cultures in a number of respects. The politics in both are open, and citizens and businesses make extensive use of both institutionalized and grass roots forms of access. The locus for development decisions rests with the public sector, and policies are based on high levels of planning and evaluation. Yet policies are conservative and limited in both cities due to low levels of support for public subsidies of private interests.

There are some cultural differences, however. Oakville emphasizes its small-town image and has a long history of growth management. In Fairborn, the large transient and older population presses for limited taxation and hence, limited service and development policies. Thus, in Oakville, growth pressures have led to limited efforts at economic development, and this emphasis on growth management marks the city as having a progressive regime. And recent efforts to perhaps limit both the inclusiveness of the system and the growth management emphasis by moving the economic development function to a public/private organization do not appear to have reduced the substantive political control over development to a significant extent. In Fairborn, the same outcome is more the result of lack of resources and a caretaker perspective. Hence, development policies in the two cities are very similar: a limited and traditional mix of marketing and modest business retention efforts and an emphasis on regulatory policies to either facilitate or control development. These are low-cost and low-risk policies.

Bureaucratic Elite-Dominated Passive Systems

Allen Park and Cornwall are similar systems in that economic development decisions are the prerogative of governmental bureaucrats. Neither community has a governing regime because, at this time, business leaders are not part of the decision-making apparatus. The overall approach of officials in both communities is passive and quite limited. In Allen Park, this stems from several economic and cultural factors. The city is a "company town," with a significant Ford Motor Company presence, and local officials have tended to allow Ford to make investment decisions and have not sought much development beyond that. Although desires for diversification and downtown redevelopment may change this, the conflictual political environment suggests that a more active development agenda may meet with citizen and business resistance. Although there is currently little business or citizen input, the business community appears to be organizing and making a bid for greater influence. Their stance appears confrontational, however, not surprising given the political history of the city. Economic development policies tend to revolve around traditional marketing efforts, DDAs, TIFAs, and some limited infrastructure investment.

Economic and cultural forces have also limited economic development initiatives in Cornwall. The city (and the Province of Ontario more generally) experienced a severe economic downturn in the early 1980s that significantly limited resources for all types of governmental activities and continues to be remembered. Although the city has recovered quite well and is beginning to create a development agenda that emphasizes high-tech and smart-city initiatives, actual development activities remain limited to industrial park development, marketing, and business retention. Although there has not been the level of political conflict in Cornwall as in Allen Park, the business community, historically "shut out" of the development process, is now organizing and pressing for a greater role. This process appears to be more cooperative in Cornwall, though business leaders still express dissatisfaction with the lack of activity on the part of government bureaucrats. Citizens appear fairly passive in Cornwall.

In both communities, local bureaucrats have tended to let development "come to them" and have been able to limit the extent of business input into the decision process. Change, however, is brewing in both cities, with business leaders taking a greater interest in development policy and a broader development agenda being discussed. Until this takes hold, economic development policies are likely to remain limited.

Bureaucratic Elite-Dominated Active Systems

Kettering and Gloucester also represent systems where governmental bureaucrats are dominant in economic development decision making. However, unlike the two foregoing cities, the approach toward development is active, innovative, and entrepreneurial. These cities are similar economically: Both are very healthy, with low poverty and unemployment. Because bureaucrats within local government make development decisions with low levels of business and citizen input, neither of these cities have identifiable governing regimes. The absence of business input is somewhat different in these communities than in the two described earlier. In Cornwall and Allen Park, local officials make no particular efforts to solicit outside opinions; indeed, they almost seem to desire to avoid them. In Kettering and Gloucester, officials are making active efforts to increase both citizen and business input. However, these have not borne significant fruit to this point. Rather, it appears that strong cultural preferences to leave decisions "to professionals," running the city as a business, and keeping politics out of development issues has kept citizen and business leaders satisfied to leave decision making to development officials.

Decision making in these cities is shaped by planning and evaluation. Resultant economic development policies are similar in their level of entrepreneurialism and innovation, although there are some differences in scale resulting from the much more limited enabling legislation environment that Gloucester operates under in Ontario. Thus, Kettering engages in small business development; land and site development, including an extremely innovative industrial reuse of a former airbase; minimal tax abatements; and quality-of-life development in the areas of the arts and education. Although unable to use financial incentives, Gloucester officials have engaged in an award-winning program of business retention and development, including visitation; business success initiatives, such as mentorships and technical assistance; and extensive marketing.

Business/Government Elite-Dominated Systems

Cadillac represents systems that, although having significant business domination, also maintain a public role in economic development. Governmental and business elites work closely together in economic development in Cadillac. There is an economic development function within the local government but also a number of private external bodies that engage in various aspects of development. All of these diverse elements appear to work cooperatively and effectively together. Indeed, as in the former two cities, "politics" is a negative word here, and conflict is simply not viewed as appropriate. The civic culture includes a strong expectation that businesses give back to the community by volunteerism and subsidy of various public activities. Obviously, there is a high level of institutionalized business input through the various external bodies. The city clearly has a stable development regime. On the other hand, citizen input is not discouraged—the business volunteer ethic appears to extend to citizens as well. Decision making in both public and private bodies is very professionalized, with each organization having its own plans. Although this might create chaos in some communities, the emphasis on cooperation in Cadillac appears to mitigate those effects. The policy approach is active and entrepreneurial, particularly in the often-complex funding arrangements typically involving state money. All types of development policies are pursued, including worker attraction programs (Cadillac's historically high unemployment rate has given way to a worker shortage due to economic growth in the area over the past decade), job training, cultural development, and brownfield development.

Comparing Across Categories

The analysis thus far has followed the case study chapters to provide continuity and to emphasize the central cultural traits in each city. It is useful to go beyond this, however, examining across categories for other possible patterns in civic culture and economic development policy. Table 11.1 provides a summary of this effort, showing a rank ordering of the cities on a variety of environmental, cultural, and policy variables.[1] Except for economic health, these admittedly impressionistic rank orders represent a reasonable summary of data from the case

(text continues on p. 352)

TABLE 11.1 Environmental Variables

1980 Unemployment		1980 Poverty		1980 Average Income (rounded)	
Kettering	3%	Allen Park	3%	Oakville	$77,000
Gloucester	6%	Kettering	4%	Gloucester	$21,000
Oakville	6%	Oakville	5%	Kettering	$19,000
Allen Park	6%	Gloucester	8%	Allen Park	$17,000
Coshocton	7%	Romulus	13%	Cornwall	$15,000
Fairborn	7%	Coshocton	13%	Fairborn	$13,000
Romulus	10%	Fairborn	15%	Coshocton	$12,500
Cornwall	11%	Cadillac	16%	Romulus	$12,000
Cadillac	12%	Cornwall	17%	Cadillac	$11,000

Unemployment Change: 1980 to 1990		Poverty Change: 1980 to 1990		Population Change: 1980 to 1990	
Romulus	−7%	Cornwall	−4%	Oakville	+27,733
Fairborn	−4%	Oakville	−1%	Gloucester	+11,675
Allen Park	−3%	Kettering	0	Fairborn	+1,598
Kettering	−2%	Gloucester	0	Cornwall	+480
Cadillac	0	Allen Park	+1%	Cadillac	−95
Gloucester	0	Cadillac	+3%	Kettering	−617
Coshocton	0	Fairborn	+3%	Romulus	−718
Oakville	+1%	Romulus	+3%	Coshocton	−1,212
Cornwall	+1%	Coshocton	+3%	Allen Park	−3,104

Overall Economic Health		
High	Medium	Low
Kettering	Allen Park (but declining)	Cornwall (but improving)
Oakville	Fairborn	Romulus
Gloucester	Coshocton	Cadillac (but improving)

TABLE 11.1 (Continued)

Government Structure—Putative		
Chief Executive	*Council*	*Party*
Strong Mayor	*Ward*	*Partisan*
Romulus	Cadillac	Coshocton
Coshocton	Gloucester	
	Oakville	*Nonpartisan*
Weak Mayor		Romulus
Allen Park	*Mixed*	Allen Park
	Coshocton	Cadillac
Manager	Kettering	Fairborn
Cadillac		Kettering
Fairborn	*At-large*	Cornwall
Kettering	Allen Park	Gloucester
Cornwall	Romulus	Oakville
Gloucester	Fairborn	
Oakville	Cornwall	

Government Structure—Real		
Chief Executive	*Council*	*Party*
Strong Mayor	*Geographical Divisions*	*Partisan*
Romulus	Oakville	Romulus
Weak Mayor	*No Geographical Divisions*	*Nonpartisan*
Coshocton	Gloucester	Coshocton
Oakville	Romulus	Allen Park
	Coshocton	Cadillac
Manager	Kettering	Fairborn
Allen Park	Allen Park	Kettering
Cadillac	Cadillac	Cornwall
Fairborn	Fairborn	Oakville
Kettering	Cornwall	
Cornwall		
Gloucester		

(Continued)

TABLE 11.1 (Continued)

	Urban Hierarchy	
Old Inner Ring	*Newer Ring*	*Isolated Node*
Allen Park	Kettering	Cornwall
Fairborn	Gloucester	Cadillac
Romulus	Oakville	Coshocton

	Competition			Country	
High	*Medium*	*Low*	*Canada*		*US*
Coshocton	Romulus	Oakville	Cornwall	Allen Park	Coshocton
Kettering	Cadillac	Allen Park	Gloucester	Cadillac	Fairborn
Fairborn	Cornwall		Oakville	Romulus	Kettering
Gloucester					

		Civic Culture Variables	
Business Input	*Citizen Input*	*Planning/ Evaluation*	*Intergovernmental Relations Quantity*
High	*High*	*High*	*High*
Coshocton	Fairborn	Oakville	Romulus
Fairborn	Oakville	Kettering	Coshocton
Cadillac		Fairborn	Gloucester
Oakville	*Medium*	Gloucester	
	Romulus		*Medium*
Medium	Allen Park	*Medium*	Fairborn
Romulus		Cadillac	Allen Park
Cornwall	*Low*	Coshocton	Cadillac
Allen Park	Cadillac		Cornwall
	Coshocton	*Low*	
Low	Kettering	Romulus	*Low*
Kettering	Gloucester	Cornwall	Oakville
Gloucester	Cornwall	Allen Park	Kettering

	Level of Conflictual Politics	
High	*Medium*	*Low*
Allen Park	Romulus	Coshocton
Oakville	Gloucester	Kettering
Fairborn	Cornwall	Cadillac

	Governing Regime		
Developmental	*Caretaker*	*Progressive*	*None*
Coshocton	Fairborn	Oakville	Romulus
Cadillac			Kettering
			Gloucester
			Allen Park
			Cornwall

TABLE 11.1 (Continued)

Poor	Combination Department	Business Leaders
Romulus	Romulus	Cadillac
Gloucester	Fairborn	Coshocton
Cornwall		
	External Body	
	Coshocton	
	Oakville	

Intergovernmental Relations Quality	*Economic Development Structure*	*Decision Locus*
Good	*Office of Chief Executive*	*Elected Officials*
Coshocton	Allen Park	Romulus
Fairborn	Cadillac	Oakville
Kettering		
Allen Park	*Independent Department*	*Bureaucrats*
	Gloucester	Kettering
Fair	Kettering	Fairborn
Cadillac	Cornwall	Gloucester
Oakville		Cornwall
		Allen Park

Economic Development Policies

Type II Policies	*Innovative/Active*	*High Financial Incentives*
High	*High*	Allen Park
Romulus	Kettering	Romulus
Coshocton	Cadillac	Cadillac
Kettering	Gloucester	
		High Demand-side
Medium	*Medium*	Kettering
Oakville	Romulus	Cadillac
(growth management)		
Fairborn	Cornwall	Gloucester
Cornwall	Coshocton	
		High Loans
Low	*Low*	Cadillac
Cadillac	Fairborn	
Gloucester	Oakville	*High Marketing*
Allen Park	Allen Park	Cadillac
		Fairborn
		Gloucester
		Cornwall

studies. The purpose of this discussion is not to provide analysis in a statistical sense but rather to explore other general patterns across cities.

An analysis story is worth mentioning here. The initial plan was to describe the rank orders of cities across the individual civic culture components: for example, the traits of cities with high planning and evaluation or the traits of cities with high business input. It quickly became clear that this was not going to work as an organizing principle because the rankings on most of the cultural variables are related. To be more specific, there are syndromes or patterns among the various cultural variables, and it simply makes little sense to analyze them individually. This supports the argument that there are cultural types or syndromes among cities composed of traits such as input, locus of decision making, how decisions are made, and so on. Thus, what follows is an examination of the rank orders based on a very similar categorization to that used for the case study chapters. In looking across the cities, it becomes apparent that Cadillac and Coshocton are similar in that the locus of power rests with either an external body or with a combination of government and private actors. Romulus, with its mayor-dominated system, stands alone. The bottom line is that inclusive cities are different in a variety of respects from elite-dominated cities, for example.

Two definitional issues need to be discussed. First, the wide range of goals identified by officials in the case studies has been collapsed into three general categories. *Social goals* are those that emphasize benefits to the community at large and include better or more diverse housing and homeownership, shopping for residents, culture/arts improvements, education, and leadership development. *Alternative goals* correspond to those examined on the survey and include small business development, economic base diversification, high-tech development, balanced business growth, tourism/hotels, and creation of local businesses. *Traditional goals* include attraction or expansion of industry, downtown development, and infrastructure development or improvement. Development policies have also been generally categorized as Type II, traditional, or entrepreneurial, and these are described more fully in the next section.

In examining the rank orders of cities on all of the variables in Table 11.1, four patterns emerge, each discussed in turn. Again, this analysis is based on identifying patterns of cities being either consistently high or low on each variable.

Fairborn and Oakville are examples of *politically inclusive* communities. They reflect the following characteristics:

City managers and high levels of citizen and business input

Governing regimes but of different types: caretaker and progressive, respectively

High levels of planning and evaluation

High levels of political input as well as conflict

A mix of social and alternative goals

Traditional development policies

In short, the politically inclusive cities have professional managers yet are still very open to community input. Parenthetically, this speaks to one of the long-standing debates in the structural reformism literature regarding the extent that city manager systems may limit the "public-regarding" tendency of unreformed systems. In these two city manager cities, it clearly does not. Indeed, in Oakville, the city council tends to predominate in policy making. The high level of input and a tendency toward political conflict—in Oakville over the relaxation of growth limitations and in Fairborn over scarce resources and particularized zoning and development location issues—appear to limit economic development to the traditional and conservative. The small-town culture in Oakville precludes an active development agenda just as the renter-driven no-tax culture does in Fairborn. Although Oakville has the economic resources for an active development agenda, it lacks the cultural "will."

It is also interesting that these two cities also are among the four with governing regimes. Here the progressive (Oakville) and caretaker (Fairborn) regimes help to manage conflict but do not appear to have activist agendas. Again, given the civic cultures, it is no accident that these are not development regimes, and the conflict management role also precludes it. Last, because local goals for development do not include industrial attraction but rather emphasize quality growth in the former and home ownership and the preservation of a small-town historic downtown in the latter, there is no future vision that would stimulate a more activist or entrepreneurial approach. An open political environment, interest representation via the regime and through grass roots efforts, decision making within the political arena, and cultural limits on governmental activism lead to conventional, traditional, and limited economic development policies.

Gloucester and Kettering are examples of *active bureaucratic-elite* communities. They manifest the following characteristics:

Healthy economies
High perceived competition
No governing regime
Low business and citizen input
High levels of planning and evaluation
Independent development departments
Medium to low political conflict
Either alternative or social goals
Innovative/entrepreneurial policies

The civic cultures in Gloucester and Kettering could not be more different than in the two previous cities. That Gloucester and Oakville share a province and Kettering and Fairborn a metropolitan area matters not at all. Rather, the cultural disdain for the political, and businesses and citizens apparently content to let government professionals deal with economic development allow those professionals to pursue an activist economic development agenda driven by strong planning and evaluation practices. It is in these entrepreneurial cities that culture and economy appear to reinforce each other. Robust economies in both cities, along with perceived competitive pressures, provide both the resources and stimulus necessary for an active and innovative economic development agenda. And there are few political or regime interests to get in the way. That the economic development policies employed in these cities are more creative than the typical tax abatements, loan schemes, or infrastructure investment has much to do with the particular goals or visions that officials—and seemingly, the larger community—share. Economic development is defined in these cities as advancement of education and the arts, quality of life for residents, high-tech development, and development and diversification of local industries.

Cornwall and Allen Park are examples of *passive bureaucratic elite* cities. They share the following characteristics:

Medium to low perceived competition
Little citizen or business input
Low levels of planning and evaluation
Traditional goals
Medium to low innovation/entrepreneurialism

In Cornwall and Allen Park, there is little citizen or business input into local economic development policy; decisions are made primarily by governmental officials. This is not to suggest that there are no political conflicts in these communities, just that there are few institutionalized access points. And in Allen Park, input appears to be avoided by local officials. Citizens have opposed bond issues for a new city hall in Allen Park, whereas business leaders in both communities express frustration with the generally passive stance toward economic development and seek greater political access. In Allen Park, this may take a confrontational stance, whereas in Cornwall, business leaders appear more interested in cooperation. In both cases, lack of pressure, limited resources, and a reliance on a few firms (in Allen Park) has led to limited and traditional economic development efforts.

Cadillac and Coshocton are examples of communities dominated by business or a *combination of business and bureaucratic elites.* They reflect the following characteristics:

Developmental governing regimes
High business input
Low citizen input
Medium levels of planning and evaluation
Business leader locus of power
Low political conflict
Either alternative or social goals
One city high on Type II
Medium to high innovation/entrepreneurialism

Cadillac and Coshocton are distinctive in that both have development regimes. In the former, the private sector entirely dominates economic development, whereas in the latter, local professionals share power with external business organizations. As expected with development regimes, business input is high and institutionalized, whereas citizen input is low. However, the civic culture in these communities mitigates the extent to which a typical development agenda is pursued as well as the extent to which public resources are devoted to private-sector interests. Instead, the culture sets expectations for businesses— volunteer time and resources to the community, pay for development, and, in Coshocton, pay reparations if they don't. Because officials in both cities emphasize such social and alternative goals as worker attraction, home ownership, tourism, and quality of life, it is not surprising that development policies are more innovative and entrepreneurial than most analyses of development regimes would suggest.

With the addition of the mayor-dominated system in Romulus, where one individual balances diverse interests through good business sense and policies that attempt to achieve a more equal distribution of the benefits of growth, these five types of cities represent identifiable local civic cultures surrounding economic development. Only in the active/elite cities is there any connection between the cultural profile and economic forces. Country or even state/province of location is not included in any of the profiles. The commonalities among cities within groups has much more to do with local cultural traits than it does with the economy, national origin, or even enabling legislation. This question of patterns in the types of economic development policies is worth some more exploration. To put it succinctly, Are there any patterns across cities if economic development policies alone are considered? This question is explored in the discussion to follow.

Patterns With Policies

To simplify policy comparisons, only three types of policy profiles are discussed: Type II policy use, traditional policy use, and entrepreneurial/innovative/active approaches to economic development. Type II policies are self-explanatory at this point. Cities with a traditional approach to economic development are those that use relatively conservative, well-tested, and low-risk policies and incentives. An innovative or active approach, on the other hand, is one where new policies are explored, creative financing arrangements are used, and risk is borne by local governments, typically in an entrepreneurial role.

Of all the case cities, Romulus and Coshocton have experimented to the greatest extent with Type II policies. Romulus has been particularly active in this area. What do these two cities have in common based on the case studies? On the surface, they both have strong-mayor forms of government, but the mayor in Coshocton did not fulfill a typical strong-mayor role, and economic development responsibility is vested in an external body. Thus, based on these cases, an inherent connection between strong mayors and Type II policies cannot be assumed. Economically, both cities have moderate levels of poverty and low average incomes. As previous literature has suggested, Type II policies are clearly not a luxury for richer cities, and it is often more stressed cities that experiment with hiring guarantees and linkage requirements (Elkins, 1995; Reese, 1998). Both cities also have high levels of intergovernmental interactions, though Coshocton's are very amicable, whereas Romulus' are quite tense. Last, officials in both cities indicate that social goals are the most important. These, then, are the only apparent patterns with Type II policy use. It should be remembered that the regression analyses also shed little light on the dynamics behind the use of Type II policies.

Looking more closely at the two cases and their particular local histories and cultures provokes several possible explanations. First, although there has been a good bit of turnover in elected officials in Romulus, in both cities, politics tend not to extend into economic development decision making. In Romulus, it appears that businesses and citizens are content to let the mayor make most policy decisions. In Coshocton, this discretion is left to the external private body. Thus, there is little political debate about day-to-day development issues. In both cities, the officials responsible for development—the mayor in Romulus and Jobs Plus officials in Coshocton—spoke about the importance of not giving away public benefits, of ensuring that firms receiving benefits pay back to the city, and of extracting reparations for those that were not "good citizens." In short, the particular officials in both cities see economic development as a give and take between the public and private sectors. The public sector would give but was prepared to take back benefits if businesses did not uphold their promises. Such a stance was simply viewed as good business by officials in both cities. And these officials were allowed to make development policy decisions without a great deal of outside influence. In short, it appears that a moderately stressed financial picture, the need to address concerns of minority residents (in Romulus), good business sense by local officials (it is important to remember that the mayor in Romulus is also a business person), and an ability to make decisions

with limited outside influence appear to lead to an experiment with
Type II policies, at least based on these two cases.

The traits of cities using an entrepreneurial, innovative, or active approach to economic development are more patterned. Kettering, Cadillac, and Gloucester are the most innovative or entrepreneurial in their
approaches to economic development. For Cadillac, innovation is most
evident in the effective mixture of private and public activity and in the
creative and often complex methods used to finance public activities.
The city of Kettering has been extremely creative in the reuse of an old
military base and in its emphasis on the arts as a form of development.
Finally, though Gloucester is more limited in what it can do by provincial law, it has conducted an award-winning business support and liaison program. What traits, then, do these three cities have in common?
From an environmental perspective, there are few patterns; Kettering
and Gloucester have robust economies, but Cadillac certainly does not.
They are, however, all city manager systems, with the manager having
substantial power in each. Perceived competition with other cities
ranges from medium to high, so it could be concluded that some level of
competition is necessary for innovative or entrepreneurial policy. Beyond this, many of the civic culture attributes appear important.

First, levels of planning and evaluation are high, and two of the three
cities leave economic development decisions to professional bureaucrats within city government. The third, Cadillac, combines the efforts
of development bureaucrats with local business leadership. In two of
these cities, there are relatively low levels of both citizen and business
input. These features link together development decisions made by
professionals, typically organized as an independent city department,
outside the glare of the political arena. Indeed, in all three cities, politics
are not viewed favorably, and cooperation is the preferred approach to
dealing with multiple interests. Business leaders have a high level of institutionalized input in Cadillac, though framed by a culture of cooperation and business volunteerism. The development goals mentioned by
officials in these cities all fall within either the social or alternative categories. It appears that intercity competition for development may spur
innovative and entrepreneurial development policies, but it is probably
not a *sufficient* condition. Entrepreneurial behavior may be stimulated
in less identifiably political environments, where economic development decisions are left to professionals and where decisions are based
on high levels of planning and evaluation.

Cities with a more traditional approach to economic development—Fairborn, Allen Park, and Oakville—are generally the opposite of the foregoing examples. Environmentally, officials in two of the three cities perceive little competition with other communities; hence, there is no external impetus for innovation. Two of the cities leave development decisions to professional bureaucrats who use relatively high levels of planning and evaluation. The main cultural difference between traditional and innovative cities is the relatively high levels of political conflict in the former. Low levels of perceived competition and high levels of internal conflict produce a conservative approach to economic development and common, low-risk, and relatively low-cost strategies. The cities employing a traditional approach to economic development not surprisingly also pursued traditional goals of business attraction and infrastructure development.

Two of the three cities with traditional approaches to economic development have governing regimes, and in the third, a nascent regime may be in the process of emerging. The regime types differ—Fairborn has a caretaker regime, whereas Oakville's is progressive—so it can not be concluded that a given regime leads to traditional approaches to economic development. But in comparing these cities to the more entrepreneurial ones, it could be argued that regimes are more likely to pursue a conservative approach to economic development, whereas bureaucratically driven processes seem to lead to greater innovation. Again, it seems reasonable that the political bargaining inherent in a regime may circumscribe the range of possibilities because any innovation becomes a harder sell to all the governing partners and interests.

This analysis leaves one city (Cornwall) unaccounted for, and Coshocton has some interesting policies beyond their recent experimentation with Type II policies, as noted earlier. The approaches toward economic development in these communities lie somewhere between innovation and tradition. Coshocton has been relatively active in the areas of downtown and tourist development. However, the downtown initiatives have been largely conducted by private organizations using private funds. The tourist initiatives include an emphasis on the historic district, summer fairs, and recreation activities that are quite creative. Cornwall has been working on a smart-city initiative to attract high-technology firms and residents. So, although not highly active or innovative, there are some interesting activities going on in these cities that separate them from the more traditional cities. In both Cornwall and

Coshocton, there is low citizen input and relatively low internal political conflict. Perceived competition in Coshocton is moderate, whereas
for Cornwall it is low to moderate. Thus, they are similar to the innovative cities in that competition is combined with low internal political
conflict. What appears to differ, then, is the extent to which decisions
are made by development professionals and how those decisions are
made. Levels of planning and evaluation are not particularly high in
these cities—much lower than in the innovative or entrepreneurial
cities. Furthermore, although decisions are left to bureaucrats in
Cornwall, they have not been particularly aggressive in their tasks. In
Coshocton, development decision making is the prerogative of business leaders in external organizations. Thus, some of the necessary conditions exist for entrepreneurial policies, but the added cultural aspect
of professionalized decision making is not as fully developed.

Last, it is interesting to note what variables *do not* appear to relate to
the overall approaches to economic development in the case cities. First,
there are no consistent patterns between the economic conditions of
communities and their development approaches. There also does not
seem to be any national pattern. Even given the more restrictive enabling legislation in Ontario, there are Canadian cities in each of the policy categories except Type II policies. The formal structure of local government also appears to play little role in development policy choice.
Although both of the high Type II cities are strong-mayor systems, at
least on paper, Coshocton does not operate as a strong-mayor system.

Nor does place in the urban hierarchy seem to determine the approach to development. Three cities each represent old inner-ring suburbs, newer outer suburbs, and isolated nodes. Although this variable
did not appear to be correlated with either process or policy in the multiple regressions, it was possible that a more careful examination in the
case studies would reveal some patterns. Basically, it did not. The three
types of cities have different visual appearance and feel—older inner-
ring suburbs look similar to each other and different from newer suburbs in terms of housing and downtown areas, for example. But this did
not translate into uniformly distinctive processes or policies for economic development. Although place in the urban hierarchy may affect
overall economic conditions and the type of built environment and
infrastructure, it does not seem to determine development processes
and policies. It is not where you are but rather how you do things that

appears important. Of all the environmental variables, only perceived intercity competition seems to affect economic development policy approach. Clearly, competition along with civic culture are more important in the overall development policy approach than environmental forces alone.

COMPARING THE CASE STUDIES TO THE PATH ANALYSIS: WORKING ACROSS METHODOLOGIES

It seems clear that, despite distinct civic cultures that are tied to economic development approaches and policies in cities, general patterns can be identified across cultures. These patterns appear to reflect the original categories guiding the case study analysis: mayor-dominated systems, inclusive systems, active elite-dominated systems, passive elite-dominated systems, and externally driven systems. These cultural categories, however, have little to do with environmental forces and even governing regime. Rather, they are shaped by history and local ways of doing things that encompass who has input, who makes decisions, how conflict is perceived and channeled, community goals, how decisions are made, and ultimately, economic development policies. The remaining question now is, How do the survey data and case analyses relate to each other? Are the same forces present in both analyses? Are the same variables important? Do both methodologies reveal similar stories about civic culture and economic development? These questions are answered in the discussion to follow.

The Regression "Story"

In looking back across the regression analyses presented in Chapter 5, a relatively parsimonious list of independent variables consistently appears to influence both local processes and policies. What variables are most frequently related to *how* economic development decisions are made? In other words, what seems to shape local goals and objectives for economic development and determines whether the overall approach is entrepreneurial and active or more traditional and passive? The resources devoted to the economic development effort, the extent to which decisions are left to professional bureaucrats, the nature of community input—business and citizen—and the extent of planning and evaluation used in making decisions are most consistently related to both goals and overall development approach. In short, input, who makes decisions, and how decisions are made are critical to understanding economic development decision processes. A similar set of variables appears consistently related to choice of economic development strategies; resources, bureaucratic decision making, having an independent economic development department, business input, planning and evaluation, the extent of entrepreneurialism in the approach to development, and local goals are most often related to the various policy types.

The nature of some of these relationships is worth reiterating here. The placement of the economic development function is important in the nature of input avenues (external placement increases business input, in-house decreases it) and the level of resources devoted to economic development. Placing responsibility for decision making with bureaucrats in the city increases the extent of planning and evaluation supporting development decisions. The nature of community input— business versus citizen—appears important in several respects. Allowing citizens greater access to the decision process appears to be associated with increased resources (which then increase planning and evaluation) and an emphasis on Type II (redistribution or equity) or social goals. Giving business interests greater access appears to increase the emphasis on alternative development goals, such as small business growth or development. Citizen and business input are not mutually exclusive, however; indeed, cities that have more avenues for one have more for the other. Thus, local systems appear to be either basically inclusive or exclusive.

The critical point is that a common set of factors—input, locus, goals, and overall approach to development—most consistently predict economic development policies. Granted, different permutations of independent variables are contained in each regression, but a summary scan across analyses clearly shows this group of variables to most consistently predict both process and policy. To be sure, environmental variables are also present in many of the equations; whereas country and residential need appear in several regressions, perceptions of intercity competition is the most prominent environmental factor in predicting economic development policies. However, no equation either relating to how decisions are made or what policies are pursued contains *only* environmental forces; policy and process are the result of a mix of environmental and cultural forces, and the environment alone is not sufficient in understanding economic development policy making.

The Case Study "Story"

As with the regression analyses, a scan across the summary of cases reveals a relatively consistent set of variables or forces that are most critical in shaping how and what cities do. Table 11.2 provides a brief summary highlighting these central features in each city. What variables seem most important? Environmental forces clearly influence choices in several of the cities. The transient population in Fairborn limits governmental resources. The severe depression in Cornwall in the 1980s is still a blow from which they are recovering, both psychologically and economically. The conflicts with county and federal governments over Detroit Metropolitan Airport permeated the discussions with local officials in Romulus. And the controversy with the Province of Ontario over municipal reorganization in the Ottawa region is ultimately leading to the demise of Gloucester as a governmental entity. The environment clearly matters. But it does not stand alone; rather, it shapes and interacts with the larger local civic culture. The variables that stand out most prominently in the foregoing summary are the following: power locus, decision-making system, local values and goals, input structures, level of political conflict, and acceptance or aversion to conflict. In short, the local civic culture variables appear most important when summarizing the essence of economic development process and policy in each community. The regression and case study analyses, although different in form and detail, tell similar stories about the centrality of local civic culture.

A comment at this point is worth making about what is *not* among the central cultural traits: governing regime. The fact that the majority of the case cities do not have regimes would be a reason to leave it off the lists. The more important and telling reason that it is not included is that for the four cities with regimes, it appears not to matter all that much. Thus, although Coshocton and Cadillac have development regimes and they are central to *how* they make decisions, their policy agendas do not

TABLE 11.2 Central Forces Affecting Economic Development

Mayor dominated
  Romulus
    Mayor locus
    Generational families, ruling "clique"
    Intergovernmental problems—airport
    Smart bargaining positions vis-à-vis private sector
    Social goals (housing, shopping, ensuring jobs for local residents)
    Type II policies

Inclusive
  Fairborn
    All interests are heard
    Transitory and senior population
    Desire for limited taxes
    Conservative approach to spending
    Political conflict over development siting
    Social and alternative goals (homeownership, base diversification, downtown
      development)
    Conservative approach to development
  Oakville
    Limit growth
    All interests are heard
    Interests organized
    Small-town image
    Decisions are made politically
    Growth management goals
    Conservative "pay as you go" approach

Bureaucratic elites—passive
  Cornwall
    Remembered effects of recession
    Keep processes closed to only bureaucrats
    Business desire for access
    Some intergovernmental conflicts
    Conservative, passive approach
    Traditional goals (attract industry, attract anything from Quebec)
  Allen Park
    Political conflict
    Keep processes closed to only bureaucrats
    Business in confrontational stance
    Rely on a few industries
    Passive stance toward development
    Traditional goals (improve infrastructure, downtown development)

TABLE 11.2 (Continued)

Bureaucratic elites—active
  Kettering
        Politics is bad
        Leave decisions to professionals
        Regional cooperation
        Professionalized decision making, high planning and evaluation
        Entrepreneurial/innovative approach
        Social goals (education, arts, increase high-paying jobs)
  Gloucester
        Run city like a business
        Leave decisions to professionals
        Intergovernmental problems—megacity
        Professionalized decision making, high planning and evaluation
        Entrepreneurial/innovative approach given provincial confines
        Alternative goals (office/hotel development, high-tech development)

Externally driven
  Cadillac
        Business/government cooperation
        High off-cycle activity
        Politics is bad, conflict is bad
        Business and citizen volunteerism
        Entrepreneurial/innovative approach
        Alternative and social goals (worker attraction, tourism, corporate leadership
            development, grow existing business)
  Coshocton
        External locus
        Little governmental involvement
        Leave private sector alone
        Business volunteerism
        Cooperation valued
        Alternative goals (small, "appropriate" business development, tourism)

---

conform to the expected give away of public resources to private interests. The local cultures in these communities dictate more social, community oriented agendas. Similarly, the cultural forces in Oakville that
lead to a progressive growth management agenda drive the nature of
the regime, not the other way around. Indeed, Oakville only marginally
has a regime because politics are widely inclusive, and the small-town
image transcends any particular group. In Fairborn, too, culture precludes any other type of approach besides a caretaker one. At root, the

civic culture shapes, defines, and limits the possibilities for regime formation and the agenda it may pursue.

Comparing the Stories

The case studies and regression analyses can be compared in two ways: first, by examining the variables most central to economic development process and policy, and second, by looking at the correspondence between what the regression analyses said about policy profiles (e.g., the profile of a high Type II or financial incentive city) and the reality of case city traits and policies. These approaches are discussed in the following sections.

Comparing Central Variables

Essentially, the regression and case study analyses are showing the same variables as being important in how and what is done in economic development. Attributes of the local civic culture are important according to both methodologies. The nature of input systems, who has access to the system, and the power locus for decision making define the culture of the economic development process and shape both the approach to economic development and resultant policies. Decision-making styles are also central in both analyses. How much planning and evaluation are conducted? How professionally driven are decisions? How entrepreneurial or innovative is the overall approach to economic development? Local goals and visions for the future are also a central component of the local culture and, indeed, were most often related to policy use in the regression analyses.

Although the case studies have allowed for greater depth and a more nuanced understanding of each local culture, the stories are essentially the same. Thus, the main difference between the two methodologies is the inability of the survey and statistical analysis to pick up such cultural traits as local history, aversion to conflict or politics, intergovernmental problems due to an airport, or the value placed on a small-town image. These forces, visible only in the case studies, shape the local civic culture in a manner not accessible to survey analysis alone. This again highlights the value of the combined methodology; the survey and case analyses complement and confirm each other. Across a number of cases and variables, the survey shows, with statistical robustness, that civic culture and the environment interact to shape local economic development process and policy. The case analysis shows how the individual local histories and environments shape local values, visions, and mores for making political decisions. In essence, they show the local civic culture at work.

Comparing Policy Profiles

Chapter 5 concluded with descriptions or profiles of typical cities extensively using each type of economic development policy discussed: financial incentives, demand-side policies, zoning policies, loan arrangements, marketing, and Type II policies. It is interesting to see how well these profiles actually describe the case study cities scoring high on each policy use. And as will become clear, the regression analyses are remarkably accurate in predicting which of the case cities emphasized particular policies.

Among the case cities, Romulus, Cadillac, and Allen Park were the cities most likely to use financial incentives, such as tax abatements and deferments. It is no accident that all of these cities are in Michigan. Ontario does not allow cities to use financial bonuses, and Michigan is among the states most free in their enabling legislation regarding tax abatements. Aside from being in the same state, the regression analyses suggested that so-called high-financial cities would be in the United States, have higher levels of residential need, feel some competition with other cities for development, leave decision making to bureaucrats, and have an entrepreneurial approach to economic development. With the exception of this last trait, the regression profile fits these high-finance cities very well. They all feel at least moderate competitive pressures and have relatively high levels of residential need. Two—Cadillac and Allen Park—leave development decisions to bureaucrats. Only one of the three—Cadillac—is particularly entrepreneurial, although Romulus clearly varies from the policy norm in its use of Type II policies.

Kettering, Cadillac, and Gloucester make the greatest use of demand-side policies where the local government acts as entrepreneur. According to regression analysis, the profile of a high-demand-side city is one where there is low residential need, high perceived competition, an emphasis on social or alternative goals, decision making by professionals, and an entrepreneurial approach to development. These traits almost perfectly match the three cities at hand. Although Cadillac had higher residential need according to the 1990 census, there has been strong growth over the past ten years to the point where there is now a worker rather than an employment shortage.

The cities of Romulus, Fairborn, Cadillac, and Oakville were the most likely to be using zoning policies either to stimulate or facilitate development, or in the case of Oakville, control development. The regression profile of a high-zoning city is one with high levels of planning and evaluation, moderate to high residential need, and strong perceived competition. These match the case cities with the exception of low residential need in Oakville; three of the four cities have high levels of planning and evaluation and officials that perceive themselves to be in competition with other cities. Cities most likely to use zoning policies according to the regression would have growth management goals, certainly true of Oakville. This is not the case in the other cities, however, where zoning is used to ease rather than restrict development. Last, the regression analysis suggests that high-zoning cities should leave development decisions primarily to bureaucrats; this is the case only in Fairborn and partially in Cadillac. The regressions here are not as accurate in predicting the high-zoning cities.

Cadillac is the only case study city making extensive use of loan arrangements to enhance development. The regression profile suggests that such a city should have professionalized decision making, relatively high levels of residential need, high levels of business input, and an entrepreneurial approach to economic development that emphasizes small business development. This profile matches Cadillac perfectly.

The case cities with the most extensive marketing programs are Cadillac, Fairborn, Gloucester, and Cornwall. As the regression analysis suggests, two Canadian cities are present here. Oakville is not marketing extensively because they are not seeking additional residential or industrial development, but they do have extensive tourist materials. The profile also suggests that high-marketing cities would be those where officials are competition with other cities, and this is the case across these cities. Two other aspects of the profile do not match the case cities at hand, however. The regression suggests that marketing cities would have high levels of business input (not the case in three of the cities) and traditional development goals. The cities in this group are more likely to emphasize social and alternative goals.

Last, the regression analysis did not provide much guidance regarding the profile of a city making high use of Type II policies other than pointing to at-large elections and having social or alternative goals. The case cities making the greatest use of Type II policies are Romulus, Coshocton, and Kettering. Although officials in these cities expressed alternative or social goals, Coshocton uses a mix of at-large and ward elections, and Kettering's council elections are all ward based. Thus, the electoral pattern does not hold.

In summary, given that the regression analyses cannot hope to capture all of the cultural nuances present in the case studies, they do a reasonably good job of predicting which case study cities will emphasize which development policies. In the case of financial, loan and demand-side policies, the correspondence is very close. Both methodologies provide consistent findings. But the shortcomings of the survey analysis for measuring local civic culture are obvious.

This chapter has provided a summary of the case studies and compared the findings of both methodologies. The primary conclusions are as follows:

Local civic culture is a necessary component in understanding local policy processes.

Although environmental forces, such as the economy and national environment, shape the local culture, they are not determinative, and development policy cannot be explained by environmental factors alone.

Although a unique civic culture can be identified for each community, there are patterns across cities in general cultural types.

The main types of local civic culture based on the case studies are as follows: mayor dominated; politically inclusive; elite dominated, passive; elite dominated, active; and externally driven.

Civic cultures can be differentiated based on the nature of input systems, who has access to the system, the power locus for decision making, decision-making styles, nature and views about political conflict, overall approach to economic development, and local goals and visions for the future.

In sum, both survey and case study methodologies point to similar cultural forces as being important in economic development policy making. Although the breadth and depth of indicators of civic culture were inherently limited in the survey analyses, the case studies clearly show that different local civic cultures can be identified based on a relatively parsimonious set of local ways of doing things. It should be noted, however, that although these civic culture attributes were found to be important using both methodologies, they do not necessarily represent a definitive set of civic culture attributes. Central aspects of local civic culture affecting economic development policy have been identified here. It is likely that the larger local civic culture that defines and delineates all aspects of local policy includes additional attributes that remain to be identified by further study.

The last chapter returns to the earlier political culture research and compares what examining local economic development through a civic culture lens can tell about local practice and policy. It suggests how past reference points can shed new light on current debates in urban political research. Does using civic culture to understand economic development processes and policies raise questions about extant "knowledge" of local economic development? Does an examination of local civic culture raise new questions to guide future research? It is to these questions that the discussion turns.

NOTE

1. Income figures for Canadian cities are in Canadian dollars. If conversions were made, those cities would be ranked somewhat lower. However, Oakville still has the highest incomes and Gloucester would remain high and Cornwall in the middle to lower range.

12

THE CIVIC CULTURE OF LOCAL ECONOMIC DEVELOPMENT

Considering Past and Future Research

The principal thesis of this analysis of economic development policy making is that local civic culture appears to frame and shape political processes and policies in each individual community and thereby play a crucial role in determining policy outputs. Several general types or categories of local civic culture have been identified. The analysis—both survey and case study—also raises a number of questions about many accepted "truths" about local economic development, specifically, and local policy making more generally.

"Who governs?" and "What difference does it make?" have been central questions of local government policy research for at least fifty years. These questions often generated methodological wars between elite and pluralist theorists, but they focused largely on the best approach to community power *case study* research. More recent studies, which led to the regime theory paradigm, built on this tradition.

Another body of research has focused specifically on questions related to economic development. This study began within this latter genre. Although its initial concern was to describe and explain economic development policies being pursued by local government officials, ultimately, it sought to explain local decision making. Given this direction, its findings began to bump into the earlier research on community power and regimes.

A broad examination of the current literature on local development, much of it presented in earlier chapters, suggests a series of reasonably shared assumptions or truths about local policy and process:

> Economic development policy making is largely about economics and, perhaps secondarily, politics.
>
> Fiscal and economic stress forces cities to approve costly incentives for private businesses.
>
> Cities employing a broad array of economic development techniques or most incentives allowed by state law are "shooting at everything that flies" and lack rational focus in their economic development efforts. This situation is exacerbated by external economic constraints.
>
> Local government structure matters in determining policy processes and resultant policies, even in the face of economic constraints.
>
> In addition to government structure, the composition of local governing regimes largely determines policies.
>
> Cities with similar governing regimes will have similar approaches to economic development.
>
> Businesses are a critical part of most local economic development regimes, and hence, development regimes will be most prevalent.
>
> Businesses will always push for incentives to lower their costs of production.

Much of this conventional wisdom comes under question when local economic development policy making is examined using a civic-culture framework. Economics, structure, and even local governing regime do not appear sufficient in explaining local process and policy. The larger local civic culture tempers and transforms these forces to create policy systems and outcomes not necessarily expected or predicted by extant ways of looking at local economic development. Furthermore, the methodological power of survey and case analysis has brought both breadth and depth to the examination of local policy making, allowing for a reexamination and reconsideration of what we think we know about local politics.

QUESTIONS RAISED BY
THE CIVIC-CULTURE APPROACH

Is it Economics or Politics or Something More?

In the wake of Peterson's (1981) *City Limits,* general debate ensued regarding the proper balance between economic—usually externally driven—imperatives and local political independence. Now, although it is generally agreed that "politics matters" and that economic determinism alone can not adequately explain local policy, it is also accepted that fiscal and economic stress drive cities to provide costly incentives to businesses (Jones and Bachelor, 1993). Yet the analysis here suggests that the determinants of local economic development policy include more than just local fiscal health, competition from other cities and nations, or even such internal political forces as governmental structure or governing regime.

Regression analyses clearly indicated that the correlates of local development policy represent a complex mix of forces that go beyond economic and governmental structure. The index of residential need, the primary economic variable, affected only three policy areas: loans, zoning, and financial incentives. In no case was it the best predictor of the policy in question. Other forces, such as governmental structure, input systems, planning and evaluation, approach to economic development, and development goals, were equally influential in determining local development policies. Case study analyses also highlighted the variable effects of the economy. For example, the most economically stressed cities—Cornwall, Cadillac, and Romulus—manifested differing approaches to economic development. In short, the economy "matters" for some policies, but it does not determine policy across the board. The factors consistently related to economic development process and policy go beyond economics and even the basics of structure and regime to encompass the larger civic culture.

Related to the focus on external economic forces is the assumption, in much previous research, that external competition and fiscal stress will produce an almost desperate attempt to try all possible economic development techniques in the hopes that something will rejuvenate the local economy. In the words of Rubin (1988), cities employing a broad array of economic development techniques or most policies allowed by state law are "shooting at everything that flies" and lack rational focus in their economic development efforts. The analysis here suggests that this is not necessarily the case, however. If decisions are dominated by professional staff and have a base of external, possibly state-level, support, "shooting" may represent a coherent or at least planned strategy. Furthermore, cities that initially appeared to be shooting (i.e., high use of traditional financial incentives, such as tax abatements) were *also* more likely to embrace demand-side policies, such as underwriting training programs, funding research and development, and operating business incubators. Cadillac represents a perfect case in point; it employs a broad array of economic development techniques yet takes creative advantage of a number of program and funding options, scans the environment to find new policies that can be adapted for local use, and has a creative, proactive, and entrepreneurial strategy. Whether a city is doing a number of economic development activities because they are desperate and haphazard in their efforts or because they are innovative and creative depends on the local culture framing how decisions are made. And this distinction can only be made through case study analysis.

Government Structure and Governing Regime: Is it the Whole Story?

Many studies of local economic development policy making have focused on the importance of local government structure. However, putative structures do not necessarily represent real dynamics. There are strong mayors dominating decision processes, and there are strong mayors who are not really very influential. Ward elections can be divisive in some cities but "public regarding" in others. Nonpartisan elections often mean just the absence of a label on the ballot because most voters know each candidate's partisan pedigree. These "facts" may seem obvious but are often disregarded in the many studies focusing on relationships between formal structure and policy outcome.

This point was well made in analysis of both survey and case study data. First, arguing that structure matters almost presupposes coherent structural forms; that is, local governments are either reformed or unreformed. In reality there is wide variation in structure and only general patterns of reform. Neither partisan nor nonpartisan elections are necessarily related to type of executive or to whether council seats are filled by district or at-large election. And few aspects of structure are related to ultimate economic development policy choice.

The general lack of relationship between structure and policy could result from two causes: Either structure simply doesn't matter, or structure is important, but cross-sectional survey research is not the best way to identify the effects. Case study analysis strongly suggests that the latter is more accurate. However, it highlights further complexities in examining the role structure plays in local policy making. Very simply, form of government seldom reflects actual operations. On paper a strong-mayor system, Coshocton really operated more like a weak-mayor/manager system, for example. Formal structure may not represent the actual structure, and that real structure may change over time. Coshocton's "weak" elderly mayor was unseated in the next election, opening the door for a return to a strong-mayor system.

Of course, much recent research—coming after Stone's (1989) *Governing Atlanta*—has moved beyond formal structure as a description of local politics to include governing regime. Regime, distinct from structure, represents the necessary coalitions and resources to govern. From the analysis here, it clearly appears that regime, too, is not broad enough to fully capture urban political systems. Economic development policies are related to a complex mixture of environmental, regime, and local cultural forces. And an excessive or single-minded focus on regime obscures the more complex social and political forces within communities. Indeed, it may even leave some cities out of the research frame because they lack regimes altogether. Five of the nine case cities had no discernable governing regime. In Romulus, the business community is not sufficiently involved in governing and does not have any ongoing institutional presence. The mayor-dominated system and the pervading civic culture precludes the development of a broader governing regime. Romulus is also a small city where politics are both familial and familiar; the mayor does not need to marshal other resources either to be elected or to govern. The situation is similar in Cornwall and Allen Park. Even the larger cities of Kettering and Gloucester do not have functioning regimes.

Furthermore, it does not appear that development regimes predominate nor can it be assumed that regimes composed of development interests will always produce development policies. The development regimes in both Coshocton and Cadillac led to policy agendas that, although clearly business friendly, also embrace expectations that businesses invest in the community through volunteerism and subsidize a large part of the city's economic development effort. The civic cultures in these communities lead away from the expected development regime agenda. In short, government structure and regime analysis both fall short in understanding and predicting local process and policy.

The Role of the Private Sector: How Much Variation is There?

The role and extent of business pressure on and input into local economic development policy-making processes has been a recurring theme of much existing research. From Peterson's (1981) limited city, Logan and Molotch's (1987) growth machine, Jones and Bachelor's (1993) sustaining hand, to Stone's (1989) development regime, the central role of capital interests has been an accepted part of the analysis and interpretation of economic development policy making. The analysis here raises a number of questions about many conventional "truths" regarding private sector influence in local governance as well. First, it is not at all clear that there is a single coherent business interest in communities. Other analysis of the survey data indicated that cities with local versus nonlocal business bases are clearly distinguishable. The nature of the base affects both how decisions are made as well as the policies that result (Reese and Rosenfeld, 2000). In the analysis here, it appears that a strong, primarily local business base can lead to greater civic volunteerism and an emphasis on alternative economic development goals. Only in cities where there is a predominant representation of branch plants or externally owned firms is the result the emphasis on traditional financial incentives predicated by much of the literature.

It also does not appear to be the case that businesses are always in a position of trying to wrest any and all incentives from local governments. Although greater levels of overall business input are associated with use of development loans and more active marketing campaigns by local governments, they do not seem to influence the use of financial incentives, such as tax abatements. More important, *both* local and nonlocal business influence are positively related to the use of Type II policies in correlation analysis. Last, where business input and involvement in both decision making and implementation is high, the result appears to be a greater emphasis on business volunteerism and support for all aspects of the community. This extends from arts to education, includes more emphasis on quality-of-life issues, and in some cases, reduces the use of public funds for economic development. Thus, corporate interests are not always pitted against public interests, and businesses do not always extract more from the local community than they contribute. In short, there are communities where the local government has been able to leverage private-sector resources in innovative ways to benefit the whole community.

LOCAL CIVIC CULTURE
AND FUTURE URBAN RESEARCH

The questions raised about conventional knowledge provide an extensive basis for future research efforts. In a general sense, the analysis here highlights the need for more extensive research in three general areas: (a) governing regimes and the connections between regimes and the local civic culture, (b) situations where the conventional wisdom seems in conflict with the current analysis, and (c) an expansion and refinement of the civic-culture approach.

Civic Culture and Regimes

The place of regimes within the local civic culture, and indeed, greater consideration of regime itself, is an area ripe for future research. The analysis here raises several critical questions about regimes. First, many cities, particularly smaller ones, appear not to have regimes, using Stone's (1989) original definition. Can regime analysis even be used to gain an understanding of governing in small places? Second, the two development regimes in the analysis reflect some anomalies. Cadillac and Coshocton have business actors fully integrated into the governing regime. By this criterion, these cities should be classified as having development regimes. However, another aspect of the definition of development regime is that probusiness policies should result. Although in neither city are policies inimical to business interests, Coshocton uses clawbacks, and in both cities, significant business resources are devoted to public-sector ends. Civic expectations in both cases require business to subsidize their own development needs. Thus, development regime actors appear to be supporting quite progressive policies. How would regime analysis explain such situations absent consideration of the larger civic culture that shapes regime forces? Similarly, cities with similar regime actors can have very different policy outcomes and vice versa. Last, the proliferation of regime types in the literature suggests that an examination of regime alone is not sufficient to understand policy and process across a wide range of cities. In short, it seems clear that a reconsideration of the role of regime, whether it is applicable to all cities, and how it fits within the broader civic culture is warranted.

Questions Raised by the Civic-Culture Focus

In addition to these questions about the sufficiency of the regime model in understanding the urban political arena, the analysis also raises questions about other aspects of the dynamics of economic development policy making that should be addressed in future research. The role of the business community in the development policy process is one such area. If there is no coherent business interest in communities, if local and extra local businesses want very different things from local governments, if businesses have a broader community vision that goes beyond just what they can extract from the public, and if growth machines and development regimes are not most prevalent across a range of cities, then how might researchers better explore the intersection between private and public sectors when it comes to development politics?

A number of pertinent, interesting, and theoretically important research questions come to mind:

What variations are there in business roles in local governance?

What forces lead to a culture of civic volunteerism?

How might city officials foster greater public-spirited business involvement in the larger community?

Are there models of business volunteerism that can be emulated by other cities?

Besides local and nonlocal business bases, what finer distinctions can be made among business interests within cities and the types of policies they pursue?

What are the different policy and governance dynamics associated with a host of other economic-base arrangements: branch plants versus headquarters, commercial versus industrial, single industry versus multi-industry?

What makes business leaders supportive of progressive/Type II policies?

Are high levels of business volunteerism and/or private-sector support of public ventures associated with better economic performance for the city?

Will building a more local business base lead to more advantageous relationships between the public and private sectors from a public interest point of view?

What are the economic and social impacts of a shift in business ownership from local to multinational concerns?

Does the presence of large, multinational firms tend to limit the aggressiveness and innovativeness of economic development policies in a large number of cities?

Second, the analysis also raises questions about how researchers measure and think about governmental structure and institutions and the extent to which they matter in determining public policy. First, because formal structure does not necessarily represent the real operating structure in communities, greater thought needs to be given to how structure or form of government is operationalized. Survey-based research needs to acknowledge that form variables may not be completely, or even largely, accurate. A safer approach is to use combined methodologies similar to that employed here to provide a sense of whether form and substance actually approximate each other. This should not be interpreted as a call for exclusively case study methodologies; rather, cross-sectional research with large data bases might be used in combination with questions explicitly designed to gauge real structural operations. Several well-written questions ought to suffice in at least providing a sense of whether a given system operates as expected.

The larger question raised about structure, however, is the extent to which it really *matters* in urban policy making. The clear argument here is that structure matters, but it represents only part of the larger civic culture. Thus, the particular mix of policies in a community results from the combined and interactive effects of environment, history, structure, and larger culture. Structure is necessary but not sufficient in understanding urban policy processes. Future research should more explicitly examine the interactions between the various forces that appear important: environmental, structural, and cultural. Such research could take two forms. One would be more extensive comparative case studies, likely longitudinal, with the main purpose being an effort to track and disentangle the various effects of these forces. The other approach would be more sophisticated modeling using large data bases. Such analysis should stress casual ordering, nonrecursive relationships, and "encompassing results" analysis that compares the parameters of rival explanatory models (Mizon and Richard, 1986). In this sense, it allows for a determination of whether environmentally or culturally driven models are better predictors of development policies or to what extent they are both valid but explain different things. This has been used on examinations of political culture at the international level with interesting results (Granato et al., 1996).

The positive relationship both in survey and case analysis between levels of business and citizen input is worth greater examination. Clearly, business versus citizen access to and power in economic development decisions is not an either/or situation. Despite conventional wisdom that suggests that many cities will give greater access to private-sector interests as a systemic response, such systems also appear more open to all types of community input. Why do business and community input appear so compatible if public and private interests are inherently at odds? Does greater citizen access counterbalance business pressures for incentives that only serve to enhance profits? Or is there some larger cultural imperative that associates the values of inclusiveness and access with a balancing of interests across diverse groups within the community?

Beyond these theoretical questions regarding the nature of business and citizen input, the analysis also highlighted methodological problems with how such input is typically measured. To the extent that large surveys have tended to measure opportunity for rather than actual access, influence, or power, findings may be misleading and may actually overstate the extent of business influence in development decisions. Survey questions must be directed at both avenues for input as well as the extent of use of such avenues, along with perceptual measures of actual power. Case study analysis can balance information on access with substantiation on the opportunity for, versus the realization of, power.

Another issue begging for more examination is differentiating between cities that are actively and innovatively experimenting with a variety of local development policies and those that are attempting everything in a desperate and almost random attempt to find something that works: the "shooting at everything" imperative. Case study research may be necessary to really understand the local dynamics. Are there other ways of doing this? Replicable and agreed on definitions of *innovation, entrepreneurialism,* and *creativity* in economic development policy use would be helpful. If researchers agreed on an operational definition of "good" policy or "cutting edge" policy, it would be it easier for scholars to identify cities with truly innovative approaches and policies and thus hold them up for emulation. The constant calls from granting agencies and higher levels of government for researchers to identify "success" stories highlights the great need not only for such operational definitions but also more research focused on the evaluation of economic development policy.

The place of race in the local civic culture is another critical area for future research. The findings here have hinted that race may be related to local political conflict and to the economic development policies pursued. However, because only one of the case cities had significant racial diversity and the Canadian cities lacked census data on race, nothing can be definitely concluded about race and civic culture. Future research on larger cities and those with greater racial and ethnic diversity should focus on questions such as the following:

Can there be a single local civic culture in the presence of diversity?

How do racial and/or ethnic cultures shape and interact with local civic culture?

Are cities with greater racial diversity more likely to have conflictual politics?

Are cities with greater diversity consistently more likely to promulgate progressive or Type II economic development policies?

How does race interact with regime within the context of the larger civic culture?

The relationship between the federal system and local civic culture also needs to be more explicitly explored. One of the criticisms of regime theory is that it does not sufficiently account for the effects of federal relationships on local power structures (Sites, 1997). Interaction with regional, state, providial, and national officials was one of the areas of focus of the case studies. However, only a few of the case cities had extensive intergovernmental relationships, and these varied widely: some extremely positive (Cadillac), others very negative (Romulus). It was difficult to tell from the cases here exactly how intergovernmental relationships affected economic development policy and practice. For example, Romulus clearly has very problematic relations with both the county and federal governments emanating from the airport. Although these issues have a direct relationship to tax base in the city and the airport affects the nature of development, it was not completely clear how the poor intergovernmental relationships affected economic development decision processes and ultimately policy, other than to provide a rallying point around which all actors in the community could agree (e.g., the county, in particular, is "bad"). Future research should target this area more explicitly to provide more detail about federal relations as well as including a broader array of situations.

Applying Civic-Culture Theory

Finally, the most important future research issue is the application of civic-culture theory. What research agenda will best allow for testing and further explication of local civic-culture theory to the understanding of local policy making? Such a research agenda should proceed in several ways. First, a replicable operational definition of *civic culture* is needed. The definition and indicators used here are reasonable and grounded in past research. However, such research has only provided limited examples of empirical definitions of culture and has been more focused on international, national, and state levels than on cities. More refinement of both theoretical parameters and empirical indicators of local civic culture would set the stage for comparable analysis. It is likely that this research has just scratched the surface in fleshing out the various types of local civic culture. With agreed-on definitions, such an effort can better proceed.

Along the same lines, this research has posited civic-culture theory for understanding economic development policy and policy making. Obviously, future research needs to expand the civic-culture approach to other urban policy areas. Is there one overall local civic culture that affects all policy areas in the same way? Within the general civic culture, are there definable variations depending on policy area? The possibility of having various shades within an overarching cultural hue is particularly salient for large cities not examined in this research. How does the diversity present in most large urban centers affect the development and maintenance of a larger shared civic culture? Or does it mitigate against the maintenance of a local culture entirely?

Last, for local civic culture to operate at the level of theory, several things must be accomplished in future research. Obviously, an operational definition needs to be created. After that, a more complete sense of the spectrum of existing cultures needs to be delineated. Ultimately, particular civic cultures need to be predictably associated with economic development approaches and policies. In short, cultural type needs to be predictive of particular policy profiles. Although establishing these connections will take time and many more studies, it is in this direction that research must go if urban scholars are to establish a theory of local development policy making. The possibility that civic culture can be used to understand other urban policy areas offers a great incentive to expand research in this direction.

BROADENING THE FOCUS: THE LOCAL CIVIC CULTURE

From Political Culture to Local Civic Culture

At this point, a final look at the application of a civic-culture framework to local policy making is useful. A reexamination of the earlier political culture analysis, even though focused on the international arena, again illustrates that the original concept has much to offer about development politics in urban areas. As Elazar (1994) initially suggested, shared patterns of understanding and action shape the local civic culture and define expectations for public roles, action, access, implementation processes, and policies. Not to reiterate the case findings here but to illustrate, it was clear that the shared tolerance for political conflict in a community, expectations of government and business roles, and attitudes about appropriate forms and nature of political access vary across communities and are intricately related to policy and process. Thus, in Cadillac, where tolerance for conflict is low but expectations for business volunteerism are high, business leaders and development administrators share power, and the resultant policies are a mixture of private subsidy of public benefits (such as support of arts and recreation) as well as the reverse (freely offering tax abatements). On the other hand, in Oakville, a higher tolerance for conflict leads to a much more open political system. However, contention in that community surrounds the extent and nature of economic growth because of a strong shared image as a small town. Shared attitudes and expectations make a difference in both how economic development is conducted and the types of policies that result.

Revisiting Kluckhohn's (1954) cultural themes is also useful at this point. To reiterate, he suggested that there are six central elements or themes composing political culture: (a) language, (b) aesthetic expression, (c) standardized orientation to life problems, (d) means to perpetuate the group, (e) individual demands for order, and (f) individual demands for survival. Although these are not all fully translatable to the urban or civic context, they point to several critical dynamics illustrated in the case studies. For example, the language used in Cadillac and Coshocton was one of "cooperation" and "volunteerism." "Politics" is used pejoratively. In Oakville, "limited growth" and "small town" were frequently mentioned. In Romulus, "good old boys" and "ruling clique" were repeatedly discussed. The language used to describe the different cities by those within the communities was different across cities but strikingly consistent internally. Similarly, desired future visions of the communities varied from "more jobs for our children" to "development of appropriate small businesses" to improved "quality of life."

Clearly, political styles differed across these cities. Although this was most evident in the differences in tolerance for conflict and expectations about the extent of access to the political system, more subtle myths or stories were also present and formed the basis of the local civic culture. For example, although no one in Romulus acknowledged a racial problem in the city, the stories told by several respondents belied that. Stories about cross burnings, conflict between youth of different races in the high school, and police actions with racial overtones all suggested that race and the challenges of a diverse community are a part of the local culture. On the other hand, a story about the mayor jumping out of his car to confront airport workers cutting down city rose bushes speaks both of the conflict generated by the airport but also of the direct and visible role the mayor plays in the community. Stories told in Fairborn about historic gambling raids and downtown businesses used to front local gambling operations provides a flavor of a community balancing new and old interests and ways of doing things. And in Allen Park, local officials talk about citizens confronting them directly about infrastructure quality and expenditure in a rather argumentative fashion. Such stories clearly illustrate not only the conflict present in the community but more essential problems that the older suburb has with infrastructure investment juxtaposed with citizen reluctance to increase tax burdens and harboring a distrust of governmental fiduciary responsibility.

"Standardized orientations" regarding access to power, the role of government in the market, the extent of governmental activity, and recruitment for public office were evident and important in the civic cultures identified here. For example, respondents in Coshocton, Cadillac, and Gloucester repeatedly spoke of limited governmental intervention in the affairs of the private sector. In Kettering and Gloucester, references to leaving economic development to administrative professionals and keeping politics out of development decisions were frequent. In Oakville and Fairborn, many comments were addressed to the importance of allowing everyone at the decision-making table and consulting with all aspects of the community before decisions were made. Different cities have different and quite evident cultures regarding how officials and citizens view the roles of various actors in the policy process. Common recruitment patterns were also apparent and varied across the cities. Most local elected officials in Romulus come from the same Catholic parish or from within the same group of generational residents. Many elected officials in Fairborn were formerly on the planning and zoning board. In Coshocton, former safety services directors often became mayors. Cultural variations in accepted views about the extent of governmental activity were also evident. In Allen Park and Fairborn, strong voter opposition to increased taxes and bond sales were evidence of a generally shared view that government should be limited. Governmental efforts to expand infrastructure or zone land as industrial in Oakville have been opposed, illustrating shared views that there should be no governmental support for increased development.

Last, individual and shared perceptions of how institutions should process competing demands and, indeed, how open political institutions should be to demands, is a central cultural factor that differentiates these cities. In the inclusive cities of Fairborn and Oakville, there is consensus that the political system should hear and encourage competing demands and that the political system is the proper forum to air such demands. In the elite-dominated cities of Cadillac and Kettering, the tolerance for political conflict is extremely low. Cooperation is emphasized over political conflict. Conflict should be channeled as group problem solving, with solutions coming from the combined efforts of professional administrators and business officials. In this sense, these latter two cities have conflict tolerances much akin to the communitarian cultures described by Swank (1996), where consensual decision making is stressed. Each of the communities also had different ways of processing demands within the system. For example, in Romulus, demands, particularly from the business sector, can go directly to the mayor. In Fairborn, there is a computer-based system for tracking citizen demands. Numerous organized citizen and business groups in Oakville have regularized access to the political arena.

As the political culture literature asserts, cultures can be more critical than objective conditions and can endure even as institutions or those conditions change. The small-town image in Oakville is apparent in all of their public materials as well as in conversations with local officials and citizens. Yet objectively, Oakville is far from a small town. The real question—and one it is still too early to answer—is how ingrained culture and institutional change will play out in this community. There are forces in Oakville that want the town to become more active in economic development, and the institutional shift from an internal economic development department to an external (although still closely tied to the city) public/private partnership suggests that there is a hope within these forces that institutional change will lead to cultural change. This remains to be seen. All indicators suggest that any alternation in the basic civic culture is going to be one of scale, not of substance. The discourse across interests within the town clearly still emphasizes growth management, governmental control of development, and limited public-sector initiative. Furthermore, the incongruence in several of the cities between putative forms of government and actual decision-making arrangements suggests that culture trumps institutions in determining both process and policy.

It should be emphasized that in no city was civic culture the only force that affected development policy. As Jackman and Miller (1996) emphasized, although culture is important, it may be more endogenous than exogenous. Indeed, culture and the economy and other environmental forces intertwine to produce local processes and policies. Local culture itself is shaped by such external forces. Consistently, however, although clearly affecting local culture and shaping what was seen as possible as far as economic development in terms of resources and even goals, external economic forces were never sufficient explanations of local development policy. As noted by Granato et al. (1996), "both cultural and economic arguments matter. Neither supplants the other. Further theoretical and empirical work is better served by treating these "separate" explanations as complementary" (626). At the end of the day, however, the research here—both survey and case study—clearly suggests that environmental or economic explanations of local policy are not sufficient. Local civic cultures must be considered to fully understand governance, process, and policy within cities.

The Centrality of Local Civic Culture

As stated in Chapter 2, local civic culture appears to be a penumbra defining what issues appear on the public agenda, how they are framed and discussed, what solutions are possible, how decisions are made, where the local leadership comes from, who has access to the political system, what interests are represented within the governing regime or whether there is a regime at all, the appropriate roles for local government, the balance between private- and public-sector interests, visions of the community, goals for the future, and ultimately, the nature of economic development policies pursued. Local civic culture, then, is broader than particular institutions or even governing regime because it encompasses the local habitus defining how individuals and groups act within the public sphere and common patterns of understanding about and behavior within the community. The local civic culture then creates the community *cum* community.

Within this larger framework, economic development decisions are part and parcel of the larger community fabric—they are inherently socially embedded. To understand development decision making through an economistic or institutional lens is akin to the blindfolded man describing an elephant. Disparate aspects of politics and process may be accurately reflected, but the overall picture is fragmented and ultimately misleading. If it is indeed as true that local governments are similar in all *unimportant* respects, then it is essential that fine distinctions in local civic cultures be explored, portrayed, and addressed.

Americans in the U.S. espouse democratic beliefs with an emphasis on locality with a vengeance. The importance of government that is "close to home" cannot be understated. For every national elected official, citizens elect literally thousands of local officials, and voters are incredibly hesitant to give up this home rule. Yet an antigovernment bias is felt across the United States. It is directed, however, at the abstract level, at the large and distant national government. It is more often than not associated predominantly with national government's power and not that of local government or local officials. Thomas Jefferson captured and epitomized the model of antagonism toward such big and distant governments. And he applied this not only to the federalists but to big, distant "urban" local governments. By far, the small, even rural, community was preferred. Some believe that the movement of the U.S. population to the suburbs from large cities reflected this Jeffersonian ideal. Democratic beliefs and antigovernment bias are a part of the U.S. civic culture. They are derived from the nation's historic relationship with England, King George, and the War of Independence.

A belief in equality is another aspect of the civic culture of the United States. From the Constitutional Convention through the Civil War, massive immigration, the Civil Rights Movement, and the continued conversation about race, beliefs in equality remain defining elements of how citizens of both the U.S. and Canada see themselves. The core arguments revolve around equality of opportunity versus equality of condition. Both sides reveal a great deal about the manner in which government's responsibilities and citizen's relationships to government are approached.

Americans are also focused on the duel concepts of marketplace and commonwealth. The love affair with free-market economies and the emphasis on individualism and individual responsibility pervade much of the thought about who U.S. Americans are as a people and how they approach government. On the flip side is the sense of commitment and responsibility for others—whether through individual acts of charity or collective acts of compassion for those less fortunate. The tension between marketplace and commonwealth also defines the civic culture, particularly in the U.S.

This dialogue about democracy, antigovernment biases, equality, marketplace, and commonwealth emerged as defining elements of the 1950s and 1960s quest to determine who governs America's cities. From John Mills to Hunter (1953), Dahl (1961), and Stone (1980, 1989, 1993), this has been the great debate of social science theory and methodology. Elite theory, pluralism, and regimes all attempt to explain the variations of the urban landscape. Although urbanization, suburbanization, industrialization, and "the new economy" have all had homogenizing effects, it doesn't require a de Tocqueville to see and realize that communities vary widely in so many ways. A drive across America may show common Interstate Highway signs, fast-food restaurants, and shopping malls—now called "generica" by some. But on exiting the highways, touring the communities, speaking with local officials and local citizens, observing the variations in policies and approaches to governance, it becomes clear that the variation is at least as great as the similarity. Why is it that Atlanta grew wildly from the 1960s to the new century, whereas New Orleans and Birmingham did not? Why doesn't Detroit have the same kind of civic infrastructure—grand buildings, parks, boulevards and institutions—that Chicago has? Why has Cleveland's rebirth been more apparent than that of Detroit? Why did New York become the port of entry and the financial powerhouse rather than Savannah or Charleston? And at a different scale, why do some small towns have vibrant downtowns, with concerts and festivals, restored and new buildings, and strong nearby neighborhoods, whereas others are barren?

It is argued here that the central defining variable of urban America is neither government structure nor the local economy. It is not local political parties, neighborhood groups, unions, or business groups. Nor is it leadership or the presence of a strong professional bureaucracy. Rather, the central factor in understanding why communities function as they do and vary as widely as they do is found in the confluence of all of the individual factors into an amorphous, unique, and defining civic culture.

When speaking with locally elected officials in Ohio, Michigan, and Ontario, it was easy to see and hear differences in their approaches to governance. Likewise, talking with representatives of citizen groups, chambers of commerce, and downtown development authorities elicited sometimes similar stories but with different beginnings, middles, or endings. Yes, the discussion of the big-box drug stores occurred again and again. But in some communities, these were sources of economic growth, jobs, and new tax revenues, whereas in others, they are encroachments on neighborhoods, threats to local businesses, and urban blight. Why? The civic culture of each community defines how regimes function, how individual citizens function, and ultimately how communities decide on one approach to public policy versus another. Civic culture is a result of multiple factors and is difficult to define but is the missing link. That is obvious in moving away from aggregate and survey data and walking the streets of a city and speaking with citizens. The goal in the case studies was to put a face on the statistics. In that process, it becomes clear that local civic culture provides an understanding of the Atlanta that was "too busy to hate" or the new Atlanta that says "let's make a deal." Just as one cannot understand America without understanding the civic culture of the nation, urban politics and urban policy cannot be understood without exploring the unique civic culture of each of thousands of local communities.

REFERENCES

Ady, R. A. 1984. Cited in Joint Economic Committee, U.S. Congress, *Industrial policy movement in the United States; Is it the answer?* Washington, DC: Government Printing Office.

Ahlbrandt, R. S., and DeAngelis, J. P. 1987. Local options for economic development in a maturing industrial region. *Economic Development Quarterly* 1 (February): 41-51.

Almond, G. A., and Verba, S. 1963. *The civic culture.* Boston: Little, Brown and Company.

Andrew, C. 1994. Federal urban activity: Intergovernmental relations in an age of restraint. In *The changing Canadian metropolis: A public policy perspective* ed. F. Frisken, 427-457. Berkeley, CA: Institute of Governmental Studies Press and Toronto: Canadian Urban Institute.

Babcock, R. F. 1987. Foreword. *Law and Contemporary Problems* 50: 1-4.

Bachelor, L. 1994. Regime maintenance, solution sets, and urban economic development. *Urban Affairs Quarterly* 25: 596-616.

Bachrach, P., and Baratz, M. S. 1962. Two faces of power. *American Political Science Review* 56: 947-952.

Bailey, R. W. 1999. *Gay politics, urban politics: Identity and economics in the urban setting.* New York: Columbia University Press.

Banfield, E. C., and Wilson, J. Q. 1963. *City politics.* Cambridge, MA: Harvard University Press.

Bingham, R. D. 1976. *The adoption of innovation by local government.* Lexington, MA: Heath.

Blakeley, E. J. 1994. *Planning local economic development theory and practice,* 2nd ed. Thousand Oaks, CA: Sage.

Boeckelman, K. 1991. Political culture and state development policy. *Publius: The Journal of Federalism* 21: 49-81.

Bohrnstedt, G. W., and Carter, T. M. 1971. Robustness in regression analysis. In *Sociological methodology* ed. H. L. Costner. San Francisco: Jossey-Bass.

Bohrnstedt, G. 1982. *Statistics for social data analysis.* Itasca, IL: Peacock.

Bowman, A. O'M. 1988. Competition for economic development among Southeastern cities. *Urban Affairs Quarterly* 4: 511-527.

Brierly, A. 1986. "State economic development policy choices." Paper presented at the annual meeting of the Midwest Political Science Association, Chicago, IL, April.

Brown, D. L., and Warner, M. E. 1991. Persistent low-income nonmetropolitan areas in the United States: Some conceptual challenges for development policy. *Policy Studies Journal* 19 (2): 22-41.

Cable, B., Feiock, R. C., and Kim, J. 1993. The consequences of institutionalized access for economic development policy making in the US. *Economic Development Quarterly* 7: 91-7.

Clarke, S. E. 1984. "The local state and alternative economic development strategies: Gaining public benefits from private investment." Discussion paper, Center for Public Research, University of Colorado, Boulder.

Clarke, S. E. 1999. "Regional and transborder regimes." Paper presented at the annual meeting of the American Political Science Association, Atlanta, GA, September.

Clarke, S. E., and Gaile, G. L. 1989. Moving towards entrepreneurial state and local development strategies: Opportunities and barriers. *Policy Studies Journal* 17: 574-598.

Clarke, S. E., and Gaile, G. L. 1992. The next wave: Postfederal local economic development strategies. *Economic Development Quarterly* 6: 187-198.

Clarke, S. E., and Gaile, G. L. 1998. *The work of cities.* Minneapolis: University of Minnesota Press.

Clingermayer, J., and Feiock, R. C. 1990. The adoption of economic development policies by large cities: A test of economic, interest group, and institutional explanations. *Policy Studies Journal* 18 (spring): 539-552.

Dahl, R. A. 1961. *Who governs?* New Haven, CT: Yale University Press.

Davies, W. K. D., and Murdie, R. A. 1994. The social complexity of Canadian metropolitan areas in 1986: A multivariate analysis of census data. In *The changing Canadian metropolis: A public policy perspective* ed. F. Frisken, 203-236. Berkeley, CA: Institute of Governmental Studies Press and Toronto: Canadian Urban Institute.

Davis, J. A. 1985. *The logic of causal order.* Newbury Park, CA: Sage.

DiGaetano, A., and Klemanski, J. S. 1993. Urban regimes in comparative perspective: The politics of urban development in Britain. *Urban Affairs Quarterly* 29 (September): 54-83.

DiGaetano, A., and Lawless, P. 1999. Urban governance and industrial decline: Governing structures and policy agendas in Birmingham and Sheffield, England, and Detroit, Michigan, 1980-1997. *Urban Affairs Review* 34 (March): 546-577.

Domhoff, G. W. 1978. *Who rules America now?* Englewood Cliffs, NJ: Prentice-Hall.

Donovan, T. 1993. Community controversy and the adoption of economic development policies. *Social Science Quarterly* 74: 386-402.

Dowding, K., Dunleavy, P., King, D., Margetts, H., and Rydin, Y. 1999. Regime politics in London local government. *Urban Affairs Review* 34 (March): 515-545.

Dubnick, M. J., and Bardes, B. A. 1983. *Thinking about public policy.* New York: John Wiley.

Eisenschitz, A. 1993. Business involvement in community: Counting the spoons or economic renewal? In *Community economic development: Policy formation in the US and UK* ed. D. Fasenfest, 141-156. London: Macmillan and New York: St. Martin's.

Eisinger, P. K. 1988. *The rise of the entrepreneurial state.* Madison: University of Wisconsin Press.

Elazar, D. 1994. *The American mosaic, the impact of space, time and culture on American politics.* Boulder, CO: Westview.

Elkin, S. 1987. *City and regime in the American republic.* Chicago: University of Chicago Press.

Elkins, D. R. 1995. Testing competing explanations for the adoption of type II policies. *Urban Affairs Review* 30: 809-839.

Erikson, R. Wright, G., and McIver, J. 1993. *Statehouse democracy: Public opinion and policy in the American states.* Cambridge, UK: Cambridge University Press.

Everitt, B. S. 1993. *Cluster analysis,* 3rd ed. New York: Halsted.

Fainstein, N. I., and Fainstein, S. S. 1983. Regime strategies, commercial resistance, and economic forces. In *Restructuring the City* ed. M. Lauria, 245-282. New York: Longman.

Fainstein, S. S., Fainstein, N. I., Hill, R. C., Judd, J., and Smith, M. P. 1983. *Restructuring the city.* New York: Longman.

Feiock, R. C. 1989. The adoption of economic development policies by state and local governments: A review. *Economic Development Quarterly* 3: 266-270.

Feiock, R. C. 1992. "The political economy of local economic development policy adoption." Paper presented at the annual meeting of the Urban Affairs Association, Cleveland, OH, April.

Feiock, R. C., and Clingermayer, J. 1986. Municipal representation, executive power, and economic development policy administration. *Policy Studies Journal* 15 (2): 211-229.

Feiock, R. C., and Clingermayer, J. 1992. Development policy choice: Four explanations for city implementation of economic development policies. *American Review of Public Administration* 22: 49-63.

Feldman, L. D., and Graham, K. A. 1981. Intergovernmental relations and urban growth: A Canadian view. In *Politics and government of urban Canada* 4th ed., ed. L.D. Feldman. Toronto: Methuen.

Ferman, B. 1996. *Challenging the growth machine.* Lawrence: University Press of Kansas.

Fleischmann, A., and Green, G. P. 1991. Organizing local agencies to promote economic development. *American Review of Public Administration* 21: 1-15.

Fleischmann, A., Green, G. P., and Kwong, T. M. 1992. What's a city to do? Explaining the differences in local economic development policies. *The Western Political Quarterly* 27: 677-699.

Flores, H. 1999. An essay on the state and the state of Latino politics. *Urban News* 13: 1-7.

Fosler, R. S. 1991. *Local economic development: Strategies for a changing economy.* Washington DC: International City Management Association.

Garber, J., and Imbroscio, D. 1996. The myth of the North American city reconsidered. *Urban Affairs Review* 31: 595-624.

Goetz, E. G. 1990. Type II policy and mandated benefits in economic development. *Urban Affairs Quarterly* 26: 170-190.

Goetz, E. G. 1994. Expanding possibilities in local development policy: An examination of U.S. cities. *Political Research Quarterly* 47: 85-109.

Goldberg, M., and Mercer, J. 1986. *The myth of the north American city: Continentalism challenged.* Vancouver: University of British Columbia Press.

Goldstein, M. L. 1985. Choosing the right site. *Industry Week* 15: 57-60.

Granato, J., Inglehart, R., and Leblang, D. 1996. The effect of cultural values on economic development: Theory, hypotheses, and some empirical tests. *American Journal of Political Science* 40: 607-631.

Granovetter, M. 1985. Economic action and social structure: The problem of embeddedness. *American Journal of Sociology* 91: 481-510.

Green, G. P. 1995. Structuring locality: Economic development and growth management in Wisconsin cities and villages. In *Local economic development* ed. N. Walzer, 159-180. Boulder, CO: Westview.

Green, G. P., and Brintnall, M.A. 1986. "State enterprise zone programs: Variations in structure and coverage." Paper presented at the annual meeting of the Midwest Political Science Association, Chicago, April.

Green, G. P., and Fleischmann, A. 1991. Promoting economic development: A comparison of central cities, suburbs, and nonmetropolitan communities. *Urban Affairs Quarterly* 27: 145-154.

Hanson, R. L., and Berkman, M. B. 1991. A meteorology of state legislative climates. *Economic Development Quarterly* 5: 213-228.

Haughton, G., and While, A. 1999. From corporate city to citizens city? Urban leadership after local entrepreneurialism in the United Kingdom. *Urban Affairs Review* 35 (11): 3-23.

Henry, I. P, and Paramio-Salcines, J. L. 1999. Sport and the analysis of symbolic regimes: A case study of the city of Sheffield. *Urban Affairs Review* 34 (May): 641-665.

Herrick, B., & Kindleberger, C. P. 1983. *Economic development*. New York: McGraw-Hill.

Hill, E. W., Wolman, H. L., and Ford, C. C. 1995. Can suburbs survive without their central cities? Examining the suburban dependence hypothesis. *Urban Affairs Review* 31: 147-174.

Hill, R. C. 1984. Economic crisis and political response in the motor city. In *Sunbelt snowbelt urban development and regional restructuring* ed. L. Sawers and W. K. Tabb, 313-338. New York/Oxford, UK: Oxford University Press.

Hunter, F. 1953. *Community power structure: A study of decision makers*. Chapel Hill: University of North Carolina Press.

Imbroscio, D. L. 1998. Reformulating urban regime theory: The division of labor between state and market reconsidered. *Journal of Urban Affairs* 20: 233-248.

Imbroscio, D. L. 1999. Structure, agency and democratic theory. *Polity* 1 (fall): 45-66.

Inglehart, R. 1990. The renaissance of political culture. *American Political Science Review* 82: 1203-1230.

International City Management Association. 1989. *Economic development survey*. Washington, DC: International City Management Association.

Jackman, R. W., and Miller, R. A. 1996. A renaissance of political culture. *American Journal of Political Science* 40: 632-659.

Jones, B. D., and Bachelor, L. W. 1984. Local policy discretion and the corporate surplus. In Urban economic development, ed. R. D. Bingham and J. P. Blair, 245-268. *Urban Affairs Annual Reviews 27*. Beverly Hills, CA: Sage.

Jones, B. D., and Bachelor, L. W. 1993. *The sustaining hand* 2nd ed. Lawrence: University Press of Kansas.

Kantor, P., Savitch, H. V., and Haddock, S. V. 1997. The political economy of urban regimes: A comparative perspective. *Urban Affairs Review* 32: 348-377.

Kieschnick, M. 1981. *Taxes and growth: Business incentives and economic development*. Washington, DC: Council of State Planning Agencies.

King, G. 1991. "Truth" is stranger than prediction, more questionable than causal inference. *American Journal of Political Science* 35: 1047-1053.

Kluckhohn, C. 1954. Culture and behavior. In *Handbook of social psychology* Vol. II ed. G. Lindzey, 921-976. Reading, MA: Addison-Wesley.

Koven, S. G. 1999. *Public budgeting in the United States. The cultural and ideological setting.* Washington, DC: Georgetown University Press.

Krmenec, A. J. 1989. Economic development policy adoption in a regional context: A study of the industrial revenue bond. *Urban Geography* 10: 251-269.

Kuhn, T. S. 1962. *The structure of scientific revolutions.* Chicago: The University of Chicago Press.

Ledebur, L. C., and Woodward, D. P. 1990. Adding a stick to the carrot: Location incentives with clawbacks, recisions, and recalibrations. *Economic Development Quarterly* 4: 221-237.

Levine, M. A. (1994). The transformation of urban politics in France: The roots of growth politics and urban regimes. *Urban Affairs Quarterly* 29: 383-410.

Levy, J. M. 1981. *Economic development programs for cities, counties, and towns.* New York: Praeger.

Levy, J. M. 1990. What local economic developers actually do: Location quotients versus press releases. *Journal of the American Planning Association* 56 (spring):153-160.

Lipsky, M. 1980. *Street level bureaucracy.* New York: Russell Sage Foundation.

Loftman, P. 1995. "The politics of evaluation research: A case study of Birmingham's prestige projects." Paper presented at the annual meeting of the Urban Affairs Association, May.

Logan, V. R., and Molotch, H. L. 1987. *Urban fortunes: The political economy of place.* Berkeley: University of California Press.

Luskin, R. C. 1991. Abusus non tollit usum: Standardized coefficients, correlations, and R^2s. *American Journal of Political Science* 35: 1032-1046.

Matulef, M. L. 1987. "Strategies for economic revitalization." Paper presented at the annual meeting of the American Society for Public Administration, Boston.

McClelland, D. C. 1961. *The achieving society.* Princeton, NJ: Van Nostrand.

McClelland, D. C. 1963. National character and economic growth in Turkey and Iran. In *Communications and political development* ed. L. W. Pye. Princeton, NJ: Princeton University Press.

McGowan, R. P., and Ottensmeyer, E. J. 1993. *Economic development strategies for state and local governments.* Chicago: Nelson-Hall.

Miranda, R., Rosail, D., and Yeh, S. 1992. "Growth machines, progressive cities and regime restructuring: Explaining economic development strategies." Paper presented at the annual meeting of the American Political Science Association, Chicago, September.

Mizon, G., and Richard, J. F. 1986. The encompassing principle and its application to non-nested hypothesis tests. *Econometrica* 54: 657-678.

Molotch, H. 1988. Strategies and constraints of growth elites. In *Business elites and urban development* ed. S. Cummings, 25-47. Albany: State University of New York Press.

Mossberger, K., and Stoker, G. 2000. "The evolution of urban regime theory: The challenge of conceptualization." Paper presented at the annual meeting of the Urban Affairs Association, Los Angeles, CA, May.

Nathan, R. P., and Adams, C. F. 1989. Four perspectives on urban hardship. *Political Science Quarterly* 104: 483-508.

Oakville Economic Development Alliance. 1999. *OEDA Activity Report, Summer 1999.* Oakville, Ontario, Canada: Oakville Economic Development Alliance.

Ohren, J. F., and Reese, L. A. 1996. "You get what you pay for: Professionalism, resources, and local economic development policies." Paper presented at the annual meeting of the Urban Affairs Association, New York, March.

Orr, M., and Stoker, G. 1994. Urban regimes and leadership in Detroit. *Urban Affairs Quarterly* 30: 48-73.

Pagano, M. A., and Bowman, A. O'M. 1995. *Cityscapes and capital.* Baltimore: Johns Hopkins University Press.

Painter, J. 1997. Regulation, regime, and practice in urban politics. In *Reconstructing urban regime theory* ed. M. Lauria, 122-143. Thousand Oaks, CA: Sage.

Pelissero, J. P. 1986. "Intrametropolitan economic development policies: An exploratory look at suburban competition and cooperation." Paper presented at the annual meeting of the Midwest Political Science Association, Chicago, IL, April.

Pelissero, J. P., and Fasenfest, D. 1989. Suburban economic development policy. *Economic Development Quarterly* 2: 301-311.

Peterson, P. E. 1981. *City limits.* Chicago: University of Chicago Press.

Polsby, N. 1980. *Community power and political theory,* 2nd ed. New Haven, CT: Yale University Press.

Putnam, R. D. 1993. *Making democracy work: Civic traditions in modern Italy.* Princeton, NJ: Princeton University Press.

Ramsay, M. 1996. *Community, culture and economic development.* Albany: State University of New York Press.

Randall, R. 1994. "U.S. and Canadian urban vitality: A metropolitan analysis." Paper presented at the annual meeting of the Urban Affairs Association, New Orleans, Louisiana, March.

Reese, L. A. 1991. Municipal fiscal health and tax abatement policy. *Economic Development Quarterly* 5: 24-32.

Reese, L. A. 1992. Explaining the extent of local economic development activity: Evidence from Canadian cities. *Government and Policy* (April): 105-120.

Reese, L. A. 1993a. Categories of local economic development techniques: An empirical analysis. *Policy Studies Journal* 21: 492-506.

Reese, L. A. 1993b. Local economic development practices across the northern border. *Urban Affairs Quarterly* 28: 571-592.

Reese, L. A. 1997a. *Local economic development policy: The U.S. and Canada.* New York: Garland.

Reese, L. A. 1997b. The use of planning methodologies in local economic development policy-making. *Government and Policy/Environment and Planning C* 15: 285-303.

Reese, L. A. 1998. Sharing the benefits of economic development: What cities utilize type II policies? *Urban Affairs Review* 33: 686-711.

Reese, L. A., and Fasenfest, D. 1996. Local economic development policy in Canada and the US: Similarities and differences. *Canadian Journal of Urban Research* (June): 100-121.

Reese, L. A., and Fasenfest, D. 1997. What works best?: Values and the evaluation of local economic development policy. *Economic Development Quarterly* 11: 195-221.

Reese, L. A., and Malmer, A. B. 1994. The effects of state enabling legislation on local economic development policies. *Urban Affairs Quarterly* 30: 14-35.

Reese, L. A., and Rosenfeld, R. A. 2000. Cross-border local development policy: An examination of spatial patterns. *International Journal of Economic Development* 2: 440-472.

Rosenfeld, R. A., Reese, L. A., Georgeau, V., and Wamsley, S. 1995. Community development block grant spending revisited: Patterns of benefit and program institutionalization. *Publius: The Journal of Federalism* 4 (Fall): 55-72.

Rothblatt, D. N. 1994. North American metropolitan planning: Canadian and U.S. perspectives. *Journal of the American Planning Association* 60: 501-520.

Rubin, B. M., and Zorn, C. K. 1985. Sensible state and local economic development. *Public Administration Review* 45: 333-340.

Rubin, H. J. 1986. Local economic development organizations and the activities of small cities in encouraging economic growth. *Policy Studies Journal* 14: 363-388.

Rubin, H. J. 1988. Shoot anything that flies; claim anything that falls; conversations with economic development practitioners. *Economic Development Quarterly* 3: 236-251.

Rubin, H. J., and Rubin, I. 1987. Economic development incentives: The poor (cities) pay more. *Urban Affairs Quarterly* 23: 37-62.

Santori, G. 1991. Comparing and miscomparing. *Journal of Theoretical Politics* 3: 446-462.

Sanyika, M. K. 1986. Balanced development. Part two: A classification of existing linkages and partnerships. *Economic Development and Law Center Report* (fall): 19-22.

Savitch, H. V., and Kantor, P. 1999. "A theory of urban development: Testing results from cities in north America and west Europe." Paper presented at the annual meeting of the American Political Science Association, Atlanta, September.

Schmenner, R. W. 1982. *Making business location decisions.* Englewood Cliffs, NJ: Prentice Hall.

Schneider, M. 1986. The market for local economic development: The growth of suburban retail trade, 1972-1982. *Urban Affairs Quarterly* 1: 24-41.

Schneider, M., and Teske, P. 1993. The progrowth entrepreneur in local government. *Urban Affairs Quarterly* 29: 316-327.

Schwarz, J. E., and Volgy, T. J. 1992. "The impacts of economic development strategies on wages: Exploring the effect on public policy at the local level." Paper presented at the annual meeting of the American Political Science Association, Chicago, September.

Sharkansky, I. 1970. *Regionalism in American politics.* New York: Bobbs-Merrill.

Sharp, E. B. 1991. Institutional manifestations of accessibility and urban economic development policy. *Western Political Quarterly* 44: 129-147.

Sharp, E. B., and Elkins, D. R. 1991. The politics of economic development policy. *Economic Development Quarterly* 5: 126-139.

Sites, W. 1997. The limits of urban regime theory. *Urban Affairs Review* 32: 536-577.

Smart, A. 1994. Recent developments in the theory of the state and the changing Canadian metropolis: Implications of each for the other. In *The changing Canadian metropolis: A public policy perspective* ed. F. Frisken, 561-579. Berkeley, CA: Institute of Governmental Studies Press and Toronto: Canadian Urban Institute.

Spindler, C., and Forrester, J. 1993. Economic development policy: Explaining policy preference among competing models. *Urban Affairs Quarterly* 29: 28-53.

SPSS. 1998. *Applications guide.* Chicago: SPSS.

Sternberg, E. 1987. A practitioner's classification of economic development policy instruments, with some inspiration from political economy. *Economic Development Quarterly* 1: 149-161.

Stoker, G. 1995. Regime theory and urban politics. In *Theories of urban politics* ed. D. Judge, G. Stoker, and H. Wolman, 54-71. Thousand Oaks, CA: Sage.

Stoker, G., and Mossberger, K. 1994. Urban regime theory in comparative perspective. *Environment and Planning C: Government and Policy* 12: 195-212.

Stone, C. N. 1980. Systemic power and community decision-making: A restatement of stratificationist theory. *American Political Science Review* 74: 978-990.

Stone, C. N. 1989. *Regime politics: Governing Atlanta.* Lawrence: University Press of Kansas.

Stone, C. N. 1993. Urban regimes and the capacity to govern: A political economy approach. *Journal of Urban Affairs* 15: 1-28.

Stone, C. N., and Sanders, H. T. 1987. Reexamining a classic case of development politics: New Haven, Connecticut. In *The politics of urban development* ed. C. N. Stone and H. T. Sanders, 159-181. Lawrence: University Press of Kansas.

Swank, D. 1996. Culture, institutions, and economic growth: Theory, recent evidence, and the role of communitarian polities. *American Journal of Political Science* 40: 660-679.

Swanstrom, T. 1985. *The crisis of growth politics: Cleveland, Kucinich and the challenges of urban populism.* Philadelphia: Temple University Press.

Turner, R. S. 2000. "Shifting regime boundaries." Paper presented at the annual meeting of the Urban Affairs Association, Los Angeles, CA, May.

Turner, R. S., and Garber, J. A. 1994. "Responding to boom and bust: Urban political economy in Houston and Edmonton." Paper presented at the annual meeting of the American Political Science Association, New York, September.

Wolman, H. 1996. The politics of local economic development. *Economic Development Quarterly* 10: 115-150.

Woodlief, A. 1998. The path-dependent city. *Urban Affairs Review* 33: 405-437.

Woodside, K. 1990. An approach to studying local government autonomy: The Ontario experience. *Canadian Public Administration* 33: 198-213.

INDEX

ABOUT THE AUTHORS

Laura A. Reese, a political scientist, is Professor in the Urban Planning Program and a Fellow in the Fraser Center for Workplace Issues, College of Urban, Labor and Metropolitan Affairs, at Wayne State University. She has published articles on urban politics, local economic development, comparative urban policy, and public personnel management in *Urban Affairs Review, Economic Development Quarterly, Journal of Politics, Review of Public Personnel Administration, Publius: The Journal of Federalism,* and the *International Journal of Urban and Regional Research.* Her most recent books are *Approaches to Economic Development* (with John Blair) and *Implementing Sexual Harassment Policy* (with Karen Lindenberg). Her current research interests focus on further exploration of local civic cultures in the U.S. and Canada, comparative studies of urban consolidation and metropolitan governance, and the identification and implementation of effective sexual harassment policies.

Raymond A. Rosenfeld is Professor of Political Science at Eastern Michigan University. He received his doctorate in Political Science from Emory University in Atlanta and has taught at Emory University, Old Dominion University, and the University of Tulsa. His research and teaching interests focus on public administration, public policy, and

407

federalism. He has published in major political science and public policy journals, including *Western Political Quarterly, Publius: The Journal of Federalism, Public Budgeting & Finance, Public Administration Review, Economic Development Quarterly, and the International Journal of Economic Development* and numerous edited volumes. Dr. Rosenfeld and a colleague (George Cox) at Georgia Southern University recently published *State and Local Government: Public Life in America*. Rosenfeld was Public Administration Fellow in 1975-1977 at the U.S. Department of Housing and Urban Development and a Fulbright Senior Scholar in 1995-1996 at the Ukrainian Academy of Public Administration in Kyiv. He has been involved in many applied policy analysis and evaluation projects for federal, state, and local governments. Currently, he is directing an evaluation of the Ameritech Technology Academy, which addresses the challenges of integrating technology into the curriculum of Michigan public schools.

Rosenfeld and Reese continue to collaborate on research that expands the notion of comparative civic culture to Canada and Ukraine.